LINGUISTIC ANTHROPOLOGY

Second Edition

LINGUISTIC ANTHROPOLOGY

Second Edition

NANCY PARROTT HICKERSON

Texas Tech University

THOMSON

WADSWORTH

Australia • Canada • Mexico • Singapore • Spain • United Kingdom • United States

PUBLISHER	Earl McPeek
ACQUISITIONS EDITOR	Lin Marshall
MARKET STRATEGIST	Kathleen Sharp
DEVELOPMENTAL EDITOR	Lisa Hensley
PROJECT EDITOR	Michele Tomiak
ART DIRECTOR	Carol Kincaid
PRODUCTION MANAGER	Andrea Archer

ISBN: 0-15-505178-4
Library of Congress Catalog Card Number: 99-068164

Wadsworth/Thomson Learning
10 Davis Drive
Belmont CA 94002-3098
USA

For information about our products, contact us:
Thomson Learning Academic Resource Center
1-800-423-0563
http://www.wadsworth.com

For permission to use material from this text, contact us by
Web: http://www.thomsonrights.com
Fax: 1-800-730-2215
Phone: 1-800-730-2214

Printed in the United States of America
10 9 8 7 6 5 4

PREFACE

This book is both a general introduction to the study of language and an overview of the contributions that linguistic scholarship has made and continues to make to anthropology. Among the topics treated in the following chapters are: the methods of descriptive and historical linguistics and milestones in the development of these fields; language acquisition, ethnolinguistics, sociolinguistics, and language planning; language typology and universals; and the origin and evolution of language. An effort is made throughout to relate linguistic issues to the major theoretical paradigms that have influenced anthropology and related fields, including cultural relativism, evolutionism, structuralism, and functionalism.

The original edition of this book, published in 1980, was essentially a reflection of several years of teaching a one-semester course in linguistic anthropology to undergraduate anthropology majors. The present edition still bears that imprint but reflects my own professional experiences and interests to a greater degree. The organization of the book is somewhat different and the content is, of course, updated. Several changes can be noted: (1) more complete treatment of the origin and diversification of language; (2) a focus on the history of ethnolinguistic theory, exemplified by changes in the analysis and interpretation of color-term systems; (3) expanded treatment of studies in the ethnography of speaking; (4) new coverage of the application of linguistic research, in language planning and other practical contexts; (5) more comprehensive coverage of historical linguistics, illustrated by reference to English and other languages; and (6) expanded discussion of field methods in linguistic anthropology.

The original edition of *Linguistic Anthropology* was designed as a module to cover the linguistic content of broad survey courses in general or cultural anthropology. Although the present edition can also serve this role, it is also appropriate as the core text of introductory courses in anthropological linguistics or language and culture; instructors can assign selected readings or exercises in line with their interests and points of emphasis (assisted by the extensive bibliography at the end of the book).

For encouraging me to write, I will always be grateful to the late David Boynton of Holt, Rinehart and Winston, and to George and Louise Spindler, general editors of the Basic Anthropology series in which *Linguistic Anthropology* was first included. I would also like to thank the following individuals for serving as reviewers for the second edition: Jill Brody, Louisiana State University; Nicholas Hopkins, Florida State University; Ina Jane Wundram, Oxford College of Emory University; and Ben Blount, University of Georgia. Finally, I thank the helpful staff of Harcourt College Publishers, including Lin Marshall, Acquisitions Editor; Lisa Hensley, Senior Development Editor; Michele Tomiak, Senior Project Editor; Carol Kincaid, Art Director; Andrea Archer, Senior Production Manager; and Caroline Robbins, Picture and Rights Editor.

CONTENTS

LANGUAGE AND LANGUAGES

Language, like *culture* or *society,* is a familiar word that subsumes and denotes a broad area of study in the social sciences. Such terms are used in a variety of ways, in many different contexts; they have general and specific, literal and metaphoric usages. An unabridged dictionary lists a dozen or more definitions of the word *language,* beginning with "the body of words and systems for their use common to a people who are of the same community or nation, geographical area, or cultural tradition"—for example, English, Hungarian, Hindi, Romany, Navajo, Yiddish, the Celtic languages, the Mayan languages, the languages of West Africa, the languages of New Guinea and the South Pacific, and so on.

A second definition, even more sweeping, tells us that *language* is "communication by voice in the distinctively human manner." In this sense, language is universal—the "gift" of language, our innate and seemingly inexplicable ability to acquire and use linguistic systems. Although, as seen here, language is usually defined as a uniquely human attribute, it is common practice (no doubt reflecting our Western culture's anthropocentric view of the world) to refer to "animal languages"—the language of the bees, birds, apes, or ants. Even genetic codes can be seen as a kind of language, as can the systems of symbols used in mathematics or physics. In popular usage, it would seem that *language* can stand for almost any medium or method of communication, and for any type of sign or symbol system. Thus, we speak of sign language, body language, computer language, the language of heraldry, of flowers, of art, and of love.

Traditionally, anthropologists have accepted the definition that limits the term *language* to *human vocal communication.* However, this can become a point of contention—although we take language to be a defining human characteristic, we are also concerned with tracing its development in the context of human evolution. When, and how, did language appear? Is there a direct evolutionary continuity between human language and the vocal communication of other species—especially the nonhuman primates? If so, can the processes of the transformation be understood? When and how did some sort of prelanguage become language?

If language is a basic human endowment, the ways of speaking characteristic of individual speech communities appear simply as variant forms of a shared mode of a universal human method of communication—*human language.* This view has become increasingly popular, especially as ongoing research reveals a number of universal features, indicating there are fundamental structural properties that underlie the surface variety of human speech.

But in the narrower sense of the term, *languages* are myriad. From this point of view, the focus is on uniqueness. There are thousands of existing languages, each one different from the others, and each reflecting and conveying the social, cultural, and ethnic diversity of humankind. Individual languages and cultures have existed for as long as there is documented knowledge of human history, and this diversity can be projected many thousands of years into the past.

In this book, the subject is both *language* and *languages*. Linguistic scholars, especially those who operate in the holistic context of anthropology, face two broad challenges, seemingly opposed to each other, yet interrelated. These experts continue a long-standing commitment to documenting the range of diversity of human languages. This task takes on new urgency as minority languages are increasingly threatened in the modern world. However, recent research on such topics as linguistic universals, language acquisition, and pragmatics has given rise to new perspectives on the nature of language. As a result, these broad linguistic interests interface with the interests of many anthropologists in topics such as cultural and biological origins, cognition, and cultural change. Linguistic studies are, perhaps more than ever before, an integral part of the anthropological perspective.

1

LANGUAGE

THE PROBLEM OF LANGUAGE ORIGINS

When did human language originate? How and why did our ancestors begin to speak? Attempts to answer these questions and to account for the development and diversification of languages are many. None of the answers so far proposed is completely satisfactory, perhaps because there is so much to explain. One approach traces the development of the vocal tract, suggesting that the ability of the higher primates to produce a variety of sounds was the starting point in a series of developments that led toward articulate speech. Another takes the development of intelligence, attested over time by a steady increase in the size of the brain-case, as the necessary precondition for the emergence of language. But what led our ancestors to begin to formulate messages in the form of words and sentences? What psychological motivation inspired half-human creatures to begin giving names to themselves and to objects in their environment, to ask and answer questions, and to formulate plans? And how did the use of language find a place in the social life of primitive hominids? The time, place, chronology, motivation, and circumstances of this complex development all have a part in the mystery, and all remain to be resolved.

Perhaps no subject has inspired more curiosity, speculation, and uncertainty as the origin of language. The uncertainty reflects the absence of solid evidence: We can never know exactly what early language was like, because speech is such an ephemeral thing. Archaeologists cannot unearth the remains of ancient words, as they can find potsherds or projectile points. The earliest writing is not very old in terms of human history. In western Asia, record keeping began around 5,000 to 6,000 years ago. This casts no light at all on the beginnings of human language, which has probably been in existence for at least 100 times as long.

Scenarios for the origin of language have been propounded by scholars, sages, and mythmakers of many nations and traditions. The sacred stories of certain cultures tell of a special creation of language, while in others it appears as part of humankind's original endowment. For example, in the biblical account, there is no specific act of creation that gives rise to language;

indeed, the act of speech itself seems to be endowed with creative force. God speaks, and the earth and its creatures come into existence:

> God said, Let the waters under the heaven be gathered together unto one place, and let the dry land appear; and it was so. And God called the dry land Earth; and the gathering together of the waters He called Seas; and God saw that it was good. . . . And God said, Let the earth bring forth the living creature after his kind, cattle, and creeping thing, and beast of the earth after his kind: and it was so. (Genesis 1: 9–10, 21)

When Adam appears, he already has the power of speech; it seems that, being made in God's image, he can speak to God just as God speaks to him:

> And the Lord God called unto Adam, and said unto him, Where art thou? And he said, I heard thy voice in the garden, and I was afraid. . . . (Genesis 3: 9–10)

Adam, too, exercises power through the use of language. By giving names to the animals, he establishes and signifies his mastery over them. It can be interpreted that this power—the power of speech—marks humans as closer to God than other forms of life, and thus superior to all of them. However, language is not always seen as a blessing. The inability to communicate with animals or to understand their vocalizations can be considered a loss or liability. The Jewish historian Flavius Josephus asserted that this was one of the penalties that humankind suffered as a consequence of exile from the Garden of Eden.

A second mystery, the diversification of languages, is also often given a supernatural explanation. In biblical tradition, the sacred language of creation evidently endured unchanged for many generations. This was the language used by Adam and Eve and their descendants until the time of the building of the Tower of Babel. Then the situation changed, again by an act of God, and the one original language became many, as a punishment for human presumptuousness:

> And the whole earth was of one language and one speech. . . . And they said, Come, let us build a city, and a tower whose top may reach unto heaven; and let us make us a name, lest we be scattered abroad upon the face of the whole world. . . .
> And the Lord said, Behold, the people is one, and they have all one language, and this is only the beginning of what they will do. . . . Come, let us go down, and there confound their language, that they may not understand one another's speech. So the Lord scattered them abroad from thence upon the face of the earth. . . ." (Genesis 11: 1–8)

As in this case, the confusion of tongues is typically seen as the result of an arbitrary or punitive act by a creator or culture hero. For example, among native peoples of California (an area where the population was split into many small tribes, speaking different languages), the mythology of the Maidu provides an explanation:

> Up to this time everybody spoke the same language. The people were having a burning (a cremation ceremony) . . . when in the night everybody suddenly

began to speak a different language. Each man and his wife, however, spoke the same. Earth Initiate (the creator) had come in the night to Kuksu (the first man) and had told him about it all, and given him instructions for the next day. So, when morning came, Kuksu called all the people together, for he was able to speak all the languages. He told them each the names of the different animals . . . in their languages, taught them how to cook and hunt, gave them all their laws, and set the time for all their dances and festivals. Then he called each tribe by name, and sent them off in different directions, telling them where they were to live. (Thompson, 1966)

Though such tales of miraculous beginnings and acts of creation are still told, few educated people today would accept them as true in a literal sense; rather, the accounts appear to mirror the enormous importance of the attributes and cultural institutions to which they are attached. After all, many people—scientists as well as laypersons—do believe that there is a qualitative difference between the intelligence of animals and that of humans. More than anything else, the mythical origin ascribed to language would seem to reflect its power and fundamental place in human life. These traditions may also project a sense of some of the negative aspects and potential pitfalls presented by the human need to communicate.

WESTERN PHILOSOPHICAL VIEWS

Throughout the history of Western civilization, the origin of language has been a favorite topic for philosophical discussion. Plato's *Cratylos* features one of the earliest recorded discussions of this issue, in the form of a debate between Socrates and another philosopher, the Sophist Cratylos. Cratylos asserts that the names of all things, as given by an original "name giver" (a god or ancient culture hero) reflect their inherent nature. He therefore proposes that knowledge of the correct—and, presumably, unchanging—names should be an important part of education. Socrates counters by inquiring how the mysterious name giver could have acquired the knowledge of things on which to base the names if there were no existing names (no words, and thus, no *language*) to provide him with that knowledge.

It would seem that Socrates' own belief was that words are coined for human use, just as a craftsperson might invent a spindle or a lathe. In effect, he was expressing a relativistic view, that the vocabulary of a language is essentially arbitrary or conventional. An implication of this view would be that language can change to meet human needs. This conforms to the viewpoint of most linguists today but may have seemed radical to Socrates' audience, whose knowledge of languages probably did not extend beyond the limits of Greece.

In the Enlightenment period (c. 1650–1750 A.D.), European philosophers renewed the discussion and speculated at great length about the origin of speech. Descartes, Rousseau, and Leibnitz are three prominent writers who elaborated on this topic, which was seen as essential to a general theory of the nature of language.

Several centuries later, these and other more recent philosophical speculations were recapitulated and criticized by a prominent German psychologist, Wilhelm Wundt,[1] in an appendix to his own two-volume treatise on language, *Die Sprache* (1911). Wundt observed that the opposing viewpoints expressed in Plato's *Cratylos*—whether language is a divine gift or an invention of human origin—continued to be the main poles around which discussion centered. However, there were also other issues involved: What is the motivation for the use of language? Is it based on imitation or on the expression of emotion? Is it the product or the cause of human intelligence? Wundt identified four competing scenarios that were prominent in the philosophical literature. He dubbed them the Invention, Imitation, Natural Sound, and Miracle theories.

The last of these, the Miracle theory, is exemplified by the biblical account: Language is a divine gift bestowed on humankind as the consequence of an original act of creation. By contrast, the linguistic scholars of the 19th century generally favored the Invention theory, which proposes that language is a human artifact, created in response to the needs of society. In Wundt's opinion this "useful fiction" was propounded and widely accepted simply because it reflected the nature of languages as we know them today. Because the connection between sound and meaning seems arbitrary and conventional in modern languages, the assumption is made that this has been the case from the beginning. However, there are obvious difficulties with the Invention scenario, which appears to assume a high development of human intelligence at a time just prior to the emergence of language. To imagine such a beginning for language—the product of a human decision about words and their meanings—presents the same dilemma that Socrates posed in his conversation with Cratylos: How could words be coined, agreement reached on their meanings, and a grammar constructed without the use of an already existing language? The Invention theory does not really attempt to answer such questions seriously.

The Invention and Miracle theories share the assumption that language has been essentially complete from the beginning, and thus the same kind of instrument that we use today. There seems to be no need to suggest a transition from a primitive or rudimentary state to languages of a modern type. However, two well-known speculative theories are attempts to do just that. One of these is the Imitation (or, more popularly, "Bow-Wow") theory—the proposal that language began with mimicry, using the vocal imitation of natural sounds. As with the Invention theory, this idea receives a degree of support from a selective sampling of present-day languages. Here, the point of

---

[1]Wilhelm Wundt (1832–1920) was the first to teach psychology as a subject independent of philosophy, beginning in 1861. Studies conducted in his laboratory in Leipzig influenced thought in both social sciences and linguistics. *Die Sprache* ("Language"), the first two volumes of his *Volkerpsychologie* ("Ethnic Psychology"), is a wide-ranging study of many aspects of language, including its origin and evolution.

THE PROBLEM OF LANGUAGE ORIGINS

departure is the fact that most languages do contain some vocabulary that appears to reflect the workings of sound imitation, or *onomatopoeia*. Pursuing this idea in the 19th century, prehistorian Sir John Lubbock, one of the founders of British anthropology, observed that, in English,

> Many names of animals, such as cuckoo, crow, peewit, &c, are evidently derived from the sounds made by those birds. Everyone admits that such words as bang, crack, purr, whizz, hum, &c . . . have arisen from the attempt to represent sounds characteristic of the object it is intended to designate. Take again the inarticulate human human sounds—sob, sigh, moan, groan, laugh, cough, weep, whoop, shriek, yawn; or of animals, as cackle, chuckle, gobble, quack, twitter, chirp, coo, hoot, caw, croak, chatter, neigh, whinny, mew, purr, bark, yelp, roar, bellow; slap, crack, smack, whack, thwack, pat, bat, batter, butt; and again, clash, flash, plash, splash, smash, dash, crash, bang, clang, twang, ring, ding, din, bump, thump, plump, boom, hum, drum, hiss, rustle. . . .
>
> I cannot but think that we may look upon the words above mentioned as the still recognizable descendants of roots which were onomatopoeic in their origin. . . . (Lubbock, 1874)

But as easy as it is to find such examples, it is also easy to dismiss imitation as a comprehensive explanation for the origin of language. Languages differ in their propensity for onomatopoeia, but none relies on it extensively as a major source of vocabulary. Furthermore, the very words that appear to have this property can sometimes be traced to earlier forms that do not. For example, *thwack, whack, bat,* and *batter* in Lubbock's list are not onomatopoetic in origin. In modern English, words that are clearly imitative (*bow-wow, choo-choo*, and the like) may be ephemeral, and they often exist alongside the more usual terms (*dog, train*); they are especially common in "baby-talk" and slang.

To accept imitation as a creative force in language, it must be put in a larger context, along with the workings of other forces. Even if it were granted that vocabulary was originally coined in this way, various processes of change would eventually have obscured the original connections between form and meaning. The Natural Sound (or "Ouch!") theory, the suggestion that language derives from instinctive emotional cries or exclamations, also demands an evolutionary scenario. In the late 19th century, Charles Darwin accepted a version of the Natural Sound theory and suggested that there was an evolutionary continuity between the vocalizations of monkeys and apes and human language. Certain recent evolutionary scenarios are elaborations on the same basic idea; however, the problem remains to explain how the transition from instinctive cries to language may have taken place.

Whatever general theory of language origin is favored, it must be emphasized that the major part of the vocabulary of all known languages is, to all appearances, arbitrary. This is easily demonstrated by comparing the names of animals, plants, heavenly bodies, and other vocabulary in a random selection of languages. For example, the English word *dog* can be translated to the French *chien*, Spanish *perro*, German *Hund*, and Russian *sobaka*. Even though these five languages are historically related, the words are obviously quite dissimilar. Adding a few other unrelated languages, we find Navajo *łeécaʔi*,

Maori *kurii*, Malagasy *alika*, Swahili *mbwa*, and Burmese *khwéi*. There is little to suggest imitation or any other kind of natural connection between these words and their referents.

It seems obvious, from the point of view of the linguist or the language student, that the important thing is not which form stands for which meaning, but that the speakers of a language agree on the selection of forms and meanings, and that they all use words in the same way: as tokens in a system of shared symbols. As a functional explanation, an insight into the way languages work, there is very little room for argument with this position. The problem remains to account for the origin and development of this kind of system. What were the raw materials out of which the plan for human language evolved? It may well be that *both* emotional cries (of pain, delight, sorrow, etc.) *and* imitative vocalizations played a part in the early growth of language. However, if this were the case, changes over the intervening years have made any direct connections untraceable; the more obvious examples of "intuitive" vocabulary drawn from modern languages are undoubtedly recent innovations.

Further, it must be observed, after surveying these "classic" ideas about the origin—and, implicitly, the nature—of language, that a disproportionate amount of emphasis has been put on *words*. It is as if a language consisted simply of its lexicon. Words are, to be sure, the stuff of language; but words are not just randomly strung together. They are ordered according to rules, reflecting an underlying structure. This structure is *syntax*, the basis for the regular patterns of phrases and sentences. We will see that, for many linguists, syntax is the most universal and defining property of language, and that this must be another piece of the "origin of language" puzzle.

LANGUAGE AND EVOLUTION

Wilhelm Wundt's own scenario for the origin of language, which he called the Evolutionary theory, was an elaboration of the Natural Sound concept. Although Wundt was not the first to suggest a direct development from non-human to human communication, he was one of the first to do so in the framework of Darwinian evolutionary biology. Like Darwin and many more recent scientists, Wundt found a clue to the origin of human language in primate behavior, specifically in the expression of emotion. His perspective was somewhat broader than that of many of his contemporaries, perhaps because he had included both speech and sign language in his own research. It was in sign language that Wundt perceived the most direct link to the expressive movements of nonhuman primates. He reasoned that early hominids would have used similar movements, primarily associated with emotions and accompanied by incidental vocalizations. These vocalizations would eventually have become the starting point for speech, while gestures lapsed in importance. The transition, he thought, would have been gradual: "If an observer were granted the power to follow the development of language step by step, he would never be in the position to say 'Here, at this moment, language begins; and there, in the immediate past, it was not yet present.' " Unfortunately, Wundt's formulation was tied to a complex—and now outdated—body of psychological theory. However, he anticipated a line of reasoning about the origin and evolution of language that can now be developed on a firmer footing, supported by experimental and field studies of nonhuman primates and a greatly expanded body of knowledge of human prehistory (Wundt, 1901, page 605).

Anthropologists usually point to four attributes that serve to define human status: upright posture, the making of tools, a high degree of intelligence, and the use of language. This complex of features developed in an African branch of the primate order, beginning more than 3 million years ago. Their emergence marks the division between creatures we consider human, like ourselves (hominid), and those that are related but subhuman (hominoid).

Although it is clear that these features are interrelated, the processes and stages in their development have yet to be clarified. More than a century ago, scientists began to debate whether, for example, humanlike intelligence evolved earlier or later than upright posture. Did tool making stimulate intelligence, or the reverse? Was Homo sapiens' large cranial capacity the product or the cause of the development of language? And, perhaps most mysterious, what role did language play in the growth of human culture and society? The degree of confusion that surrounded these issues can be seen in the reception originally given the famous "Piltdown Man," a putative fossil hominid unearthed in England in 1912. This fraud, supposedly of great antiquity, was actually a crude composite of a recent human brain-case and the jaw of an ancient ape. At the time, however, such a combination of features seemed believable, and Piltdown Man was hailed as the "missing link," validating a popular view that the transition from ape to human began with the emergence of human intelligence.

In the subsequent decades, archaeology and human paleontology have matured as sciences, and the general outlines of the hominization process have become fairly clear. The process began, not with a great increase in intelligence, but with the acquisition of upright posture. The australopithecines (or "man-apes") of eastern Africa, 4 to 6 million years ago, walked upright, although they were not as completely adapted to sustained upright posture as are their modern descendants. Some 4 million years ago, the small Australopithecus afarensis known as "Lucy" had a small brain and long arms, like those of brachiating apes. However, her lower skeleton—particularly the shape of the pelvis—attests to her upright posture and adaptation for walking. The early australopithecines were probably at home in the trees as well as on the ground. Their evolutionary status is still debated; taxonomically, they are not included in the human genus but are considered transitional to it. One species—probably Australopithecus africanus—is now thought to have been the ancestral population from which genus Homo evolved.

Upright posture, in turn, was functionally linked to the development of a new specialization of the hands, not just for grasping and tree climbing but for manipulative activities that would eventually include the making and using of tools. Upright posture and bipedal walking were followed by changes in the shape and proportions of the head and face, including rounding and expansion of the brain-case, flattening of the face, and reduction of the jaw. Lucy's cranial capacity was apelike; at approximately 450 cc, it was no greater than that of a chimpanzee. Two million years later, roughly contemporary with the last of the australopithecines, *Homo habilis* had a cranial capacity of around 750 cc and is clearly associated with a tradition of tool making—a definite indication of the beginnings of human culture.

Where, in the expanding body of knowledge of human prehistory, is there evidence for the origin of language? Can a case be made that a biological adaptation for the use of language was already present in the ancient hominids? The evidence is hard to come by, but increasing interest in these questions has led to new investigations. Attention now focuses on progressive changes in two areas: the vocal tract and the brain.

THE BIOLOGY OF LANGUAGE

THE VOCAL TRACT.   The anatomical feature that is basic to our biological specialization for speaking had its origin as a side-effect of the acquisition of upright posture. This is the *pharynx,* the portion of the vocal tract linking the oral cavity and the larynx, which contains and protects the vocal cords. In most mammals, the oral cavity leads immediately to the larynx, but in the higher primates the windpipe became bent and somewhat lengthened, as the skull rotated to a position atop the spinal column (rather than suspended at the end of it). In humans, this part of the windpipe, the pharynx, is much elongated and serves as a resonator in the production of speech sounds. (See Figure 1.1.)

Biologists consider speech to be an overlaid function of the vocal tract because there are no unique structures that are exclusively associated with speech. However, the pharynx and the oral and nasal cavities do serve to modify vocalic sounds (forming the vowels of speech), and the tongue is the primary articular of consonants. In the course of human evolution, it appears that specific modifications in the size and shape of the vocal tract, changes in the proportions of the mouth and jaw, and an overall reduction in the size of the teeth (providing additional space for movements of the tongue) have all operated to facilitate speech. These modifications account in large part for the distinctive facial configuration of modern *Homo sapiens.* Thus, it would appear that the presence of such modifications in prehistoric populations should serve as a clear indicator of the use of spoken language.

Philip Lieberman was one of the first investigators to seek objective evidence for the presence of a biological capacity for language, by examining and comparing the skeletal remains of ancient human and nonhuman primates. Lieberman, a linguist, worked in cooperation with biological anthropologist Edward Crelin. They wanted to trace the relative development of the pharynx, which

FIGURE 1.1 THE SPEECH APPARATUS.

(1) The vocal cords; (2) the pharynx; (3) the oral cavity; (4) the nasal cavity.

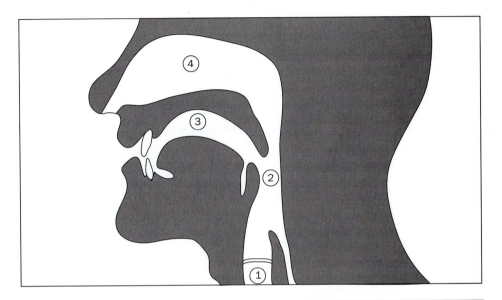

they saw as the primary organ of speech. This presented a problem, however, because the windpipe is formed entirely of soft tissue; the vocal cords are cartilaginous, and the delicate hyoid bone, which buttresses the pharynx, is rarely recovered in ancient remains. Skeletal materials alone could not be relied upon for a direct indication of the size or proportions of the pharynx.

Lieberman and Crelin carried out an innovative experiment. Working with human fossils, they used a modeling compound to reconstruct the vocal tract. Then they developed a computer program to calculate the range of vocalic sounds that such a vocal tract could produce, in order to make comparisons to the phonetics of modern human languages. The most controversial study, which heightened interest in their approach, was an analysis based on an assembly of Neanderthal fossils. Lieberman and Crelin's conclusion was that the vocal tract of the "Old Man of La Chapelle-aux-Saints" was "inherently incapable of producing the range of sounds that is necessary for the full range of human speech." Specifically, they asserted that the opposition of high front, high back, and low central vowels (phonetically, [i], [u], and [a]) which is a universal feature in languages of the world, could not have been present (Lieberman & Crelin, 1971).

This study raised a number of questions. Although some critics rejected the methodology outright, much of the controversy appears to hinge on the issue of the position of "Neanderthal man" in the overall framework of human evolution. For some, the study suggested that the Neanderthals were so primitive as to lack language entirely. This interpretation is attractive to those who see Neanderthal as a failed side branch of hominid evolution. To others, the Lieberman and Crelin research seemed compatible with the capacity for a rudimentary language, perhaps appropriate to a direct ancestor of modern humans.

In a series of studies different in methodology but similar in aim to those of Lieberman and Crelin, J. Laitman identified a skeletal feature that is associated with elongation of the pharynx and, presumably, the presence of language. Laitman found that the base of the cranium (*basicranium*), which borders the upper respiratory tract, varies in its configuration in a way that directly relates to the size of the pharynx:

> In mammals where the larynx was placed high in the neck such as cats, dogs, monkeys and apes, the basicranium was relatively non-flexed (flat). Only older [adult] humans showed a larynx placed absolutely lower in the neck, and only these individuals exhibited a markedly flexed basicranium. . . . Human infants . . . showed basicrania which closely resemble those of other primates . . . [and] exhibited a larynx placed high in the neck. (Laitman, 1976)

Laitman's findings can be closely related to those of Lieberman and Crelin. The larynx forms the lower end of the pharynx; therefore, the lower its location, the longer the pharynx. In Laitman's terms, then, a marked flexion of the base of the cranium is a progressive trait, indicating a developed pharynx and the presence of—or at least the capacity for—language. As he remarks, this feature is absent in human infants; the larynx begins to descend during the first 18 months of life, and the pharynx becomes progressively more elongated as the individual matures (Laitman, 1976).

By taking measurements at five key points along the base of the cranium, Laitman was able to calculate and compare the degree of flexion in modern and fossil skulls. These clearly reveal the unique conformation of the adult *Homo sapiens* basicranium and provide a basis for evaluating future paleontological finds in order to arrive at a more complete picture of human evolution as it relates to language.

Although the pharynx is essential to the production of the vocalic sounds used in speech, many other features asssociated with speech may have developed in response to selective pressures. G. Krantz attempted to trace the development of a series of traits that differentiate the skull of *Homo sapiens* from that of *Homo erectus:* increased cranial capacity, the size and shape of the vault (both related to the configuration of the brain); the location of the occipital condyle (related to the restructuring of the pharynx), and a backward and downward shifting of the tongue (also a consequence of the changes in the pharynx); the flattening of the face; reduction in the size of teeth; and reshaping of the nose and chin (see Figure 1.2). In Krantz's view, all of these are interrelated parts of the hominization process, and all are consequences of the emergence of language: "This interpretation of the sapiens transformation is based only on the development of full vocal communication, presumably of phonemic speech" (Krantz, 1980).

FIGURE 1.2

Lateral view of skulls and supralaryngeal passages of newborn (A), Neanderthal (B), and adult man (C). On supralaryngeal passages, NC—nasal cavity; T—tongue; P—pharynx (after Lieberman and Crelin, simplified). Reprinted with permission of Macmillan Publishing Co., Inc. from *On the Origins of Language* by Philip Lieberman. Copyright 1975 by Philip Lieberman.

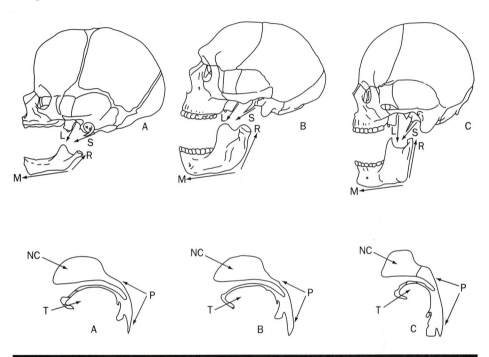

The cumulative impact of the studies by Leiberman, Laitman, and Krantz, and others in a similar vein, has been to reveal the mainstream role of language in human evolution. It now seems obvious that the distinctive human vocal tract was shaped by selective processes and that it should be considered a specialization for speech, just as the human hand is specialized for the use of tools.

THE LANGUAGE-SPECIALIZED BRAIN.   Through the early stages of human evolution, biological changes are paralleled by evidences of the emergence of culture. The use of language appears to have developed in concert both with increasing human intelligence and with habitual tool use. In turn, tool use may have mitigated against the use of gestures. The size of the brain increased enormously, from the australopithecine average of 400–500 cc, to more than 700 cc in *Homo habilis*, to around 1,000 cc in *Homo* *erectus,* to more than 1,400 cc in *Homo sapiens.* This growth consisted almost entirely in the thickening and convoluting of the *neocortex,* the outermost layer and evolutionarily the most recent portion of the brain. Development of the neocortex is unique to mammals, is most marked in the higher mammals, and is especially prominent in the primates. This outer layer is superimposed on the brainstem and midbrain, which control vital functions such as breathing and trigger emotional and other automatic responses. In humans, the neocortex is the seat of cognitive functions, such as spatial perception, memory, anticipation, judgment, and control. In relation to behavior, the neocortex appears to supplement and, in part, to take over certain functions of the brainstem and midbrain. Via the neocortex, learning and conscious decision making have replaced or overriden the automatic or unconscious responses that are triggered by these more ancient parts of the brain. This means that speech, like other forms of behavior (gustatory, sexual, social, etc.) is learned and consciously controlled rather than purely instinctive. It is, as a consequence, culturally patterned.

Humans have brains that resemble, but are larger than, those of other members of the primate order. Even in the brainiest of these—the gorillas and chimpanzees—we find a cranial capacity that is less than half of the human norm. And this is only part of the story: Our brains are not just larger, they are also developed in special ways. Most of this specialization is seen in the neocortex, and much of it appears to be related to the use of language. Some of the more salient features of the human brain are:

1. An enlargement of the occipital (posterior) lobe is characteristic of all primates, including humans. This area is associated with vision, a sense that is highly developed in the more arboreal primates but continues to be of great importance to humans. By contrast, all primate brains are underdeveloped in the areas associated with the sense of smell (which is highly developed in carnivores).

2. Primate brains show a strong development of the temporal lobes. This is especially pronounced in humans. Functions located in this region include the analysis of visual and auditory stimuli, which facilitates the recall and reactivation of past experience.

3. The frontal lobes are enlarged in the higher primates, especially in *Homo sapiens.* The characteristic of a high, bulging forehead is recognized as a distinctively human trait. The neocortex here is folded and convoluted, greatly increasing its total surface area. Much of this region consists of motor and sensory areas, of which those associated with the fingers, the hand, and the tongue and mouth are especially large.

4. The human brain exhibits *lateralization,* that is, the two hemispheres differ in size and configuration and are differentiated in function. This is a departure from the more general mammalian tendency to bilateral symmetry and is far more marked in *Homo sapiens* than in other hominids. Dominance of the left hemisphere is linked to dextrality

(right-handedness), which is characteristic of all human populations. Further, in all right-handed and most left-handed individuals, language functions are concentrated in the left hemisphere.

5. Finally, it has been suggested that a degree of lateralization, perhaps related to language, exists in a subcortical region of the brain, the hippocampus. This is the seat of limbic functions, relating to emotional arousal, and of cognitive mapping having to do with spatial memory. It appears that the left half of the hippocampus may also have some connection with deep-structural syntactic patterns that are universal in, and unique to, human language. R. Wallace suggests that this is an overlaid function—that linguistic transformations are "analogs of mapping functions" in the hippocampus (Wallace, 1989).

Although individuals in several mammalian species, including the non-human primates, exhibit brain asymmetries and preferences in using their limbs, only humans show a marked bias toward dextrality. M. Corballis believes that dextrality was prevalent in hominids as early as *Australopithecus robustus* and *Homo habilis* and that specialization of the hands developed in concert with bipedalism and tool use—the left hand routinely used for holding, the right for manipulating and operating. Presumably, these cognitive changes would have developed over time, along with the emergence of language. While the left hemisphere controls many language functions, other functions are concentrated in the right hemisphere, notably spatial orientation and visual pattern processing. Corballis generalizes the division of functions as "the left . . . for analytic processing, . . . the right . . . for holistic processing" (Corballis, 1989).

Full development of lateralization came late in hominid evolution, making possible an increase in the complex functioning of the brain without a substantial increase in cranial capacity. Further, the concentration of related functions in either the left or right hemisphere may constitute a kind of economy— coordination of functions can be more direct and responses more rapid than would be the case if the loci were widely separated. Thus, several speech functions, including articulation and word memory and associations, are located in adjacent regions of the left hemisphere, while spatial orientation and concepts of proportion are predominantly right-brain functions. It is tempting to think that, in both cases, we see evolutionary developments of great significance in the hominization process, giving us the potential for language, tool making, and mathematical, artistic, and other distinctively human skills.

Initial identification of the primary speech areas was achieved, for the most part, by means of investigations undertaken to diagnose the cause of speech impairments and aphasias. *Broca's area* (named for its discoverer, French physician and physical anthropologist Paul Broca) was identified in 1861, through autopsies conducted on aphasic patients. These patients exhibited problems in speech production; they were unable to articulate speech sounds although their comprehension was unimpaired. The area implicated in such cases, associated with control of the motor functions of

FIGURE 1.3   LANGUAGE AREAS OF THE BRAIN.

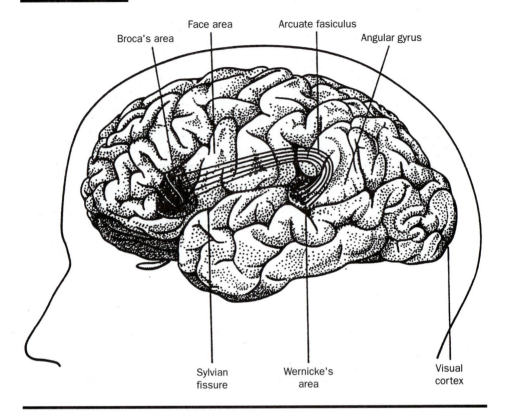

speech, is situated in the left frontal region (see Figure 1.3), adjacent to areas that control other delicate and precise motor functions (of, for instance, the fingers and the hand). Similarly, *Wernicke's area* is best known because of its linkage to aphasic symptoms. Damage to this area, situated nearby in the left parietal region, usually results in an aphasia characterized by disturbances in language comprehension and in garbled or incomplete sound production. Other identifiable language areas include the *arcuate fasiculus*, a bundle of nerve fibers linking Broca's and Wernicke's areas, and the *angular gyrus*, which is thought to mediate between visual and auditory centers.

Directly or indirectly, then, several unique or specialized features of the human brain have a connection with the use of language: special language-function centers, areas for perception and association, for memory, and for fine muscular control and coordination (of the lips, tongue, glottis, etc.). There are linkages between the auditory, motor, and associational areas involved in speech, as well as right-brain areas that are less specialized but essential to overall comprehension of speech, including associations of emotion, symbolism, cultural content, and so on.

ANIMAL COMMUNICATION
AND HUMAN LANGUAGE

For a behavioral perspective on the nature of human language, let us consider it in the broader context of animal communication. For any species, communication serves a variety of functions connected to foraging, predation, defense, mating, and other activities. Information comes in many forms and can be apprehended through any, or all, of the senses—touch, vision, hearing, smell, and even taste provide information—and all of these can play a role in communication among individuals and groups. In various mammals, visual, auditory, tactile, and olfactory signals (singly or in combination) may serve to indicate sexual readiness. An animal's cries of alarm or distress can give a warning of danger to any others that are within earshot; and the actions of one individual foraging for food will telegraph information about the availability of food to others. We humans are apt to think first of the intentional messages that we send through language, and of the deliberate use of gestures and facial expressions. However, much of our communication is instinctive and unintentional. A look of fatigue, concern, surprise, or elation; a sigh, grimace, shudder, or tear: These convey messages that may be more revealing than words. We share this instinctive kind of communication with nonhuman species. More often than not, however, we accompany our body language with verbalization. (Redundancy is a common feature of communication, whether human or nonhuman.)

ARMY ANTS AND HONEY BEES. Communication is supremely important for all social animals; it is the glue that links numbers of individual organisms into a larger whole. This is as true of ants and bees as it is of humans. Some of the characteristics of complex society (organized communities, a hierarchical structure, and a division of labor) that bespeak the importance of communication in human life appear to have parallels in the life of social insects. These insects seem to hold a special fascination for human observers, who tend to attribute humanlike qualities to their communities and coordinated activities. (In 1998, two feature-length films, *Antz* and *A Bug's Life,* presented highly romanticized views of life in an ant colony.)

For sheer numbers, few animals can rival the colonies of the several species of *army ants,* which are found in the tropical rain forests of Africa, Asia, and the Americas. Colonies follow cyclical patterns of movement that are triggered by stages in the reproductive life of the solitary females or "queens," who periodically deliver between 20,000 and 30,000 eggs. The colonies—often called "troops" or "tribes"—are predominantly made up of males, ranging in size from "major" to "minim"; these play a variety of roles in defense, food gathering, and caring for the young during the pupal and larval stages.

The movements of a colony fall into two phases: quiescent periods of "bivouac" interspersed with nomadic "marching" and "raiding." The latter type of activity, during which hundreds of thousands of ants sweep across the landscape, consuming any and all dead or inactive animals and insects in their path, has especially excited the imagination of observers. Terms such as "phalanx," "officers," "skirmishes," and "maneuvers" abound in the writings of authors who have described encounters with army ants. Until 20th-century scholars like T. C. Schneirla made systematic studies, both in the field and in a laboratory setting, most observers did not hesitate to explain ant behavior in terms that suggest tactics and deliberation, "as if the creatures could reason, exchange information, take purposeful action and feel tender emotions" (Schneirla & Piel, 1948).

But anthropomorphism, as Schneirla and Piel point out, can actually explain nothing about the social life and organization of insects. Communication of a sort does take place, and it is as essential to ant society as it is to human, but it has little in common with human communication through language. Learning, which plays a considerable role in shaping the behavior of all mammals, reaches its maximum importance in *Homo sapiens*. By contrast, ants, like other insects, have a minimal capacity for learning; virtually all of their behavior is genetically determined, the product of natural selection.

Ants are almost completely deaf and blind. Vision is limited to the discrimination of light and darkness, and hearing amounts only to the detection of vibrations transmitted through the ground. Still, ants—like humans—are in constant contact and communication with one another. But is this communication analagous to human language? The ants' chief organs of perception are their constantly moving antennae, through which they make tactile and chemical determinations. It is not information about the outside world that is exchanged, but chemical secretions. The cohesion of the colony arises from the exchange of these substances, *pheromones* or "co-enzymes," that are essential to the survival of all. The enzymes are species specific and even differ slightly between colonies of the same species. They are constantly traded as the ants touch, lick, and nuzzle one another.

How does a colony of some 150,000 ants perform the complex series of maneuvers that might appear to be planned and coordinated by a chain of command? Their behavior alternates between inactive periods of "bivouac," when the queen delivers thousands of eggs, and "march," when the entire colony moves in search of food. When ants are on the march, activity begins at dawn, stimulated by light, and increases as the day grows brighter. Soon, the ants begin to throng in a churning mass until a raiding column breaks forth along a path of least resistance. Once movement has begun, the rest of the colony follows along a trail of droplets secreted by the anal glands of those in the lead. Smaller and medium-sized ants move, tightly pressed, along a central path, while the larger and more ungainly are crowded to the sides—an arrangement that has suggested the identification of the larger ants as "drill sergeants" or "works majors." At any obstacle, the numbers of ants pile up until a critical mass is achieved, eventually breaking through to continue the march. Once begun, it is pressure from the rear that keeps movement going from dawn until nightfall. Any quarry is quickly engulfed, and movement goes on, following "the principles of hydraulics even more closely than those of military tactics." In other words, it is essentially directed by chance factors—the character of the terrain, natural obstacles, and the location of booty (Schneirla & Piel, 1948).

Both ants and bees have long appealed to popular fancy as symbols of industry and cooperation. Animal behaviorist Karl von Frisch conducted studies that revealed hitherto unsuspected intricacies of bee behavior and also clarified basic differences between insect and human communication. In an early experiment, von Frisch placed sheets of paper smeared with honey in a spot where they were eventually discovered by a lone forager bee; within a period of moments, dozens or hundreds of bees appeared. "How," he wondered, had the "first-comer . . . announced her find to the other bees in the hive?" (von Frisch, 1953) His studies would involve both long observation under natural conditions and the use of specially designed hives and equipment that enabled him to view the colony at close range.

Of von Frisch's many findings, attention has focused on the behavior that he characterized as "dancing." When a forager returns to the hive, traces of pollen on her body convey the identity of the flower species, and the honey that she disgorges is a sign that a rich source has been discovered; but it is through the "dance" that the location of the source is made known. This is a series of gyrations that are performed either out-of-doors on a flat surface or in almost total darkness on the vertical panels of the hive. In the *round dance*, performed when the food source is nearby, the bee begins whirling in narrow circles, turning first clockwise and then counterclockwise. Other bees contact her with their feelers and mimic her movements, until she is followed by a "comet-tail of bees." She may pause to disgorge more honey and then repeat the dance, and may eventually fly out again. But whether or not she returns to the source, others do, and they will also dance. Von Frisch concluded that the vigor of the dance gives an impression of the richness of the source; the scent, apprehended through the feelers, reveals the variety of the flowers; and, as the bees fly out to scour the area, an odor released by the original forager's own scent glands provides a clue to the right location. The *wagging dance* is performed when the distance to the food source is greater.

It is the wagging dance that enables bees to fly as far as 3 miles in a given direction, to the precise location of a food source. In this dance, the forager runs clockwise in a semicircle, then makes a turn and moves—with a wagging movement of her abdomen—along a straight line back to the starting point. She then makes a counterclockwise semicircle, returns to the starting point, and repeats the pattern. Von Frisch found that the pace of the dance was directly related to distance from the source—if around 100 yards, the turns followed one another in quick succession, but if distances were greater, the runs were slower and the intervals longer. He remarked that the bees "must possess a very acute sense of time, enabling the dancer to move in the rhythm appropriate to the occasion, and her companions to comprehend and interpret her movements correctly" (von Frisch, 1953).

"DIALECTS" IN BEE-DANCING
In 1962, Karl von Frisch expanded his original observations, comparing the behavior of several kinds of bees from different regions of Europe. He found variations on the same patterns that he had originally described in the Italian honey bee *(A. Mellifera ligustica)*. His observations are summarized in Figure 1.4.

FIGURE 1.4 DIALECTS IN THE LANGUAGE OF THE BEES.

The dwarf bee dances on a horizontal surface. All others dance on a vertical surface. The speed of the wagging dance carries distance instructions. The more rapidly the bee performs its wagging runs, the shorter is the distance. The figures in the squares represent the number of wagging runs in 15 seconds for each distance and kind of bee (von Frisch, 1962).

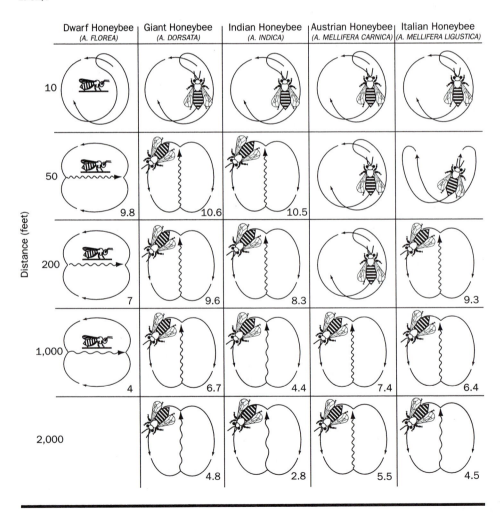

Finally, it is the orientation of the straight-line axis of the wagging dance that indicates the direction of the route. The bee's superior spatial orientation is made possible by its special sense of vision; its compound eye can take in a wider range and more successive impressions than the human eye, and it also has a sensitivity to polarized light (that humans do not experience). Bees always move in a straight line, at a certain angle in relation to the sun; the axis of the dance repeats this angle. This is perfectly straightforward when the dance is performed out-of-doors with the sun in view; in the hive, however, the force of gravity appears to replace the sun, and the angle is thus the degree of deviation from the vertical. Despite the apparent complexity of the maneuver, the dance is a reenactment in miniature of the forager's flight—and it transmits the information that enables others to repeat it.

Linguists have found the "dancing" of honey bees especially interesting as an example of animal communication that appears to embody some of the principles of human language—for example, *displacement*, the ability to "talk" about referents that are removed in time or space. Von Frisch himself appears to suggest other similarities, referring to the round dance and the wagging dance as "two different words of the bee language." However, he also points out basic differences between insect and human communication: Bees fail to respond when a test situation requires that they deviate from their accustomed routine. They rely entirely on inborn reactions and respond only to "those factors . . . to which they have been accustomed since prehistoric times." Bee dancing is not language in any real sense; the dances are not words, but they *are* signs, performed and understood instinctively. The intricacy and complexity of the message may approach human language; but in being genetically programmed, rather than learned, it could not be more different (von Frisch, 1953).

Mammals, like insects, have characteristic patterns of social life in which communication plays an important role. Their patterns are more variable and adaptable than those of the social insects. This greater flexibility is a direct consequence of their greater intelligence. While insect behavior is genetically programmed and is essentially fixed, mammals are quicker to learn and thereby to modify their behavior. In the evolution of reptiles, birds, and mammals there has been a general tendency toward increase in the size and complexity of the brain; this roughly corresponds, in functional terms, to increased reliance on learning.

Numerous field studies of animal behavior reveal intricate and flexible behavior patterns in which the importance of communication is evident. These tendencies are especially strong in the case of social animals, including the various species of the canine family, which includes coyotes, dingoes, jackals, and wolves.

THE SOCIAL LIFE OF WOLVES.   Wolves are native to a broad expanse of arctic, subarctic, and temperate habitat extending across Eurasia and most of North America. At present, their numbers are depleted throughout much of this area; in the United States, efforts have recently been made to reintroduce wolves to parts of their earlier habitat, which includes several national parks.

Like ants and bees, wolves have a longtime prominence in Western folklore—largely as familiar symbols of evil, aggression, and sometimes male sexuality.

The wolves of European tradition usually appear as individuals (the "Big Bad Wolf," for example); this is somewhat ironic, since wolves are a prime example of social animals. Their social groups (packs) range in size from 2 to 30 members; most packs have between 10 and 20 members. Pack members stay together year round, cooperating in hunting, playing, and caring for their young. Like all social animals, wolves depend to a great extent on communication, both within the pack and between packs.

Wolves are carnivores. The numbers in the pack and the size of its territory are both highly variable, conditioned by features of habitat and the kind of prey available. In settings in which small animals constitute most of the prey—mice, rabbits, and so forth—wolfpacks are small; where deer, the most common prey, predominate, packs are of medium size—around 8 or 10 animals; if moose or elk is hunted, at least five to six adult wolves must cooperate in the hunt, and the size of the pack is correspondingly larger. Territories of neighboring packs may overlap slightly; or, if population pressure is low, there may be a buffer zone. In any case, boundaries are scent marked, and territory will be defended against intruders. There must be sufficient resources to sustain the pack; if the prey is depleted, the wolves may have to move elsewhere.

The wolves' year falls roughly into two periods. In fall and winter, the pack is usually on the move, scouring the territory and following prey. Mating takes place in late winter; food is usually more plentiful in the spring and summer, when cubs are born and raised through their first months. Social organization is hierarchical. A typical wolfpack is led by two dominant animals—the alpha male and alpha female. In most cases, these are the only animals that breed, and, as a result, the pack normally produces a single litter of pups.

Membership of the pack may largely consist of the older and younger offspring of one breeding pair, but there is some flexibility. Members occasionally leave and strangers are accepted, with the effect that a rough balance is maintained between pack size and food supply. The "lone wolves" (male or female) usually leave as young adults, to hunt alone or perhaps to join another pack. These isolated males and females sometimes bond and form the nucleus of a new pack.

Scent marking by urine serves to indicate territorial boundaries, trails, and important environmental features. When traveling, an alpha male scent marks roughly every 2 minutes. These marks are thought to be important as an aid to hunting and as a way to help younger wolves establish a cognitive map of the territory. Dung is also used to mark territory. More frequently, it appears to be used as a warning of danger. It is well known that wolves defecate on traps; trappers tend to take this personally, but it is more likely done as a caution to younger pack members.

Contrary to popular belief, the wolf's howling is not directed at the moon, and wolves do not howl while on the chase. Howling seems to function to assemble the pack: One or two begin to howl, and others soon arrive to join in. When wolves howl in concert, each individual takes a different pitch. Their blend of voices, with audible overtones, has a powerful impact on the human ear. According to one observer, "any more than two sound like a dozen" (F. Harrington, quoted in Grooms, 1993). The sound can carry as far as 6 miles—an unforgettable experience to any campers within earshot. Howling is not conversation; neighbors do not respond in kind. More likely, the howl is a message of pack unity and territoriality.

Within the pack, there is constant communication by look, posture, and physical contact, with minimal vocalization. Most social relationships have their source in litters born to the dominant breeding pair or their predecessors. These relationships begin with the ties of affection among littermates and in the play-fighting that establishes a hierarchy within the litter. The young adults that leave the pack are often aggressive and independent individuals, who may eventually have a dominant role in a new pack. However, the solidarity of the pack is important to survival; lone wolves seldom survive unless they are able to join with or create a new pack.

Dominance relations are mirrored in facial expressions and body language. A lower-ranking animal approaches an alpha male or female with body lowered, tail down, and ears laid back, and may lick or nuzzle the dominant animal's face. Retracting the corners of the mouth to reveal the teeth in a "submissive grin" or flashing the whites of the eyes are additional signals of submission or acquiescence. An alpha male's fixed stare and low growl, with teeth exposed, can quickly end a squabble and restore peace. The position of the tail is a sign of status—most pack members carry their tails down, while the alpha pair carry theirs high. Markings of the fur seem to emphasize details of the face and posture—the dark tip of the tail gives it greater visibility, the wolf's black lips are outlined by white hairs in the muzzle and lower jaw, and the ears are lined with white hairs and rimmed with dark.

Much of the communication is low-key and subtle. Wolves rarely bark. A quiet "woof" may indicate surprise or give a warning; growling is rare as a serious threat, though common among pups at play. Low whines or "social squeaks" are greetings or invitations to play. When one pup is fed, it may squeak to call the others. B. H. Lopez, after observing wolves in captivity, concluded that "squeaks were repeated often enough to be recognized; these were associated with certain specific behaviors, leading one to think of them as true bits of communication" (Lopez, 1978). Wolves have an extremely acute sense of hearing and so may have no need for loud vocalizations in intragroup communication. Some observers believe that in hunting, wolves may rely more on this sense than on the sense of smell (Lopez, 1978; Grooms, 1993).

FIELD STUDIES OF PRIMATE COMMUNICATION

Anthropologists take a special interest in the social behavior of the nonhuman primates. Because humans are part of the primate order, comparisons with other branches of this order can provide a general baseline for an objective approach to our own behavior. Diet, reproduction, territoriality, social organization, gender roles, communication—all of these, as elaborated in the setting of human culture, grew out of broad underlying primate patterns. The most informative comparisons may be those made with primates that are phylogenetically closest to the human line: the Old World monkeys and apes.

The past three to four decades have seen a strong wave of interest in the study of monkeys and apes in their natural habitat. Primatology developed as an arena for interdisciplinary cooperation—environmentalists, biologists, psychologists, and anthropologists are among the scholars most involved in this research area. Typically, field studies do not deal directly with communication as such. More often, the focus is on ecological adaptation or social organization. However, an unanticipated effect of these studies has been to give anthropologists a greater awareness of the integral place of communication in the adaptation of all primate species, and this in turn gives depth to our perspective on human communication.

BABOONS AND OTHER MONKEYS. A pioneering study, directed by S. L. Washburn and I. DeVore, set a standard for subsequent research on primate social groups. In the late 1950s, Washburn and DeVore performed a long-term study of savanna baboons living in wildlife preserves in South Africa. These Old World monkeys share with humans the distinction of being predominately terrestial (ground dwelling), by contrast to the arboreal (tree-dwelling) adaptation characteristic of most primate species. The parallel in adaptation was a factor in the choice of this particular species for study.

Baboons are extremely social animals, living in compact "troops" of between 20 and 250 individuals. Since they often inhabit open savanna country, baboons come in contact with carnivorous predators such as lions and hyenas. The strength of their social organization, which keeps members of a troop always in contact and organized for defense, is the key to the successful adaptation of baboons. Ubiquitous primate traits, as characteristic of baboon as of human life, include the protracted dependency of infants and the critical role of learning as preparation for adulthood. Infant baboons are constantly in contact with their mothers; they are carried, first on the belly and, after the first month or two, on the back. An infant explores its territory as the mother moves with the troop, learns to feed by observing and imitating her, and receives constant attention in the form of grooming by the mother. Baboons of all ages spend time daily in mutual grooming; this is a kind of tactile communication that reinforces solidarity among troop members.

Juvenile baboons play, test their strength against one another, and establish a dominance hierarchy that is of lasting importance in the maintenance of social equilibrium. Although baboons have a number of distinctive vocal calls that serve as warnings and signals of aggression, they are usually quiet—far more so than more arboreal primates. Their silence may, in part, be explained by the danger of attracting nearby predators. It also reflects the compactness of the baboon troop—members are almost always within eye contact of one another and respond to visual, rather than vocal, cues.

According to Washburn and DeVore, "it is not unlikely that the major system that mediates interindividual behavior for baboons is one of visual cues from facial expressions, intention movements, and attitudes . . . auditory, tactual, and olefactory cues are of descending order of importance" (Washburn & DeVore, 1961).

CHIMPANZEES AND OTHER APES. Gorillas and chimpanzees are much closer to humans, in phylogenetic terms, than are baboons. Their habitat varies but usually includes both forest and open areas; in either setting, adults spend much time on the ground, while the smaller juveniles are more arboreal in habit. Gorillas are the largest of the primates and probably, next to humans, the most intelligent. Chimpanzees appear to have an extraordinarily flexible type of organization, with small social groups scattered unevenly over a large area of forest. Their social groups (or "bands") are smaller than the troops of baboons, and the membership is less stable, with individuals occasionally leaving or joining various bands. Frequent "hooting" calls and drumming on tree trunks serve to maintain contact among groups, keep each aware of their neighbors' locations, and sometimes serve as signals for a large gathering or "carnival."

Within the bands of gorillas and chimpanzees, there is constant communication among individuals. This combines vocal, facial, and gestural signals. Primatologist Jane Goodall observed many instances of such behavior and discerns a general similarity between chimpanzee and human nonverbal interaction:

> One significant aspect of chimpanzee behavior lies in the close similarity of many of their communicatory gestures and postures to those of man himself. Not only are the actual positions and movements similar to our own but also the contexts in which they often occur. When a chimpanzee is suddenly frightened he frequently reaches to touch or embrace a chimpanzee nearby. . . . Both chimpanzees and humans seem reassured in stressful situations by physical contact with another individual. . . .
>
> When two chimpanzees greet each other after a separation, their behavior often looks amazingly like that shown by two humans in the same context. Chimpanzees may bow or crouch to the ground, hold hands, kiss, embrace, touch, or pat each other on almost any part of the body, especially the head and face and genitals. A male may chuck a female or an infant under the chin. . . .
>
> Many of [the chimpanzee's] games are like those played by human children. The tickling movements of chimpanzee fingers during play are almost identical with our own. The chimpanzee's agressive displays are not dissimilar to some of ours. Like a man, an angry chimpanzee may fixedly stare at his opponent. He may raise his forearm rapidly, jerk back his head a little, run toward his adversary upright and waving his arms, throw stones, wield sticks, hit, kick, bite, scratch, and pull the hair of a victim. In fact, if we survey the whole range of the postural and gestural communication signals of chimpanzees on the one hand and humans on the other, we find striking similarities in many instances. It would appear, then, that man and chimp either have evolved gestures and postures along a most remarkable parallel or that we share with the chimpanzees an

ancestor in the dim and very distant past; an ancestor, moreover, who communicated with his kind by means of kissing and embracing, touching and patting and holding hands. (Lawick-Goodall, 1971)

Chimpanzees (unlike baboons) are extremely noisy; they accompany their physical displays and communicative gestures with a large repertoire of screams, hoots, pants, and chattering sounds. They have, second only to humans, the most varied repertoire of vocalizations of any primate species. Field researchers have been able to identify some 45 different chimpanzee vocalizations, all with identifiable situational meanings (e.g., excitement, surprise, food discovery, and sexual arousal). In this respect, as in their use of gesture and body language, chimpanzees provide a likely model for the communication patterns of our own protohominid ancestors.

THE PRIMATE BASELINE FOR HUMAN LANGUAGE

In *Primate Behavior and the Emergence of Human Culture,* Jane Lancaster (1975) commented that the natural communication systems of monkeys and apes are "extraordinarily complex" in comparison to those of many species of birds and mammals. Part of this complexity lies in the fact that primate communication is largely "multimodal"—that is, it involves the simultaneous use of vocalization, body movements, facial expressions, and, at times, touch or olfactory stimuli. In the threat behavior of baboons, for example, three or even four of these sensory channels are typically involved in sending or receiving a composite message. An additional consideration that makes animal communication difficult to analyze under any but close field conditions is the fact that the social context may be essential to interpreting the meaning of a signal: The baboon's ritualistic threats, for example, may be taken seriously in one situation but ignored or taken as a bluff in another.

Primate signals are usually graded. A particular type of vocalization will vary in intensity through a continuous series of changes in volume or duration. This grading of signals, as Lancaster points out, is quite different from the songs of many birds, which are unique and easily identifiable as to function or situation. It is also different from human language, in which messages are built up syntactically, of separate, discrete parts. Lancaster concedes this difference but points out the basic similarity to the paralinguistic and kinesic aspects of human communication: ". . . these systems have little relationship with human language but much with the ways our species expresses emotion through gesture, facial expression, and tone of voice" (Lancaster, 1975). It is on this basis that, as Jane Goodall observed, human observers often find the reactions of other primates intelligible and familiar.

Note that the general functions of primate communication are primarily emotional and agonistic. Vocalizations register alarm, threat, challenge, excitement, arousal, and so forth. Facial expressions and bodily movements similarly serve to mediate social relations, including those of dominance and submission. Physical contact, as in grooming, serves to establish and cement social solidarity. All of these find close parallels in human behavior—in tone of voice, expressive gestures, posture, body language, and facial expression.

What is most obviously missing in nonhuman primate communication, *vis-à-vis* human language, is *reference;* monkeys and apes communicate feelings, intentions, rivalries, and status, but they rarely appear to communicate *about* anything. Naming, identifying, indicating, describing—the informational content of language—is missing.

Language, as Lancaster sees it, "provided human beings with a tool by which they could communicate information to others not only about their own emotional states but also about social relationships and the physical environment."

The course of evolution taken by human language parallels, and seems to have a common cognitive basis with, the evolution of technology and tool use. Philip Lieberman discerns similarities between the cognitive patterns—roughly, the mental maps or plans—that underlie the chipping of stone tools of the sort made and used during the Paleolithic (or Old Stone Age) and general syntactic patterns typical of human language. Both, he would argue, are overt expressions of patterns in the mind. Exemplified in material culture, these patterns are initially crude but emerge more fully as technique is developed. As exemplified in language, patterns become elaborated through coinage of vocabulary and utilization in the context of human society. Thus, the parallelism that Lieberman discerns would hold that universal patterns, in language as in material culture, have a common mental basis and that over time, both have diversified and become more complex (Lieberman, 1975).

Language did not begin all at once; it was built slowly and cumulatively, out of many parts. Names, or nouns, are one basic component; like tools, they serve to separate and control the materials, things, and creatures of the environment. Language also incorporates the culturally patterned ways in which love, concern, alarm, fear, hatred, and other human emotions are expressed. The grammar of language codifies spatial and temporal relations, the logic of cause and effect, and the sequencing of events. It gives a means for relating the past to the present and planning for the future, for understanding relationships and weighing probabilities. The categories of language give rise to concepts and metaphors, extending knowledge of the concrete and immediate to the abstract and general—the basis for an encompassing "world view." As a finished product, language has all the complexity we need for social interaction, coordination of activities, division of labor, teaching and learning, ritual and worship, and the perpetuation of human knowledge across the generations.

Although we may never be able to reconstruct the social life and communication system of early humans in detail, the studies of field primatologists like Sherman Washburn, Jane Goodall, Dianne Fossi, and Birute Galdikas provide insight into the behavioral parameters within which our ancestors may have functioned. *Australopithecus africanus,* the diminutive primate that seems the most likely precursor of the hominid line, may well have been as social as the present-day African apes. However, as ground dwellers, the australopithecines would probably have lived in somewhat more compact groups than the chimpanzees, perhaps somewhat similar to those of baboons, which are tightly structured for defense. Like other semi-terrestrial primates, they would have retreated to the trees when danger threatened but would have found their greatest security in a strong network of social relationships.

Like the other higher primates, our australopithecine ancestors must have relied on several different kinds of communication. Touch, facial expressions, and gestures were important, just as they are for today's gorillas, chimps, and bonobos. In addition, it seems certain that vocal communication was just as prominent, perhaps more so. As innovations were made in social life—in cooperation and coordination of activities, diversification of gender roles, the sharing of responsibilities in parenting or group defense—they would have been matched by changes or innovations in the vocal repertoire. Social networking, facilitated by communication, gave them an advantage over other species, and natural selection operated in favor of this aspect of their adaptation. Over time, a vocally talented group of primates became even more so, outstripping even the versatile chimpanzees.

EXPERIMENTAL STUDIES OF PRIMATE LANGUAGE ABILITIES

Additional insights into primate communicative potential have come from studies carried out under laboratory conditions. In this case, researchers have focused attention on the learning ability and performance of individual animals. Although most of the early studies were carried out with chimpanzees as subjects, the scope has more recently widened to include gorillas, orangutans, and other primates. This research was initiated by, and still remains largely the domain of, behavioral psychologists, though linguists and anthropologists have also been participants. These studies have been of great interest for anthropologists interested in primate psychology. They provide a basis for reconstruction of the cognitive baseline from which human consciousness developed.

Beginning around 1950, a series of experiments pursued the objective of teaching elements of human language to nonhuman primates. These studies were consistent with a long tradition of the use of animals for psychological experimentation. Years earlier, a pioneer experiment in chimpanzee learning was carried out by psychologists W. N. and L. A. Kellogg, who, in the 1930s, raised an infant chimpanzee in their home together with their own son. The boy and chimpanzee—approximately the same age—were given a parallel series of intelligence tests, and their progress was described in numerous published and filmed reports. It was obvious that the chimpanzee, Gua, was physically ahead of the boy, Donald, and Gua scored higher in most tests through their first year and a half of life—roughly up to the age when language begins to play an important role in human learning (Kellogg, 1968).

The Kelloggs did not attempt to teach Gua to speak, though they believed that he understood many English phrases. In subsequent studies, several researchers have attempted to go farther in focusing specifically on language. K. J. Hays and C. Hays succeeded in teaching a home-raised chimp, Vicky, to pronounce three words in appropriate situations: *mama, papa,* and *cup.* After long and laborious efforts, however, it became obvious that the production of speech sounds was physically difficult for Vicky—her articulations were slow and awkward, and her vocal repertoire remained extremely limited. Later studies, while continuing the use of chimpanzees as subjects, generally shifted to concentrate on nonvocal forms of language. This was, in part, a reaction to the consistent failure of the animals to learn to speak (despite an obvious intelligence and aptitude for various kinds of mimcry). It also reflects the influence of field studies that, as we have seen, revealed the prominence of gesture communication among primates in the wild (Hays, 1952).

Subsequent primate language studies have taken divergent directions. Certain projects continue the earlier efforts to teach a modified form of human language in a social setting, with the use of manual word signs rather than speech. In effect, the emphasis appears to have been on the acquisition, retention, and use of vocabulary. An early project of this type was under-taken by R. A. Gardner and Beatrice Gardner, who undertook to teach American Sign Language to a chimpanzee.

The Gardners stated that their primary interest was in the processes of learning. Their main subject, Washoe, was between 8 and 14 months of age when she was caught in the wild. The research design may not have taken into account the fact that, prior to capture, Washoe had already lived for several months in a social environment rich in vocal and gestural interaction. She was evidently regarded, more or less, as a blank slate—a *tabula rasa*—for the purpose of experimentation. However, a gesture system was chosen as appropriate: "We reasoned that gestures for the chimpanzee should be analogous to bar-pressing for rats, key-pecking for pigeons, and babbling for humans" (Gardner & Gardner, 1969).

American Sign Language (ASL) is a widely used system made up of signs that are *iconic* (that is, they have some resemblance to their referents; see Figure 1.5) and others that appear to be arbitrary. The crew of research assistants received training in ASL (though few were fluent ahead of time). They endeavored to expose Washoe to this language in a relaxed social environment, in much the same way that a child would be exposed to a spoken language. Sounds such as clapping, whistling, and laughing were permitted—but only sounds that a chimpanzee might imitate; speech was not used.

The Gardners were relying on the chimpanzee's natural penchant for imitation. However, direct imitation of signs was not much in evidence. Rather, Washoe demonstrated delayed imitation, using a sign spontaneously after observing it over a period of time. For example, when her teeth were brushed after meals, instructors introduced the sign for "toothbrush." Her own first use of this sign came after several months, when she surveyed the contents of the Gardners' bathroom and signed "toothbrush."

FIGURE 1.5

Two of Washoe's signs: "book" and "baby." From *Apes, Men and Language* by Eugene Linden, illustrations by Madelaine Gill Linden. Copyright 1974 by Eugene Linden. Reprinted by permission of the publisher, E. P. Dutton.

Washoe: "book"   *Washoe: "baby"*

Games were invented to elicit imitation, and any of Washoe's movements that resembled signs were encouraged and reshaped. This evidently had the effect of increasing her manual "babbling" (random activity of the arms and hands), upon which new signs could be built. Researchers gave Washoe credit for creating new signs and sign combinations—"bib" (when she indicated a desire to be fed by outlining the shape of her bib on her chest) and "watermelon" (when she used signs for "candy" and "fruit" in combination). By the age of 3, Washoe had learned 35 signs, and eventually would acquire an active vocabulary of at least 85.[2] Once she had learned signs, the chimp used them creatively, transferring them to new contexts and extending them to new referents. For example, "flower" is an iconic sign, made with the hand cupped to resemble a flower and touched to the nose; Washoe learned it early and generalized it to flowers of all sorts. When she went on independently to apply this sign to a variety of odors, the ASL sign for "smell" was introduced. Thereafter, she was able to make the distinction but sometimes persisted in using "flower" in "smell" contexts. In another case, the sign "open" was introduced in reference

---

[2]This is a conservative count, since a sign was not considered to be established until three different observers reported it as occurring in an appropriate context. It is likely that Washoe's innovations still continue, since she is still alive and well and is the mother and grandmother of signing chimps.

to certain doors. Washoe transferred it, first to other doors, and then to containers, the refrigerator, briefcase, jars, and eventually even water faucets.

The Gardners' published accounts of their project included the assessment that "the most promising results have been spontaneous naming, spontaneous transfer to new referents, and spontaneous combinations and recombinations of signs" (Gardner & Gardner, 1969). It can be seen that, as in much of the earlier work on language origins, the emphasis is principally on vocabulary and especially on naming. Other language-learning experiments have turned the focus to syntax, rather than vocabulary.

The Gardners did observe that Washoe used signs in combinations, and she sometimes put together amazingly long sequences of them. For example, when Susan, a research assistant, stepped on Washoe's doll, her recorded reaction was: "Up Susan, Susan up, mine please up, gimme baby, please shoe, more mine, up please, please up, more up, baby down, shoe up, baby up, please more up . . . you up" (Jolly, 1972). However, the Washoe study was not designed to deal with extended discourse or with functional parallels to language; the numbers and sequences of signs were not treated analytically.

In another watershed study, psychologist David Premak undertook a project to deal specifically with the acquisition and use of syntactic rules. Premak introduced a young chimpanzee, Sarah, to the use of colored tokens in a variety of shapes. The tokens, which represented words, had to be arranged in a particular order to produce acceptable sentences. Premak used a standard behaviorist approach, rewarding Sarah with treats when she performed successfully. Along the same lines, psychologists at the Yerkes Primate Center worked with Lana, a chimpanzee who proved to be adept at keying in her responses on a specially designed computer keyboard. Beyond the reward for correct responses, delivered by machine, there was no interactive use of language in these studies. This type of research continues, although many linguists are, once more, inclined to skepticism, doubting that the apes' performance is truly "linguistic." True, Lana can use her keyboard to produce sentences like "Please * machine * give * Lana * candy" to obtain a desired reward. However, critics suggest that her performance is the result of operant conditioning, not language competence. (The criticism may be justified, but it seems rather like giving Professor Higgins the credit for Eliza Doolittle's success at the ball!)

Although the great majority of these language experiments were conducted with chimpanzees, a young gorilla named Hanabi-Ko (or Koko) first made the news in 1978 because of her startling achievements in language learning. Koko was given instruction in American Sign Language and, unlike Washoe, was also exposed to spoken English. Her trainer, Francine Patterson, speaks and signs simultaneously. Koko claims a signing vocabulary of more than 500 signs and has an aural comprehension of several thousand words (Patterson & Linden, 1978).

Another study of considerable recent interest involves Kanzi, a young male bonobo. Bonobos (*Pan paniscus*) were earlier known as "pigmy chimpanzees," but they are now recognized as a third variety of African ape, on a par with chimpanzees and gorillas. They resemble chimpanzees but differ both anatomically and behaviorally in details that appear remarkably humanlike. For example, bonobos show a definite tendency to dextrality; they wave, gesticulate, beg, and sign predominantly with the right hand. This is evidence that there is some development of the lateralization of the brain that is, in humans, associated with language.

Kanzi began language learning as an observer of his older sister's training. He soon outpaced her and has been the principal subject of studies by S. Savage-Rumbaugh of Georgia State University. Like Koko, Kanzi was exposed to spoken English; his training also included the use of lexigrams, printed symbols similar to those used by Sarah, each of which stands for a single word. Kanzi answers questions by manually selecting these symbols in a printed layout. According to Savage-Rumbaugh, Kanzi constructs sentences with some regularity of grammatical ordering—a controversial development since many linguists have decried the achievements of earlier experimental animals like Washoe because of their evident inability to acquire rules of syntax. Savage-Rumbaugh observes that language training helps apes to elaborate and refine their cognitive skills. She believes that, with language, apes are better able to cooperate with one another—and also with humans (Savage-Rumbaugh, 1976).

Still, F. de Waal and F. Lansing make a point that would be seconded by many anthropologists. They see attempts to impose human language on nonhuman primates as a "thoroughly anthropocentric enterprise." After observing the obvious intelligence of animals like Kanzi and other experimental subjects, they wonder, "What do these apes normally . . . use all this brain power for?" They suggest that more serious study of their natural communication systems could be rewarding (De Waal & Lansing, 1997).

THE NATURE OF ARCHAIC LANGUAGE

In 1911, when Wilhelm Wundt wrote his chapter on the origin and evolution of language, he did so in violation of a longstanding tacit agreement among philologists and other linguistic scholars of the time. If Wundt had submitted his manuscript to a reputable linguistic journal, it would very likely have been rejected out of hand. In 1865 the Linguistic Society of Paris had declared that contributions dealing with the origin of language would no longer be accepted for publication. The society evidently took the position that the problem was insoluble, leading only to idle speculation. Other professional societies and journals followed suit, and the subject of language origin and evolution became virtually taboo. In the prestigious new field of linguistics, scholars tended to emphasize the gap or discontinuity separating human and animal communication, arguing that the differences were qualitative rather than simply quantitative. Language, unlike the instinctive communication of animals, was held to be a symbolic system—a cultural creation, the product of human intelligence.

With a few exceptions, it was not until the middle of the 20th century that the issue was once again raised. Charles F. Hockett initiated the new wave of discussion in a series of publications in which he made a serious effort to suggest how the gap between animal cries and human language might have been crossed.

THE ORIGIN OF LANGUAGE: THREE SCENARIOS

CHARLES HOCKETT: DESIGN FEATURES. Hockett listed 13 "design features" that he saw as basic to language (as shown in Figure 1.6). Of these, he identified the last four (displacement, productivity, traditional transmission, and duality of patterning) as being uniquely human. The others are shared with various animal species, especially with mammals and birds. Therefore, Hockett reasoned that features 1–9 were present in prehuman vocal communication (as they are in the call system of gibbons, for example), while features 10–13 would have developed later and in approximately this order.

These four key features deserve a brief discussion: *Productivity* means the ability to formulate new messages. Nonhuman species such as gibbons (apes) and baboons (monkeys) typically have an unchanging set of a dozen or or more calls, with identifiable general meanings such as alarm, danger, or discovery of food. They thus partake of features 6–8 as well as the lower numbered features, which are shared by many other animals. However, their call systems appear to be nonproductive; that is, new calls are not invented, and the existing calls are not combined. In other words, these are closed systems, while human languages are open systems that can take in or coin new words and sentences. Hockett suggested that "blending" of calls constituted the first, perhaps accidental, step toward an open system, leading to an increase in vocabulary.

By *displacement*, Hockett meant the ability to refer to some thing or event that is not present. Certain other animals (bees, for example) exhibit what might be called displacement, but those closest to humans do not. Their vocalizations generally occur in the presence of the stimulus, as when the sight of a predator elicits a danger call. Hockett thought that displacement, like productivity, began to develop fairly early in human history and gradually increased in importance. He compared displacement to the carrying of sticks and stones, which is "like talking today about what to do tomorrow." That is, both give an indication of foresight or planning.

A *productive* system is one that can grow. This complements the feature of displacement, which implies an increase in the use of verbal signals since they can be used in more and different situations. Perhaps at this point one would be tempted to refer to the system as a language. However, the most characteristic feature of human language may be *traditional transmission—*

FIGURE 1.6   THIRTEEN DESIGN FEATURES OF LANGUAGE.

Adapted from "The Origin of Speech" by Charles Hockett. Copyright 1960 by Scientific American, Inc. All rights reserved.

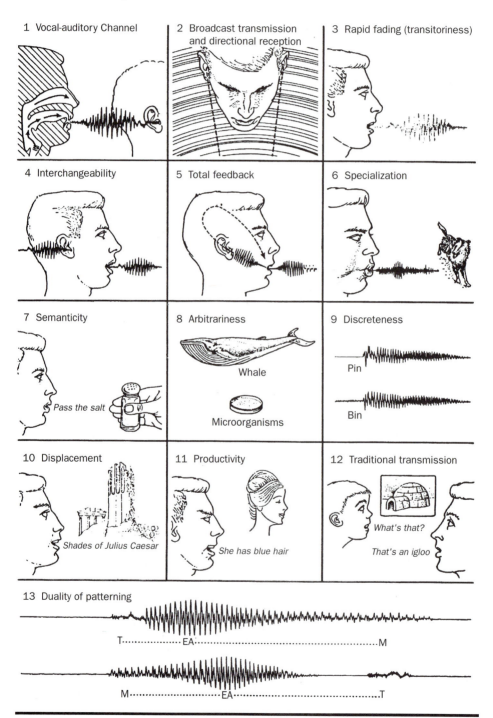

1 Vocal-auditory Channel

2 Broadcast transmission and directional reception

3 Rapid fading (transitoriness)

4 Interchangeability

5 Total feedback

6 Specialization

7 Semanticity
Pass the salt

8 Arbitrariness
Whale
Microorganisms

9 Discreteness
Pin
Bin

10 Displacement
Shades of Julius Caesar

11 Productivity
She has blue hair

12 Traditional transmission
What's that?
That's an igloo

13 Duality of patterning
T·············EA···························M
M···························EA·············T

this is what links it most closely with culture. Although the potential for using languages, the innate general ability to do so, is biologically transmitted, specific languages are taught and learned. They are passed on traditionally, generation after generation, from older speakers (who already know the language) to younger ones (who acquire it). In turn, language enables humans to learn other things, through tradition rather than by direct experience. Even at a very early stage of human development, Hockett pointed out, such learning would have a survival value: "A child can be taught how to avoid certain dangers before he actually encounters them."

The most complex of the design features, and the one that Hockett thinks must have developed relatively late in human history, is *duality of patterning*. This feature is common to all modern languages but may have originated only when simpler systems became overloaded, so to speak. If we assume, as Hockett does, that the earliest human languages were built by "opening up" a primate call system and adding additional elements to it, we can imagine that it might grow from perhaps a dozen up to 100 or more elements. A vocabulary of this size would be much more extensive than any known set of primate calls and probably be sufficient for a rudimentary human culture. But, according to Hockett, "There is a practical limit, for any species or any machine, to the number of distinct stimuli that can be discriminated, especially when the discriminations typically have to be made in noisy conditions" (Hockett, 1960).

An improvement over this state of affairs, then, is a system of language built of elements of two types: (1) a small number of meaningless sounds or *phonemes* (most languages use between 20 and 40) that combine in regularly patterned ways to form (2) a large number of meaningful units—*morphemes*, words and phrases. All modern languages, built on this plan, have a virtually limitless capacity for expression. If we follow Hockett's view of the evolution of language, this step is the most dramatic and, perhaps, the hardest to comprehend.

Articles by Hockett and by Hockett and Ascher excited a great deal of interest and marked the real beginning of modern efforts to investigate the problem of *glottogenesis*, the origin of language. In time, other scholars partly rejected or revised Hockett's list of design features, and he himself has added to it. In retrospect, the most obvious and perhaps most telling criticism of Hockett's approach is this: He appears to think of language almost entirely in terms of vocal communication. This gives the discussion an unnecessary bias, since the modern human type of communication is adopted as a standard.

For a more balanced comparative approach, it should be realized that language, as we know it, is unique and highly specialized in its principal reliance on vocalization. It is not enough to seek a direct continuity between the multimodal communication of other species, in which vocalization may play a minor role, and human language, in which vocalization is primary. Instead, there must be continuity of a broader sort in order to account for the transformation of the older type of system. In the years since Hockett's scenario was published, numerous field studies of chimpanzees and other primates have drawn attention to the complexity and subtlety of their gestures and other nonvocal communication. Detailed study of these systems may eventually serve to further narrow the gap between human language and its antecedents.

An initial effort in this direction was offered by anthropologist Gordon Hewes. In a series of publications during the 1980s, Hewes became the leading spokesperson for a gestural theory of the origin of language, reminiscent of the views earlier proposed by Wilhelm Wundt. An important part of Hewes's contribution was an extensive review of origin theories, accompanied by a two-volume bibliography. This subject, a favorite topic of discussion prior to the mid-19th century, was virtually discovered anew in the 20th.

GORDON HEWES: GESTURE THEORY. Like Hockett, Hewes looked to primate studies for a perspective on human behavioral innovations. He observed that the vocalizations of nonhuman primates differ fundamentally from those that make up human speech in that they are not under voluntary control but are triggered by various emotional and environmental stimuli. Further, they "do not appear to be signals directed toward others, but are broadcast, like human screams, shrieks, or groans, whether others are present or not" (Hewes, 1973). By contrast, their manual manipulative behaviors "are voluntary and based on . . . cognitive analyses of situations primarily apprehended visually." For this reason, chimpanzees like Washoe, who have succeeded in signing, have failed in spoken language. By analogy, Hewes reasoned that early hominids, still lacking both the specialized cortical areas for perception and motor control of articulation, and the vocal tract adaptations necessary for speech production, would likely have developed a rudimentary language based on gestures.

Cultural traditions such as tool making, Hewes assumed, were learned and passed from generation to generation by visual observation and imitation. Similarly, Washoe and other chimps have learned and transmitted signing behavior either by imitation or by "molding," when instructors positioned and guided their learners' hands through the proper movements. "Chimpanzees," according to Hewes, "exhibit behavior which can be regarded as the substrate for a gestural language," consisting of "attention-orientation . . . , arm and hand gestures, facial expressions, body postures, and incipient locomotion, any of which may be accompanied by vocalization." A manual-gesture language model "has the virtue of following the line of least biological resistance, in that it demands no changes—at least for a very long period—in neural or bucco-laryngeal anatomy or function, other than in the direction of greater precision or control" (Hewes, 1973). The assumption, then, is that hominization involved the growth of a vocabulary of manual signs and arm, body, and facial gestures. Some or all of these movements may have been accompanied by involuntary vocalizations, which still remained secondary. At the same time, Hewes believed that the hunting way of life could have exerted selective pressures for "cross-modal analysis" of animal cries and other environmental noises and eventually prepared the way for the transition to vocal language (Hewes, 1973).

SIGNS Logicians and semioticians have devised elaborate classification systems of signs and symbols, according to their functions and the relationship between speaker and referent. In the present discussion, only three main types are distinguished:

1. *Natural signs (symptoms, indices)*. Natural signs are not intentionally produced for the purpose of communication but can be used by an observer as a source of information about the condition or intention of the sender or source. A physician can diagnose illness by observing symptoms such as fever, coughing, or other behavior of a patient. Parents recognize an infant's cry as a sign of distress and learn to distinguish between cries that indicate hunger, discomfort, or distress. A baboon recognizes the signs of alarm in a nearby herd of gazelles at the approach of a lion and takes to the trees for protection. A dog's owner can read the animal's panting as a sign of thirst or fatigue; and even a plant's poor color or loss of foliage serves as a sign to the gardener, communicating a need for water or nutrients.

2. *Intuitive signs (iconic, deictic, demonstrative, etc.)*. An icon is a copy, representation, or image. Thus, iconic signs are based on imitation or depiction of some recognizable feature or attribute of the referent of the sign. Iconism can take many forms—vocal imitation, as of bird or animal calls; graphic depiction, either realistic or conventionalized (as in a cartoon or advertising logo); or physical mimicry. Obviously, the Imitation ("Bow-Wow") theory of language origin is based on the principle of iconism; so also, but less obviously, is the Natural Sound ("Ouch!") theory, since words like *ouch, ho-hum,* and *kerchoo* are recognizable as imitations of involuntary vocalizations.

Deictic and demonstrative signs serve to call attention and to indicate location or direction. Demonstrative gestures are the most obvious, and perhaps most primitive, examples, corresponding in spoken language to *here, there, come, stop,* and so on. Pronouns that distinguish among speaker (first person), hearer (second person), and other (third person) also have a deictic function. This three-way distinction is a universal in languages of the world.

3. *Arbitrary signs (symbols).* The association between symbol and referent is a cultural convention. Both icon and symbol are human creations, and an iconic sign may be simplified or conventionalized; however, the iconic sign retains a recognizable connection with its referent. There may be a progression over time from icon to symbol, as the sign becomes increasingly conventionalized (see Figure 1.7). In the case of a symbol, the connection between sign and referent appears wholly or partly arbitrary to the degree that it must be learned outright. The association between the phonemes of a language such as English and the letters of the alphabet (A, B, C, etc.) is symbolic, as is the connection between most words (apple, book, cat, dog, etc.) and their referents. Languages, as we know them, are built up of dense networks of symbols, as are cultural institutions such as art, literature, religion, and politics.

FIGURE 1.7 TWO SIGNS OF THE ZODIAC.

Leo

Scorpio

The figures on the left have an iconic resemblance to their mythic referents, while those on the right are so conventionalized as to be unrecognizable. On another level, the signs themselves are symbols of the 12 segments of the lunar calendar.

Hewes's formulation is not in outright disagreement with Hockett's but would put the steps that Hockett envisions into a larger context; thus, the transition to spoken language becomes a longer and more complex process. This extended transition period appears reasonable in terms of the time frame for human evolution that is documented by the paleontological discoveries of the past several decades. An obvious implication of the gestural hypothesis would be that cognitive and neural developments that are basic to language, whether spoken or signed, began well before the modifications of the vocal tract that support speech. In this perspective, the problem that looms the largest may be not the ultimate roots of language itself, but the shift from gesture to speech as the dominant modality.

SWADESH: INTUITIVE LANGUAGE.   Hewes reasoned that a language based on gestures could have developed out of a natural communication system similar to that of nonhuman primates and suggested that speech was a later development. A suggestion as to how the progression from gesture to speech could have come about appeared in a posthumous publication of writings of Morris Swadesh,[3] a distinguished linguist and anthropologist. Swadesh framed his ideas in the context of a broad evolutionary typology of languages, from archaic to modern times. However, he looked for clues to the nature of the archaic stage in the behavior of modern humans, as well as in that of primates and other animals.

---

[3]Morris Swadesh (1909–1967) was an innovator in methods of linguistic analysis, classification, and comparison. With an early interest in the origin and distant relationships of languages, he developed *glottochronology* as a tool for investigating linguistic prehistory (see chapter 4). Swadesh taught at Yale and other U.S. universities and had a long association with the National University of Mexico.

Swadesh observed that there often seems to be a connection between movements of the hands and those of the lips and tongue. He noted that pointing is universally used as a demonstrative gesture; a finger, the chin, or the pouted lips may be used. He believed that early humans communicated by means of both gestures and vocal calls—expressive, imitative, and directive (roughly corresponding to natural, iconic, and deictic signs). At first, oral gestures, perhaps involuntary, accompanied manual gestures; the vocalizations produced in this way eventually became sufficient to carry the message, and the manual gestures became secondary (as they remain today). At this stage a kind of sound symbolism prevailed, which, in Swadesh's view, is still to be found as a minor component of many modern languages. Vocalizations would have been graded, with sounds varying along several dimensions—in length, loudness, pitch, rounding, nasalization, and so on. Thus described, Swadesh's archaic "intuitive" language roughly corresponds, in Hockett's terms, to early language prior to the innovation of *duality of patterning*—the segmentation of words into discrete, meaningless sounds (phonemes).

It is in the vocabulary of modern languages that Swadesh found the scattered bits of evidence he cited to support his ideas about the nature of archaic vocabulary. Like earlier theorists, he reasoned that anomalous tendencies in word formation could represent survivals from an earlier period. Often, he suggested, the shape of objects was "imitated in human gestures and from there [passed] into vocalization." These were oral gestures: The lips are flexible and could be used to copy shapes ranging from rounded to flat. Then, air passing through this space produced "a resonance that is related to their shape." Thus, noises, actions, and shapes were named, following a set of general principles. According to Swadesh:

1. Stops represent hard impact, nasals soft impact or resonant vibration, and continuants free vibration.
2. Vowels indicate shape, in accordance with the kind of vibration that goes with each form of resonating space.
3. Labials (*p, m*) give the effect of flat surfaces slapping together, dentals (*t, n*) the contact of a point, and velars (*k, ng*) that of blunt objects.
4. The two consonants of a vocable permit the definition of a complex sound, from first contact to final fading, the shape of each of two colliding objects, or a three-dimensional shape defined by its form at each end.

Swadesh believed that he could recognize primitive word roots, as they conformed to these principles; a few selected examples will illustrate his approach:

1. *pek*—Flat base to blunt point, impact of flat on blunt (or the opposite); principally associated with objects and qualities: bone, hard, white. Examples: (English) *pack, peck, pick*; (French) *bec*, beak; (Mayan) *p'ek'*; (Latin) *pectus*, chest.

ARCHAIC LANGUAGE IMAGINED

In *The Clan of the Cave Bear*, Jean M. Auel tells the story of a Cro-Magnon (modern *Homo sapiens*) child who is adopted and cared for by a Neanderthal clan. Auel draws on archaeological sources in describing the Neanderthal culture; much of the interest in the story derives from her contrasting depictions of two human groups that are, in many respects, alien to each other—as when the old shaman Creb tries to teach the child, Ayla, the clan's ways of communicating:

Creb had spent time with Ayla nearly every day . . . trying to teach her their language. The rudimentary words, usually the more difficult part for Clan youngsters, she picked up with ease, but their intricate system of gestures and signals was beyond her. . . .

Starting the lesson, he pointed to the tree with his staff.

"Oak," Ayla quickly responded. Creb nodded approval, then he aimed his staff at the stream.

"Water," the girl said.

The old man nodded again, then made a motion with his hand and repeated the word. "Flowing water, river," the combined gesture and word stated.

"Water?" the girl said hesitatingly, puzzled that he had indicated her word was correct but asked her again. . . .

Creb shook his head no. He had gone over the same kind of exercises with the child many times. He tried again, pointing to her feet.

"Feet," Ayla said.

"Yes," the magician nodded. . . . Getting up, he took her hand and walked a few steps with her. . . . He made a motion and said the word "feet." "Moving feet, walking" was the sense he was trying to communicate. . . . He made the gesture again, exaggerating it so much it almost meant something else, and said the word again. He was bent over, looking her squarely in the face, making the motion directly in front of her eyes. Gesture, word. Gesture, word.

What does he want? What am I supposed to do?. . . She knew he was trying to tell her something. Why does he keep moving his hand? she thought.

Then the barest glimmer of an idea came to her. His hand! He keeps moving his hand. She lifted her hand hesitatingly.

"Yes, yes! That's it!" Creb's vigorous affirmative nodding almost shouted "Make the signal! Moving! Moving feet!"

With dawning comprehension, she watched his motion, then tried to copy it. . . . She made the gesture again saying the word, not understanding what it meant, but at least understanding that it was the gesture he wanted her to make. . . .

Suddenly, like an explosion in her brain, she made the connection. Moving on feet! Walking! . . . The hand movement with the word "feet" means walking! Her mind raced. She remembered always seeing the people of the clan moving their hands. . . . standing, looking at each other, moving their hands, saying few words, but moving their hands. Were they talking? Is that why they say so little? Do they talk with their hands? . . .

The girl paused for a moment, then turned and ran away from him. After running back across the small clearing, she waited expectantly in front of him again, a little out of breath.

"Running," he motioned as she watched carefully. It was a different movement; like the first, but different.

"Running," her hesitant motion mimicked. . . .

Creb was excited. The movement was gross, it lacked the finesse of even the young children of the clan, but she had the idea. He nodded vigorously and was almost knocked off his seat as Ayla threw herself at him, hugging him in joyful understanding.

The old magician looked around. . . . Gestures of affection were confined to the boundaries of the fire. But he knew they were alone. The crippled man responded with a gentle hug and felt a glow of warmth and satisfaction he had never felt before.

—JEAN M. AUEL, 1981

2. *mek*—Soft and broad set on something hard, associated with buttocks, belly, cheek, big. Examples: (English) *mackle, main, . . . mega-, might, mass . . .* ; (Tsimshian) *mik,* mature; (Nisenan) *muk,* big; (Nez Perce) *mexshem,* mountain; . . . (Yucatec Mayan) *muk,* big; . . . (Quechuan) *maqma,* broad; (Old Irish) *mochtae,* large; (Hittite) *makkes,* large. . . .

3. *men, mel, mer*—Vibratory sound, broad soft base to soft point. . . . Examples: (English) *fen, penis, pin, fly, flit . . .* ; (Samoan) *malu,* soft; . . . (Basque) *malsho,* soft; (Arabic) *mals,* smooth, soft . . . ; (Latin) *mollis,* soft. . . . (Swadesh, 1971)

Thus, Swadesh presented much the same sort of lexical examples as Lubbock had but explained the initial formation of vocabulary as a by-product of oral gesturing rather than simple sound imitation. It is the widespread occurrence of similar patterns that suggest their antiquity; but in no single language do these patterns occur with any regularity. Swadesh pursued his discussion tentatively, with examples of forms that "were collected by a broad sweep; the question is whether they give the impression of relationship." Unlike most linguists of his time, he was intrigued by the question of remote relationships among languages and with evidence which might confirm the common ancestry of all languages. The search for remote relationships has been continued by more recent scholars, including J. Greenberg and M. Ruhlen (see chapter 4); like Morris Swadesh, they feel that the most widely distributed features of language may be the most ancient.

FROM ARCHAIC TO MODERN LANGUAGE

The growth of language, once begun, must have continued as a protracted feedback process. If superior communicative abilities gave our primate ancestors an advantage over competing species, natural selection favored features that enhanced those abilities. Anatomical and behavioral facets of language developed apace, interacting with and reinforced by other aspects of biological and cultural evolution.

All of the hominoids have volitional control of manual operations and use the hands selectively for brachiation, grooming, feeding, gesticulating, and using tools. Apes use a variety of gestures as signs (to threaten, for begging, etc.); bonobos have been observed to invent new gestures. Early hominids probably made similar use of gestures; thus, a lexicon of visual signs could have arisen prior to the shift to vocal language. The shift from gestures to vocal signs (in Hockett's terms, the "opening up" of the primate call system) may be considered the first great transformation in the evolution of language.

The use of vocal signs developed apace, as increasing corticalization and lateralization facilitated the volitional control of articulatory movements. The presence of the pharynx was initially a by-product of upright posture; enhancement of this feature, as seen in *Homo sapiens,* represents a kind of evolutionary fine-tuning of the vocal tract as a sound-producing instrument.

A preference for vocal communication may first have arisen as an accommodation to other behavioral developments, including the increasing use of tools; it may also be functionally related to social and demographic conditions, such as population growth and territorial expansion of hominid groups.

In the hominid line, the steady increase in the size of the brain and, especially, the enlargement of the neocortex is associated both with cognitive developments and with the fine motor control that is reflected in manual dexterity (the basis for refined and specialized tool making) and in precise articulatory movements (the basis for the phonetic contrasts used in language). Neural centers of language processing, located in the left hemisphere, are identifiable in *Australopithecus* and *Homo habilis* endocasts but are fully developed only in *Homo sapiens.*

Lateralization is also indirectly linked to upright posture, which promoted the differential use of the hands for manipulation and tool use; artifacts associated with *Homo habilis* indicate right-handedness. Thus, it would seem that tool making and language, both associated with the left hemisphere, had their beginnings at least 2 million years ago. Both progressed slowly at first, and both had a rapid florescence in the Upper Paleolithic period, beginning roughly 150,000 years ago.

According to M. Corballis, a "characteristic that modern human language and the construction of complex tools share is *generativity*"—the "power of combining elements, using rules to generate novel assemblages, be they words, sentences, or multipart tools" (Corballis, 1989: 499). Our endowment with this left-hemisphere property means that we have a unique ability to "construct representations from parts" (the parts being abstract units that Corballis calls *geons*). Perception and recognition proceed by segmenting an image into geons; these, in turn, can be mentally manipulated, combined, and recombined to generate new forms—whether technological inventions or novel sentences. The complex syntactic structures of modern languages are a case in point.[4]

By contrast, the right hemisphere appears to be specialized for holistic perception and for analogic (rather than symbolic) representations; it is the seat of spatial orientation and skills involving pattern recognition. Corballis suggests that the right hemisphere is actually "specialized by default"; that is, it retains the more generalized operating principles characteristic of pre-*sapiens* hominids and shared with other species. His formulation is, admittedly, debatable; other scholars describe the functional balance between the right and left brain in somewhat different terms. In any case, most human cognitive functions, including those of language, depend on the involvement of separate, but coordinated, right- and left-brain processing.

---

[4]Corballis observes that, "given a limited number of elements and rules for combining them," it is relatively easy to construct words and sentences; "deconstruction—analyzing a construction into its component parts—is much more difficult" (Corballis, 1989: 500).

The archaic language of the early hominids evolved slowly, from the Lower to the Middle Paleolithic era. This was intuitive language, built of iconic (imitative or descriptive) and deictic signs and incorporating natural agonistic responses brought under cortical control. The lexicon was built of *phememes*—indivisible units, each unique in meaning. "Blending" or combining of these units may have enhanced their usefulness; however, as Hockett points out, there was a practical limit to the overall size of the vocabulary and, thus, to its potential for adaptation to new cultural needs.

A second great transformation, leading from archaic to modern language, may have begun more than 100,000 years ago; it culminated around the time of the great cultural florescence of the Upper Paleolithic period. The basis of this transformation was a shift from phememic to phonemic structuring, culminating in the overall language plan that Hockett calls "duality of patterning." Phonemes are, in effect, linguistic *geons*, abstract sound units that can be combined and recombined into a multitude of linguistic forms; they are the stuff of languages as we know them.

Hewes suggests that the original advantage of a phonemic system may have lain not so much in its potential for building a greatly enlarged vocabulary, as in the facilitation of word access and retrieval of information. It seems that the larger the vocabulary, the greater the difficulty that individuals experience in finding just the right word or phrase, in speaking and in decoding speech. Our mental filing system appears to be organized, in effect, alphabetically—words are accessed on the basis of their phonemic composition (do, dock, dodge, dog, doge, dogma, etc.). This kind of system is far more efficient than one in which vocabulary is stored and accessed according to meaning, as was probably the case with the "phememes" of archaic language.

Of course, this sweeping transformation was not planned and deliberately introduced; it was a natural development, a consequence of a steady increase in the functions of language beyond the capacity of the older system. Once the change was begun, it may have proceeded quite rapidly; presumably, populations that had access to this new style of language would have been at an advantage over others. In Hewes's estimation, this "phonemic revolution" in language would have been complete by the end of the Middle Paleolithic era—early enough to have influenced the languages carried by *Homo sapiens* to all regions of the globe. This was the last stage of the sapienization process; selection favored, as it still does, verbal fluency and comprehension skills.

One important feature remains: *Syntactic rules* are a basic structural component of all languages. Syntax undoubtedly emerged and grew in complexity as part of the overall evolution of language. D. Parisi has proposed a three-stage process, which can be roughly correlated with the transformations already proposed:

Type I: Pre-syntactic. This type of system is closed, and the messages are unvarying. The number of meaningful units is limited; they cannot be divided into smaller elements and cannot be combined. Parisi takes animal communication systems such as those of the higher primates to exemplify type I.

Type II: Lexical. A type-II system would be semi-open and nonsyntactic. Here, a message is made up of lexical units (phememes or indivisible "words"); new units can be added, though the total lexicon would be limited, and new combinations can be made of existing units. The meaning of a message can be derived solely from the meanings of its parts, in situational context. For Parisi, the "sentences" produced by very young children and by language-trained chimpanzees appear to approximate this type of construction, at least in the respect that they are often ambiguous. For example, a child's "Mommy sock" can be interpreted as a statement, "(This is) Mommy's sock," or as a request, "Mommy, (I want my) sock."

If the speakers of a type-II language added to its lexicon and used it productively, in new situations, problems of assembly and interpretation would undoubtedly arise. Ambiguities can be resolved by common sense or extralinguistic clues. Thus [*dog cat chase] would be understood as "The dog chases the cat," utilizing the basis of general knowledge of the behavior of dogs and cats; or it could be made clear by pointing to a specific animal or animals. However, really new experiences, Parisi comments, would be difficult to talk about without errors.

There are no existing type II languages, but Parisi proposes that this was a transitional type between animal communication and human languages as they exist today; thus, it would have emerged during the archaic phase of language evolution.

Type III: Syntactic. The type-III system is open and productive; new messages can be freely coined. In this case, *assembly instructions* are part of the message itself. Each word provides some instruction on how it is to be used (as noun, verb, conjunction, etc.), and word order, pauses, intonation, and other features play a role in processing and interpreting messages. All existing languages are built on this general plan, though differing greatly in the number and complexity of syntactic rules (Parisi, 1976).

Thus, Parisi proposes a logical progression, from syntax-free animal communication to modern languages in which syntax is essential. His formulation would certainly be criticized by those linguists who, like Chomsky, consider syntax to be the defining characteristic of language, reflecting fundamental patterns of human cognition. If this is the case, syntax should characterize language from the beginning. Further, research in language acquisition has indicated that children's early speech is not completely asyntactic but encodes simple syntactic rules that appear to be universal (see chapter 2). Moreover, Parisi, like Hockett, evidently limits his argument by considering only *vocal* communication. The status of his type II is suspect, since most of the actual development of language is telescoped into type III.

It is tempting to think that the emergence of syntactic rules may have begun with the shift to a completely vocal language; syntax, in effect, would have replaced the use of visual clues (such as pointing) in clarifying the intent of the message. Syntactic "assembly rules" would then have become increasingly important and increasingly complex as humans came to rely on the use of a multipurpose language to convey a broad range of meanings in a variety of situations.

THE ORIGIN OF LANGUAGES

All languages change over time, and words—even those of fairly recent origin—can change to the point that their original forms and meanings are no longer recognizable. For this reason, the study and comparison of modern and recent languages, which can yield valuable information about their historical relationships, cannot serve as a direct route to their distant origins. At the same time, we must assume that the processes of change have been constant, from early to late. If the starting point was a natural communication system of the type that can be observed in nonhuman primates, the direction of change was toward the culturally patterned and seemingly arbitrary type of system characteristic of modern speech communities. Several kinds of changes have already been posited as essential steps in this evolutionary process:

1. A long-term, gradual shift from from a multimodal system with heavy reliance on visual/gestural communication to one in which the auditory/aural channel predominates.
2. A phased transition from instinctive (limbic) to volitional (cortical) motivation of most vocalizations.
3. Adoption of traditional transmission, productivity, and displacement as design features.
4. Supplanting of natural signs by iconic signs and, eventually, by symbols.
5. Growth of lexicon, from a limited set of signs to a vocabulary of at least 10,000 words in fully evolved languages.
6. Development of syntactic structures, incorporating transformational rules.
7. Adoption of the phonemic principle, replacing unitary phememic structures.

Items 6 and 7 correspond to the design feature *duality of patterning*. Accordingly, all modern languages are built of meaningless sounds (phonemes) that, in regular patterns of combination, form the meaningful units (morphemes, words, sentences). According to Hockett, the introduction of duality was a response to the overloading of earlier and more primitive structures. "Words" of the earlier type (phememes) would have been indivisible units, each unique in form and meaning.

All of these developments are reflected in the nature of language as we know it, that is, they are *universal* features, present in all known languages, past and present. It is doubtful that any of these were instituted as sudden changes or deliberate inventions. Rather, they are the cumulative product of slow incremental changes—changes that represent responses to natural selection, in the context of a reciprocal relationship between biological and cultural evolution.

Against this background, we now want to understand the origin not of *language,* but of *languages.* Today, as through all of recorded history, the languages of the world number in the thousands. In view of this diversity, it would seem reasonable to ask, "Do all human languages have a common origin?" The issue—as with the question of the origin of races—is one of *monogenesis* versus *polygenesis;* and, as with the question about races, serious scholars have argued for both positions. I would answer "yes" to both questions, but I realize that the choice between "yes" and "no" depends, at least in part, on one's definition of *human* and the point in time at which common ancestry is sought. Ultimately, all of humankind does have a common evolutionary heritage, and language is as much a part of that heritage as upright posture, scanty body hair, and a fully opposable thumb.

Human life, at present and in the documented past, is characterized by diversity. The diversity of languages is no less remarkable than the diversity of physical types or of cultures. The evolutionary developments fundamental to language, as listed above, set the stage for the diversification of languages. In every case, the progressive developments—for example, volitional motivation, traditional transmission, and productivity—are those that increase the potential for change. Thus, we are endowed with the ability to build vocabulary, create symbols, coin metaphors, and, in general, adapt our languages to our needs. Ancient languages changed, as modern languages do, through processes of invention (new combinations or "blends," iconic signs, and the like) and diffusion or borrowing (via migration, trade, and other contacts among groups). Paleolithic tool traditions and art motifs diffused throughout vast regions of the world; it is reasonable to believe that linguistic innovations spread over the same routes. In Figure 1.8, steps and stages in the development of language are represented, paralleling the course of human evolution and the growth of culture.

Hominids, like the other primates, were originally animals of tropical and semi-tropical provenance, but they eventually dispersed into a wide range of ecological zones. It appears that Africa, the continent in which hominization began, was the cradle from which evolutionary changes would spread through the world in a series of waves. The transition from *Australopithecus* to *Homo* took place in Africa, where *Homo habilis* is identified as the first tool maker, at a time depth of around 2,000,000 B.P. A skull of *Homo habilis* found near Lake Tanganyika shows clear indications of some brain asymmetry and the presence of Broca's area. These suggest the presence of some sort of prelanguage—an expanded repertoire of calls or gestural signs.

FIGURE 1.8	STAGES IN BIOLOGICAL, CULTURAL, AND LINGUISTIC EVOLUTION.

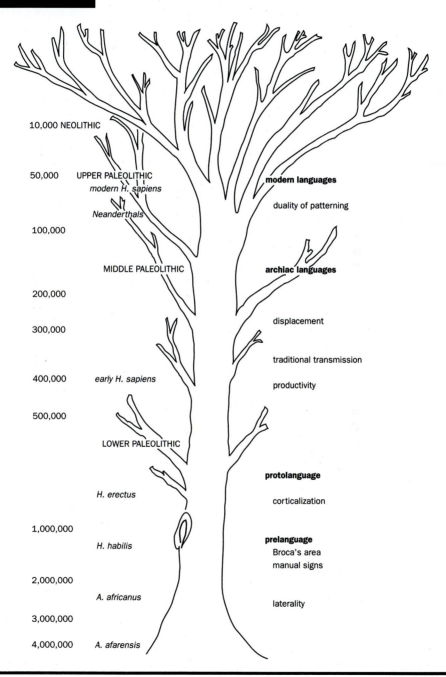

The time-scale is at the left. Cultural eras are given in capital letters; paleontological milestones are indicated in italics. The tree represents the growth of language and its diversification. Stages and important developments in the evolution of language are indicated in their approximate sequence, in the right-hand column.

During the Lower Paleolithic period (roughly between 1,500,000 and 200,000 B.P.), the range of *Homo erectus* extended from South Africa to China. The protolanguages of *Homo erectus* may have been largely intuitive, combining iconic signs with imitative or emotive calls, but there was surely a degree of variation, which grew as time and space increased the separation of regional populations.

During the Middle Paleolithic (c. 200,000 to 50,000 B.P.), archaic *Homo sapiens* populations spread through much of the Old World. Their ability to control fire and their use of tools for hunting and for processing the flesh and pelts of large herbivorous animals enabled these human groups to move into the cold climates of northern Europe and Asia. Opinions differ about the evolutionary status and relationships of the variety of physical types that were present in the world during this period, and it is possible that in some areas the more primitive *Homo erectus* and more progressive *Homo sapiens* types coexisted. It is easy to imagine that clear-cut differences separated populations, but it is more likely that there was simply a wide range of physical variation—including variation in intelligence and, perhaps, in language potential. For archaic *Homo sapiens*, with a cranial capacity virtually identical to that of modern humans, and with well-developed tool traditions and other evidence of cultural activity, it cannot be doubted that language had come to play an important role in socialization and coordination of activities. This was archaic language, with simple lexicon and rudimentary syntax, but it was transmitted by learning, and it reflected the distinctive cultural traditions of local speech communities. Marginal populations, including the "classic" Neanderthals of Europe who were virtually isolated by the climatic conditions of the last Ice Age, may have been less advanced in the development of language (as Lieberman and others have suggested); however, the direction of evolution is clear. During the transition to the Upper Paleolithic period, between 100,000 and 50,000 B.P., the human population became increasingly modern in physical type, and the variety of cultures and languages increased.

The earliest indications of physically modern *Homo sapiens* are found in Africa and the Near East, at dates in the vicinity of 100,000 B.P. Around 50,000 B.P. they began to appear in Europe, and small founder populations may have reached New Guinea and Australia shortly thereafter. The complexity of material culture and the rate of cultural change became much advanced over earlier periods, and the distinctiveness of particular styles and traditions makes it possible for prehistorians to identify and trace the development of individual cultures and cultural complexes. Distinctive blade tools, a varied material culture, and the first appearance of representational art are the hallmarks of the Upper Paleolithic and are clearly associated with modern humans—and so, it is inferred, is language as we know it.

Some linguists see language as the catalyst that led to the cultural "explosion" of the Upper Paleolithic. Scholars have even argued that language itself had its beginning as recently as 35,000 B.P.—perhaps due to a single mutation (as suggested by Noam Chomsky). This position, which ignores the biological, paleontological, and primatological comparisons that have been discussed here, is very close to a 20th-century version of the Miracle theory of language origin. But it *is* very likely that the Upper Paleolithic saw the emergence of fully modern languages, with the feature of duality of patterning, and that the rapid pace of cultural change and diversification during this period was paralleled by an equally rapid increase in the number and variety of languages.

The dispersal of modern *Homo sapiens* was not an organized campaign of conquest and colonization. It was simply the gradual expansion of an evolutionarily successful subspecies, with assets of superior technology, social organization, and communication skills. This took place incrementally, with bands fissioning (as population increased beyond the 100 to 150 persons typical of hunter-gatherer groups) and gradually extending their territories. When these groups confronted earlier populations, they may have coexisted peacefully and eventually interbred and merged. Organized warfare is not characteristic of historic hunter-gatherers, nor is it likely that it was in antiquity. Cultural innovations diffused, as did language traits. In regions that had archaic populations, a substratum of earlier culture and language may have blended with the language and culture of new arrivals. Thus, some of the unique features of various language groups today could be survivals from an earlier stage in the overall evolution of language.

Note that much of the evidence about human origins and evolution is controversial and that radically different theories are still under discussion. M. Wolpoff is one biological anthropologist who defends a modified theory of multigenesis, arguing that human populations in different world areas evolved from archaic times in a parallel fashion, with sufficient gene flow between areas to maintain species unity (Thorne & Wolpoff, 1992). However, there is a growing tendency to accept the idea, advocated by C. Stringer, that the transition to biologically modern humans first occurred in a single area—either the sub-Saharan area or northern Africa (Stringer, 1990; Stringer & McKie, 1996). Descendants of this population would then have dispersed, either dispatching, overwhelming, or merging with earlier archaic regional populations. I am, in a general way, following Richard Leakey (and my own inclinations) in advocating the third of these alternatives (Leakey, 1994).

The dispersal of the Upper Paleolithic *Homo sapiens* population created a worldwide network of small speech communities. Prior to the Neolithic period, which began around 10,000 B.P., all of humankind consisted of hunter-gatherer groups, most of them living as nomadic or semi-nomadic bands. At this level of sociopolitical organization, populations are small, and territories are large. In language, this is reflected in localized languages—typically, each band or group of intermarrying bands constitutes a speech community. Even during the Neolithic period, when the introduction of agriculture stimulated a marked increase in the population of various world areas, tribes—like bands—generally would have constituted discrete speech communities.

What this means is that a great diversity of languages and small language families (as seen in the Americas or Australia prior to European colonization) is a more ancient condition than one in which large continental areas are dominated by one or a few large language groups (as in Europe or North America today). Despite the natural tendency of languages to split and diversify, there were far more languages in the world even a century ago than there are today, still more before 1500 A.D., when the Age of Discovery began, and even more around 1000 B.C., before the Aztecs, Romans, and other civilizations began the sort of empire building that imposes the language of the conqueror on subject peoples. In chapter 4 we will discuss some of the ways in which linguistic evidence can help in reconstructing historical events such as the migration, expansion, or merging of specific peoples and cultures.

2

Language Acquisition
and Socialization

How do babies acquire language? Human infants are not born with the ability to speak, but everywhere in the world, they cry and coo and babble. Before long their babblings begin to sound like words—words in the languages spoken around them. Words lead to sentences, and eventually all children become conversationalists, participating in verbal repartee, asking and answering, arguing and joking. This happens in every human society—but how?

In Western societies, where literacy and formal education have long been entrenched, we sometimes have the illusion that language must be taught. It *is* an illusion. Despite the hours that schoolchildren devote to reading, writing, and "language arts," these exercises are all, in a sense, frills. The most basic human knowledge, competence in one's native language, is gained without formal instruction, and, at times, it is mastered under the most adverse conditions. How does this happen? One longstanding explanation holds that language is learned outright, as children listen, observe, and mimic their elders. An opposing theory proposes that there is an inborn capacity for language, which develops and expands naturally as a child matures. This is a version of the classic argument between *nature* and *nurture:* Are we the product of our biological heritage or of the environment in which we grow and develop? A reasonable view is that, in most cases, both play a role; however, most interested scholars have tended to take a partisan position, emphasizing either learning or genetic programming as the basis for the development of language in the individual.

The philosopher John Locke (1632–1704), one of the most famous and influential figures in Western intellectual history, described the human mind as an "empty cabinet." He used this metaphor to underline his belief that knowledge is acquired—not innate—and to assert the importance of education. This was a liberal view in Locke's time, since it implied that members of both the upper and the lower classes were products of their environments. Thus, Locke minimized the importance of birth and inheritance. In 20th-century anthropology, the theory of *cultural relativism* echoes Locke's view that individuals are shaped by their life experiences and social milieu. As applied to language, this would mean that the individual plays a relatively passive role, simply learning and retaining the forms of speech current in the family and community.

This was a popular view early in the 20th century. Linguists who held it were strongly influenced by behavioral psychologists such as J. B. Watson and B. F. Skinner, who propounded the importance of the *conditioned response*. According to Skinner, words and their meanings and appropriate uses are all acquired through conditioning. If a baby's babbling resembles an acceptable word ("Daddy," for example), the baby is rewarded with smiles and attention, and that particular response is thereby reinforced. Other babbling is ignored and gradually becomes less frequent. Similarly, a child may, at first, apply words in a hit-or-miss fashion, modifying or adjusting his or her usage as it meets with approval or disapproval. One child, for instance, might use "kitty" for small animals, "doggie" for larger; another may greet all adult males as "Daddy." But children are usually eager to please, and so their behavior, including speech, is gradually shaped by social conditioning.

Upon reflection, however, a total application of this approach appears simplistic; it does not explain how individuals acquire subtleties of language such as connotations and extensions of meaning or how they come to use particular words in new constructions that they have never had the opportunity to hear. Since the 1950s, linguistic theory has been strongly influenced by a different view of language acquisition, a view that also has a distinguished philosophical tradition.

The French philosopher René Descartes (1596–1650), a near contemporary of John Locke, advocated the view that knowledge and perception are based on innate ideas or structures in the mind. These shape the interpretation of experience, rather than the reverse. As applied to language, this view would imply that the basic structures of language are already present in the mind at birth. The particulars of individual languages must be acquired, it is true, but these are like icing on the cake; the basic patterns are innate.

The most influential modern spokesperson for this viewpoint has been Noam Chomsky, who bases his discussion on the study of syntax. According to Chomsky, the major categories of language (such as subject, predicate, object) reflect a specific type of mental organization that is uniquely human. Language comes to the child easily and rapidly through the operation of an inborn "language acquisition device" (LAD); innate patterns in the mind serve as a model or template against which the child can match and sort out the forms of the specific language of his or her surroundings. In acquiring language, the child would be testing and discarding or modifying hypotheses until the proper set of grammatical rules were established (Chomsky, 1968).

Developmental psychologists and educators, influenced by Chomsky's formulation, have taken syntax as the key marker in studies that trace the acquisition of language. For the most part, these studies have taken English-speaking children as their subjects. Chomsky uses the term *deep structure* for the innate part of language. In his view, speech transforms deep structure into specific *surface structures*—words and sentences. Thus, transformational linguists seek to formulate rules which, applied in sequence, account for the surface structures of particular languages. In research on language acquisition, observations are planned and experiments designed to discover when, at what age, and in what order the transformations and surface structures of adult speech are acquired.

Studies of English sentences as used by young children reveal a typical course of development. At first, utterances are short, usually one-word (*holophrastic*) sentences, often accompanied by gestures, such as pointing or waving. Interpretation of the child's intention depends at least as much on situational context as on the spoken word—thus, "Mommy," spoken with a smile and with upraised arms, is interpreted as a request to be picked up. It is in the next, two-word stage that syntactic patterns begin to emerge. Two-word (or two-part) sentences make up a very large proportion of the speech of children between, roughly, 18 months and 3 years of age. Collection and analysis of this data has revealed a number of characteristic features, including a typical grammatical structure. It is these structural similarities, overriding other cultural or linguistic differences, that linguistic researchers find to be of great interest.

Typically, at this stage, an English-speaking child's sentences are built of a combination of two classes of words; some researchers have labeled these the *pivot class* and the *open class*. The pivot class has relatively few members, and new words are added slowly; words such as "byebye," "hi," "more," "allgone," "see," and "nightnight" are representative of this group. The open class has more members and takes in new words more rapidly; these are, for the most part, names of pets and family members, favorite toys, foods—for example, "Mommy," "Daddy," "teddy," "shoe," "boat," "plane," "milk," "cookie." Sentences, then, usually include one word from each group— "Byebye Sally." "See Daddy." "Allgone milk." "Nightnight teddy."

This type of construction is typical of children's earliest speech in English, and close parallels have been described in Russian and other European languages. Over time, vocabulary becomes larger, sentences grow longer, and the number of word classes and types of sentence construction increase. The infant's pivot class includes words that will eventually be re-sorted as adjectives, verbs, salutations, and so forth. The open class is always the larger, consisting at first of the names of family members, toys, pets, and familiar household objects; it closely approximates the adult category of nouns, but these will eventually be differentiated into nouns of different types—names and proper nouns, mass nouns, singulars, and plurals.

A familiar characteristic of young children's speech is that it is *telegraphic*. That is, short words such as pronouns, prepositions, conjunctions, or even verbs (such as *is* or *can*) are often omitted, and so are the endings that distinguish tenses in verbs or show possession in nouns. Thus, for example, a child who has just begun to string two, three, or four words together may say such things as: "See plane." "Adam make tower." "Cat stand up table." "Pop go weasel." "Where Ann pencil?" The elements—words or parts of words—that are omitted are usually those that are unstressed in adult speech. These are gradually added later, in the older child's speech (McNeill, 1966).

Many studies of children's speech have focused on the progressive differentiation of sentence types and the acquisition of transformational rules—rules for the transformation of simple sentences into negatives, questions, and more complex sentences. Very young children may use only the simplest, most basic sentence constructions; real diversification and variety come with the addition of rules for expansion and transformation. One of the first to be acquired is the transformational rule for forming negative sentences. Progressively, this may go through a number of stages. Thus, in response to the question "Do you want some food?": (1) "No want some food." (2) "I no want some food." (3) "I don't want no food." (4) "I don't want some food." (5) "I don't want any food."

The linguist's interest in the acquisition of transformational rules does not simply reflect an interest in children's speech *per se*. Rather, it is one approach to a hierarchical ordering of syntactic rules, with the premise that these reflect the structure of human mentality. It appears that the priorities affecting the acquisition of language have some relationship to the processing of more complex sentences by adult speakers and to other types of cognitive processing—for example, loss of linguistic competence in individuals affected by aphasias and speech disorders. It may also be argued that, to a degree, the unfolding of language in the individual recapitulates the course of evolution of language in the human species.

BIOLOGICAL CORRELATES OF LANGUAGE ACQUISITION

Eric Lenneberg,[1] a psychologist whose interests overlapped those of both linguists and anthropologists, proposed that one of the most basic foundations for human language lies in our ability to generalize and to form categories of phenomena. According to Lenneberg, a number of interrelated physiological processes are involved in this human cognitive capacity, a capacity that is actualized or developed as behavior during the long period of immaturity that characterizes the human species. Thus, to Lenneberg, the complex *cognitive function* that is the basis for language is seen as a species-specific biological endowment, unique to humankind.

As a psychologist, Lenneberg based his argument primarily on case studies of language acquisition by children, comparisons of normal children with

---

[1]Eric Lenneberg (1921–1975) was professor of psychology and neurology at Cornell University. His doctoral dissertation at Harvard University, a study of language-deficient children, was the basis for *Biological Foundations of Language*—a work that anticipated later research on properties of the brain and vocal tract (described in chapter 1). Lenneberg also attracted anthropological interest through experiments designed to test the relationship between semantic categories and verbal response (Lenneberg & Roberts, 1956). This work provided the basic methodology that was subsequently used by Berlin, Kay, and other anthropologists in cross-cultural studies of color categorization (see chapter 5).

those whose language ability was impaired, and clinical observations of patients with language-related conditions such as aphasia. He proposed that there are uniform stages in the speech development of most children, whatever their language and the conditions under which they learn it. These stages parallel and are related to the general course of human growth and motor development. A few of the important "milestones" marking language development are

Age	Stage
12 weeks	Cooing, vowel-like and pitch-modulated
20 weeks	Addition of consonantal sounds (fricatives, aspirants, nasals), though these are still very different from the mature language
6 months	Cooing changes to babbling, resembling one-syllable utterances
12 months	Identical sound sequences are replicated; words are emerging ("Mamma," "Dadda," etc.)
24 months	Vocabulary of more than 50 items; beginning to join words in two-word phrases
36 months	Vocabulary of about 1,000 words; intelligible utterances; grammatical patterns of adult language (with mistakes)

According to Lenneberg, this general course of development is universal and is largely a contingency of biological maturation. However, the particular language that is acquired depends on the individual's social environment, and a deficient environment may limit development. Pursuing this point, Lenneberg cited studies of children in institutions and other "deficient" environments, including the physically normal children of deaf parents. In this last instance, the children were compared with a control group of children reared by speaking parents:

> "The environment of the two groups of children differed in two ways: (1) the amount, nature, and occasion of adult vocalization heard by the babies differed significantly, and (2) the baby's own vocalizations could never be responded to by a deaf mother, who, we discovered, could not even tell whether her child's facial expressions and gestures were accompanied by silence or noise. The babies born to hearing parents appeared to vocalize on the occasions of adult vocalization, whereas the babies born to deaf parents did not. Nevertheless, they made as much noise and went through the same sequence of vocalization development with identical ages of onset (for cooing noises) as the control group." (Lenneberg, 1967)

Although Lenneberg drew heavily on studies of English-speaking subjects, some observations by anthropological investigators are cited in support of his position; they generally indicate that progress in language development appears to parallel the acquisition of motor skills, though there may be some variation in absolute age. Lenneberg asks, rhetorically: "Why do children normally begin to speak between their 18th and 28th month? Surely it is not because all mothers on earth initiate language training at that time. . . ." (1967).

The answer, evidently, is that human children are biologically programmed to begin speaking at this time and will do so unless they are severely impaired or unless the environment is severely limiting. It should be emphasized, however, that not all children employ the same strategies in their efforts to use language. One child may build a large vocabulary of single words—used in combination with appropriate gestures—before undertaking any longer utterances; another may remain speechless longer and begin using whole sentences sooner. Some children are observed to imitate sentence intonation patterns while chattering in nonsense syllables, while others are precocious in their mastery of syntactic rules. Some seem eager to learn socially, but others practice the repetition of words and sentences in bed at night or while playing alone. The general stages that have been outlined are just that; they do not apply to all children in exactly the same way (Jolly, 1972).

Although Lenneberg's observations are not necessarily at odds with Chomsky's model, it must be emphasized that Lenneberg put language development in the broader context of individual growth and maturation. If the capacity for language unfolds or emerges in stages, apace with a child's physical growth, there would seem to be no need to posit the existence of a special language acquisition device. This is an underlying premise in the work of psychologist Dan Slobin, who asserts that "in acquiring language, children use general learning mechanisms which develop as they mature" (Bavin, 1995). Slobin's influence has been felt in fields as divergent as education, social psychology, sociolinguistics, and cultural anthropology since about 1980. Recent studies in this tradition rely heavily on ethnographic research and emphasize the active role of the child as a participant, as well as the influence of the social environment, in the development of linguistic competence.

THE LANGUAGE GAME

A normal child comes into the world ready and eager to undertake the task, or to play the game, of language acquisition. The child will always take the initiative in this game, beginning by experimenting with sounds and sound combinations and by attempting to link sounds to meanings. In acquiring vocabulary and discovering the rules of grammar, as well as in learning the social conventions that affect his or her use of speech, each child must find the solution to an endless succession of riddles. In the end, the prize is mastery of the particular set of rules that one society has chosen to live by.

PLAYING WITH SOUNDS

A human infant seems to be almost constantly experimenting with the use of his or her vocal tract, producing and modifying sounds. At the same time, monitoring the speech events that go on all around, the infant has a model to work toward. Various studies have revealed that, within days after birth, newborns have already become attuned to the phonemic patterns of the speech community into which they are born—just as quickly as they are able to distinguish colors, or to discriminate between familiar and unfamiliar faces. There is a common belief that a babbling infant produces a wide range of sounds more or less at random, eventually homing in on those to be used in his own language. In fact, the baby's immature vocal tract and lack of teeth limit the range of sounds that can be produced; labial and alveolar consonants (m, b, d, etc.) and central vowels (i, ə, a) normally predominate. Important phonemic contrasts (including some that the child is able to perceive) may be merged in early speech.

To begin speaking, a child must gain sufficient muscular control—learning which movements will produce which sounds—and learn which of these are important. Those that are important are those that carry information; the first step in determining this is to identify the ways that they contrast. This is an ongoing process over the first 2 to 4 years or so. For example, an 18-month-old English-speaking child may use only a single medial stop—which sounds like a *d*—in words like *Jill* [dɪə], *dear* [dɪə], *doggie* [dodi], *Tommy* [dami], *Daddy* [dadi], *Give me* [dɪmi], *stomach* [dəmi], *kitty* [dɪdi], or *sticky* [dɪdi]. Objectively, all these words seem very much alike—but not to an adoring parent!

As the child's vocabulary grows larger, the confusion could increase; however, at the same time, he or she is becoming more adept at articulating the necessary contrasts in the sound system. Thus, the child who began speaking English as described will be able to distinguish medial from velar stops (d from g), voiced from voiceless (d from t), stops from affricates (d from j), and so on. The same list of words, for a 2-year-old, might be transcribed as: [jɪl], [dɪə], [dogi], [tami], [dadi], [gɪmi], [təmi], [kɪti], [tɪki]. Not perfect, by adult standards, but much easier to understand and much less ambiguous.

Of course, a child who is growing up as a Russian speaker has to acquire a somewhat different set of phonological rules; a Navajo-speaking child, yet a different set. But each one, as he or she matures, eventually masters the points of contrast (or *distinctive features*) at work in a particular language. There may be a generalized sort of order to be seen in all this. According to Roman Jakobson, a linguist who developed the analysis of language in terms of distinctive features (see chapter 3), the contrasts such as voicing, nasality, and affrication are acquired successively in much the same order by children everywhere. This order is, it is interesting to note, approximately the reverse of the order in which the contrasts are lost by persons suffering from certain speech disorders, such as aphasia (Moskowitz, 1973).

THE PUZZLE OF SYNTAX

The two-part sentences typical of early childhood described earlier seem to reflect an intuitive perception of relationships that can be termed *predication*: the linking of two entities as actor and object, cause and effect, means and end, possessor and thing possessed, and so on. Beyond the predicative relationship, the constructions are relatively undifferentiated, and they may be ambiguous in terms of an adult grammatical system. For example, as recorded by one linguist, a child was heard to say "Mommy sock" in two different situations—when the mother was putting a sock on her own foot (subject–object), and when the child picked up her mother's sock (possessor–thing possessed). The child's speech is telegraphic; that is, some parts are omitted, and the meaning can be interpreted only in the context of the particular situation (Bloom, 1973).

The child's subsequent development, then, will include the acquisition of an expanded vocabulary and the know-how for forming more complete, and less ambiguous, sentences. By around age 2, the English-speaking child should soon progress to something like "Mommy put on sock" and "Mommy's sock." Both of these are still grammatically incomplete and will be further differentiated as question, command, or statement as the child masters the intonation patterns (early) and grammatical transformations (later) to form these different types of sentences: "Is Mommy putting on her sock?" "Mommy! Help me put my sock on." "Is this Mommy's sock, or mine?" "Why is Mommy's sock on the floor?" and so on.

When we contemplate the acquisition of large sets of particular rules, we are left with a picture of almost endless diversity in languages. Our young English speaker must learn to pay particular attention to word order, to both intonation and the use of the "WH" words (*Why? Where?* etc.) in asking questions, and to such tricky matters as the placement of the verbal particle (*on, off*). A Russian- or German-speaking child will eventually master an involved system of gender categories and case forms; each language has its own set of complexities, but none presents problems too difficult for a normal child to solve within the first 6 to 7 years of life.

Despite wide differences in the structural patterns of languages, some broad generalizations can be made about the acquisition of grammatical rules cross-culturally. Slobin makes the following observations, among others:

1. Inflections at the ends of words—suffixes and post-positions—are learned earlier than prefixes and internal changes in words. Thus, *Mommy's* might occur sooner than *to Mommy*.

2. Standard word order is learned early; deviations from standard word order may be interpreted as if they *were* in standard order. In English, one effect of this is that young children often misunderstand passive constructions—for example, *The girl is pushed by the boy* could be misunderstood as *The girl pushes the boy*.

3. Present tense is learned before any other tenses or time indicators.

4. General rules and rules applicable to larger classes are learned before rules for special cases. This is very noticeable in children's use of English, since almost all children generalize the rules for making past-tense verbs (saying *knowed, runned,* and *hurted*) and plural nouns (such

as *sheeps, childs,* and *mouses*). Typically, an unmarked form is learned first (in English, the singular noun); the most common type of marking is learned next (*key/keys, doggie/doggies*); the marking is then overgeneralized (here, applied to any and all nouns); and, eventually, the exceptions are learned (*child/children, man/men*) and the adult system is finally complete (Slobin, 1973).

Slobin comments that the forms of children's speech, in its early stages, appear much more similar, across language boundaries, than the fully elaborated forms used by adult speakers. Transformational linguists would interpret this to mean that the underlying deep structures of the grammar are "hard-wired" in the nervous system and that these provide the point of departure for the greater variety of sentence patterns that are developed in different languages. However, ongoing cross-cultural research on language acquisition appears more attuned to the specifics of different languages than to the recurrence of common patterns.

A Guessing Game With Words

From what has been said about the acquisition of syntax, one could probably predict how the system of meanings, the *semantic structure,* of a particular language is acquired. Children must, of necessity, begin to learn meanings on the basis of specific examples. They generalize from these examples, and they must then correct and reformulate their definitions until the appropriate set of categories is achieved. If a child learns—as children in our own society often do—to identify picture-book animals as *kitty, doggie, bunny,* and so on, they will generalize these terms to take in more examples and new experiences. Sometimes, too, the name of a household pet will be used as a term applied to other animals. One psychologist tracked his own child's acquisition of words for animals: At 21–22 months of age, the child applied the cat's name, Timothy (abbreviated as "Tee"), to all animals, while a toy dog was called "goggie." "Goggie" was soon extended, replacing "Tee" in application to small dogs. By 23 months, "Tee" had been further narrowed by the successive introductions of "hosh," "pushie," and "moo-ka." Finally, at 24 months, a compound term, "biggie-goggie"—first applied to a St. Bernard, then to other large dogs—narrowed the range of "hosh" and completed the approximation of major adult categories for these familiar animals (with subcategories, such as breeds of dogs and cats, still to be learned). It is interesting that one distinction that was obvious to the child from the beginning—the difference between a real animal ("Tee") and a toy (the first referent of "goggie")—was blurred in his 2-year-old vocabulary (Lewis, 1955).

It is easy to see that a process as flexible as this can be applied to many types of cultural knowledge. It would appear that young children typically begin with the immediate experience of objects and individuals within the family or household and structure the larger world on the basis of this experience—with the help of the older individuals around them. Most of that help is given through language; thus, the child learns that certain things are grouped together, emphasizing their similarities (as toy dogs, small dogs, large dogs), while other things are set apart, emphasizing their differences (as horses and cows). Anthropologists have pointed to the important role of language in shaping or influencing the individual's perception of the world (see chapter 5); case studies of children, such as that by Lewis, reveal some of the processes through which the individual comes to terms with the categories imposed by language.

WHO AM I?

Children never acquire language in isolation. While they are learning words, grammatical forms, and meanings, they are also becoming familiar with some of the social settings in which speaking occurs. Bambi Schieffelin and Eleanor Ochs, linguistic anthropologists with an interest in language acquisition, draw a distinction between two separate but overlapping areas of concern: *socialization to use language,* and *socialization through the use of language.* In the first, the focus is on the ontology of language itself, with emphasis on the interplay between the child and the social environment and the mechanisms through which linguistic competence is achieved. As for the second, the focus of study is the use of language for sociocultural ends—engaging children in the mix of values, status relations, and communication patterns appropriate to their ethnic and social milieu.

Schieffelin and Ochs (1986) point out that "ordinary conversational discourse is a powerful socializing medium." This generalization is confirmed by a series of *microanalytic* studies by sociolinguistic researchers—studies that deal in detail with children's verbal interaction in school, play, and other social settings. Events are filmed and recorded and, at the same time, careful observations are made of behavior. Special attention is paid to certain types of interaction and behavioral routines, such as turn taking, role playing, and the acquisition of social skills such as politeness or the utilization of usage patterns appropriate to different social situations.

An important assumption in these studies is that connections will be found between language socialization and world view—that is, the "microanalytic" studies of children's discourse are expected to reveal patterns consistent with broader ethnographic accounts of the "cultural beliefs and practices of the families, social groups or communities into which the children are socialized" (Schieffelin & Ochs, 1986). This can be illustrated by reference to Schieffelin's studies of Kaluli children in New Guinea. She comments that Kaluli children's requests (for food, assistance, etc.) require considerable verbal competence: They must "select the appropriate set of linguistic resources, including expressive words to elicit compassion, vocatives to frame the request within a particular relationship based on sharing, morphemes to mark affect such as intimacy . . . , affect-marked pronouns to elicit pity, . . . syntactic constructions to put the agent in focus in addition to the use of a whining voice, which Kaluli call *geseab*" (Schieffelin & Ochs, 1996). Put into a larger cultural context, Schieffelin sees the early socialization of children to use appropriate linguistic forms as part of a broader program of socialization that emphasizes sharing and exchange relations. In Kaluli society, "sharing, reciprocity, and exchange . . . organize and give meaning to social life" (Schieffelin & Ochs, 1986).

In American society, children may learn that there are times when children are expected to speak—even to show off their verbal skills or to dominate the conversation—and that there are also times when they must be quiet, be "seen but not heard," or even be excluded entirely. Culturally distinctive patterns of interaction are early impressed on children through socialization routines. Ochs contrasts two types of responses to young infants' vocalizations, the "expressive guess" and the "minimal grasp." The first is typical of U.S. middle-class mothers, who will guess what the baby might be attempting to communicate and expand on it; the infant is assumed to have communicative intent, and every effort is made to interpret the message. By contrast, Ochs finds that Samoan infants are not viewed as conversation partners, and their vocalizations are not interpreted—they may simply be asked to repeat themselves. By and large, Samoan children are expected to listen and watch until they have knowledge to contribute. The willingness of American mothers and other caregivers to engage in one-on-one conversations with young children is more the exception than the rule; in Samoa, as in many other cultures, "infants fill the role of overhearer and not addressee and are thus socialized into multi-party interactions" (Bavin, 1995).

In small-scale societies, where roles are fairly undifferentiated and where numbers of people of different ages and sexes often work together—a peasant village, for example—a child might be able to observe and learn firsthand almost all of the speech patterns of adult life. However, there are many societies in which adult male and female worlds are relatively segregated; little boys (cared for by women) have little or no opportunity to learn to act and speak like men. In such cases, there may be a prescribed initiation period or rite of passage when boys are separated from their mothers and female kin; formally or informally, they are taught male skills, including the kinds of speeches, rituals, jokes, bragging, or recounting of history and mythology that are the cultural prerogatives of men. Girls may seem to have an easier time of it because they often remain with their mothers and learn adult women's ways of behaving and speaking by imitation and participation—although, in the process, they may be cut off from opportunities to achieve status and social prestige.

In the complex hierarchical societies of the modern world, roles are many and varied and numerous dialects, levels, and styles of speaking can be discerned in most communities. There are unique regional dialects, accents that are considered urban or rural, and special vocabulary choices or mannerisms that serve to identify a person's ethnic group or social class, educational background, or occupation. There are also styles of speaking deemed appropriate to formal or informal settings, work or play; and subtle differences

A STUDY OF CHILDREN'S REGISTER KNOWLEDGE

In the context of studying language socialization, Elaine S. Andersen examined children's acquisition of *register knowledge*—the kind of variation in usage that is related to social roles and settings. Adults modify their speech to fit the situation. When and how do children become aware of this kind of code switching, and how early is it reflected in their pretend role playing? Andersen provided puppets and let children (ages 4–7) do the voices as they played with the puppets in family, medical, and schoolroom settings.

Andersen observed that every child in every context used features such as pitch, volume, and intonation to distinguish roles: "Pretend fathers all used deep voices, frequently spoke louder than any other family member. . . . Mothers spoke with higher pitch than fathers, and often used exaggerated intonation." Children playing the role of baby made appropriate phonological substitutions—"aw wedy" for "all ready" and the like.

Older children were able to maintain these role-playing distinctions more consistently than younger children and may have exhibited more familiarity with some of the settings (the classroom setting, for example). But all children revealed knowledge of vocabulary and topics characteristic of family roles, and even of the doctor's office. In the family setting, pretend fathers "talked mainly about going to work, 'firing the secretary,' having meetings or building a new 'repartment' building."

In analyzing her material, Andersen became aware of the use of verbal forms that linguists call *discourse markers*—words or phrases that function to initiate topics and/or control the flow of conversation. In Andersen's study, *well, okay,* and *now* often appeared to signal a speaker's "intention to take or hold the floor." These forms were frequently used by children playing higher-status roles, as in the following examples (f = father; m = mother; c = child):

1. m: How many guests should we have at the party?

   f: **Well,** I'm the father, I have to ask you that question. Because you're the mother. . . .

2. f (to child): **Okay now,** Mother will read you a story. I don't have a story. Your mother does.

In the classroom setting, the use of these forms showed a clear connection with authority; teachers not only used them most frequently but sometimes "stacked" them in sequences of two or more (t = teacher, g = girl, b = boy):

3. t: **Now then,** there's one thing I have to tell you. . . .

4. t: **Okay, well now** . . . have you ever been to school, or is this your first time?

And when those playing child roles used these markers, it was almost always a boy talking to a girl:

5. b: (I want to) play kickball.

   g: Oh me too. Can I play?

   b: **Well,** girls aren't allowed to play.

   (girl kicks ball)

   b: **Well,** now you have to get it.

   b: **Well,** run around the bases.

In a parallel study of French children, much the same picture emerged, with words such as *alors* "well" and *bon* "good" used for the most part by children in the roles of parent, doctor, and teacher. In comparing the two studies, Andersen observes that "by the time children arrive at school, they are already well aware of even the most subtle sociolinguistic markers, though their skill at using these markers increases over the elementary school years" (Andersen, 1996).

between men's and women's speech. Besides all this, children have a special status, not just as boys or girls (learning to be men and women), but as *children*. We provide institutions, organizations, sports and games, films, recordings, television and computer programming, books and magazines, clothing, furniture, and much other equipment—all designed exclusively for children and adolescents. There is much in the way of specialized knowledge, vocabulary, and verbal lore that goes along with all this, defining a special domain of children.

With all this diversity, however, there is also a great deal of room for individual variation. Some of the reasons for this are obvious: Families are on the move; the makeup of households often changes; individuals play different social roles; and children learn from a variety of mentors—parents and other family members, friends, teachers, and the role models of the mass media. Even though a child is likely to begin speaking like his or her parents, the child may not; and as he or she grows older, the influence of other role models (peers, teachers, rock stars, media personalities) will almost surely be stronger than those in the home.

Perhaps the most important linguistic preparation for adult life that children can receive in a complex society comes in the experience of *code switching*. Children may learn, first of all, the language that they hear at home; but by participating in different social roles and situations, they learn the forms of speech appropriate to each one. A little girl may learn to "talk like a lady," but she also must learn to talk like one of the guys if she wants to be accepted on the Little League team; a boy may practice "talking tough" but will not be permitted to talk that way at Sunday school or synagogue. A family may have private phrases, jokes, or pet names, which should be used only at home and not in public. Children learn to speak more politely or "correctly" at school, more casually or with more slang on the playground. They may even find it necessary to switch from one language to another if the language of the home is not that of the school or larger community.

Linguistic variety is a fact of life and has reached a peak in our contemporary world. Everyone has some ability in code switching because no one speaks in exactly the same way in all situations. It seems likely, however, that children who learn to use this general ability with greatest facility can also function most comfortably in a variety of adult roles.

THE EFFECTS OF SOCIAL ISOLATION

Special insights into the development of language can be gained by looking at cases in which normal circumstances have not prevailed. For example, as Lenneberg indicated, it is instructive to observe the hearing children of deaf parents, if only because their development—under the most difficult conditions—so closely parallels that of children in a normal environment. Similarly, certain researchers have studied the case histories of children with physical handicaps that affect their ability to speak. Such research can be oriented both toward understanding the effects of impairment on the acquisition of language and toward the development of therapeutic methods to overcome or bypass the impairment.

There are many cases in which isolation, either physical or social, has kept children from normal contacts with a larger speech community; the consequences of such isolation can be alarming. The most famous such case is probably that of Victor, the "Wild Boy of Aveyron," a child approximately 11 years of age who was found roaming the French countryside in 1797. Victor's case is by no means unique but is one of the few recorded in detail because of the attention of a young physician, Jean M. G. Itard, the newly appointed director of a school for the deaf in Paris. When Victor was placed in his care, Itard soon realized that the boy was not deaf; further, Itard defied the initial diagnosis that the boy was half-witted and set out to educate him. He succeeded up to a point—Victor soon acquired the basic conventions of social behavior and was able to understand some spoken language. He even learned to read at an elementary level—but he was never able to speak.

Other so-called feral children—children who have been returned to human society, sometimes after years of living in isolation—have much in common with the "wild boy." Like Victor, these children often appear to be mute and do not appear to recognize speech sounds as such. It is difficult or impossible for them to recapitulate the stages of development they have missed, and more so when the child is Victor's age or older. In 1920, two such children were discovered in rural India, reportedly living with a pack of wolves; they were taken in and cared for by missionaries. The younger girl, Amala, around 5 years of age, soon began to walk erect and to speak; however, she died within a year. Kamala, who was several years older, survived; she was less able to adapt to human society and never learned to produce sounds intelligibly (Brown, 1958).

Much more numerous than cases of feral children are those of children whose contacts with society are limited or made difficult by the restrictive social conditions under which they are forced to live. Few have been as well documented as that of Genie, a 13-year-old girl who came to the attention of California social workers in 1970. Genie had been kept imprisoned in her bedroom since infancy; she spent her nights in a crib and her days tied to a potty-chair. She was never spoken to and was punished if she made any sounds. Over the course of the next decade, she was cared for in a series of institutions, under the ministrations of therapists and educators, and her cognitive and language development was carefully monitored. She did begin speaking, at first in single words, and then in two-word constructions reminiscent of the speech of normal 2-year-olds. Her vocabulary continued to grow, but she was not able to go beyond about a 3-year-old level in the acquisition of syntax—her sentences were rudimentary, generally without plurals, prepositions, and such. She was never able to live independently, and efforts to continue her education were eventually discontinued. Some of Genie's sentences: "Want milk." "Mike paint." "Applesauce buy store." "I want Curtis play piano" (Bickerton, 1981).

From Victor to Genie and other similar cases, most accounts are anecdotal, and many are poorly documented; however, all report a degree of isolation and neglect that leaves the children psychologically damaged as well as linguistically impaired. Although the ages of the children are sometimes only estimated, observations seem to support the notion that there is a critical span of years—roughly, the first 12 or 13 years—during which a child is, in a sense, "programmed" for the acquisition of language. Beyond these years, individual success varies, and some learning clearly can take place, but the chances of successfully acquiring normal language ability are very slim.

TWIN LANGUAGE

Twins are seldom socially isolated; however, the special bond that twins have with each other often seems to set them apart from all others—even from other family members. This separateness provides the setting for, and seems to be intensified by, the development of "twin language." It has been estimated that around 50% of twins develop the special words and phrases that make their conversations unintelligible to outsiders.

What is the nature of "twin language"? Do these children actually *invent* a language of their own, as some have supposed? Actually, close study of specific cases indicates that the vocabulary is largely derived from "baby-talk"—either the phonologically simplified forms typical of early language acquisition, often in very reduced or contracted form, or the deliberate simplifications invented by parents. Further, dialogues between twins are usually rapid, terse, and accompanied by gestures, facial cues, and other conversational shortcuts that decrease the likelihood of intelligibility to observers.

Normally, the use of a special code of this sort is curtailed or ceases entirely by the time formal education begins; many twins who are known to have passed through a "twin language" phase have lost all memory of it by the time they are adults. Retention into later childhood is very rare; when this occurs, it probably attests to an unusual degree of isolation or separation from social contacts outside the immediate family. A startling case was reported in 1977, in newspaper and magazine accounts of twin girls who, at 7 years of age, had retained the use of their own special language.

Gracie and Ginnie not only shared what appeared to be a full-fledged private language, they did not speak either English or German (the languages that they heard at home) or Spanish (the main language in their San Diego neighborhood). When they entered school, they were at first classified as retarded; later, when the nature of their problem became more obvious, they were enrolled with speech therapists for intensive training in speaking English.

The little girls appeared to be very shy, relying socially on each other almost exclusively. In their home, the parents spoke English to each other and German to a grandmother who knew no English. Tests revealed that the twins understood both these languages perfectly well, but they seldom tried to use them. Besides *Mommy, Daddy,* and a few English nouns, they got by with nonverbal signals and, most often, their private form of speech.

One of the most interesting details in this case is the report that Gracie (the elder by around 5 minutes) usually took the initiative in inventing vocabulary. Sometimes, according to their father, Gracie "would hold up an object, and after a brief exchange the girls would agree on a name for it." In this way, they developed a large vocabulary that bears little superficial resemblance to either English or German. However, some words apparently are phonological transformations of adult speech (probably originating in "baby-talk"). For example, *topit* for "stop it" and *gimba* for "camper" may come from English; but other words are unrecognizable, such as *dine* for "pen." As is usually the case, one of the difficulties in recognizing words, and in transcribing and analyzing their conversations, lay in the extreme rapidity of their speech.

It seems clear that a multilingual environment contributed to these twins' linguistic isolation. As F. Davis and J. Orange (1978) point out, many children grow up in a home where two languages are spoken and learn both quite successfully, but others do not. They may confuse the two and learn neither perfectly. *Idioglossia,* a term that includes twin language and other private codes, is a common enough phenomenon, but in this case it may have become more important and have been retained longer than usual, as a sort of compensation for the difficulties presented by the environment in which the two children found themselves. It would appear that they tried to adapt to this environment as they experienced and understood it—a world that included three languages, each closely tied to a separate social category. English was their parents' language, German was identified with their grandmother, and Spanish was the language of the outside world. Thus, it may have seemed quite reasonable to invent a fourth to serve their own special relationship.

3

A WORLD OF LANGUAGES

Since the time of Plato and Aristotle, Western philosophers and academicians have never ceased to discuss grammar and logic or to spin theories about the nature of language in general. The perspective is typically somewhat ethnocentric, since these scholars' views have been, for the most part, grounded in their knowledge of European languages with long-established literary traditions. Greek and Latin have played a special role in shaping our ideas about the nature of language. For centuries, these were the languages of great cultural importance in the Western world, associated with literature and scholarship, political and judicial power, and established religion. Latin maintained its prestigious position throughout western Europe until the time of the Renaissance and beyond. Not only did learned men know little or nothing about the languages of Africa, Asia, and unexplored regions of the world, they also gave short shrift to the vernacular speech of their own countries. The Germanic, Slavic, Celtic, Basque, Finno-Ugric, and other dialects spoken by rural populations throughout Europe were seldom reduced to writing and received as little scholarly attention as Mbuti or Yupik.

Latin, on the other hand, was the object of intensive study, both out of respect for its literary importance and because of its practical value. Many textbooks and treatises dealt with Latin grammar; this was important because persons who spoke Spanish or Dutch or English as their first language were obliged to learn Latin if they were to obtain a higher education and improve their status in life. Greek was also of interest to international scholars as a vehicle of philosophy and religion. Some considered it to be a more ancient and more perfect language than Latin. The emphasis on Greek and Latin was so pervasive that when, around the turn of the 16th century, modern languages such as English were deemed worthy of study, they were described and taught according to a plan developed with the classical languages. Centuries of study of Latin set a precedent for the presentation of English grammar, even though the two languages differ significantly. The influence of this tradition is still felt, when we use terms like *genitive, ablative,* and *vocative* in parsing the structure of English sentences.

European horizons expanded in the Age of Discovery. By the end of the 17th century, explorers, traders, and missionaries had visited six of the seven continents. The Enlightenment period of the late 17th and the 18th centuries was characterized by a new current of intellectual curiosity. There was a

growing interest in the civilizations and cultures of the world and an awareness of the variability of the human condition. Out of this curiosity came
some of the early speculative anthropological writing by such philosophers
as Montesquieu, Voltaire, and Rousseau.

By the 19th century, there was a growing body of scholarship devoted to
the classical languages of Asia. Hebrew had long claimed a special importance as the language of the Old Testament. Biblical scholars believed that
Hebrew was the first language of humankind, or at least the direct descendant of the language that was given to Adam and Eve at the time of Creation.
One view held that all the languages of the world had been split apart, so to
speak, at the time of the Tower of Babel; all, therefore, were distorted or
transformed versions of the original divine language. Early studies in comparative linguistics were thus motivated by the hope of "repairing Babel"
and revealing the nature of humankind's first language.

Accounts of the Chinese language, beginning with the journals of Marco
Polo, excited a special sort of curiosity, since Chinese appeared radically different from the languages of the West. With its short, uninflected words and
fixed word order, Chinese seemed to be a more "logical" language than the
familiar European tongues; one writer even suggested that Chinese might
be the lost language of Creation. What they knew of the Chinese writing
system aroused the special admiration of Western intellectuals. The alphabetic scripts of Europe, in which letters stand for speech sounds, can be read
and understood only by persons who know each individual language. By
contrast, the Chinese script employs signs that stand for ideas, or units of
meaning. Persons who speak the several different tongues of China (Mandarin, Cantonese, and so on) are all able to use the same writing system,
each pronouncing the words of the individual's own language or dialect.
Writing can, therefore, serve as a means of communication across language
boundaries. In polyglot Europe, the use of Latin was by this time waning,
and it no longer served adequately as an international language. The idea of
developing an international writing system, modeled after the Chinese,
seemed an excellent one, and European intellectuals (Leibnitz, for one)
expended much effort in analyzing and comparing languages in order to
invent such a system.

These efforts failed. No international written language was ever widely
accepted, and efforts to devise one dissipated as a philosophical, rather than
a practical, undertaking. However, the analytical approach to language that
went into the project played a part in the future development of linguistics.
It led, indirectly, to the development of new theories of semantic structure, to
a consideration of universal and variable features of language, and to
attempts to deal with the many difficulties encountered in translation—all of
which are still key issues in the study of language.

In the modern era, cultural and linguistic horizons have been extended by
the acceleration of travel and trade, providing a growing amount of information about the world and its peoples. Between the 15th and 19th centuries—
the years of European exploration and colonization of the globe—several

historical circumstances promoted a broader perspective on the nature of language and, more importantly, on speech in its myriad forms. Explorers had a constant need for translators, a need that only increased over time as the great powers established a worldwide network of colonies. In the wake of the explorers came missionaries, who saw the study of languages as a prerequisite to preaching and translating the scriptures. Early interest in the variety of languages of the world is exemplified by the *Mithridates* of Johann Christoff Adelung, a four-volume work completed in 1817 that presented, as a basis for comparison, the Lord's Prayer translated into 500 languages.

An indirect impetus to the growth of linguistic scholarship came with the emergence of modern national states and the ideology of democracy, which has swept the globe in the modern era. The populism that was part of this movement gave rise to a new interest in the customs, folklore, music, and vernacular language of the common people. Linguistics and folklore studies developed as related disciplines in the 19th century, as exemplified in the research of Jakob and Wilhelm Grimm. These scholars, devoted to the study of their own Germanic traditions, were contemporaries and colleagues of the founding fathers of anthropology, whose studies extended to prehistory and the nonliterate peoples of the earth. One link between these fields of study was the conviction that language, as a vehicle of thought and an expression of human nature, could provide a unique kind of data for comparative and historical studies.

THE DESCRIPTIVE STUDY OF LANGUAGES

As long as linguistic research was essentially limited to the languages of Europe and the rest of the literate world, scholars based their analytic and comparative studies primarily on written documents. They tended to identify *language* with *writing*, as many educated people still do today. However, the study of non-Western languages presented an entirely different problem, since most did not, and many still do not, have an established form of writing. Moreover, those languages that do have a long literary tradition employ a variety of writing systems, many of them highly conventionalized and each with its own particular quirks of spelling and punctuation. Comparison of these is an art in itself. Spelling rules may vary considerably, even between very closely related languages such as Spanish and Portuguese.

There is, of course, no natural association between speech sounds and written symbols. Writing systems are, at best, only imperfect ways of recording spoken language. Those of us who learned to read and write English as our first language are aware of some of the inconsistencies of our spelling system. For example, the letter *o* stands for three sounds that most speakers can—if they listen carefully—distinguish as different in the words "No, not now," and for a fourth in the second syllable of "button" (a vowel similar to but higher than that written as *u* in the first syllable); double this same letter, and it stands for still different sounds, as in "schoolbook").[1] We are also accustomed to oddities such as the *gh,* which a spelling reformer might want to replace with *g* in *ghost* or *f* in *enough* and leave out entirely in *bright* or *though.* Our own spelling conventions usually cause us little concern because we are so thoroughly accustomed to them. But it would be quite another thing to attempt to use English orthography to transcribe the words of an unfamiliar language or to try to read back those words as transcribed by another observer—whose first language is perhaps French or German—with a different tradition of spelling and pronunciation.

Linguistically untrained travelers and explorers often attempt to record the names of people and places and cultural vocabulary (terms for plants or animals, artifacts, dances, ceremonies, etc.) from native languages of the Pacific, the Americas, and other world areas. If their transcriptions are compared, many inconsistencies are revealed that, under some circumstances, can be a cause of confusion. Thus, the name of the *Tlingit* tribe of northwestern North America is found in various travelers' accounts (German, French, Danish, English) as *Thlinkit, Tlinkit, Thlinkeet, T'linkets, Klen-e-kate,* and *Klen-ee-kate.* The neighboring Chinook people of Washington and Oregon have been called *Chinuk, Tshinuk, T'sinuk, Tschinuk,* and *Cheenook;* and the Cherokees of the Southeast appear variously as *Tschirokes, Chirokis, Chelekee, Shannaki,* and *Tsalagi*—and this is just a sampling of the many versions of these names in the literature of the exploration of North America (Powell, 1981).

In part, this lack of agreement simply reflects the different spelling conventions of the reporters. For example, the consonantal sound that an English writer would normally write as *ch* (the initial in *Cherokee* and *Chinook*) would probably be written as *tch* by a French writer and as *tsch* by a German writer. But in part also, there are variations in transcription that derive from the reporters' efforts to deal with speech sounds that partly resemble, but also differ from, sounds in their own languages. This undoubtedly accounts for variant spellings of the initial consonant in *Tlingit,* a lateral affricate sound (written as *tl, thl, t'l,* and *kl*), and the variation between a resonant *r* and *l* in *Cherokee.*

A focus of interest among linguistic researchers at the end of the 19th century was this problem of accuracy and consistency in transcribing the sounds of languages, however unfamiliar. Franz Boas,[2] who was familiar with many Native American languages and cultures, was well aware of the

---

[1]The first three, in the author's pronunciation, are [oʷ], [a], and [æ]; in *button* the first is [ə], the second [ɨ], and the last two [u] and [ʊ].

[2]Franz Boas (1859–1942) was born in Germany, where he received his Ph.D. in geography. After immigrating to North America, Boas became influential in establishing anthropology as a university, rather than museum, discipline; at Columbia University, he set the pattern for the holistic organization of the field (with cultural, biological, and linguistic subfields) that still prevails. His research was multifaceted, but his most lasting contributions are in the study of Native American languages and cultures; for much of his life, he pursued studies of the Kwakiutl of British Columbia.

need for a solution to this problem. Boas observed that, in human languages, ". . . [t]he number of sounds that may be produced . . . is unlimited. In our own language we select only a limited number of all possible sounds. . . . A comparison of the sounds of the well-known European languages—like English, French and German; or even of the different dialects of the same languages, like those of Scotch and of the various English dialects—reveals the fact that considerable variation occurs in the manner of producing sounds, and that each dialect has its own characteristic phonetic system" (Boas, 1911).

In other words, the human speech organs can produce great variety in sounds, from which any individual language or dialect uses only a fractional part. For the development of linguistic science, it was essential to arrive at an accurate, objective method for identifying and recording speech sounds—a standard system of *phonetic transcription*. The most comprehensive such system is the International Phonetic Alphabet, compiled late in the 19th century by a group of European linguistic scholars. Phoneticians trained in the use of the IPA are able to capture minute variations of pronunciation with great accuracy.

The need for accurate transcription becomes most obvious in the study of "exotic" or unfamiliar languages that do not have standardized writing systems to guide the non-native student. However, as Franz Boas pointed out, we also find remarkable phonetic differences among dialects of the same language, even though they may employ the same writing system—the many dialects of British, American, Australian, and other varieties of English, for example. Dialect studies could hardly be conducted with accuracy if the linguist relied on the standard written forms.

Franz Boas's own primary concern was with the study of aboriginal languages, which were, at the time, generally nonwritten. His discussion abounds in examples of speech sounds that are characteristic of Native American languages but are quite different from those common to European languages. Sounds such as those shown in the examples given above had proved difficult to analyze and transcribe. However, this typically anthropological interest in the unique features of certain languages was balanced by a concern for the discovery of underlying basic principles shared by all.

SPEECH VERSUS LANGUAGE

Ferdinand de Saussure,[3] one of the most famous linguists of his time, is considered the founder of modern structural linguistics. Fundamental to Saussure's teachings was the distinction that he drew between *parole* (speech) and

---

[3]Ferdinand de Saussure (1884–1939) was educated in, and made significant contributions to, Indo-European comparative linguistics. In his later career, he was professor of linguistics at the University of Geneva. His ideas have continued to be influential through the posthumous *Course in General Linguistics*, which was compiled from lecture notes by two of his students, C. Bally and A. Secheheye.

langue (language). Speech, according to Saussure, is individual and particular; it provides the raw material from which a linguist is able to determine the system of a language. He regarded language as a *social fact*,[4] arising as a set of conventions shared by a community of speakers. Since they hold this shared understanding, members of the speech community are able to use the language quickly and spontaneously as a tool for transmitting information. (In other words, we do not have to think about articulating speech sounds or constructing grammatical sentences; as we acquire our language, these processes become automatic—and so we can give our attention to formulating and interpreting the messages conveyed by the sounds.)

Saussure's distinction between speech and language became widely accepted in 20th-century linguistics and is basic to the ways in which languages have traditionally been described and analyzed. On this foundation, the American linguist Leonard Bloomfield[5] (1887–1949) formulated the principle of the *autonomy of language* as an object of study. According to this principle, the patterns of language operate with regularity and are therefore subject to scientific study. Thus, linguistic research can lead to the discovery of empirically valid synchronic (structural) or diachronic (historical) laws. Students who followed Bloomfield's teachings, as propounded in the widely used text *Language* (1933), found linguistic systems, made up of shared sets of lexical forms and grammatical paradigms, to be the appropriate targets of study. The implication is that, for most purposes, the linguist does not need to describe the range of variation among speakers; much of this variation can be safely ignored, and a single speaker can serve to exemplify the system of the language. Bloomfield's assumptions seem very similar to those that were, in the same era, common in cultural anthropology. In the traditional anthropological approach, it was the regular, habitual, socially shared patterns of behavior that were the focus of study, and it is these that were put forward in an ethnographic description of culture.

An alternative way of distinguishing between speech and language is to see the latter as a plan or design, a mental abstraction shared by speakers and manifested in their individual acts of speaking; such a view also has its parallels in theories that view cultures as shared plans or "blueprints" for action. In recent decades, both linguists and cultural anthropologists have questioned and often departed from normative assumptions of this sort; it will be seen in chapter 7 that sociolinguistics is based on the study of variation rather than the shared features of language.

---

[4]Saussure was a contemporary of, and was undoubtedly influenced by, the sociologist Emile Durkheim; a *social fact,* as defined by Durkheim, exemplified the power of society to shape and constrain the individual.

[5]Leonard Bloomfield (1887–1949) was a dominant figure in American linguistics in the first half of the 20th century. His earlier views reflected Wundt's mentalistic psychology, but his influential book *Language* (1933) reveals the growing influence of behaviorism. By training, Bloomfield was a Germanic scholar, but he also made important contributions to the study of nonwritten languages, including those of the Austronesian and Algonkian families.

In the work of Noam Chomsky, an American linguist of great influence since the publication of *Syntactic Structures* (1957), *competence* and *performance* appear as terms that approximate the time-honored opposition of *language* and *speech*. However, there are somewhat different underlying assumptions, in that Chomsky considers the basic structures that constitute linguistic *competence* to be at least partially innate. Individual competence develops partly on the basis of clues that are revealed in the speech of others; but it is also the expression of an inherent human capacity for language. Proceeding from this assumption of a basic human endowment, Chomsky's methods give priority to defining the abstract form of any language, or its *deep structure*, primarily through introspection. For the most part, he has based his findings on introspection and his intuitive knowledge of his native language, English, which then serves to exemplify properties that are put forward as universal. Since he regards it as essential to build on the insights of a native speaker, Chomsky appears to discount the efforts of linguists who study languages empirically, on the basis of a *corpus*, or collection, of speech data.

Although it was an outgrowth and refinement of earlier structuralist theory, at times Chomsky's approach seems to reverse long-established working procedures in linguistics. However, despite an enormous influence in both general and applied linguistics, the enduring impact in linguistic anthropology may simply be to complement—but not to replace—a traditional interest in the distinctive patterns of individual languages.

APPROACHES TO LINGUISTIC DESCRIPTION

There are two different broad strategies of gathering data for language studies. In accord with the Chomskian strategy, the larger units of speech can be taken as the starting point. These might be whole utterances or the segments of utterances marked by pauses, by change of speaker, by shift of topic, and so on. Such segments can be progressively broken down, or rewritten, into component units such as sentences and phrases, and these into still shorter units, such as words or groups of words with identifiable functions. One can go on, working down from the longer to the shorter, to identify progressively smaller "building blocks" of language—speech sounds, or even the components of individual sounds. This approach, which gives priority to syntax—the broad logical relationships among words and phrases—is most conveniently applied to the analyst's own language. It rests on a "native speaker" competence as a guide to segmenting stretches of speech and certainly does not resemble the approach that a foreigner would take in learning a new language.

An opposite approach is to begin with the minutiae of speech, to become proficient in identifying speech sounds (recognizing, pronouncing, and writing them down); using them in single words or short utterances and learning how these are built up; and finally, discovering the rules for combining these units into longer grammatical sentences and longer utterances. This more closely parallels the way in which a non-native speaker's learning of a language is usually undertaken.

Both of these general strategies, the method of "working down" and the method of "working up," are useful approaches for gaining certain types of insight into the structure of language. When doing field research, anthropological linguists have usually studied languages that are foreign to them and of which they often have little or no prior knowledge. They have, therefore, tended to follow the procedure of "working up," uncovering the structure of the language bit by bit and, in the process, becoming part of a community of speakers as well as acquiring a valuable source of insight into the culture of that community.

For this kind of situation, linguists have developed field methods that are equally applicable to any natural language and that can be relied on to provide a comprehensive description of the *phonology* (the system of sounds), *morphology* (the meaningful units and structure of words), and *syntax* (the structure of phrases, sentences, and larger units) of language. These are the three levels of structure usually included in a descriptive grammar.

PHONOLOGY: LANGUAGE AS SOUND

Phonology is a general term that encompasses many aspects of study of the sounds of language. A pair of terms distinguish two subordinate areas, *phonetics* and *phonemics;* each of these has its own methods and objectives. The concern of phonetics is the precise identification and description of speech sounds, either by specifying the manner of production (*articulatory phonetics*) or by analysis of acoustic properties (*acoustic phonetics*). Articulatory phonetics is the usual choice for linguistic research, especially in fieldwork situations. Accuracy depends on the linguist's skill in perception and transcription, achieved through training and practice. Acoustic analysis of speech sounds using laboratory equipment can be more precise but is time consuming and is not compatible with fieldwork. It provides a useful resource for solving specific problems and has contributed substantially to linguistic theory.[6] The best-known demonstration of acoustic phonetic techniques is probably in the acoustic analysis of individual "voice prints," which has important forensic uses.

Phonemics is an interpretive or functional, rather than purely descriptive, type of analysis. The objective of phonemic study is to reveal the system—the organization and functioning—of the set of sounds of any language. The analysis is aimed at identifying the *phonemes,* which are functional units or categories of sounds; their *allophones,* or variations; and the rules of order, combination, and selection that are characteristic of a particular language. In their phonetic inventories, languages may differ markedly from one another; however, it seems remarkable that any and all of the sounds that occur in

---

[6]The sound spectrograph and related technology have many uses, such as the definition of individual "voice-prints"—as distinctive as fingerprints—for forensic purposes.

human speech can be identified, described, and classified according to the same basic principles.

ARTICULATORY PHONETICS

Humans produce speech by coordinated use of (1) the natural flow of air exhaled from the lungs; (2) *voice,* a harmonic sound originating in vibrations of the vocal cords, which are set in motion by the flow of air; (3) modifications of this sound in three resonating chambers—the pharynx, the mouth, and the nasal cavity; and (4) articulations that obstruct or constrict the passage of air through these chambers. (See Figure 1.1.)

1. In all natural languages, most of the sounds used in speaking are produced with the use of egressive (exhaled) air. With the help of muscular movements that control the vocal cords, the flow of air causes a vibration of the cords; this produces *voice.* Further, with the help of articulations, which constrict or partly block its passage, the egressive air produces frictional or explosive *noise.* Voice and noise are the two kinds of sound used in speech. Only a few languages make use of ingressive sounds, sometimes called *clicks,* along with the more usual egressive sounds. The Khoisan languages of the Bushman and Hottentot peoples of South Africa are the best known of these.

2. Vibration of the vocal cords is controlled by a complex system of muscles in the laryngeal area of the throat. The degree of tension and the speed of vibration of the vocal cords affect the pitch and quality of the voice. There can be rapid alternation between tensing of the cords, with accompanying vibration (voice), and relaxation, with lack of vibration (voicelessness). The contrast between voice and voicelessness is basic to the patterning of all languages. Thus, vowels are normally voiced (though they may also be modified by devoicing, or whispering); consonants may be either voiceless (as English *p, t, k, f,* and *s*) or voiced (as *b, d, g, v, z, m, n,* and *r*).[7]

3. The greatest flexibility of the speech apparatus is found in the region between the larynx and the lips. It is in this area that the human vocal tract has its greatest biological adaptation for speech. The supralaryngeal tract is divided into three main resonating chambers: the pharynx and the oral cavity, which are the most important and the most flexible, and the nasal cavity. The size and shape of the first two of these resonators can be varied in several ways, but most importantly by the movements of the tongue. The tongue, a large muscular mass, can be pushed forward or drawn back, changing the size and proportions of

[7]The reader may become aware of the presence or absence of voice by placing the fingertips lightly on the larynx ("Adam's apple") to detect the vibration of the larynx. For a start, contrast a long "Sssss!" (voiceless) with "Zzzzzz!" (voiced); then go on to compare various voiced and voiceless consonants, pronouncing them between vowels and in other environments.

the pharyngeal and oral cavities. When the tongue is drawn back, the pharynx is constricted and the oral cavity is enlarged; when the tongue is pushed forward, the relationship is reversed. The tongue can also be raised and lowered. Pushing the lips forward or drawing them back is another way of enlarging or restricting the size of the oral cavity.

These movements are responsible for most of the distinctive differences in the quality of vowels. The vowel in *feet*, for example, is produced by pushing the tongue to the front and raising it high in the mouth; the pharyngeal cavity is enlarged, and the oral cavity is small, constricted even more by drawing back the lips. The reader may form the articulation of this vowel and then contrast it with the vowels of *foot, fought*, and *fat*; notice the movements of the tongue and lips, which change the size and shape of the oral cavity.

Another change in resonance is brought about by opening or closing off the nasal cavity via muscular movement of the velum (the soft palate). The velic valve can be open or closed; it is open for nasal consonants like *m* and *n*, and for other sounds, usually vowels, that are "nasalized" (French has a number of such vowels).

4. So far, it has been indicated that speech sounds are ordinarily formed with exhaled or egressive air; that voice can be present or absent, as can nasal resonance; and that the shape and proportions of the main resonators can be varied a great deal, mainly by gross movements of the tongue. Additional smaller movements of portions of the tongue and of other *articulators*, which obstruct or interfere with the flow of air through the pharyngeal and oral cavities, account for many of the distinctions among consonants. The tip, blade, and back of the tongue, and the lips are flexible articulators, touching or forming a narrow constriction with the teeth, alveolar ridge (just behind the teeth), palate, or velum. Phoneticians refer to these articulations by naming the *point of articulation* rather than the *articulator*. For example, an alveolar consonant is formed with the tip of the tongue touching (or almost touching) the alveolar ridge, as in the initial sounds in *tip, dip, sip, gyp,* or *zip*.

Thus, consonants can be partly identified by naming the place or *point of articulation;* they are further identified by *type of articulation*. The main types are: (1) *stops*, formed with the air passage completely closed; (2) *nasals*, with closure of the oral cavity and opening of the nasal resonator; (3) *trills* or *flaps*, characterized by a series of brief closures (for example, the tongue-tip trill [ř] of Spanish or the uvular flap [ʀ] of French or German). Because of phonetic similarity, trills and flaps are often grouped together with (4) *laterals*, in which the tongue is in contact with some point of articulation, while air escapes on one or both sides (as in the initial and final sounds in *little*). A lateral may have some frictional noise, depending on the force with which the air escapes. Frictional noise is absent or light for English [l]; with stronger and more audible friction, [ɬ] is usually classified as a fricative.

5. *Fricatives* are formed by narrowing the air passage. There is audible frictional noise due to this constriction, as in the initial sounds of *fit*, *sip*, *ship*, and *thin* (f, s, š, θ: voiceless fricatives), and *vine*, *zip*, and *then* (v, z, ð: voiced fricatives).

6. The term *affricate* identifies speech sounds that are a combination of stop and fricative—a complete closure released with frictional noise. English examples are the initial and final sound in *church* (č) and the initial in *jam* and *ginger* (ǰ). A speech sound foreign to English but common in Native American languages is [λ], a combination of [t] plus the fricative [ɬ]; this is the intial sound in the native pronunciation of *Tlingit* (described earlier).

Although the International Phonetics Alphabet is important in providing an established standard for accuracy, today's linguistic scholars seldom follow its arcane and complex orthography in every detail. In practice, most rely on a smaller selection of symbols, largely drawn from or modified from letters of the Roman alphabet. Many individuals find these to be simpler to use in the field, and—more importantly—they are preferable because they eliminate the need for expensive specialized typewriter keyboards, printer's fonts, and other supplies. The IPA has not served its original purpose of standardization, but it serves as an unambiguous point of reference for resolution of differing transcriptions or clarification of unique or unusual phonetic details.

Figure 3.1 presents a basic set of phonetic symbols, adequate for transcribing the sounds of most natural languages; additional symbols can be added when needed.

To the single-letter symbols that stand for vowels and consonants, diacritic marks can be added for "narrow," or detailed, phonetic transcription. In Figure 3.1, the subscript caret and dot are examples of such combined representations (as in [ṱ] and [x]). Use of diacritics enables the fieldworker or interviewer to record whatever distinctions or variations are found to be of interest in a particular language, or even in a particular individual's speech, while still relying on a fairly limited number of basic symbols. The specific diacritic marks that are used vary considerably and may even be chosen *ad hoc* to deal with particular cases; the following are a few of that the author relies on:

subscript caret [ʌ] beneath a letter indicates a fronted articulation;

subscript [ ] stands for a backed or retroflex articulation;

raised [ʸ] or ['] following a letter indicates palatalization of a consonant, or "y-off-glide";

raised [ʰ] or [ᶜ] stands for aspiration;

raised [⁼] for definite absence of aspiration;

raised [ˀ] for glottalized release (simultaneous glottal stop);

raised [ʷ] for labialization (simultaneous lip-rounding);

[̥] below a letter, or use of a capital letter, for devoicing of a normally voiced speech sound (thus, [m̥] or [M]).

Skilled phoneticians rely on a combination of experience in selective listening (analyzing and comparing the sounds of diverse languages) and mimicry (imitating these sounds); this training, in turn, helps them to identify articulatory movements and to identify new sounds. Linguistic students usually receive phonetic training of this sort, holding sessions with native speakers of various languages or working with recorded materials in academic courses in field methods and analytic methods. A beginner can start to practice phonetic transcription while listening to recordings of his or her own speech and by noting variations in pronunciation by individuals in the home, in the classroom, or in the media.

FIGURE 3.1 PHONETIC SYMBOLS.

Consonants

	Bilabial	Labiodental	Dental	Alveolar	Alveopalatal	Velar	Uvular	Glottal
Stops								
(voiceless)	p		t̪	t	tʸ	k	q	ʔ
(voiced)	b		d̪	d	dʸ	g	ɢ	
Affricates								
(voiceless)			c	č				
(voiced)				ǰ				
Fricatives								
(voiceless)	ɸ	f	θ	s	š	x		h
(voiced)	ƀ	v	ð	z	ž	γ		
Nasals								
(voiceless or devoiced)	m̥			n̥	ñ̥	ŋ̥		
(voiced)	m		n̪	n	ñ	ŋ	N	
Flaps, Trills				ř, r		ɾ	R	
Laterals				l,ł		!		
Semivowels								
	w			r	y	(w)		

Vowels

	Front	Center	Back
High	i (b*ee*t)	ɨ (j*u*st)	u (b*oo*t)
	ɪ (b*i*t)		ʊ (b*oo*k)
Mid	e (b*ai*t)	ə (*a*bout, b*u*tt)	o (b*oa*t)
	ɛ (b*e*t)		
Low	æ (b*a*t)	a (p*o*t, c*a*r)	ɔ (b*ou*ght)

<table>
<tr><td>REGIONAL DIALECTS IN AMERICAN ENGLISH</td><td colspan="2">If a student listens carefully, compares, and attempts to transcribe a list of words as pronounced by several</td></tr>
</table>

REGIONAL DIALECTS IN AMERICAN ENGLISH

If a student listens carefully, compares, and attempts to transcribe a list of words as pronounced by several different speakers, some points of variation will be discovered. Some of the variation may be idiosyncratic, but it may also reflect differences in the ethnic or regional background of the individuals. All of us are aware of this kind of variation and may be able to identify with fair accuracy a southern, New England, or Texas accent. Henry Lee Smith was a virtuoso in his knowledge of regional speech variation. From 1939 to 1941, Smith conducted a radio program in which, on the basis of a brief interview, he was able to guess the location—sometimes even the urban neighborhood—where individuals had grown up or lived. Later, Smith held an academic position in linguistics; his analyses of English phonology and syntax were influential in his field and were also the basis for developing teaching materials that have been widely used in American elementary and secondary schools.

The following words are drawn from a list that Smith used in defining and distinguishing among eight dialect areas: eastern New England, western New England, central Atlantic Seaboard; northern Middle West, Midland, coastal South, Southern Hill, and Far West. Examples given here represent (A) eastern New England, (B) Midland, and (C) coastal South.

	A	B	C
"merry"	mɛri	məri	mɛri
"marry"	mæri	mɛri	mæri
"Mary"	meəri	meᵊri	meʸri
"wash"	wɔš	waš	wɔʸš
"water"	wɔtər	watər	wɔᵊtər
"greasy"	griᵊsi	grizi	grizi
"ash"	æᵊš	æyš	æyš
"ask"	æᵊsk	æsk	æᵊsk
"about"	əbæʷt	əbæʷt	əbæʷt
"park"	pæːk	park	paːk
"penny"	pɛni	pɛni	pɪni

(Trager, 1972)

FROM PHONETICS TO PHONEMES

Skill in phonetic transcription can be a useful tool to any anthropological field-worker, whether primarily interested in language or not. However, accurate transcription is a basic necessity for linguistic research, since it is the essential means for obtaining an objective visual record of speech. This record becomes the raw material for further study and analysis. The phonetic transcription documents the use of language by an individual speaker. Comparisons with other individuals will reveal a range of minor variations—variations that do not interfere with understanding and that will not necessarily become part of the phonemic record. For a descriptive study of a language, research at this point is directed toward phonemic analysis—determining the relationships of speech sounds to one another, noting points of similarity and difference among them, specifying their occurrence in the flow of speech, and grouping them into functional classes that constitute the *phonemes* (the distinctive phonological units) of particular languages.

A turning point in the history of modern linguistics was the discovery that the sounds of languages vary not only in number and selection but also in their patterning into functional units. In the passage quoted earlier, Franz Boas commented on the variation that he had found in the sounds of Native American languages; he went on to observe that "each sound is nearly fixed, although subject to slight modifications which are due to accident or to the effects of surrounding sounds." With this remark, he anticipated the concept of the *phoneme,* a concept that was to be developed more fully by linguists such as Leonard Bloomfield, Edward Sapir, and Morris Swadesh (Boas, 1911).

The "modifications" mentioned by Boas amount to what later linguists would term *free* and *conditioned* forms of allophonic variation. A *phoneme* can be defined as a class or group of sounds (*allophones*) that vary in either of these two ways. As an example of conditioned variation, we can consider some of the phonemes of English. If we are native speakers of English, we are aware of the three voiceless stop *phonemes* (*p, t, k*) as separate and distinct units of sound. We are not usually so aware of the variations (*allophones)* that occur when we use these phonemes However, it is easy to detect some of this variation. To do so, the following experiment can be undertaken.

Pronounce each of the voiceless stops in word-initial position, followed by a vowel: *pot, top,* and *cop.* If you hold your hand—or, better still, a piece of paper—in front of your mouth, you can detect a fairly strong puff of breath, or *aspiration,* as the initial *p, t,* or *k* is released. To indicate this aspiration, a phonetician might write the segments as [p^h], [t^h], and [k^h].

Now put the same three consonants in a different word environment, with each of them as the second in a sequence (as in *spot, stop,* and *Scot*). In this case, you will find that there is little or no aspiration as the stops are released. To indicate the difference, they might be written phonetically as [p$^=$], [t$^=$], and [k$^=$].

In these examples, the variation between [p^h] and [p$^=$], [t^h] and [t$^=$], and [k^h] and [k$^=$] is automatic. In English, the choice between aspirated and unaspirated release is conditioned by the phonological environment. In this case, the conditioning factor is the position of the consonant in the word (either word-initial or second position, preceded by *s*-). Because the variation is automatic, native speakers of English are not normally aware of the choices, or, indeed, that there is any variation in the sounds at all.

The other type of variation, *free variation,* may also be observed in these same words, as they might be pronounced by different speakers or at different times. All of them have voiceless stops in word-final position; some individuals, when reading a list of the three words—*spot, stop, Scot*—will strongly release or aspirate all the final consonants, while some will not.

THE PHONEMES OF AMERICAN ENGLISH

In this list, English phonemes are grouped according to method of production (stops, affricates, fricatives, nasals, resonants, semivowels, and vowels. Within these categories, similar phonemes are listed in sequence (p, b, and so on), with examples that illustrate contrasts in initial, medial, and word-final position.

Stops:	/ p /	pill, copper, tap
	/ b /	bill, robber, tab
	/ t /	till, later, bat
	/ d /	dill, ladder, bad
	/ k /	kill, locked, tack
	/ g /	gill, logged, tag
Affricates:	/ č /	chill, botched, match
	/ j /	Jill, budged, Madge
Fricatives:	/ f /	fill, huffle, gaffe
	/ v /	village, hovel, gave
	/ θ /	thigh, ether, wreath
	/ ð /	thy, either, wreathe
	/ s /	sill, possum, gas
	/ z /	zeal, poison, gaze
	/ š /	shill, passion, gash
	/ ž /	—, leisure, beige
	/ h /	hill, ahead, —
Nasals:	/ m /	mail, hammer, seem
	/ n /	nail, banner, sin
	/ ŋ /	—, banger, sing
Resonants:	/ r /	rip, barrow, store
	/ l /	lip, dollar, stole
Semivowels:	/ w /	will, lower, —
	/ y /	yell, layer, —
Vowels:	/ i /	beat, beet
	/ ɪ /	bit
	/ e /	bait, hate
	/ ε /	bet
	/ æ /	bat, battle
	/ a /	bottle
	/ ə /	but, between, bitter
	/ ɔ /	bought
	/ o /	boat
	/ ʊ /	book
	/ u /	boot

Thus, *spot* could end either with a final [tʰ] or a [t⁼]. Again, the variation would not be noticed unless called to one's attention. However, it is not automatic, and therefore not predictable, though probably related to rate and style of speaking. The English language also has a set of voiced stop phonemes: *b, d, g*. These occur in fewer environments and show less variation than do the voiceless stops. The distinction between voicing and voicelessness is important in English, separating sets of fricative and affricated phonemes as well as stops.

When linguistic students first become aware of the regular allophonic variation in the sounds of their own language, they may leap to the assumption that this variation is natural and inevitable—that the same patterns of variation can be expected in any and all languages. But this is not the case. Patterns of allophonic variation *are* found in all languages, but not the *same* patterns of variation. Languages differ from one another both in their inventory of sounds and in the ways that those sounds are patterned in relation to one another (in other words, the differences are not only phonetic, but also phonemic).

A simple illustration of this fact can be seen in a short list of words drawn from closely related African languages, Zulu and Swahili (Gleason, 1955). In both languages, the phoneme /o/ has two allophones, or variants: [o] and [ɔ], as seen in the following words (which are written phonemically *except* for these allophones):

Zulu		Swahili	
bɔna	see	bɔma	fort
bɔpha	bind	nɔmbe	cattle
mɔsa	despoil	ñɔña	nurse
imɔtɔ	car	nɔŋa	strangle
iboni	grasshopper	ndoto	dream
umosi	one who roasts	mboga	vegetable
lolu	this	soka	ax
umxoxi	storyteller	jogo	rooster

The reader might pause and inspect these two lists; the choice between [o] and [ɔ] comes "naturally" to both Zulus and Swahilis, but the rules differ— what are these rules? The solution to the Swahili problem is fairly obvious: [ɔ] occurs when the next phoneme is a nasal consonant (m, n, ñ, ŋ), and [o] is used in all other environments.

In Zulu also, the choice of allophones is conditioned by what follows, but in this case it is the next *vowel* that is important: [ɔ] is used when the next vowel is low (/o/, /a/, or /e/) and [o] when the next vowel is high (/u/ or /i/). This is an example of a phenomenon called *vowel harmony*, which is highly developed in a few European languages (Hungarian and Turkish, for example) but not unknown in other areas. Small phonetic details of this sort make it very difficult to learn to speak a second language like a native. Speaking fluently but with a "foreign accent" means that the individual either retains the phonological rules of his or her native language or has not internalized those of the second—or, more likely, both.

PHONEMIC THEORY

Early in the 20th century, formulation of the phonemic principle launched a period of florescence in modern linguistics. New generalizations were inspired by a growing familiarity with the languages of the world, written and nonwritten. This led to new questions and inspired an eagerness to study and compare a wider sample of hitherto unrecorded languages. As the body of work grew, linguistic methods became more sophisticated. Much of the theoretical discussion in linguistic books and journals of the mid-century was focused on restating and clarifying definitions of the phoneme and related concepts.

Franz Boas had approached the concept of the phoneme as a structural unit when he remarked on the phenomenon of variation in the sounds. It appeared that the discovery of regular patterns in the occurrence of these variant sounds, or *allophones,* could provide an objective basis for defining the phonemes of any language. A new development came when Boas's student Edward Sapir—one of the giants of modern linguistics—observed that the phoneme could also be considered a psychological unit in the functioning of language. Sapir came to this realization when he observed the ease with which Native American consultants could read his phonemic transcriptions of their speech—he had captured the important (phonemic) distinctions and omitted the unnecessary (allophonic) details.

A third and equally influential definition of the phoneme would come out of the long-established comparative tradition in the study of European languages. Ferdinand de Saussure emphasized the distinction between the *diachronic* (or historical) orientation of this tradition and the newer *synchronic* (descriptive or functional) approach. Saussure expressed dissatisfaction with the piecemeal way in which earlier comparative scholars had dealt with linguistic data, often simply working with words and isolated forms taken out of context. It was his view that languages should first be analyzed synchronically, as systems in which each part is related to each other part. In turn, change could be seen as a process affecting the whole fabric of language.

Consistent with his emphasis on the understanding of languages as systems, Saussure formulated a functional definition of the phoneme, based on contrast, or *opposition,* as a structural principle. Individual speakers may vary among themselves, and the same individual may not always pronounce the same words in the same way; yet this does not interfere with communication. We hear and interpret speech, the particular utterances of particular speakers, within a frame of reference provided by the overall patterning of a given language. For example, speakers of English actually vary considerably in their articulation of the phoneme /s/; some pronounce it forcefully, with considerable frictional noise; some more lightly; some with the tip of the tongue near the teeth, and others with the blade of the tongue near the hard palate (an important contrast in some languages, but not in English); and some even with an accompanying whistle—but none of this is important for intelligibility. The important thing is that English /s/ contrasts with the phonemes that resemble it most closely, that is, /z/, /š/ (the *sh* sound) and /θ/ (the voiceless *th* sound), so that "sip," "ship," and "zip"; "sin" and "shin"; and "sink" and "think" all remain distinct.

From Saussure's viewpoint, then, it is the fact of opposition, or contrast, between speech sounds that defines them as phonemes. This principle of opposition has broad applicability in linguistic theory and is the basis for a number of approaches. One formulation, which became the basis for a comprehensive view of language structure, is *distinctive feature analysis,* given its definitive formulation in the book *Fundamentals of Language* by Roman Jakobson and Morris Halle (1956). Their approach to language has been compared with—and, in fact, appears to have inspired—the structuralist approach in anthropology advocated by Claude Levi-Strauss. Applied to phonology, the goal of analysis is the discovery of the contrastive features that differentiate the phonemes of any language.

The terminology used by Jakobson and Halle (and other members of the "Prague School" of linguistics) is derived from an acoustic, rather than an articulatory, approach to phonology. As an example, the consonants of

Mohawk (an Iroquoian language), as analyzed by P. Postal, are constituted of seven distinctive features identified as *consonantal, sonorant, vocalic, grave, nasal, compact,* and *interrupted.* It can be seen that each consonant differs significantly (*i.e.,* is in contrast with) all of the others in at least one of these features (Postal, 1964).

	n	*r*	*w*	*y*	*k*	*p*	*t*	*s*
consonantal	+	+	+	+	+	+	+	+
sonorant	+	+	+	+	−	−	−	−
vocalic	+	+	−	−				
grave			+	−	+	+	−	−
nasal	+	−						
compact					+	−		
interrupted							+	−

Comparisons with the phonological systems found in other languages indicate that the total inventory of distinctive features is limited. Twelve of these were named by Jakobson and Halle, who proposed that the features are universal, underlying the phonemic systems of languages everywhere. According to Jakobson and Halle, the "supposed multiplicity of features" sometimes said to characterize different languages is "largely illusory," since the apparent differences can be interpreted as just so many manifestations of the same limited stock of oppositions. Their claim, of universal principles in the structuring of phonological systems, anticipated by several decades a recent wave of interest in linguistic universals.

MORPHOLOGY: THE STRUCTURE OF WORDS

Phonology is the study of the sounds of language without consideration of meaning. The smallest segments that carry meaning—*morphemes*—can be isolated and their meanings identified by essentially simple procedures of contrast and comparison. However, discussion of the distribution, variation, and rules that govern the occurrence of morphemes can become quite intricate. After the initial identification of these segments, there may be problems in determining whether those that are similar in form have meanings in common, and vice versa—decisions that, in turn, will lead to treating two or more segments as variants (allomorphs) of a single morpheme or as separate morphemes. The major points of disagreement among linguists, however, do not usually concern segmenting or identifying the meaningful units of language, but instead focus on interpretive statements of grammatical structure—the formulation of an ordered series of rules for building larger and more complex grammatical structures out of simpler ones. For present purposes, we will not pursue an extended discussion of issues of this sort. Students who continue in the study of linguistics will become familiar with current approaches to language description, preferably with the assistance of classroom instruction and the application of analytic methods to specific language data.

In reconstructing the evolutionary history of language, Charles Hockett pointed to "duality of patterning" as the design feature that supports the level of complexity characteristic of existing human languages. All known languages are built on this plan, which involves two types of structural elements. The first of these are the units of sound, or *phonemes;* the second consists of the meaningful units, or *morphemes;* these in turn combine to form larger structures (words, phrases, sentences, and so on).

IDENTIFYING MORPHEMES. Morphemes may be short—at times only a single phoneme—or may be several phonemes in length; in any case, they are the minimal building blocks that have identifiable meaning; they cannot be reduced or analyzed further. In all languages, words and sentences are made up of morphemes, one or more phonemes in duration, that occur in orderly sequences and combine in accordance with regular rules of order. However, even though this generalization is simple in principle, it can be difficult to apply in specific cases. For example, most speakers of English would probably agree with the author of a popular textbook (Gaeng, 1971) in his analysis of the English sentence: *Yesterday John ran away with the baker's younger daughter.*

yester + day John ran a + way with the bake + er + s young + er daughter[8]

   1   2   3   4 5   6   7   8   9   10 11 12   13   14

However, some English speakers might suggest that (1) *yester-* (which otherwise occurs only in *yesteryear*) is not separable, and that *yesteryear* should be considered a single element.[9] Many would reason that (4) *ran* includes a past-tense morpheme marked by the change of the vowel of the present tense form (*run*). And it is likely that a few individuals would hesitate to divide (5) *a-* and (6) *-way*, considering *away* to be an irreducible unit (despite the fact that a similar initial vowel also occurs in *aground, afloat, ahead,* and so on). Conversely, some might argue that (14) *daughter* could be divided into *daught-* and *-er,* since a similar *-er* occurs in other kinship terms like *father, brother,* and *sister* (a weak argument, since the initial syllables do not occur alone or in any other constructions). Even linguists may disagree on issues of this sort, especially when irregular or archaic forms are involved.

---

[8]This analysis divides the sentence into *segmental* morphemes only; actually, it is incomplete as it does not include *suprasegmental* morphemes, e.g., intonation and stress. The overall meaning of the sentence would be affected, for example, by using a final rising intonation (questioning) rather than the expected falling intonation (statement). It would also be changed by putting strong stress on the third segment (emphasizing *John*) or the 12th (emphasizing *younger*).

[9]A popular song of the 1960s, *Yester-me, Yester-you, Yesterday,* shows that this morpheme is in fact separable, for aesthetic effect if not in ordinary usage.

In any language, at any given time, the inventory of morphemes is finite in number. They may be counted in the hundreds or thousands, but in any case they are fewer than the words and other constructions that can be built from them. Thus, a list of morphemes would always be shorter than the lexicon, or dictionary, of a language—though languages differ in the degree of freedom with which morphemes can be combined productively to form new vocabulary. It is, however, typical that most can enter into a variety of combinations.

Let us return to the English sentence, *Yesterday John ran away with the baker's younger daughter.* We quickly recognize most of the morphemes in this sentence because we are familiar with them, alone or in combination, in many different contexts. Thus, *John* is immediately recognized as a personal name; *day* occurs alone and in words such as *days, daylight, midday, half-day,* and *Saturday.* We know *bake* as a verb (*bakes, baked, baking*) and recognize it as the stem of words like *baker, bakery,* and *half-baked.* We can quickly make comparisons to other words in our vocabulary and should recognize the *-er* of *baker* as the same ending (the "agentive") that also occurs in *miller, teacher,* and *player.* By contrast, the *-er* of *younger* would be identified as the "comparative" suffix seen in *older, fatter,* and *jollier.* We find *baker's* to resemble, in form and meaning, such words as *cook's, captain's, boss's,* and *George's,* since all include the "possessive" morpheme *-s.* Finally, numerous past-tense verbs such as *baked, wanted, cooked,* and *laughed* can be juxtaposed to the irregular *ran* (which resembles the others in meaning but is dissimilar in form).

So far, we are proceeding on the basis of intuitive knowledge of our own language and are looking at familiar words in their written forms. For a more methodical study, a linguist might begin by collecting large amounts of speech data, phonemically transcribed, and then proceed to compile lists of words and phrases that can be compared to reveal similarities in form and meaning. In the process, some regular patterns of variation would also become apparent; these may be obscured by the conventions of our writing system. For example, the possessive suffix that we write as *-s* appears, phonemically, as /-z/ in *baker's,* /-s/ in *cook's,* and /-əz/ in *George's;* these are identical with three alternate forms (or allomorphs) of the plural morpheme. One of the key problems in the morphemic analysis of many languages is to formulate the rules for such alternations. Linguists often use special symbols in such statements. For example, -Zi might stand for the plural and Zii for the possessive morpheme in English, and the rules for the occurrence of allomorphs could be stated as a formula:

$$/\text{-əz}/ \text{ following s, z, š, ž, č, ǰ}$$
$$\text{-Z} \rightarrow /\text{-s}/ \text{ following other voiceless consonants (p, t, k, f, θ)}$$
$$/\text{-z}/ \text{ following other voiced consonants (b, d, g, v, d, m, n, ŋ, r, l, y, w)}$$

Concise rules or formulas can simplify the description of a language by relating allomorphic variation to the environments in which the morphemes occur. As in this case, the formula may simply state explicitly the patterns of the language that the native speaker follows intuitively. A more awkward problem arises concerning the status of irregular forms such as the limited number of English plurals that do not follow such regular rules (*geese, oxen, mice, children, radii,* and so forth). Some linguists might treat all of these as additional variants of -Zi, determined or selected by the particular bases with which they combine. Others would leave such items out of the description of the grammatical system as such and simply list them as exceptions; the description would then focus on the regular, productive formations.

MAJOR AND MINOR MORPHEMES. In English, as in most languages, the many morphemes from which the lexicon is built can be divided into two main groups: major morphemes, or *bases,* and minor morphemes, or *affixes.* Numerically, bases always constitute the larger group, but individually, these are apt to occur less often than most of the affixes, some of which are used again and again with great frequency. Bases are said to carry the basic meaning of any word, which can be modified or changed by various affixes. In our sample sentence, some of the bases can be identified as: *John, run, way, bake,* and *young.* The affixes include the *-er* and *-s* in *baker's* and (according to our analysis) the *a-* of *away* and the infixed *-a-* of *ran.*

Affixes fall into three distributional types according to their sequential position in combining with bases. It is convenient to speak of *prefixes, suffixes,* and *infixes.* Some languages include all three of these affix types, but most seem to have a preference for one and may make little or no use of the others. English makes use of both prefixes and suffixes. Suffixing, however, is more common and is far more productive in forming new vocabulary. As seen in the example, an inventory of English affixes would include many that are productive (freely used in new combinations) and others that are nonproductive. Some of the elements that can be identified as affixes (like the *a-* in *away* or *afar,* some of the uncommon plural forms, like *oxen* and *children,* or the *de-* and *per-* in *deceive* and *perceive*) come down to us from earlier historical periods and now occur in only a handful of words. They are not apt to be used in forming new vocabulary. On the other hand, the -Zi plural suffix and several suffixes that form new verbs or adjectives (like *-ize, -ify,* and *-ish*) are used much more freely. Native speakers of English know immediately how to form the plural of a noun, even though we may never have heard the word before. When a new word is coined or is borrowed from another language—like *sputnik* from Russian or *igloo* from Yupik (Eskimo)— we can immediately speak of *sputniks* and *igloos* (even though the plural forms are *sputniki* and *iglut* in Russian and Yupik, respectively).

DERIVATION AND INFLECTION. An important distinction must be drawn between two types of morphological processes, *inflection* and *derivation,* both of which typically proceed through the use of affixes. Inflectional affixes combine with word bases (simple or derived) to add information such as *tense, aspect, number, gender,* and the like. Inflectional morphemes are very prominent in languages like Latin and Greek, in which all verbal forms include the marking of person, number, and tense by suffixes. They are much less prominent in English and many other languages.

Derivation is a process of word formation. Derivational affixes are added to existing words or bases to form new words. This may bring a change in the grammatical class (from noun to verb, for example) or a change in meaning, or both. The word *baker* is derived from the verb *bake* by the addition of the agentive/instrumental suffix -*er*; it is, technically, a deverbal noun—the suffix simultaneously changes the meaning and identifies the grammatical status of the word. Of course, both *bake* and *baker* are familiar words that have been part of the English vocabulary for centuries, but -*er* is still a productive affix— we still use it to form new verbs: *Swinger, bopper* (or *be-bopper*), *surfer,* and *rapper* are 20th-century examples. Other productive suffixes include:

-*ify,* which is added to nouns and adjectives to form verbs. For example, from nouns we get *beautify, glorify, objectify;* from adjectives, *simplify, falsify.* In *Alice's Adventures in Wonderland,* Lewis Carroll coined the words *uglify* and *uglification;* he could do this, and we understand what these words mean without any explanation because the words conform to regular processes of English word formation. A recent example with this suffix is *Disnify,* which means, approximately, "to make cute and appealing."

-*ize,* similar to -*ify.* Some examples, from nouns: *magnetize, carbonize;* from adjectives, *slenderize, digitalize.* This suffix has often been used to coin the names of processes, based on personal names: *pasteurize, macadamize, mercerize;* also *vulcanize,* from the name of the Roman god of fire, Vulcan.

-*(i)cation* and -*tion,* derive nouns from verbs, as in *communication, abolition, confirmation;* and, with derived verbs, *beautification, uglification,* and *rationalization.*

-*ish,* derives adjectives from nouns: *childish, kittenish, boorish.*

-*(i)an,* derives adjectives from nouns: *American, Christian, Elizabethan, Boasian.*

-*ful,* derives adjectives from nouns: *healthful, beautiful, soulful.*

-*y,* derives adjectives from nouns: *healthy, hearty, fuzzy, lovey-dovey.*

-*ist,* derives nouns from verbs, nouns, or adjectives: *conformist, separatist, terrorist; Marxist, functionalist, racist.*

-*able,* derives adjectives from verbs: *acceptable, bearable, doable, eatable.*

-*ite,* derives nouns from nouns (often from personal names): *Luddite, Mennonite, Trotskyite, Chomskyite.*

un-, derives verbs from verbs, adjectives from adjectives: *undo, undress, unknown, unproductive, unfunny, undoable.*

re-, derives verbs from verbs: *reform, reappear, rerun, remake.*

ex-, derives nouns from nouns: *ex-wife, ex-Republican, ex-addict.*

super-, *derives nouns from nouns:* superhuman, superstar, supernova.

Compounding is another productive process, building new words by combining existing words: *hotcake, pancake; suitcase, handbag, carryall, backpack;*

baseball, homerun, two-bagger, pinch-hitter; basketball, free-throw, scoreboard; knockout, knockdown; poorhouse, bighouse, lighthouse; blackout, blackbird, black-belt, blackjack; catbird, catcall; and so on. The meaning of a compound word may be, more or less, the sum of its parts, but this is not always the case. In 1974, Fromkin and Rodman observed that "a *blackboard* may be green or white"; at present, *chalkboard* is in general use and may eventually replace the older term.

Contemporary English also includes a great variety of acronyms, blends, and other innovative word formations that are based on the written language. *Acronyms* are words formed from the initials of a phrase or, often, the name of a government bureau or organization, for example, *NASA, UNESCO,* and *CREEP* (the Committee for the *Re-e*lection of the President, notorious during the Watergate period). This device first became popular during World War II, with acronymic names applied to military units such as the *WAACs* (*W*omen's *A*rmy *A*uxiliary *C*orps), *SWAT* (*S*pecial *W*eapons *A*nd *T*actics), and *ANZAC* (*A*ustralian-*N*ew *Z*ealand *A*rmy *C*orps). It is now so common that organizations sometimes deliberately choose names that will provide catchy, meaningful, or at least pronounceable acronyms—for example, *MADD* (*M*others *A*gainst *D*runk *D*riving), *PETA* (*P*eople for the *E*thical *T*reatment of *A*nimals), and *LASSO* (*L*inguistic *A*ssociation of the *S*outhwest. Technology also inspires such words as *scuba* (*s*elf-*c*ontained *u*nderwater *b*reathing *a*pparatus) and *radar* (*ra*dio *d*etecting *a*nd *r*anging).

Blends (or *telescoped words*) are similar, made of segments of longer expressions. Typical examples are *smog* (from *sm*oke and f*og*) and *motel* (*mo*tor ho*tel*). Lewis Carroll seems to have popularized this method, inventing words that he dubbed "portmanteau terms." More recently, B. Berlin and P. Kay, the authors of a study of color terminology, coined the word *grue* as a label for the color field overlapping *gr*een and bl*ue.*

Finally, note that we sometimes simply use abbreviations as words—*TV, CD,* the *USA,* the *NBA.* There seems to be a narrow line between abbreviations and acronyms—we familiarly refer to the *UN* (using the abbreviation) but make acronyms of its various branches—thus, *UNESCO* and *UNICEF.*

The productive resources of any language are limited, but it is always possible to form new words, to talk about novel experiences or flights of fancy, and to name inventions or discoveries. For these needs, the regular patterns of derivation, by the use of affixes, compounding, or other processes, normally suffice. In addition, words may be borrowed from other languages, along with the artifacts or behavior patterns that they denote. It is unlikely that any language is completely regular and consistent in its rules and patterns. Like English, languages generally have loose ends and outdated or atrophied parts. These reflect the fact that all languages change; they sometimes offer evidence of earlier stages in the history of a language or may provide clues to its remote relationships with other languages. In *oxen,* for example, we have a form that once was a common type of English plural; in *men* and *geese* we see traces of ablaut (internal change), a characteristic way of forming plurals in Germanic languages related to

RICH HALL'S SNIGLETS

During the early 1980s, comedian Rich Hall was a regular performer on HBO's "Not Necessarily the News," presenting *Sniglets:* "words that don't appear in the dictionary, but should." In these ephemeral lexical creations, Hall employed the typical processes of English word formation: iconism, compounding, derivation, incorporation of Greek and Latin elements, acronyms, and word blends—always with a comic twist. Some examples, culled from *Sniglets* (1984) and *More Sniglets* (1985):

alponium	*n.* (chemical symbol: Ap) Initial blast of odor upon opening a can of dog food.
aquadexterous	*adj.* Possessing the ability to turn the bathtub faucet on and off with your toes.
bathquake	*n.* The violent quake that rattles the entire house when the water faucet is turned to a certain point.
busblender	*n.* The device at the front of the bus that tosses your fare around for a while, then swallows it.
charp	*n.* The green, mutant potato chip found in every bag.
coeggulant	*n.* The white things in a plate of scrambled eggs.
detruncus	*n.* The embarassing situation of losing one's bathing shorts while diving into a swimming pool.
eastroturf	*n.* The artificial grass in Easter baskets.
erdu	*n.* The leftover accumulation of rubber particles after erasing a mistake on a test paper.
eufirstics	*n.* Two people waiting on the phone for the other to hang up first.
fenderberg	*n.* The large glacial deposits that form on the insides of car fenders during snowstorms.
gladhandling	*n.* The frustrating attempt to find and separate the ends of a plastic sandwich or trash bag.
hozone	*n.* The place where one sock in every laundry load disappears to.
keyfruit	*n.* The one apple or tomato in the stand that, when removed, causes all the others to tumble down.
lactomangulation	*n.* Manhandling the "open here" spout on a milk carton so badly that the "illegal" side must be used.
napjerk	*n.* The sudden convulsion of the body just as one is about to doze off.
opup	*v.* To push one's glasses back on the nose.
otisosis	*n.* The inability to meet anyone else's eyes in an elevator.
peppiér	*n.* A waiter whose only apparent function is to walk around and ask diners if they want ground pepper.
phonesia	*n.* The affliction of dialing a phone number and forgetting whom you were calling just as they answer.
piyan	*n.* (acronym: "Plus If You Act Now") A miscellaneous extra item thrown in on a television ad.
profanitype	*n.* The special symbols used by cartoonists to replace swear words (asterisks, stars and so on).
slottery and vendication	*n.* A public misdemeanor in which a person loses money to a vending machine and tries to exact revenge by kicking it.
spork	*n.* The combination spoon/fork you find in fast-food restaurants.
twinch	*n.* The movement a dog makes with its head when it hears a high-pitched noise.
xiidigitation	*n.* Effort to determine the year a movie was made by deciphering the Roman numerals at the end of the credits.

English; and *radii* and *fungi* bear witness to the influence of Latin on English language and culture. Latin plurals, especially, tend to be replaced by plurals that follow the regular pattern; people are likely to say *radiuses* and *funguses* rather than using the "correct" Latin plural.

THE DISCOVERY OF "PRIMITIVE" LANGUAGES

Early attempts by missionaries and other travelers to record and translate the languages of aboriginal peoples were usually accompanied by negative stereotypes and assumptions of racial and cultural inferiority. Native peoples were often labeled as "savages," and their languages were assumed to be crude, lacking the nuances and sensitivity of the languages of "civilized" peoples. There were stories of tribes who could not express themselves adequately without the use of gestures. Native Americans were routinely caricatured as speaking in grunts and monosyllables, accompanied by sign language. Even as the study of aboriginal languages progressed, questions were still raised about their "evolutionary" status. Were they, in some way, deficient? There were persistent rumors that "primitive" languages lacked both fine distinctions and abstractions.

These issues were addressed by linguist Archibald Hill in a short paper that is now considered a classic. Hill examined statements, repeated again and again over the years in many publications, that presented the Cherokee language as "primitive" in having many specific terms but lacking general and abstract concepts. An example that seemed to support this stereotype originally appeared in the writings of John Pickering, dated 1823; the primary source of the information was a Reverend Buthrick, a missionary to the Cherokees. In the Cherokee language, according to Pickering, ". . . thirteen [sic] different verbs are used to express the action of *washing*. . . ."

1. Cu tu wo	I am washing myself, as in a river
2. Cu le stu la	I am washing my head
3. Tse stu la	I am washing another person's head
4. Cu cu squo	I am washing my face
5. Tse cu squo	I am washing another's face
6. Ta ca su la	I am washing my hands
7. Ta tse ya su la	I am washing another's hands
8. Ta co su la	I am washing my feet
9. Ta tse ya su la	I am washing another's feet
10. Ta cung ke la	I am washing my clothes
11. Ta tse yung ke la	I am washing another's clothes
12. Ta cu te ya	I am washing dishes
13. Tse yu wa	I am washing a child
14. Co we la	I am washing meat

Pickering, and those who later reprinted this example, followed a traditional practice of dividing Native American names and other words and phrases into separate syllables, which seldom have any relationship to the grammatical structure of the language. Thus, the actual meaning of the phrases remained a complete mystery. Hill first undertook to identify the Cherokee words and rewrite them phonemically. The analysis into morphemes was assisted by Floyd Lounsbury, an authority on Iroquoian languages. The corrected word list, along with the literal translations, is as follows (a nasal vowel, similar to French /a/, is written as v):

1. k-ata-wo	I-reflexive-bathe (in a stream)
2. k-ali-sdul-e	I-reflexive-head-wash
3. tsi-sdul-e	I-(someone's) head-wash
4. k-a-gvsk-wo	I-him/it-face-wash (bathe)
5. tsi-gvsk-wo	I-(someone's) face-wash (bathe)
6. de-k-asul-e	plural object-I-extremity-wash
7. de-tsi-ya-(a)sul-e	plural object-I-him-extremity-wash
8, 9	identical with (6), (7)
10. de-k-vgil-e	plural object-I-clothing-wash
11. de-tsi-y(a)-vgil-e	plural object-I-him-clothing wash
12. de-k-atiy-e	plural object-I-dish (or spoon)-wash
13. tsi-yvw(i)-e	I-person (?)-wash
14. k-owil-e	I-meat-wash

Beyond the morpheme-by-morpheme translations, Hill does not discuss the grammatical system in any detail. However, several comments may be made on the basis of Lounsbury's analysis: First, the examples consist of inflected forms of two different Cherokee verbs, /-wo/ *bathe* (usually in a stream, as a rite of purification); and /-e/ *wash*. These verb stems are found in word-final position and are preceded by two to four additional morphemes. Among these are the first-person prefix that appears in two variants or allomorphs, /k-/ before vowels and /tsi-/ before consonants. Examples 1 and 2 contain two different reflexive prefixes. Examples 6 to 10 include an initial prefix that marks a plural object. Finally, most of the examples illustrate a rare pattern that is distinctive of Iroquoian languages—the incorporation of the noun object in the verb: /-sdul-/ *head, /-gvsk-/ *face, /-asul-/ *extremity (hand or foot), /-vgil-/ *clothes, /-ati(y)/ *dish, and /-owil-/ *meat. (Some of the incorporated nouns, marked by *, may be archaic; they are not the usual forms in modern Cherokee.)

Hill concludes that the Cherokee language, "so far from being over-specific, is a language like other languages, possessed of order and system. . . . We do not find fourteen totally unrelated expressions for washing, but two morphemes only, which differ in meaning, and which enter into a whole series of systematic constructions" (Hill, 1952).

STRUCTURAL VARIETY

An emphasis on descriptive methods that are appropriate and equally applicable to all languages is essentially a 20th-century concern. Through the first half of the 20th century, linguistic anthropologists took the fact of diversity as a point of departure—they seem to have been persuaded that anything is possible in language and emphasized the development of a methodology that could discover and deal with the unique or unexpected. In "American Indian Grammatical Categories," Edward Sapir[10] compared the types of morphemes and sentences representative of seven Native American languages. In so doing, he was able to build on a body of previous research, by himself and others, devoted to the study of many individual languages. Sapir was an influential figure in a historical period in which there was a strong emphasis on methods in linguistics—methods that should enable the linguist to analyze and describe objectively any and all human languages.

Sapir began his discussion of "American Indian Grammatical Categories[11] with the observation that ". . . within the confines of the United States there is spoken today a far greater variety of languages—not dialects, not slightly divergent forms of speech, but fundamentally different languages—than in the whole of Europe" (Sapir & Swadesh, 1946). In fact, Sapir comments further, even the state of California contains a wealth of native languages of greater diversity than any comparable area in the Old World. Unlike most of the languages of Europe, these American Indian languages are not known to have a common origin, and in both sounds and structures they present "the most bewildering diversity of form."

Because of this variety, Sapir felt that studies of American Indian languages had, even as early as the 1920s, contributed greatly to knowledge, to a sampling of the total range of variation in the phenomena of language, and to an eventual understanding of the psychology of language and thought. All human languages, he asserted, can be reduced to "a common psychological ground"; but the ground cannot be adequately understood or mapped "without the perspective gained from a sympathetic study of the forms themselves."

Sapir noted the existence of several very widely distributed linguistic features. All the familiar patterns of European languages, he wrote, can be found in those of aboriginal America. But none are universal, and some are encountered that are unique or rare. In order to explore the diversity that he found so impressive, Sapir used the device of translating a single English sentence into several Native American languages, pointing out some of the characteristic grammatical features of each. The languages used here are Wishram, Takelma, Southern Paiute, Yana, Nootka, Navajo, and Yokuts—all languages of the west or southwest, and all languages that Sapir had studied in the field.

---

[10]Edward Sapir (1884–1939) came under the influence of Franz Boas while studying at Columbia University. Sapir described several languages of the western United States and also made contributions to ethnology and psychological anthropology. His *Language* (1921) and other writings are still widely read; he was an influential teacher at the University of Chicago and Yale University, training many of the next generation of linguistic anthropologists.

[11]The article was written by Sapir in 1929 but edited and published by Morris Swadesh in 1946, several years after Sapir's death.

English:	He will give it to you.
Wishram:	ačimluda (a-č-i-m-l-ud-a)
	will-he-him-thee-to-GIVE-will
Takelma:	ʔospink (ʔok-t-xpi-nk)
	WILL GIVE-to-thee-he or they (in future)
S. Paiute:	maɣavaaniaakʔanaʔmi (maɣa-vaania-aka-ana-ʔmi)
	GIVE-will-visible thing-visible creature-thee
Yana:	baːjamasiwaʔnuma (baː-ja-ma-si-wa-ʔnuma)
	ROUND THING-away-to-does or will do-unto-thou (in future)
Nootka:	ʔoyiː ʔaːqλateʔic (oʔ-yi-ː-ʔaːqλ-ʔat-eʔic)
	THAT-give-will-done unto-thou-art
Navajo:	neidoːʔaɬ (n-aː-yi-diho-ʔaɬ)
	thee-to transitive-will-ROUND THING (in future)
Yokuts:	ma-m waːn-en taː-ni
	THEE-obj. GIVE-will THAT-at

In discussing these examples, Sapir emphasized (as had his mentor, Franz Boas) the contrasts in *obligatory* categories. The psychological unity of humankind is evident in the fact that the English sentence *can* be adequately translated into all the others; but each language must include information that may be omitted in others. In English, for example, we must indicate the *gender* of the third-person actor (masculine) and object (neuter), as well as *number* (both are singular); and we specify the time when the action occurs by the *tense* of the verb (future). We do not need to indicate, as speakers of some languages do, the size or shape of the object, whether or not it is visible, or whether the action was observed by the speaker. Some of Sapir's comments on each of the translations is summarized as follows:

Wishram: The construction is highly *agglutinative*—that is, it is easily analyzable into a number of separate morphemes. The order of these is fixed. Wishram makes pronominal gender distinctions that are sometimes arbitrary (as in German or French); thus, the third morpheme is "him" (the referent being defined as a stone). The base of the Wishram construction, "give," is in sixth position; note that tense is marked twice, both initially and finally.

Takelma: As in Wishram, a number of elements are strung together, but Takelma is more *fusional*. The separate morphemes are, so to speak, fused together so that the boundaries are obscured. The verb base is the first element; this morpheme ("will give") includes the idea of future time, as does the final pronominal element. Gender and number are not indicated; this could be done by adding independent pronouns but, according to Sapir, this would also amount to an unusual emphasis on this information. Finally, the third-person object is not formally indicated but is simply assumed (in the presence of a transitive verb).

Southern Paiute: As in Wishram, the construction is agglutinative but allows more flexibility in the order of morphemes. Two obligatory distinctions determine the choice of object and subject pronominals (the third and fourth elements)—that is, animate versus inanimate, and visible versus invisible.

Yana: The base is the initial element of the construction, as in Southern
Paiute and Takelma; it indicates both movement and a classification of
shape (the stone is classified as a "round thing").

Nootka: The initial base "that" (or "that one") refers to the thing given
(the stone). The second morpheme is a suffix that indicates *aspect,* an
obligatory category; the aspect here is "momentaneous" (other possible choices would indicate greater duration or repetition of the action).
Tense, indicated by the third element, is an optional category.

Navajo: The base is the final element in the word and, as in Yana, it indicates a classification ("round object") as well as movement. Future
time is indicated both by the verb base as well as by an affix. Note that
the actor is not formally indicated; a third-person actor is implied by
the absence of a first- or second-person pronominal element.

American Indian languages, Sapir noted, are often characterized as *poly-
synthetic.* All six of the examples so far discussed illustrate this general tendency; that is, they combine a large number of meaningful elements into a
single word. However, the last example, Yokuts, was chosen to illustrate an
opposite tendency—superficially, at least, more similar to the English in
number and length of words. Here again, the third-person actor is normally
omitted. Sapir paraphrases the meaning of the construction as "will present
thee at (or with) it" (Sapir & Swadesh, 1946).

SYNTAX: THE STRUCTURE OF SENTENCES

In traditional linguistic approaches, the focus of study is a specific corpus of
data. Phonology, morphology, and syntax are considered to be three semi-
independent levels of analysis. Phonology treats the sounds of language and
their combinations; morphology, the regular patterns and sequences of morphemes in the formation of words; and syntax, classes of words and their
combinations in the formation of phrases and sentences. One way to
approach the study of syntax is to examine the freedom with which words
and phrases can be substituted in specific contexts, or *frames.* For example,
consider the sentence: "The tall young man next door is a basketball player."
For the words *the tall young man next door* we can substitute *the tall man, the
young man,* and *the man next door*—but not **the tall young, *the young next door,*
or, with changed order, **the young tall man.*[12]

If this sort of procedure is systematically continued, classes of words and
phrases will emerge that have the same *privileges of occurrence*—that fill the
same slots in constructions and thus have the same grammatical functions.
Although this could be done simply by collecting and analyzing samples of
recorded speech or written text, it can be done more easily by relying on the

---

[12]According to linguistic convention, asterisks indicate hypothetical or unacceptable forms.

judgments of a native speaker. The difference between the two techniques may seem subtle, but it is major from a theoretical point of view: The first would be an objective analysis of a corpus of linguistic data, while the second would put reliance on introspective and possibly subjective judgments.

Similar to the use of frame sentences, but methodologically more elegant, *immediate constituent* (or *IC*) *analysis* proceeds by breaking down sentences through successive binary divisions. This follows an assumption, common among linguists and cognitive scientists, that the human mind processes information (both in the building up and in the breaking down of structures) by dualities. Thus, "The : young man / who : lives . next door // is / a : basketball . player." is divided into immediate constituents as follows: The first division (//) is into subject and predicate clauses; the division of the subject clause into its immediate constituents (/) yields *the young man* and *who lives next door;* the first of these is next divided (:) into *the* and *young man;* and so on. As before, the objective is to arrive at word classes, based on patterns of phrase construction and substitutability of words and phrases—but also yielding an understanding of sentence structure as a "hierarchy of IC's" (Gleason, 1961). Some of the considerations that, in various languages, serve as a guide to the analysis of sentence patterns are the occurrence of inflectional morphemes that signal word relations (markers of case, number, and gender), and patterns of intonation, stress, and word juncture.

More contemporary approaches to syntax have built on the earlier structuralist methods but approach the problem in a somewhat different way, usually describing languages in terms of rules for the production of sentences. These rules are believed to be similar in type from language to language and are limited in number. A *transformational-generative* (T/G) analysis is a concise statement of rules that yield acceptable (grammatical) sentences for a specific language. Theoretically, the number of sentences that may be produced is infinite. In principle, the emphasis is on the creative aspect of language; a generative grammar is not limited to description of a particular corpus of data, since speakers of any language are always capable of producing new grammatical utterances.

An important consideration in T/G and related approaches to syntax is the distinction that Noam Chomsky has drawn between *competence* (an individual's intuitive knowledge of the rules of grammar) and *performance* (what individual speakers actually say). Related to this is the separation of *deep structure* (the abstract form of a sentence) from *surface structure* (its realization as a string of words and morphemes). It is on the level of deep structure that differences among languages are thought to be minimal or nonexistent because the relationships here are conceptual and are thought to be determined by the structure of the human mind. Chomsky developed a series of models for the conversion of deep structure (which includes both syntactic and semantic components), through several stages of syntactic processing, to phonological realization in actual speech.

Transformational-generative analysis begins with the largest syntactic units (S, sentence) and proceeds to break the sentence into successively smaller parts (NP, noun phrase; VP, verb phrase; N, noun; A, adjective; and so on) through a series of "rewrite" rules (symbolized by an arrow, →). Thus:

$$S \rightarrow \quad NP\ VP$$
$$NP \rightarrow \begin{cases} \text{(Det) N} \\ \text{Pn} \end{cases}$$
$$VP \rightarrow \begin{cases} \text{V (NP)} \\ \text{is Adj} \end{cases}$$

Det: the, this

N: student, girl, clerk

Pn: it

V: saw, remembered, wrote

Adj: energetic, pretty, impossible

A formulaic statement of this sort is a mini-grammar that will generate several acceptable English sentences: *The student saw the girl. The girl remembered the student. The student remembered it. The clerk remembered the girl. The clerk wrote it. The clerk is pretty. The girl is energetic.* One can easily add more words to increase the productivity of such a *phrase-structure grammar.* Generative rules of this sort are called *phrase-structure rules.*

The addition of a series of *transformational rules* will make it possible to derive other sentences of various types from the simple *kernel* sentences shown above: questions, exclamations, negative sentences, and complex or compound sentences, which are interpreted as combinations of simpler ones. Thus: *Did the student see the girl? The clerk did not remember the girl. The pretty girl remembered the clerk. The girl the student remembered was energetic.* The ultimate objective would be to discover the complete set of rules that make it possible for a native speaker to produce sentences that will be understood and accepted by other speakers.

Great reliance is placed on the insights of native speakers in assessing the acceptability of sentences and in explaining how derived sentences are related to simpler sentences. Therefore, many T/G linguists have worked primarily on the basis of their own use of language. However, comparative studies based on this approach have suggested an overriding similarity among languages in their use of syntactic rules and structures. Increasingly, T/G and related theories have had a significant impact on anthropological discussions of language. Syntax has become a focus of interest in anthropological textbooks and journals, perhaps in part because it appears to reflect cognitive processes more obviously than phonological or morphological structures.

LANGUAGE UNIVERSALS

This book began with an examination of the origin and evolution of human language and a look at the sources of diversity in languages. An effort is being made throughout the book to balance the particular and the general, mindful both of anthropology's longstanding commitment to cultural relativism and of the underlying unity of the human evolutionary heritage. The horizons of contemporary anthropology have been much expanded by recent discoveries in human paleontology and prehistory; it is now possible to trace our evolutionary development in far greater detail than could be done in earlier generations. It seems appropriate, then, that linguistic scholars have revived an earlier interest in the origin and common heritage of languages, expressed in new efforts to discover features that reflect this heritage. For a number of linguists, their studies of topics as diverse as phonology, syntax, language acquisition, sociolinguistics, taxonomy, and pidgin and creole studies have begun to converge; what emerges is a shared interest in *language universals.*

Charles Hockett was, indirectly, one of the initiators of the recent research on language universals. In developing his theory of the origin of language (discussed in chapter 1), Hockett defined certain "design features" that he saw to be universal in human languages and either rare or absent in the communication of other species. He isolated *productivity, displacement, traditional transmission,* and *duality of patterning* as features that marked the transition from pre-language to language. Subsequently, Hockett has extended the list, adding: *prevarication,* the fact that linguistic messages can be false or meaningless; *reflexiveness,* the ability to communicate about language itself (as well as anything else); and *learnability,* meaning that humans are not limited to just one language but can acquire others. (These last three are not basic in the same sense as those in the original list but are extensions of them.)

In 1961, speaking at the Dobbs Ferry conference that opened up language universals as a subject for serious discussion, Hockett made several additional observations. For example, he noted that:

- all languages have intonation systems; "intonational" and "non-intonational" messages are transmitted simultaneously.
- all languages have deictic morphemes, including at least one for speaker (I/me) and one for addressee (you).
- all languages have proper names, denoting individuals.
- all languages have at least two basic orders of magnitude in grammatical patterning (morphology, syntax).

- in phonology, all languages employ the contrasts of consonant/vowel and stop/nonstop; include at least two contrasting stop positions; and use contrasts of vowel color.

These were fairly impressionistic assertions, reflecting Hockett's own familiarity with a number of languages but not substantiated by systematic research on universals *per se*. However, the suggestions that he made have been pursued and have helped to set the direction for future study. Joseph Greenberg, the organizer of the Dobbs Ferry conference, has been a leader and innovator in studies that employ wide and methodically selected linguistic samples and arrive at generalizations based on statistical correlations and typological classification. Universals defined on this basis are sometimes referred to as *Greenbergian universals*.

A second, and quite different, inspiration to the discussion of language universals emerged from the transformational-generative linguistics of Noam Chomsky. In this case, linguistic features are described in abstract terms, as attributes of a "universal grammar" that is posited as an innate property of the human mind. Universals defined via the transformational-generative approach are designated as *Chomskian universals*.

THE TYPOLOGICAL APPROACH. Greenberg and his associates have described several types of universals, based on the level of correlation or association of features:

1. *Unrestricted universals* are those that characterize all of the sample (and, presumably, all human languages), the presence of a contrast between vowels and consonants, the grammatical distinction between nouns and verbs, and the use of intonation are acknowledged as unrestricted universals—and thus become, in effect, part of the definition of *language*.

2. *Statistical universals* are those that appear in most, but not all, languages. It is always possible that features thought to be unrestricted universals will eventually fall into this category if further research uncovers exceptions. For example, "All languages have nasal consonants" is a statistical universal. The exceptions are a handful of languages, concentrated in northwestern North America, well under 1% of the languages of the world. In such a case, when the statistical universal appears to be the norm, attention may focus on the exceptions: What explains their deviation from the norm?

3. *Implicational universals* are features present in a restricted set of languages. They are described by the statement "If Y exists in a language, then X must also be present." For example, Greenberg reports that an alveolar affricate phoneme *ts* (or *c*) always implies the presence of the fricative *s*; there are, thus, three groups of languages: those with both *s* and *ts*; those with *s* but without *ts*; and those with neither. The other logical possibility—with *ts* but without *s*—does not occur (Greenberg, 1978).

4. The most productive research has come by using variation in selected features as the basis for typological classification. At the Dobbs Ferry conference, Greenberg first presented a classification of languages based on the relative order, within sentences, of three basic elements: nominal subject (S), verb (V), and nominal object (O). This typology has subsequently been discussed in several publications.

Greenberg observes that sentences such as *The boy drank the water* can be found in all languages. Thus, in a sample of seven languages:

English: the bóy dránk the wáter
        S   V   O

Russian: mál'čik výpil vódu
        S   V   O

Turkish: çoçúk suyú içtí
        S   O   V

Arabic: šáraba lwáladu lmāʔa
        V   S   O

Hausa: yārō yášā ruwā
        S   V   O

Thai: dègchaaj dyym nàam
        S   V   O

Quechua: wámbra yakúra upiárqan
        S   O   V

As in these examples, subject, verb, and object can be identified and abstracted from other ideas (tense, gender, number, and so on) that may or may not be expressed in each language. There are, logically, six possible orders in which these three components might occur: VSO, SVO, SOV, VOS, OSV, and OVS. However, Greenberg found only the first three as normal word order in a representative sample of languages.[13] These three (VSO, SVO, and SOV) differ from one another only in the placement of the verb; they have in common the fact that the subject precedes the object. This, then, appeared to be a universal, possibly reflecting, according to Greenberg, "a general set of psychological and physiological preferences" common to all humankind.

Since this claim was made, exceptions have come to light: Hixkaryana, of the Carib family, is one of a small number of languages with OVS as normal

---

[13]Most languages do permit some variation in word order, often expressing variation in emphasis.

word order; all known instances are located in the Amazon forest region of South America. But the real significance of the word-order typology became apparent when it was shown to have predictive value. That is, if it is known that a language is Type I (VSO), Type II (SVO), or Type III (SOV), then other features of its grammatical system can be predicted with some degree of accuracy. Thus, languages of Type I employ prepositions almost exclusively, while those of Type III (in many respects the "polar opposite" of Type I) usually have postpositions; Type II languages are more variable. There are similar positive correlations between the word-order types and the relative order of nouns in a genitive expression, the position in the sentence of interrogative particles or affixes, and the relative order of main and subordinate verbs. Refinements and extensions of these correlations have been undertaken by a number of linguists. It remains one of the most valuable results of the typological approach to universals (Greenberg, 1961, 1966; Comrie, 1981).

THE GENERATIVE APPROACH. The notion, advocated by Noam Chomsky, that there is a universal mental grammar, stored in the brain, has been called "*the* central theoretical construct of modern linguistics" (Jackendoff, 1994). If this is accepted as a premise, it becomes the goal of linguistic theory to understand the mental operations that derive the "surface structures" of particular languages from the abstract "deep structure" that reflects innate patterns embedded in the human mind.

Chomsky and linguists influenced by him have approached this goal through in-depth study of individual languages, relying on the judgment of native speakers about the acceptability of grammatical constructions. In effect, the linguist's own language is analyzed in depth to provide a model of the general nature of language. Some of the features attributed to universal grammar are

- a basic sentence structure (S → NP VP).
- hierarchical tree patterns that fit into the larger components (NP, VP).
- the property of recursiveness (incorporation of sentences into longer sentences).

Early work in the generative tradition was largely confined to the study of English; more recently, it has been extended to a wider range of languages (still largely Western). To accommodate structural diversity, there has been a concern with the identification of *parameters*—points at which variation is allowed. One such parameter is *pro-drop*, which permits the dropping of unstressed personal pronouns. Spanish is a pro-drop language: Both "*Yo tengo*" and "*Tengo*" are acceptable as sentences; in English, "*I have*" is acceptable, but "** Have*" is not. Other parameters have to do with word order—such as whether adjectives and other modifiers precede or follow nouns, for example.

On the whole, the typological framework, which approaches the search for universals empirically through comparison of a wide range of individual languages, has proved more compatible with the general perspective of anthropology than the generative framework. One may question the positing of an abstract mental template for grammar, as well as the use of English as the primary basis for judgments about the nature of language. In the opinion of Bernard Comrie, "Simple transference of a model that handles English syntax reasonably well often produces a distortion of the syntactic nature of . . . other languages." Comrie does not deny the possibility of eventually arriving at a universal theory of syntax, but he is convinced that such a theory must be defined empirically, on the basis of comparative study (Comrie, 1981).

It may be observed that the two different approaches described here are not *necessarily* incompatible. Each aspires to what the other does not: Study via the generative method seeks to characterize a native speaker's understanding of his or her own language, while typological studies search for points of objective similarity in linguistic forms. In fact, some cross-fertilization and a degree of cooperation have taken place, in the context of conferences and workshops dealing with specific linguistic issues (such as discourse, word order, passive constructions, or case marking). In this text, treatment of topics as diverse as language acquisition, color terminology, terms of address, and pidgin and creole languages may be seen to reflect a universalizing perspective.

FIELDWORK IN LINGUISTIC ANTHROPOLOGY

Linguists, like cultural anthropologists, must deal face to face with other human beings in order to collect the data for their studies. Any linguistic study, whatever its scope, is based on a body (usually called a *corpus*) of methodically collected speech data. Some linguists find their data very close at hand—in fact, for a *generative* grammar (an analysis of a native speaker's internalized competence), a linguist may rely on his or her own judgments about "well-formed" and "ill-formed" constructions.

However, serving as one's own data source is not the usual practice. Linguistic anthropologists usually work with one or more "informants" or *consultants*,[14] whose speech is recorded, either directly in phonetic transcription or on tape, to provide the corpus of data for study and analysis. Data can be collected close to home: in the linguist's own office, for example, where colleagues or students might provide information on their own languages; on a busy street or in a crowded railroad station, where data could be recorded for a survey of speech variation; or in a selected venue such as a church, school, or business firm, perhaps to provide data for a sociolinguistic study

---

[14]*Informant* is the term traditionally used to identify native speakers used as the source of information about a language or culture; in recent decades, the term has acquired negative political implications, and *consultant* is more often used.

(see chapter 7). However, pursuing the anthropological tradition of *fieldwork,* linguists also travel to distant locations, where they often study aboriginal or Third World languages; much of the analysis may be done on the spot with the cooperation of native consultants.

In the past it was commonplace (and even today it is not unusual) for a linguistic anthropologist to begin a field study without having substantial prior knowledge of the *target language,* the language to be studied. There are still many small languages and language groups that remain to be methodically studied and described, and some that do not have established writing systems. But even if earlier studies can be consulted, it may be best to begin a study more or less from scratch, by listening, mimicking, and transcribing words and phrases in order to become familiar with the sounds of the language. There are often significant differences in dialect within an area, even between groups that claim to speak the same language, and changes can occur over time. Any researcher should take pains to record data accurately and objectively rather than relying outright on the work of previous investigators. Comparisons can be made and points of difference investigated after an initial analysis is done that satisfactorily accounts for the primary data on which the study is to be based.

Linguistic fieldworkers use three basic techniques to collect data:

1. *Direct eliciting.* This is initiated by the linguist, who simply asks questions in order to obtain responses from the consultant. For example: What is the word for *God?* For *beauty?* How do you say, *"The sky is blue?"* or *"The flowers smell sweet?"* How do you count from *one* to *ten?* Some direct eliciting is probably unavoidable. For several reasons, however, this may be the least desirable method for anthropological purposes. First, the very questions chosen will impose unintentional cultural biases; any of those listed above might have this effect, calling as they do for translation of abstractions (*God* and *beauty*), color categories, sensory impressions, and numerical concepts—any of these might have no one-to-one equivalent in the target language.

   Further, with direct eliciting comes a danger of unintentionally influencing the grammatical form as well as the content of the responses. A consultant may attempt to give literal translations of words or phrases, even if a different construction would be more idiomatic or culturally appropriate. Word order could easily be influenced by the model presented by the linguist's question, or syntactic rules might unintentionally be simplified for easier comprehension. C. F. Ferguson has dubbed this sort of distortion "foreigner talk"— speech that is simplified or otherwise adapted to the patterns of the interrogator's language.

   But the most fundamental drawback of direct elicitation is the fact that it can reveal only what the interrogator can conceive of, or is able to ask for—and here the linguist may be limited by the resources of his or her own language. Unique or unusual semantic or structural features of the target language, potentially of great theoretical interest, could be misunderstood or overlooked if one were to rely on direct elicitation alone. For example, eliciting of verbal paradigms could lead to confusion if an English-speaking researcher were to routinely ask for translation equivalents of English constructions. The consultant might respond by attempting to be explicit about time (which could be optional in the target language, rather than obligatory as it is in English) or by trying to adjust a two-tense system (e.g., past and non-past) to the past, present, and future categories called for in English and other European languages. The gender and number categories of English verbs could also cause problems in translation—Lokono, for example, has only two gender categories (masculine and non-masculine), and grammatical gender categories of any kind are completely foreign to many languages. An effort to obtain basic grammatical information of this sort by direct elicitation can be quite daunting, especially when the researcher has little initial fluency in the target language. (See the discussion of language and world view in chapter 6.)

2. *Participant observation.* The linguistic fieldworker can emulate the cultural anthropologist in becoming a participant observer, simply monitoring and taking notes on verbal behavior. This is an important and very useful strategy when the fieldworker has gained a degree of fluency in the target language but is a very slow approach for obtaining the basic data for a descriptive grammar. Participant observation may be the best—perhaps the only—way to obtain truly natural speech data for a study of verbal dueling, joking, and other conversational gambits. At the same time, speech events of this sort can be videotaped for detailed analysis, also utilizing the assistance and commentary of a native consultant

3. *Collection of texts.* American anthropology has traditionally emphasized the collecting of texts as a source of information on cultural traditions and as the raw material for language study. Typically, a consultant is asked to recount historic events, describe cultural practices, or narrate events of daily life, recall childhood experiences, and so on. The text is recorded without interruption; the objective is to avoid any sort of direction or limitation that might influence or restrict either content or style. Subsequently, the text can be translated and analyzed, phrase by phrase or word by word, with or without the assistance of a native speaker (the narrator or another) as translator or commentator.

A combination of recording texts and direct eliciting, with the linguist's questions aimed at complementing and clarifying the content of the texts, constitutes the most common fieldwork practice of linguistic anthropologists. This offers a way into the grammatical structure of the target language while avoiding or minimizing the potential distorting effects of direct eliciting alone. And, as a bonus, the anthropologist may gain valuable cultural as well as linguistic data.

STUDYING A NATIVE AMERICAN LANGUAGE "IN THE FIELD"

In 1951, after completing a master's thesis based on library research, I was eager for my first fieldwork experience. Following the example of my professional role models—Franz Boas, Edward Sapir, and my own mentor Carl Voegelin—I intended to study a Native American language. The opportunity came when I accompanied my anthropologist husband to Guyana, in South America. When we settled in Danielstown, the coastal village where he was to survey socioeconomic conditions, I hoped that I could study the Arawakan language that was indigenous to the region.

Prior to embarking on the Dutch freighter that carried us from New York to Georgetown, the Guyanese capital, I had poured over language maps of South America and searched for information on Guyanese Arawak, or Lokono. The only substantial work that I was able to locate, by a Dutch scholar, was based on 19th-century religious texts and Bible translations; it was full of verbs like *baptize-da*, *praise-da*, and *circumcize-da*, and was more confusing than helpful. Of more interest to me were articles by Douglas Taylor, an amateur linguist who would later build a reputation as the leading authority on West Indian languages. Taylor had recently begun studying so-called Island Carib, a nearly extinct language of the Lesser Antilles that was said to be related to Lokono. I hoped eventually to explore the nature of the relationship; copies of Taylor's publications went with me to serve as a rough guide and basis for comparisons as I began to collect data.

In the Guyana of the 1950s, Native Americans seemed virtually invisible. The great majority of the population, concentrated in the coastal zone, was (and is) of African and East Indian descent. Both governmental officials and the Church of England priest who oversaw the small native reserves in the Essequibo district assured me that the Lokono language was defunct—that "Nobody speaks it anymore." I doubted that this was truly the case and was eventually relieved to find that it was not. In fact, I was fortunate indeed to find that a native speaker of Lokono was living in Danielstown. Edna Fredericks knew the language well, and she welcomed the opportunity to help me learn. She became my first and most important Arawakan consultant.

Over the next several months, I would spend most mornings on the front porch of the small cottage that Edna shared with her fisherman husband Joseph, and two children. When I arrived for my first session, 3-year-old Joanie was much in evidence. My interest in the little girl eased our initial encounter. When Edna commented that "Joanie has a new dress," I immediately asked her to repeat the remark in her own language. Opening my notebook, I tried to write the sentence phonetically and then read it back to her; she corrected my errors, I made changes in my transcription, and our working relationship was begun.

Unfortunately, I no longer have my notes on that first morning's work. However, I recall that I continued by using the initial sentence—*Joanie has a new dress*—as an eliciting frame. That is, I would change one or two words at a time in the English sentence, asking each time for translation into Lokono, in order to elicit and identify the morphemes and, at the same time, to introduce additional vocabulary—thus, "Joanie has a blue dress," "The girl has a blue dress," "She has a blue dress," "She has a yellow dress," "I have a new dress," "Do you have a new dress?" and so forth. When this palled, I elicited vocabulary—mostly body parts and other nouns. When I left that day, I thought rather smugly that I had learned quite a bit about sentence patterns, had filled several pages with word lists, and had what I considered to be a complete list of Lokono color terms (something that I found of particular interest). As far as color terms are concerned, I would later realize that things are seldom as simple as they seem, and I would drastically revise the list. (See chapter 6.) Before long I would come to realize the shortcomings of my initial eliciting technique. However, at the time, I felt that I was off to a good beginning.

As the Lokono sessions continued, a daily routine gradually took form. After a few days, my eliciting had become repetitive and my consultant seemed bored. It began to dawn on me that I should obtain material that did not depend, in form or content, on leading questions of the sort that I had asked on the first day. Further, even though my consultant and I both could communicate in English, our dialects were not always mutually intelligible. I thought that I understood Edna's Creole English well, but I sensed that she was sometimes confused by my North American dialect, especially when pressed to make fine distinctions in meaning. My best recourse seemed to be to begin each session with a short text of some sort—I would ask her to tell me, in Lokono, about her daily routine, her family, or events in her childhood on the Pomeroon River, far to the north of Danielstown.

Eventually, Edna began to recall folktales and to enlarge on Arawakan cultural traditions, and the texts became longer. My first task of the morning was to transcribe these texts phonemically, as rapidly and accurately as I could, noting the breaks that seemed to separate phrases in her narration.[15] Then I would read it back, phrase by phrase, for her corrections (of omitted syllables, misheard sounds, misplaced accents) and for a rough translation. The text was not yet completely segmented into separate words—that would come later, in the process of close translation and morphemic analysis.

The third time through a text was the longest and most tedious. One by one, each segment (word or phrase) became the basis for eliciting, with questions aimed at defining word boundaries and isolating and identifying the component morphemes. In my notebooks (small exercise books sold in the local shop as school supplies) I routinely transcribed the text on the left-hand page, leaving space between lines for translation, and reserving the facing page for notes taken and comments made during eliciting. The following brief text is an example drawn from one of our early sessions:

Transcription: 1 depéroŋsa (a)buáka / 2 makotáičita / 3 čičikidónua maosúañi /
E.F. translation: 1 My puppy sick. / 2 He don't want to eat. / 3 He does fall often. /
4 dáičiŋ tokáritua / 5 baríka akotáhu dàsikiŋ tómuŋ /
4 I think he hurt himself / 5 Withal I does give food to him /
6 abúaŋdomaŋ makotáičita / 7 mabúaŋbenàŋ / 8 úsa tókoton tóra /
6 because he sick, he don't want to eat / 7 When he ain't sick / 8 he does eat good /
9 hamáiroŋ dašikíŋtoŋ tekénoma /
9 Anything I give him, he does eat /

And here are a few comments, which touch on some but by no means all of the points of interest in the text:

1. First, the transcription is not completely phonemic. Although some phonetic details I might have indicated earlier have been omitted, there are also changes that I made later that are not reflected here. The [č], for example, which occurs only before the vowel [i], was later reinterpreted as a variant of the phoneme /t/; thus

čičikidónua would be rewritten as /titikidónua/. Similarly, the [ñ] would be

[15]Ideally, I would have recorded these texts on tape. The lightweight battery-powered tape recorders now in use were not yet available. I did take with me a large cumbersome wire recorder; however, the only available electricity—from a gasoline-powered generator at the village rum shop—was so erratic that the quality of the recording was very poor.

rewritten as /n/ and the [š] as /s/—these allophones also occur only before /i/. The vowel segments [o] and [u] were often hard to distinguish; thus [usa] might have been (and in other texts was) written as [osa]. When there are any doubts of this kind, the best policy is to write down exactly what one hears; this phonetic detail may be useful later, when a decision about the phonemic status of the vowels can be made.

2. The first notes that I made after transcribing the text concerned the initial segment. I do not remember exactly what questions I asked, but I wrote down the following in my notebook:

| péro | *dog* | pérosa | *puppy* |
| depéroŋ | *my dog* | depéroŋsa | *my puppy* |

Comparison of "dog" and "my dog" makes it possible to isolate a prefix /de-/ and suffix /-n/. I was already familiar with the prefix, which—with variable vowel—indicates first-person singular possessor with nouns, and actor with verbs (compare with "I think" and "I give" in the text). I would later learn that the suffix /-ŋ-/ is the most common of several variants of a morpheme that I would call a "subordinator" or "possession-marker"; it must follow some, but not all, nouns when the person-marker prefixes are used—thus, /dakábo/ *my hand*, but /depéroŋ/ *my dog*.

I suspected that /-sa/ might be the same morpheme that I had elsewhere recorded as /osa, -sa/ *child*, as in /dása/ *my child*. At this point, I tentatively interpreted /perosa/ *puppy* as, literally, "dog's child (or offspring)." This seemed to be confirmed later, when I ran across a parallel in /kárinasa/ *egg* (from /karina/ *chicken, fowl*).

3. Many of my facing-page notes on this short text are concerned with segments that can be matched, in the translation, with references to food and eating: /makotáičita/ *he don't want to eat;* /akotáhu dàšikiṇ/ *I does give food;* and /úsa tókoton/ *he (it) does eat good.* Attempting to clarify these, I asked questions to elicit the forms: /dákota/ *I eat,* /dakotáičika/ *I want to eat,* and /makotáičida/ *I don't want to eat.* Leafing back through earlier texts, I also find /bókota/ *you eat,* /uákota/ *we eat,* /uakotófa/ *we will eat,* and /wajíli makotáičika/ *the man don't want to eat.* By comparing these and other constructions, I was beginning to recognize a number of prefixes and suffixes and to have some sense of the workings of Lokono grammar. (For a translation and analysis of a longer Lokono text, see Hickerson, 1954.)

LANGUAGE AND WRITING

Despite its prominence in our lives today, writing has not always been a component of our culture. As we have seen, speech is everywhere, and at all times a part of human life; our specialized nervous systems and vocal tracts testify to our evolution as speaking animals. But writing is a fairly recent achievement; unlike language, it *is* an invention. Writing is an artifact of culture that meets the needs of human life in certain times and places but is absent in others. Anthropologists distinguish between *preliterate* and *literate* societies and usually take literacy as a marker of civilization. However, some have suggested that, with our reliance on electronic communications media, we may be on the verge of a *postliterate* stage of history.

In other words, there are social conditions under which writing was invented and has been of use; and it is conceivable that there are conditions under which it will fall out of use (though there may still be a few literate specialists who can decipher the ancient records of our civilization). In origin, writing is an elaboration or specialization of a much more ancient and universal type of human activity: graphic representation, including drawing and the use of marks for counts and tallies. People in other times and places have used conventionalized drawings, or *pictographs,* as signs of identity, sacred symbols, records of historical events, and the like. In a study of Paleolithic artifacts, A. Marshak demonstrated that evidence of such records—for example, pictographs and tallies that appear to record the passing of seasons, phases of the moon, and number of days—can be found far back in prehistory. (See Figure 3.2.) Graphic representations of events and concepts may be almost as ancient as *Homo sapiens* (Marshack, 1972).

We still make use of signs that resemble pictographs, to give

  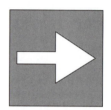

warnings, restrictions, or directions

As you can see, such signs may be simplified and highly conventionalized, but they encapsulate complex messages. Pictographs may resemble writing, but there are basic differences: In writing, there is a one-to-one relationship between structural units of language (words, syllables, or individual phonemes) and the drawn or printed symbols. There is a linear order in writing that follows that of speech. And while only selected information can be encoded in pictographs, a real writing system can transmit anything that can be put into words.

Still, writing evidently had its origin in conventionalized drawings. Both the "letters" of Western alphabets and the "characters" used in Chinese and Japanese writing can be traced back to pictorial origins: The letter *A,* for example, is descended from ⅄ *aleph* ("ox"), apparently a stylized drawing of the head of an ox. Similarly, the Chinese character 日 *ri* ("sun," "day"), was earlier written ⊖, which is interpreted as a drawing of the sun. In both cases, early writing comes closer to pictorial forms than do later systems, in which the symbols have become more conventionalized and abstract (Gelb, 1963).

From its beginnings in pictorial representation, writing has followed two diverging lines of development. Modern writing systems can usually be placed in one or another of these traditions, although the two have sometimes merged and have influenced each other in a variety of ways. Writing systems of the first type are *logographic* (or *ideographic*); essentially, they employ symbols that stand for lexemes—whole words or units of meaning. In the evolution of such a system, pictures of things (the sun, for example)

FIGURE 3.2

Two sides of an engraved bone "knife," Magdalenian culture, Upper Paleolithic. The designs are animal heads, serpentine lines, branches, and other vegetation forms; according to the archaeologist, A. Marshack, the two faces represent images of the spring and autumn. Copyright 1972 by Alexander Marshack.

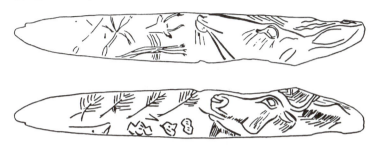

may be generalized or extended to stand for related and associated things or qualities (such as day, light, or brilliance). The Chinese writing system (see Figure 3.3) is perhaps the best modern example of a system that is basically logographic (though it also incorporates elements of other types).

In a logographic writing system, the individual signs are whole units that have meaning; they cannot ordinarily be analyzed into smaller parts, and there is no direct connection between these units and the sounds of speech. Such a writing system is difficult to learn because there may be approximately one written symbol for each item in the vocabulary; an erudite knowledge of classical Chinese literature requires control of several thousand characters—there are said to be around 50,000 in all. This level of literacy is rare and requires years of study. However, logographic writing has its advantages; the most positive feature is perhaps the fact that, since the characters stand for meanings and not for sounds, the same writing system can be used by speakers of different dialects or even different languages. What is required is cultural similarity and a shared system of meanings. The main "dialects" of Chinese (Mandarin, Cantonese, Suchow, Hakka, and others) are quite different from one another and not mutually intelligible when spoken; however, the use of a common system of writing facilitates communication and has, over the centuries, helped to maintain the unity of the Chinese cultural sphere.

The second line of development appeared first in western Asia and has given rise to the majority of the world's writing systems. In this case, pictorial signs came to stand for phonetic units rather than for units of meaning. In principle, signs of this sort resemble the kind of word puzzle called a *rebus*.

The two kinds of signs—logographic word signs along with those of the rebus type—are found together in early writing systems of the eastern

FIGURE 3.3 MODERN CHINESE WRITING.

Reprinted from *A Study of Writing* by I. Gelb by permission of The University of Chicago Press. Copyright 1963 by The University of Chicago Press.

疆 畯 口 其 用 不 田 令 吉 惟
克 臣 口 用 獻 顯 人 尹 庚 十
其 天 口 朝 于 魯 克 氏 寅 又
萬 子 口 夕 師 休 拜 友 王 八
年 克 降 享 尹 揚 稽 史 才 年
子 其 克 于 朋 用 首 趩 周 十
子 日 多 皇 友 作 取 典 康 又
孫 易 福 且 昏 旅 對 善 穆 二
孫 休 眉 皇 遘 盨 天 夫 宮 月
永 無 壽 且 克 惟 子 克 王 初
寶 永 考
用 令 其

Mediterranean area such as Egyptian and Hittite (see Figure 3.4). However, the rebus idea eventually won out and, in turn, was the basis for a more economical and flexible type of writing, the *syllabary*. By around 5,000 years ago, there were a number of written languages of the syllabary type in use in western Asia; the most famous of these is the West Semitic syllabary, the ancestor of modern Hebrew and Arabic scripts.

A perfect syllabary would contain a written symbol for each different syllable used in a language. The number of these varies from language to language, but most would have between 50 and 100—a larger number of signs than in our alphabet, but much fewer than is required in a logographic system, where signs represent individual words or concepts. The Hittite syllabary, used in Syria between 1500 and 700 B.C., exemplifies this principle.

In the course of time, some syllabaries were simplified by reducing the use of the original signs to only the most common syllables; additional consonants or vowels were then indicated by diacritic marks. This anticipated the idea of the alphabet, since some individual phonemes are separated out of the larger unit, the syllable. Many of the ancient writings of the Near East,

FIGURE 3.4 THE HITTITE HIEROGLYPHIC SYLLABARY.

Reprinted from *A Study of Writing* by I. Gelb by permission of The University of Chicago Press. Copyright 1963 by The University of Chicago Press.

	a	e	i	u
Vowels	a 'a			
Nasals				
ḫ				
i̯	ia iā			
k/g				
l				
m				
n				nu nú
p/b				
r				
s				
ś				
t/d				
w				
z (=ts)				
Syllables of unknown value				

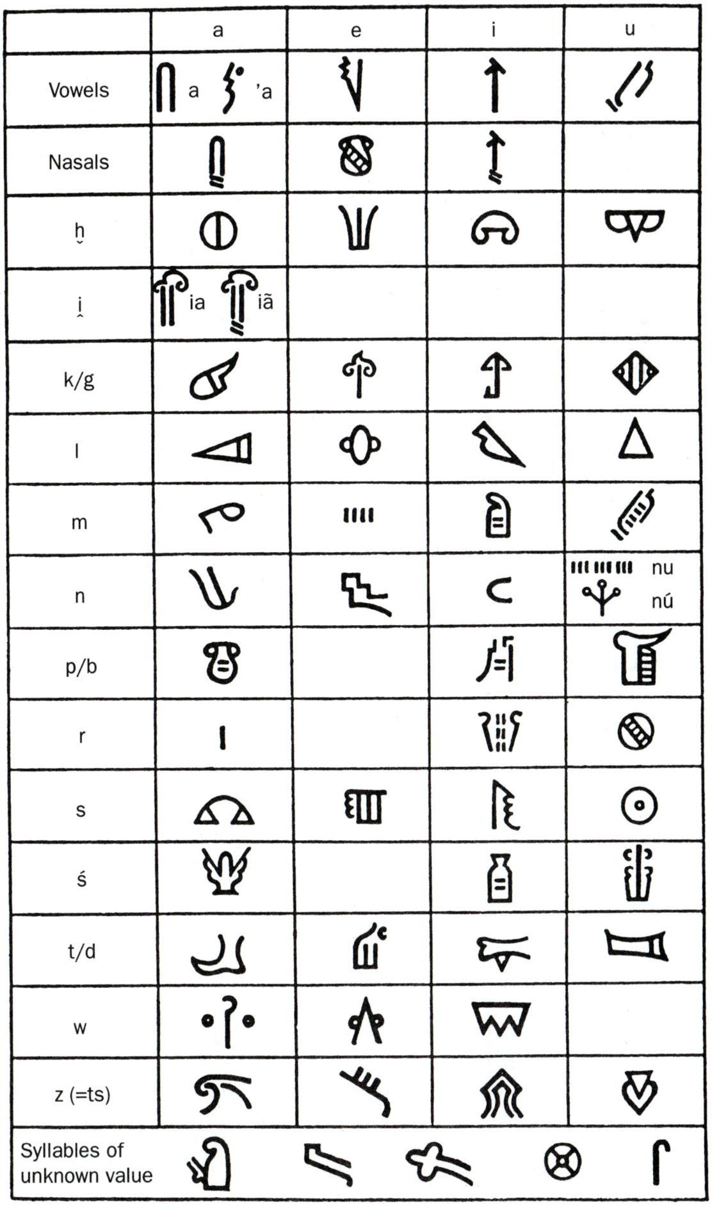

which survive in the form of cuneiform inscriptions on baked clay tablets, represent this type of syllabary. In the Old Persian writing system, for example (600–400 B.C.), there are signs that stand for consonants followed by *a* (the most common vowel) or for the consonant alone, and there are separate signs for three vowels (*a, i, u*); the total number of signs is 36 (see Figure 3.5).

FIGURE 3.5   OLD PERSIAN SYLLABARY.

Reprinted from *A Study of Writing* by I. Gelb by permission of The University of Chicago Press. Copyright 1963 by The University of Chicago Press.

	a	i	u		a	i	u
Vowels	𒀀	𒐊	𒐋				
b	𒁀	𒁀+i	𒁀+u	l	𒇷	𒇷+i	𒇷+u
č	𒋡	𒋡+i	𒋡+u	m	𒈠	𒈪	𒈬
ç	𒊬	𒊬+i	𒊬+u	n	𒈾	𒈾+i	𒉡
d	𒁕	𒁲	𒁺	p	𒉺	𒉺+i	𒉺+u
f	𒉘	𒉘+i	𒉘+u	r	𒊏	𒊏+i	𒊒
g	𒂵	𒄀+i	𒄘	s	𒊓	𒊓+i	𒋢
h	𒄭	𒄭+i	𒄭+u	š	𒊭	𒊭+i	�+u
ḫ	𒄩	𒄩+i	𒄩+u	t	𒋫	𒋫+i	𒌅
y	𒅀	𒅀+i	𒅀+u	ṯ	𒊐	𒊐+i	𒊐+u
j	𒍣	𒍣+i	𒍣+u	w	𒉿	𒌑	𒉿+u
k	𒆠	𒆠+i	𒆬	z	𒍝	𒍝+i	𒍝+u

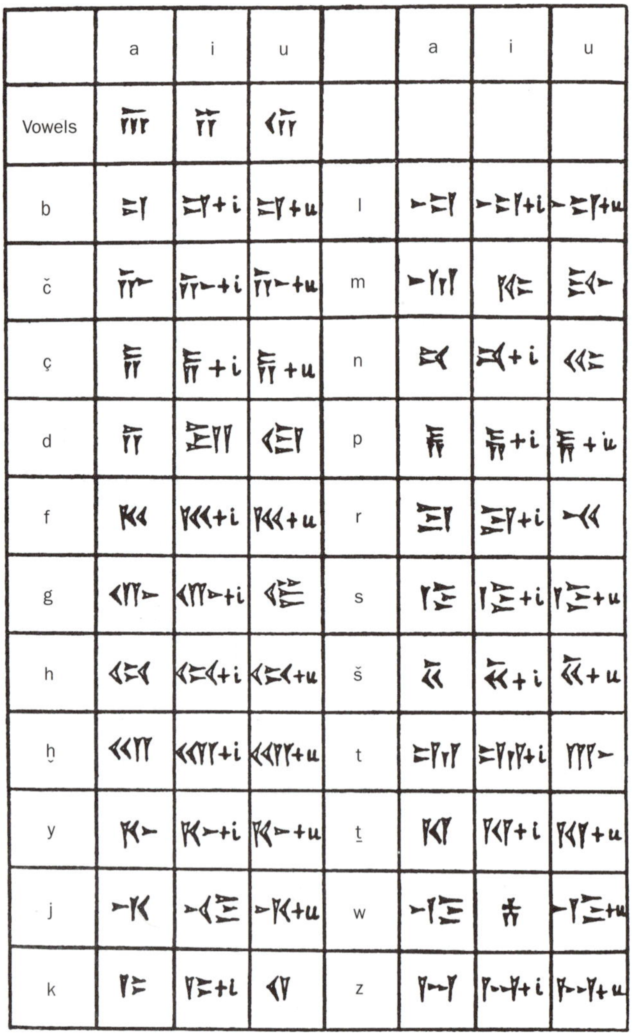

The West Semitic syllabary used by the Phoenecians was still more condensed than the Persian in that most of the signs stood for consonants *with or without* a following vowel. In the Semitic languages, vowels are dropped or added, depending on the grammatical or syntactic function of the word in which they occur, and can often be predicted on the basis of context. Therefore, it was a convenient simplified form of writing to omit them, at least in recording business transactions (the main context in which Phoenecian writing is known). The signs were as few in number as in an alphabet, and they became the basis for alphabetic writing when borrowed and adapted to the Greek language (as seen in Figure 3.6). This happened some time before the eighth century B.C. (Gelb, 1963).

FIGURE 3.6 COMPARATIVE CHART OF GREEK AND WEST SEMITIC WRITINGS.

Reprinted from *A Study of Writing* by I. Gelb by permission of The University of Chicago Press. Copyright 1963 by The University of Chicago Press.

| | West Semitic | | | | | | | | | | | Greek | | Latin |
AHĪRĀM	RUWEISEH	AZARBAʿAL	YEHIMILK	ABĪBAʿAL	ELĪBAʿAL	ŠAPATBAʿAL	MEŠAʿ	ZINCIRLI	CYPRUS	SARDINIA	Old	Late	
K	K	✳	K,K	✳	✳	✳	✳	✳	✳	✳	⊅, A	A	A
⅁	⅁	⅁	⅁,⅁	⅁	⅁	⅁	⅁	⅁	⅁	⅁	⋺, ⅍	B	B
⌐		⌐		⌐	⌐	⌐	⌐	⌐	⌐	⌐	⌐, ⌐	Γ	C (& G replacing Z)
◁	◁		△		△	△	◁	△,△	△	△	△	Δ	D
⅊			⅊				⅂	⅂	⅊	⅊	⅊, ⅊	E	E
Y		Y	Ψ	Y	Y	Y	५	५	५		⅌, Y, V	(Y at end)	F (& U,V,Y at end)
I	I	I		I	I	ᴐ	ᴐ	I			I	Z	(Z at end)
⊠	⊟	⊟	H,⊟	⊟	⊟	⊠	⊠		⊟		⊟	H	H
⊕				⊖	⊖	⊕		⊖				⊗, ⊕	⊖	
⅂	⅀	⅀	⅀		⅀	⅂	⅂	⅂	⅂	⅂	⟨, ⟩	I	I
Ψ	Ψ	Ψ	Ψ	Ψ	Ψ	Ψ	⅄	⅄	⅄	⅄	⅂, ⅄	K	K
⌊		⌊	⌊	⌊	⌊	⌊	⌊	⌊	⌊	⌊	⌊, ∨	Λ	L
⅃		⅃	⅃	⅃	⅃	⅄	⅄	⅃	⅃	⅃	ᵐ	M	M
⅄	⅄	⅄	⅄			⅄	⅄	⅄	⅄	⅄	⅄	N	N
⊥		⊥					⊥	⊥			⊥	⊥	(X at end)
o	o	o	o	o	o	o	o	o	o	o	o	O	O
⌐	7:ᵊ	⌐		⌐	⌐	⌐	⌐	⌐	⌐	⌐	⌐, ⌐	Π	P
	ⱨ		λ	ⱨ			ⱶ	ⱶ		ⱨ		⅄, ⅃	(M)	
		φ			⅄	φ	φ	φ	φ	φ, φ	(φ)	Q
⅂			⅂	⅂	⅂	⅂	⅂	⅂	⅂	⅂	⅂, P	P	R
w		w	w		w	w	w	w	w	w	⟨, ⟩, ⟨	Σ	S
+,X		+	X		⊬	+	X	⊬	⊬	X	T	T	T
												Y,φ,X,Ψ,Ω	U,V,X,Y,Z

A PRECURSOR
OF WRITING IN
WESTERN ASIA

One of the earliest documented writing systems is the Sumerian. Clay tablets unearthed at the site of the ancient city-state of Uruk, dated at roughly 4000 B.C., are inscribed with signs, some of them clearly pictographic and others seemingly abstract; like the Egyptian writing of a millennium later, this system evidently followed the rebus principle. Since the excavations at Uruk in the 1920s, other Sumerian sites have been explored, and numerous examples of written texts have been studied—but only partly deciphered. In 1978, archaeologist Denise Schmandt-Besserat published the results of an investigation that has uncovered the source of many of the enigmatic written symbols, tracing them to the very beginnings of the Neolithic revolution in western Asia.

Schmandt-Besserat's research began in 1969 as a broad study of the uses of clay in the Near East. As she surveyed museum collections of clay artifacts, the earliest of which dated to around 9000 B.C., she began to notice—along with bricks, beads, and figurines—an "unforeseen category of objects: small clay artifacts of various forms." Roughly, this category included spheres, disks, cones, crescents, and other shapes, most of them between 1 and 2 centimeters in their largest dimension. Most had been modeled from clay by pinching and rolling, some bore added marks made by incising, and all had been hardened by fire. Once on the track of these types of objects, Schmandt-Besserat found examples in virtually all available collections of artifacts from western Asia. Many reports neglected to mention them, and those that did described them in a confusing variety of ways, from "objects of uncertain purpose" to "children's playthings," "game-pieces," "phallic symbols," and "amulets."

Despite these varied and imaginative descriptions, Schmandt-Besserat was impressed by the fact that there was great continuity in form and variety of the objects, from the earliest Neolithic sites up to the Bronze Age city of Susa, at around 3000 B.C. and Nuzi, in Iraq, at around 1500 B.C. It was at these two sites that archaeologists found similar objects in a context that suggested their use as tokens in an accounting system. Cuneiform texts in the palace archives at Nuzi referred to tokens being "deposited," "removed," and "transferred" when economic transactions were made, cattle were slaughtered, or sheep were moved from one pasture to another. Hollow egg-shaped tablets, or *bullae*, were found that contained tokens. On the surface of one of these was an inscribed list of 48 animals; and inside, there were 48 clay tokens. There were no intact bullae at Susa, but it appeared that a similar accounting system was used there.

Schmandt-Besserat believes that the use of tokens began, early in the Neolithic period, when farmers found a need to keep track of allocations of crops and animals—for current needs, storage, barter, and the like. Around 5000 B.C., as populations grew and political systems became more centralized, a new need for official record keeping arose—the collection of taxes in kind. The basic inventory of token types continues, but more subtypes appear, with the addition of painted lines and dots. A large percentage of the tokens were perforated; those representing a single transaction may have been strung to keep them together.

By the time of the Bronze Age, beginning around 3500 B.C., the growth of cities, development of craft specializations, and expanded trade networks brought a proliferation in types and subtypes of tokens. During this period the practice of enclosing tokens in clay envelopes began. At Susa, many bullae bear the impress of two personal seals—likely the parties to a transcrion; the tokens, representing the kind and quantity of merchandise, were sealed inside. Then, to make it possible to determine the contents, images of the tokens were preserved on the surface—either by pressing the tokens themselves into the clay or, more often, by inscribing it with a stylus. Thus, one could read the contents without destroying the clay envelope in the process.

Almost inevitably, it would seem, the hollow bulla with enclosed tokens was superceded by the use of a solid clay tablet, with a two-dimensional portrayal of the tokens—and, thus, a written record. At the same time, the system was expanded to accommodate functions other than the recording of economic transactions. Schmandt-Besserat demonstrates the continuity from tokens to writing, showing that the shapes of individual tokens can be matched with many of the characters in the earliest Sumerian inscriptions as shown in Figure 3.7 below (Schmandt-Besserat, 1978).

FIGURE 3.7

Eight of the 52 tokens that D. Schmandt-Besserat was able to identify, matched with incised characters in early Sumerian inscriptions.

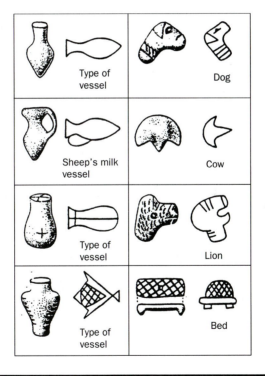

The Greek writing system is the first considered to be truly alphabetic; that is, there is a separate written symbol for each vowel and each consonant, a total of 22. There were further modifications when the alphabet was later adapted to Latin and other western Mediterranean tongues. Alphabetic writing spread from Greece and Rome to northern and western Europe, through trade, conquest, and administration. Latin was the official language of the Roman Empire, and the Latin alphabet was adapted to the writing of other languages as well. Later, under the aegis of the Christian religion, use of the Latin alphabet was carried far and wide by missionary priests of the Roman Catholic Church, while the Greek alphabet was adopted in the parts of eastern and central Europe (Russia and the Balkans) where the Greek Orthodox denomination prevailed.

In the Far East, the logographic Chinese system has been modified in a number of ways over the years; for example, there are "phonetic" signs that may be used in combination with logographic signs in order to distinguish among the several possible meanings that these might have. Syllabic and alphabetic orthographies have also been devised, but the system in general use is still basically logographic. Japanese writing was derived from the Chinese by adapting Chinese characters to stand for phonetic segments; thus, the originally logographic system was converted into a syllabary.

Of the three main types of writing—logographic, syllabic, and alphabetic— the syllabary appears to be the most "natural," judging by the fact that this type has been invented again and again. Full-fledged logographic systems are few, and it would appear that the principle of the alphabet has arisen only once.

New writing systems of the syllabary type, such as the Cherokee "alphabet" invented by Sequoyah in 1821, are built on the same general plan as that of the ancient Hittites. The Cherokee syllabary (shown in Figure 3.8) has 85 symbols, many of them adapted from the shapes of the English alphabet. The symbols correspond almost perfectly to the syllable structure of the Cherokee language. When introduced to the Cherokee people, the syllabary was quickly accepted, since only a few hours of instruction were required for a speaker of the language to learn to use it. This writing system was widely used in official documents and a newspaper, *The Cherokee Phoenix,* before the Cherokees' printing press was destroyed during the American Civil War. Since that time, it has been used primarily in private correspondence and in religious services. Recently, there have been new efforts to promote the use of the Cherokee language, and publications have increased, especially for educational purposes.

Another ingenious syllabary was invented in 1840 by J. Evans, a missionary, for the writing of Cree, Ojibwa, and neighboring Algonkian dialects. The Evans syllabary (see Figure 3.9) spread widely in Canada and was modified for use by speakers of Yupik. It is still used in personal correspondence and other private functions, though the Canadian government has officially adopted a Latin orthography for native languages (Walker, 1975).

In contrast to the syllabary, the principle of the alphabet seems to have been invented only once. All existing alphabetic systems are, directly or indirectly, derived from those of the Greeks and Romans, and thus have much in common; they have evolved and diversified within, roughly, the past 2,000 years. A curious alphabet that at first glance would appear to be an exception is the Celtic *Ogham* script, a linear code that is known from inscriptions dated to the second to fourth centuries A.D. Tradition links this script with the Druidic priesthood. However, Ogham (or Ogam) was very likely

FIGURE 3.8 CHEROKEE SYLLABARY.

Cherokee Alphabet					
D a	**R** e	**T** i	δ o	O u	i v
S ga O ka	**F** ge	**y** gi	**A** go	**J** gu	**E** gv
ℓ ha	**P** he	**Ə** hi	**F** ho	**Γ** hu	**Ꮁ** hv
W la	**ℓ** le	**P** li	**G** lo	**M** lu	**Ꮕ** lv
ℓ ma	**α** me	**H** mi	**Ꮆ** mo	**Y** mu	
Θ na **t** hna **G** nah	**Λ** ne	**h** ni	**Z** no	**ꓝ** nu	**O** nv
Ꮖ qua	**ω** que	**P** qui	**V** quo	**ω** quu	**ε** quv
U sa **ω** s	**4** se	**b** si	**Ꮅ** so	**ꝸ** su	**R** sv
L da **W** ta	**S** de **Ꮦ** te	**J** di **Ꮧ** ti	**V** do	**S** du	**ℓ** dv
δδ dla **L** tla	**L** tle	**C** tli	**Ꮸ** tlo	**Ꮽ** tlu	**P** tlv
G tsa	**V** tse	**Ir** tsi	**K** tso	**J** tsu	**C** tsv
G wa	**ℓℓ** we	**Θ** wi	**ℓℓ** wo	**ꝸ** wu	**6** wv
ℓℓ ya	**β** ye	**ꝸ** yi	**ꝸ** yo	**Gꝸ** yu	**B** yv

inspired by Mediterranean writing systems, by way of trade contacts that reached Britain at least a century before the Roman colony was established there in the first century B.C. More or less contemporaneous with this Celtic alphabet, the earliest Germanic runic inscriptions come from the third century A.D. This was ancestral to several later alphabets, including the Anglo-Saxon, Gothis (East Germanic), and Scandinavian.

It should be obvious that no writing system or set of symbols has a necessary association with any particular language or language family. Instead, the distinctive characteristics of individual orthographies have developed as they have been inherited, borrowed, adapted, and modified. New letters are invented while others fall out of use, signs are converted from representing syllables to single phonemes, diacritic marks are added or dropped, the phonetic value of a sign changes over time, and so forth.

Typically, writing has begun in the context of politically complex centralized societies; it may have served commercial interests first, but it has also been intimately associated with the hierarchies of both church and state. Writing has diffused from one geographical area to another with the spread of empires and world religions. Although a need for literacy may be stimu-

FIGURE 3.9

The James Evans syllabary as adapted to Moose Cree by John Horden in the 1850s, reproduced from Willard Walker, "Notes on Native Writing Systems and the Design of Native Literacy Programs," *Anthropological Linguistics* (May 1969), which was based on a chart of the Cree syllabary in C. Douglas Ellis, *Spoken Cree West Coast of James Bay, Part 1*, The Department of Missions (M.S.C.C.), The Anglican Church of Canada, Church House, 600 Jarvis St., Toronto 5.

	e	i	o	a	Nonprevocalic
Vowel only	▽	△	▷	◁	
p	V	∧	>	<	‹
t	U	∩	)	(	⸲
c	⌐	⌐	⌡	∪	⸲
k	q	ρ	d	b	❭
m	⌐	⌐	⌐	L	L
n	⬝	σ	⸱	ɑ	⸱
l	⌐	⌐	⌐	⌐	⌐
s	⌐	⌐	⌐	⌐	⌐
š	⌐	ʃ	⌐	⌐	⌐
y	⌐	⌐	⌐	⌐	•
r	⌐	⌐	?	⌐	⌐

lated by technological changes and economic growth, writing itself has been more directly linked with religion. In the present century, many Catholic and Protestant missionaries have devoted themselves to the study of native languages in Africa, Oceania, and the Americas. Their first objective is the development of alphabets for translating the Bible and other religious literature into native languages; linguistic study is thus an essential part of the religious mission. The Summer Institute of Linguistics is one major organi-

OGAM IMAGINED

In his Sister Fidelma novels, Peter Tremayne (the literary pseudonym of Peter Beresford Ellis, a prominent Celtic scholar) chronicles the travels of a seventh-century Irish nun, Fidelma of Kildare, who is a *dalaigh*, qualified to gather evidence and appear before courts of law. In *The Spider's Web*, Fidelma is dispatched to a remote village where a young man, both blind and deaf, has been wrongly imprisoned for the crime of patricide. Fidelma is able to question the youth when she learns that he was raised and cared for by a "wise woman" and healer, who taught him the ancient Ogam "finger code."

Ogam was the earliest form of writing among the people of the five kingdoms and consisted of short lines drawn to, or crossing, a base line, representing the twenty characters of the alphabet. The ancients claimed that the god Ogam, patron of literacy and learning, had come to the southwest of Muman, the place of all primal beginnings and instructed the wise ones in the use of the characters, so that they could journey through the land and even across the seas to show people how they might write. The alphabet was often inscribed on wands of hazel or aspen and many grave markers of stone were inscribed in Ogam. It had fallen into disuse with the introduction of the new Latin learning and alphabet into the kingdoms. Fidelma had studied the old system and alphabet as part of her education, for many texts were still to be found written in the archaic form.

She could suddenly see how such a simple form of alphabet might be used as a means of communication by manual gestures. Gadra was watching her changing expression. . . . "Do you want to test it for yourself?" he asked.

Fidelma nodded eagerly.

"Take his palm. Hold it upright and use the line of the second digit as the base line down to the heel of the hand. Introduce yourself by writing your name in the Ogam characters."

Fidelma cautiously took the youth's hand.

Three strokes to the right of the base line for F; five dots on the base line with the tip of her finger for I; two strokes to the left of the base line for D; four dots on the line for E; two strokes to the left for L; a diagonal stroke across it for M and a single dot for A. She made the movements fairly slowly and cautiously. Then she paused, awaiting a response.

The young man, an eager smile on his lips, took the left hand, which she offered him, and held it palm up. Then came his finger against the palm. A diagonal for M; two dots on the line for O; a slight pause before four dots for E and then four strokes to the right for N. Moen.

(Tremayne, 1997)

FIGURE 3.10 THE OGAM SCRIPT.

B L F S N　H D T C Q　M G NG Z R　A O U E I

zation that prepares missionary linguists for the project of Bible translation; the training of these missionaries emphasizes phonemics as the basis for practical writing systems.

Even though writing may be introduced in the service of a particular religious sect or denomination, its introduction often marks the beginning of other social changes; literacy promotes modernization and enables isolated communities to participate in national and international political movements. For this reason, political leaders often welcome the help of missionaries in developing writing systems and introducing literacy programs, even though they may not share the religious motives of the missionary organization. For example, the Summer Institute of Linguistics has worked in collaboration with governmental agencies in Latin American countries such as Peru and Mexico to promote common educational goals.

LANGUAGE AND HISTORY

Prior to the 20th century, the study of language had a prevailingly historical orientation. Popular interest in the sources and historical relationships of the languages and peoples of Europe and the Orient inspired a substantial body of careful, detailed research. Many of the issues and insights that emerged from this early scholarship continue to occupy the attention of modern linguists. However, interpretation of historical issues can now rest on a richer data base as the result of modern descriptive and structural analyses.

Grammarians and philologists of the Enlightenment period had spoken of "older" and "younger" languages and sometimes judged modern languages (such as English or French) to be degraded or imperfect in comparison with classical Latin or Greek—as these, in turn, would presumably have been in comparison with the divine language of Creation. The key to a more comprehensive view of the nature of language and a more realistic understanding of the relationships among languages was a new concept of the dynamics of linguistic change. This was the crucial development in the linguistic science of the 19th century.

Historians usually date the beginnings of modern linguistic science from 1786, when Sir William Jones[1] published a paper calling attention to points of similarity among Sanskrit (the classical literary language of India), Greek, and Latin. The revolutionary aspect of Jones's assessment of these similarities was his belief that the three must be related *by common descent* from some earlier or ancestral language. This proposal of "genetic" relationship as an explanation for similarities among languages was very much in the spirit of the times, as theories of evolutionary change—both in nature and in the development of society—would become the dominant paradigm in the 19th century. This new and more dynamic perspective replaced the relatively static view that languages, like natural species and human institutions, were created or divinely inspired more or less in accord with biblical tradition.

Sir William Jones and his successors broadened the horizons of Western knowledge by demonstrating that grammatical and lexical resemblances linked

---

[1]Sir William Jones (1746–1794), who served in India as a superior court judge, was an Orientalist and avid scholar of languages who translated, published, and thus introduced Muslim and Hindu works to the West. Jones's findings concerning the common ancestry of Sanskrit, Greek, and Latin were presented in his presidential address to the Asiatic Society in London in 1786.

Greek and Latin to Sanskrit and, by implication, to other, possibly more distant linguistic kin. Over the following century, many scholars participated in the comparative and historical study of the Indo-European family of languages; among these were Rasmus Rask (1787–1832), Jakob Grimm (1785–1863), and August Schleicher (1821–1868). In 1814 Rask, a Danish linguist, published an essay on the Icelandic language in which he defined the interrelationships of the Scandinavian languages and, in more general terms, their place in the Germanic branch of Indo-European. This essay has come to be appreciated as one of the earliest rigorous applications of the comparative method in linguistics. Between 1819 and 1837, Jacob Grimm compiled an encyclopedic German grammar that traced points of similarity among the major divisions of the Germanic tongues. The text identified the regular correspondences of consonants in these languages to others more distantly related (in particular, to Greek, Latin, and Sanskrit, as they were considered immediate descendants of the earlier parent language). The formula that summarizes these correspondences became the cornerstone of later comparative work; it is still commonly referred to as Grimm's Law and is discussed later in this chapter.

A half-century after Jones's initial proposal, August Schleicher[2] undertook the task of reconstructing words and forms of the Indo-European parent language. In order to obtain more complete data for this project, Schleicher researched and wrote a grammar of Lithuanian—a language which, until that time, had never been a subject of scholarly interest. Published in 1857, this was one of the first field studies of a vernacular language, based on speech rather than on literary texts.

By the late 19th century, the general outlines of the Indo-European family of languages had been defined; less was known about other languages and the dynamics of linguistic change. Linguistic scholars were very much aware of contemporary developments in the natural and social sciences, and some saw linguistic change as analogous to processes of evolution. August Schleicher characterized language as a kind of living organism that is born, lives, gives birth to offspring, and eventually dies. He charted the genetic relations among languages in the form of a family tree—a form in which they are still often presented—although many linguists now find fault with this kind of analogy between languages and biological organisms. Schleicher also proposed a typological classification of languages, based on descriptive concepts formulated by the influential scholar and philosopher Wilhelm von Humboldt.[3]

[2]August Schleicher (1821–1868), a professor at the University of Jena, was an innovator in attempting to study languages scientifically in an evolutionary framework. Three major aspects of his work are his grammar of Lithuanian, his typology of languages (as isolating, agglutinating, and inflecting) and the *Stammbaum* theory, which represented the relationships among Indo-European languages in the form of a "family tree."

[3]Wilhelm von Humboldt (1767–1835) was a Prussian educator and diplomat. His interest in languages led him to study the Basque language and to undertake a major work on the ancient Kawi language of Java. The latter work, which was published posthumously, includes an essay expressing his ideas concerning the importance of language as expressing and influencing the development of culture. In this respect, Humboldt anticipated and may have influenced later theorists such as Sapir and Whorf.

Schleicher described three structural types, which he proposed as evolutionary stages in the general development of language. In the *isolating* or analytic type, a word is a single, unanalyzable unit; Chinese is the classic example of this type. In the *agglutinative* or synthetic type, words are composed by the mechanical combination of parts (bases, prefixes, and suffixes); Turkish is an example. In inflectional languages, words change in form to express a variety of meanings but are not easily analyzable into discrete morphemes; this type is exemplified by Latin, Greek, and most other Indo-European languages. Linguists still find Schleicher's categories useful as a convenient way to characterize linguistic structures, although few languages conform closely to the typical patterns.

The evolutionary implications that Schleicher attached to his typology have long since been discredited. An accumulation of evidence drawn from languages of the world and the testimony of documented histories of individual languages would soon cast doubt on this and other theories of universal and inevitable stages in the evolution of either language or culture. However, typology remains an interest of modern linguistics, and new approaches to typology play a part in recent efforts to identify universal features of language.

THE COMPARATIVE METHOD IN LINGUISTICS

The early focus of study in comparative linguistics, following the lead of Sir William Jones and his contemporaries, was the large group of languages that includes Germanic, Romanic, and Slavic branches and extinct languages such as Sanskrit, Greek, and Latin. Earlier known as Indo-Germanic, this is now called the Indo-European family of languages. The standards of language description and methods of comparison that were developed in the study of Indo-European have since been applied to many other language groups.

The comparative study of a group of languages aims, first of all, to confirm or disprove the relatedness of the languages included. The accepted proof of relationship is not simply the existence of similarities, but the discovery of regular parallels—or *correspondences*—in the phonemes and grammatical patterns of the several languages. Beyond this, comparisons enable linguists to reconstruct the forms and meanings of earlier times, reaching back to the remote common ancestor of the group of related languages. A reconstruction attributes to an earlier stage those features that are shared by daughter languages and suggests forms that seem likely to have given rise to features that are divergent but similar. Such a reconstructed language is identified by the prefix "proto-"; thus, proto-Germanic is the reconstructed ancestor of the Germanic languages, while proto-Indo-European represents a still earlier stage, ancestral to Germanic and all other divisions of Indo-European. (Hypothetic forms attributed to a protolanguage are usually marked by an asterisk.)

This procedure of comparison and reconstruction resembles, in a general way, the method a biologist might use in classifying and tracing the evolutionary relationships of plants or animals. For example, a comparison of the hands of various anthropoids (monkeys, apes, and humans) would lead one to the conclusion that the common ancestor of these closely related animals had a hand with five prehensile fingers, including a short, opposable thumb, and with flat nails on all the fingers—features shared by most existing species of this suborder. It becomes obvious, then, that the elongated fingers of the gibbon and orangutan, the atrophied thumb of the spider monkey, and the relatively long, rotatable thumb of *Homo sapiens* are all specializations or adaptations away from the general pattern. Obviously, too, these specializations developed at a later time than did the general features that are shared. A natural scientist, studying such a problem of taxonomy, can sometimes draw on the evidence of fossils from earlier geological periods that supplement (and may revise) the conclusions that can be reached on the basis of comparison of living creatures alone.

Similarly, a linguist might compare French *terre,* Spanish *tierra,* and Italian *terra* (all meaning "land") and come to the conclusion that the earlier form must have been very similar to those in the daughter languages. In this case, the existence in written documents of the Latin form *terra(m),* with the same meaning, serves something of the same function as fossil evidence for the biologist. However, this kind of confirming documentary evidence is not always at hand and is never available when we are dealing with languages that do not have a long history of writing. Therefore, the comparative linguists' reconstructions are usually based on the general evidence of grammatical parallels and the more specific evidence of cognate words.

Indo-European

Cognate words are words that can be shown to have a common origin; that is, they are descended from forms that were present in the ancestral language. The following list presents several examples of Indo-European cognates, with examples from Sanskrit, Greek, Latin, and English (as a representative of the Germanic subfamily). In the final column, each letter stands for a set of corresponding sounds in the cognate words.

	Sanskrit	Greek	Latin	English	
1.	pitár	patér	pater	father	*p
2.	trájah	trejs	tre:s	three	*t
3.	kravih	kréas	crûor	(O.E. *hreaw*) raw	*k
4.	pad	póda	pedem	foot	*d
5.	yugá-	zugón	iugum	yoke	*g
6.		kannabis		hemp	*b
7.	bhratar	phra:ter	fra:ter	brother	*bh
8.	vidháva	e:itheos	divido	widow	*dh
9.	hári	khólos	helvus	gold	*gh
10.			porcus	pork	—

The regularity in these phonological correspondences in consonants and vowels is taken to be the only convincing proof of common origin. Those that are noted in this list are stated in summary form as Grimm's[4] Law:

1. Where the Indo-European parent language had *voiceless stops (p, t, k)*, the Germanic cognates have *voiceless fricatives (f, th, [θ], h)*. Items 1-3 in the previous list give examples of this set of correspondences.

2. Where proto-Indo-European had *voiced stops (b, d, g)*, Germanic cognates have *voiceless stops (p, t, k)*. Note, especially, items 4-6.

3. Where the ancestral language had *aspirated voiced stops (bh, dh, gh)*, Germanic cognates have *voiced stops (b, d, g)*. Items 7-9 include examples of this type of correspondence. It is less obvious than the other types because the aspirated voiced stops have also been lost in Greek and Latin.

Once the regular patterns of correspondences have been established, linguists can determine whether individual lexical pairs that show resemblances are true cognates. Sometimes resemblances are simply coincidental. More frequently, they are words that have been borrowed from one language by another. It can be relatively easy to identify these, especially if they are recent borrowings; they may actually resemble each other more closely than true cognates. Item 10 is an example: English *pork* is a borrowing from French and closely resembles the French form; the true Germanic cognate is Old English *fearh*, retained in modern English *farrow* (newborn pig).

Note in comparing the words shown here that the consonant correspondences appear to be more regular than those of vowels. This has been obvious from the time of early comparative studies. Later corrections and modifications of Grimm's formulas have been concerned with explaining irregularities and apparent exceptions to the regular patterns of consonant correspondence, and also with efforts to reconstruct the proto-Indo-European vocalic system and its reflexes in the modern languages. This involves many subtle changes in vowel quality because vowels are affected by position in the word, stress, and other factors.

Karl Verner (1846–1896), a Danish linguist writing in the late 19th century, explained some apparent exceptions to Grimm's Law that arose from the location of stress in the protolanguage; his formulation is sometimes referred to as Verner's Law. In 1878 Ferdinand de Saussure was able to explain the seemingly erratic behavior of many vowels as caused by the influence of a type of laryngeal (*h*-like) consonant that, as he demonstrated, had been present in the ancestral language but was lost in the descendant languages. Grimm and other pioneers of Indo-European study had discovered the basic

---

[4]Jakob Grimm (1785–1863), together with his brother Wilhelm Grimm, was a renowned collector of Germanic folktales and songs. As a philologist, his precise demonstration of the relationships among Germanic languages established the principle of phonological correspondences among related languages, which has subsequently been widely applied in historical linguistics.

patterns and rules of correspondences, and their work was the point of departure for many later modifications, new discoveries, and more sophisticated formulations.

LANGUAGE, TIME, AND HISTORY

Demonstration of relationships among languages, with the prospect of tracing their origins and reconstructing their ancestry, holds an obvious interest for anthropologists. In 1916, Edward Sapir, one of the most original minds among anthropological linguists, wrote the important essay "Time Perspectives in Aboriginal American Culture," which called for the use of linguistic information—together with the distribution of culture traits and other types of "direct and inferential evidence"—to solve complex historical problems. There are two types of questions that historically oriented anthropologists can hope to answer with the help of linguistic data: (1) Can the prehistoric cultures studied by archaeologists—which often can be assigned fairly exact dates—be identified with or related to historical cultures or speech communities? (2) Can reasonably accurate dates be determined for the origins, separations, or movements of known population groups in the absence of solid archaeological data?

Problems of this sort can be very difficult to resolve. However, there are methods that are designed to deal with them, bringing linguistic data into use along with other types of information. One of the most productive of these methods relies on *lexical reconstruction.* The reconstructed vocabulary of a protolanguage can provide information about certain aspects of culture. The process of reconstructing vocabulary, by means of the comparative method, leads almost inevitably to hypotheses about the ancient culture: Words that can be shown to be cognates in the daughter languages are, by definition, reflexes of words that were in existence when the protolanguage was spoken. If these cognates have approximately the same meaning in all or most of the languages, then a reasonable inference can be made about the original meaning in the protolanguage.

Studies in lexical reconstruction have used reconstructed terms for plants, animals, and similar vocabulary as evidence for defining features of habitat or environment. Attempts have also been made to use vocabulary as the basis for inferences about subsistence pursuits, social and kinship systems, religious concepts, political and military life, and so forth. The most voluminous studies of this sort have been devoted to the homeland and culture of the proto-Indo-Europeans, but the approach is also increasingly attractive to specialists in the study of other language groups. For example, a major work on proto-Athabascan kinship by an ethnologist, D. F. Aberle, and a linguist, I. Dyen, constitutes both an important test of the method and a contribution to an issue of theoretical interest to social anthropology—the origins of matrilineal kinship in certain Native American societies (Dyen & Aberle, 1977).

Lexical reconstruction achieves results of interest to anthropology through comparisons that make use of "cultural" vocabulary—vocabulary that might be expected to vary as culture itself varies. For example, reconstructed cultural vocabulary might lead us to conclude that the people who spoke a particular protolanguage were big-game hunters, agriculturalists, or maritime folk; lived on dairy products or meat or grain; believed in nature spirits or worshipped their ancestors—depending on the richness or paucity of the vocabulary in particular areas.

On the other hand, there is rarely any distinctive cultural information to be gained from the terms for eating, breathing, walking, or talking; or for body parts, earth, water, wood, or stone. Such things are universal or inevitable in the human experience. But this type of "culture-free" vocabulary has proved especially valuable as the basis for a method of arriving at (or at least approximating) dates for the existence of ancient language communities and the time periods during which groups of related languages may have dispersed. This is *lexico-statistical dating*, or *glottochronology*, a method developed by Morris Swadesh. Like Sapir, Swadesh was a specialist in the study of Native American languages and was intrigued by the challenge of tracing their origins and historical relationships.

Seeking a method for measuring linguistic change and assessing relationships, Swadesh observed that cultural vocabulary sometimes remained stable over long periods, while at other times it might change quite rapidly. Words for plants or animals, for example, can be lost if the environment changes or if people migrate from one area to another, and technical vocabulary may increase rapidly in response to inventions or cultural contacts. On the other hand, *basic* or "culture-free" vocabulary would appear to be relatively immune to such nonlinguistic influences. If this proved to be the case, Swadesh reasoned, the rate of change would be minimal, and the degree of change found in any given case should serve as a sort of index of elapsed time.

Pursuing this idea, Swadesh and several of his associates formulated and refined a list of basic vocabulary items—first, in a shorter (100-word) and then in a longer (200-word) version. The basic vocabulary was tested in preliminary studies of a number of languages for which more than 1,000 years of documentation is available, including Chinese, Egyptian, Greek, and Latin (together with its daughter Romanic languages). It was found that in these cases, when earlier and later vocabularies could be compared, the rate of change in the basic lexicon was surprisingly uniform; words were lost and added, or replaced, at the rate of approximately 18 to 20 out of 100 in 1,000 years' time.

When a percentage figure based on this initial study (.805/1,000 years) was taken as a constant, it became possible to estimate the time of separation of related languages simply by counting shared or cognate items in the basic list. This calculation can be done by listing words in parallel columns, examining the pairs of words one by one, and judging them as "same" (+) or "different" (–). Then, using a standard formula, the count can be translated into

| AN EXERCISE IN GLOTTO-CHRONOLOGY |

Swadesh's 100-item diagnostic list is given here, together with vocabulary from two Native American languages. Lokono (or "true Arawak") and Garifuna (or Central American Island Carib) are languages of the Arawakan family. Douglas Taylor, who compiled the vocabularies, studied Lokono in Surinam and Garifuna in Belize.

English	Lokono (Arawak)[5]	Garifuna (Central American Island Carib)
1. I	dai, dei	nuguia; M.S. au (K)
2. thou	bɨi, bii	buguia; M.S. amoro (K)
3. we	oai, oei	uagia
4. this	tho(h)o / li(h)i	lua / lea (nonmasc./ masc.)
5. that	thora(h)a; lira(h)a	tura; lira (nonmasc./ masc.)
6. who?	halika(n)	ka, kata-
7. what?	hamaha	= 6
8. not	ma-; kho(ro)	ma-; ua (K)
9. all	hara(-)	sụ (gubai)
10. many	io(h)o	gibe
11. one	aba(-)	abana, aba
12. two	biama, bian	biama, bia
13. big	(i)firo; (i)fili-	uairi-
14. long	oadi-	migife- (K)
15. small	ibi-; sioko	niorao-
16. woman	hiaro	hịaru; M.S. uori (K)
17. man	oadili	eieri; M.S. uogori (K)
18. person	loko	mutu
19. fish	hime	udu(rao) (K)
20. bird	kodibio	dunuru (K); soso
21. dog	peero	aụli
22. louse	iehi, -ie	ịe
23. tree	ada	ueue (K)
24. seed	isii, -si	t-ila; t-ii
25. leaf	adobona, -bona	-bana
26. root	ɨɨkirahi, -ikira	-ilagola
27. bark	adada, -da	-ura
28. skin	ɨda, -da	= 27
29. flesh	sirokoho, -siroko	-ogorogo
30. blood	ɨthihi, -thina	hitao, -ita
31. bone	abonaha, -bona	-abu
32. fat	iki(h)i	-agole
33. egg	kodibiosa, -sa	t-ii (cf. 24)
34. horn	-(o)koa	arigai
35. tail	i(h)itoko; -i(h)i	-ili
36. feather	(o)bara, -bara	= 25
37. hair	=36	-idiburi
38. head	isii, -si	icogo, icigo
39. ear	-dike; koioko	= 34

[5]Taylor's transcriptions differ considerably from similar forms recorded by Hickerson in Guyana; for example, his /th/ and /kh/ are aspirated stops that, in most cases, correspond to Hickerson's /t/ and /k/. Differences between the two may, for present purposes, be ignored.

40. eye	-kosi	-agu
41. nose	sirihi, -siri	igiri
42. mouth	-reroko	-iuma
43. tooth	arii, ari	-ari
44. tongue	-iee	-ieie
45. claw	-bada	-(u)bara
46. foot	-koti	-(u)gudi
47. knee	-koro	-gacorogo
48. hand	-khabo	-(u)habu
49. belly	-dibeio	-(u)ragai
50. neck	-noro	-igiina
51. breast	-dio	-uri
52. heart	-oasina; oloa	anigi
53. liver	-bana	= 25
54. drink	(a)thin (v.t.); (a)than (v.i.)	ata, gura-
55. eat	(e)kin (v.t.); khoton (v.i.)	aiga, hau-
56. bite	ridin	agoragua
57. see	dikhin	ariha
58. hear	kanabon	agaba
59. know	aithin	subudi-, subuse- (K)
60. sleep	donkon	arumuga
61. die	(h)odon	aue, hila
62. kill	farin	afara
63. swim	thimin	afuliha (K)
64. fly	morodon	ahamara
65. walk	konan	aibuga
66. come	andin	acolora; niobui (K)
67. lie	torodon	rau-
68. sit	balatin	niuru-, -(n)iu
69. stand	dinamin	rarama-
70. give	sikin	iciga; ru-
71. say	aakan; dian	erega, ariaga
72. sun	hadali	ueiu (K)
73. moon	kathi	hati
74. star	oioa	uaruguma
75. water	oniabo, -nia	duna (K)
76. rain	oni	huia; M.S. gunubu (K)
77. stone	siba, -siban	dobu (K)
78. sand	mothoko	sagau (K)
79. earth	hororo, -orora	mua
80. cloud	oraro	huariu; ube(h)u
81. smoke	koreeli	gumulali
82. fire	hiki(h)i; -ihime	uatu (K); -(i)leme
83. ash(es)	balisi	baligi
84. burn	bithin, bithan	aguda, guda
85. path	oaboroko; abonaha	oma (K); -emari (K)
86. mountain	hororo sin (= 79 + 38)	uobu (K)
87. red	kore(e)-	funa-
88. green	imoro-	urigi-
89. yellow	hehe-	dumari
90. white	harira-	haru-
91. black	khareme-	uri-
92. night	orika; kasakoda	ariabu
93. hot	there-; oerebe-	hara-; baca-

94. cold	mimili-	dili-
95. full	(h)ebe-	buị
96. new	(h)emelea-	iseri (K)
97. good	sa-	buidu (K)
98. round	balala-	giriri-
99. dry	oaa-; sare-	mabai-
100. name	-iri	-iri

(Taylor, 1977)

Arawakan is a large family, widely distributed in South America (IIIA in Figure 7.8) but most concentrated in the tropical forest region and centered on the Amazon River system. Lokono is spoken in an ecological setting similar to that in which the protolanguage developed and diversified, appears to be conservative, and is regarded as a typical Arawakan language. The native languages of the West Indies appear to have been largely Arawakan, having spread northward from the continent at an unknown date. Those Arawaks that settled on the small islands of the Lesser Antilles were strongly influenced by contacts—both friendly and hostile—with Caribs, members of another South American family (IIC in Figure 7.8). The impact on their language was so strong that early explorers mistakenly identified these islanders as "Island Caribs," partly because of the "men's language," which incorporated much Carib vocabulary. (See chapter 7.)

The "Island Carib" language of the West Indies is effectively extinct, although Douglas Taylor was able to collect vocabulary from a few individuals on the island of Dominica during the 1950s. However, Garifuna (or "Central American Island Carib") is a direct descendant, spoken by a racially mixed population whose ancestors were relocated from St. Vincent to the coast of Central America around 1800. In the list above, "M.S." identifies terms used exclusively by men, and "K" marks terms that Taylor has identified as being of Carib origin.

In comparing the Lokono and Garifuna lists, it can be assumed that when two or more forms are listed, the first should be preferred (assumed to be the most common). Exceptions are numbers 4 and 5, where a distinction between masculine gender (with l-) and nonmasculine (with t-) is made in both languages. Lacking an expert's knowledge of Arawakan etymologies, one must simply be guided by overall similarities in identifying correspondences.

By my count, there are 37 probable correspondences between the Lokono and Garifuna vocabularies (and 4 possible correspondences).[6] Following Swadesh's formula, this would suggest roughly 2,000 years of separation from a common ancestor. It might be noted that if the men's speech were taken as the norm, the differentiation would be greater, and that the large number of Carib (K) loanwords must be taken into consideration in any attempt to relate the linguistic data to archaeological and other historical evidence (see Taylor & Rouse, 1955; Hickerson, 1992).

---

[6]Items 2, 3, 4, 5, 8, 11, 12, 16, 17, 22, 24, 25, 27, 28, 29, 30, 31, 35, 38, 40, 41, 43, 44, 45, 46, 48, 53, 54, 55, 62, 70, 73, 80, 83, 90, 95, and 100. (I marked items 6, 47, 51, and 93 as questionable.)

years of separation. The formula is: $t = \log C (2 \log r)$, where t = time (in thousands of years), C = percentage of cognates, and r = the constant rate of retention (Swadesh, 1959; Gudschinsky, 1956).

Few linguists would accept the resulting time estimates at face value; yet glottochronology still excites interest among many anthropologists as a method that is fairly easy to apply and that yields tangible results. If genetic relationships and a relative chronology for the separation of languages have already been established by the comparative method, lexicostatistical dating can provide a starting point for attempts to link this chronology with other historical evidence—most obviously, with the findings of prehistoric archaeology.

TRACING INDO-EUROPEAN ORIGINS

Since the development of the techniques of lexical reconstruction in the mid-19th century, many scholars have undertaken to describe the culture and identify the original homeland of the ancient Indo-European people. Linguistic evidence, supplemented by the calculations of glottochronology, points to the existence of proto-Indo-European (as a single language community or, perhaps, as a group of closely related languages or dialects) at a time depth of around 5000 to 6000 B.C. Much effort has gone into attempts to identify the early Indo-Europeans with known prehistoric cultures, to locate their original homeland, and to trace the migratory movements and demographic processes that gave rise to the historic array of languages and cultures. The complexity of these problems obviously defies simple solutions.

There was, at first, an inclination to suppose that classic Sanskrit was the closest to the protolanguage and that the early location might have been in India. However, the lexical data clearly discredit this suggestion. The proto-Indo-European language had terms for trees such as birch, beech, oak, willow, and fir (but not fig, olive, or grape); for wolf, bear, lynx, and fox (but not for elephant, monkey, or tiger). There are cognate terms that refer to cattle, sheep, horses, pigs, and goats; to barley, bees, and honey; to the hedgehog, turtle, beaver, otter, and salmon. Clearly, the weight of evidence drawn from the reconstructed lexicon appears to point to a forested terrain and a temperate climate, suggesting a European environment, possibly lying between the Mediterranean and the Baltic Seas. In particular, the co-occurrence of beech trees, salmon, and turtles has prompted some researchers to identify an area along the coast of the Baltic Sea as the "proto-Indo-European homeland" (Thieme, 1964).

Another long-standing theory suggested that the Indo-European speakers might be identified with people living in the Danube basin around 6000 B.C. (exemplified by a site called Starcevo). These were early farmers who may have adopted agriculture through their trade contacts with the Mediterranean. Their improved subsistence practices would have been followed by an expansion in population and, eventually, by migrations into new territories It is possible that they first moved into areas that were not productive for the small communities of hunter-gatherers already present (Claiborn, 1977).

However, while the reconstructed vocabulary gives indications of the presence of both domesticated plants and animals, the weight of the proto-Indo-European lexicon seems to be toward pastoralism; the number of words associated with cattle and sheep is particularly large. This presumed pastoral bias has led some to suggest a homeland located farther to the east, perhaps in the steppes of Russia or central Asia. One suggestion is that an early pastoral horse-raising people called the Kurgans, who are thought to have migrated into Europe from the steppes of Russia in the fifth century B.C., may have been speakers of an ancestral Indo-European tongue.

A long-standing impression that the territorial expansion of the early Indo-Europeans must be in some way related to the spread of Neolithic culture has recently been restated in somewhat different terms by archaeologist Colin Renfrew. Renfrew's views reflect a tendency in modern archaeology to reject theories of wide-ranging migration as explanations for the spread of languages and cultures. He favors a *processual* model, which proposes that the Neolithic way of life—based on agriculture and the use of domestic animals—had a slow, incremental spread through Europe, with population density increasing and the frontier advancing northward and westward, generation after generation. In the process, an early form of Indo-European ("Old European") would have been diffused, its subsequent differentiation reflecting, to some extent, the influence of the earlier regional populations (Renfrew, 1987). Renfrew is probably correct in downplaying the role of long-distance migrations and conquests, but it should not be forgotten that such events have played a role in recorded history—and may have done so in the prerecorded past—with influences on both languages and cultures that remain to be discovered.

Established views of the development and dispersal of the Indo-European family have been complicated in the 20th century by two additions to the roster of languages—Hittite and Tocharian. The ancient Hittite civilization, well known to classical archaeologists and Old Testament scholars, developed in Anatolia (part of modern Turkey). In 1935, the decipherment of Hittite cuneiform texts both revealed a language that is unquestionably Indo-European and also provided the earliest evidence of writing associated with this family. Further, the same texts include names and other vocabulary that appear to represent an early form of Sanskrit (or a closely related Indic language); this would suggest that trade and/or diplomatic relations already existed between two early centers of civilization—Anatolia and India.

The date of c. 1500 B.C. assigned to the Hittite texts is, of course, much more recent than the estimated antiquity of proto-Indo-European. However, the Hittite writing system, employed in the codification of laws and record keeping, must have developed in the context of a mature society. The Hittite civilization itself appears to have evolved *in situ* in Anatolia (Turkey) over the course of many centuries, as an integral part of the eastern Mediterranean region within which agriculture had its beginnings around 8000 B.C. With this in mind, it appears that Hittite may be central to the question of Indo-European origins rather than peripheral.

On balance, it may be posited that the formation of the of Indo-European family began around 10,000 years ago with a cluster of interrelated populations, speaking somewhat differentiated dialects, living in Anatolia and neighboring regions south and east of the Caspian Sea (the location of present-day Armenia). These people were among the first to adopt the Neolithic way of life; their communities grew, and after a number of generations they began to push into new territories. Early dispersal may have led some settlers westward, in the direction of Greece and the Balkan regions; some eastward, toward the Persian plateaus; and others southward, toward India. Early centers of civilization developed in all of these areas; Sanskrit, Hittite, Avestan, and Greek had developed writing systems by 2000 to 1500 B.C.

While these complex and urbanized societies were developing, the dispersal continued in frontier regions, and the increasing separation of regional populations meant a greater linguistic differentiation. Over many centuries, incremental advances pushed Indo-European pioneers westward and northward through most of Europe. Diversification of the northern and western subfamilies may have begun in a "staging area" north of the Black Sea and south of the Baltic (the environment suggested by much of the reconstructed plant and animal terminology). The precursors of the Italic, Celtic, Germanic, and Balto-Slavic subfamilies became separated; their subsequent movements and interactions bring us to the dawn of European history.

It may have been along the eastern fringe of this staging area, perhaps in the steppes of Russia, that some Indo-Europeans adopted a nomadic, pastoral way of life with an emphasis on horsemanship. The Tocharians, who lived in northern Mongolia between the 12th and 15th centuries A.D., represent this pattern—and are, by far, the most eastern representatives of Indo-European prior to the modern period.

DISCOVERING PROTO-ALGONKIAN

During the 1920s Leonard Bloomfield began a comparative study of Algonkian, an important family of Native American languages. This was an important milestone in the history of linguistics because the study was undertaken as a test case; Bloomfield was applying the comparative method to a group of languages that lacked the early written materials that had played a large role in the study of Indo-European and other Old World families.

Many traditional linguistic scholars felt that written documentation was essential for a comparative study and the reconstruction of a protolanguage; Bloomfield disagreed. He did make use of existing studies of Algonkian languages by earlier scholars, but for primary data he relied on his own field research on four centrally located languages: Cree, Ojibwa, Menomini, and Fox. Working with speakers of these four languages (easily accessible from his academic base at the University of Chicago), he was able to facilitate his comparative study by gathering parallel data—a considerable advantage over research that draws information piecemeal from a variety of sources.

Because of his concentration on languages of the Great Lakes area, Bloomfield was less familiar with the more peripheral divisions of the Algonkian family—the languages located in the Great Plains (such as Cheyenne and Blackfoot), those of the southeast (like Delaware and Shawnee), and those of the northeast (including Micmac, Abenaki, and several extinct languages of New England). Therefore, he limited the scope of his study and called the reconstructed ancestral language Proto-Central Algonkian (or PCA) (Bloomfield, 1946). Additional research would be necessary to bring the more far-flung representatives of the family into the picture.

English	Fox	Cree	Menomini	Ojibwa	PCA
man	ineniwa	iyiniw	eneeniw	inini	*elenyiwa
stone	asenya	asiniy	aʔsen	assin	*aʔsenya
louse	ihkwa	ihkwa	ehkuah	ikkwa	*ehkwa
kettle	ahkohkwa	askihk	ahkeeh	akkik	*axkehkwa
duck	šiišiipa	siisiip	seeʔsep	šiišiip	*šiiʔšiipa
my grandmother	noohkomesa	noohkom	noohkomeh	nookkomiss	*noohkomehsa
I place him	netasaawa	nitahyaa	nettaaʔnaw	nintassaa	*netaʔlaawa

Later Algonkianists—many of them Bloomfield's own students—have broadened the scope of the comparative studies that he initiated. Other Algonkian languages, not included in his original study, were found to conform well to the outlines established for proto-Central Algonkian; little modification was necessary. Proto-Algonkian is now well established, and comparisons have been extended to demonstrate the existence of more remote relationships (I, Macro-Algonkian, Figure 7.7). Bloomfield's work launched an ongoing tradition of Algonkian research and also inspired similar work on other aboriginal language groups in North America—Athabascan, Siouan, Salishan, and others.

THE PROTO-ALGONKIAN HOMELAND.   The combined efforts of several Algonkianists have produced a body of comparative research that may be second only to that dealing with the Indo-European tongues. In 1967, F. Siebert published a study that utilized reconstructed proto-Algonkian terms for 55 species of plants, animals, birds, and fish as the basis for delimiting the geographical area inhabited by the ancestral Algonkians. There are terms for widespread species of temperate and subarctic North America such as the common raven, golden eagle, great horned owl, and pileated woodpecker; porcupine, squirrel, moose, skunk, and bear; and familiar American trees such as elm, white spruce, maple, and willow. However, just as in the case of Indo-European, a few species are critical: Siebert's conclusions relied especially on the proto-Algonkian terms for woodland caribou, harbor seal, and lake trout. The original community of speakers must have lived in an area where all three of these were present, a requirement that narrows the search to areas adjacent to the upper St. Lawrence River, Hudson's Bay, and the Great Lakes. On the basis of these and other considerations, the core area, at around 1200 B.C., appears to have been located "between Lake Huron and Georgian Bay and the middle course of the Ottawa River, bounded on the north by Lake Nipissing and the Mattewa River and on the south by the northern shore of Lake Ontario, the headwaters of the Grand River, and the Saugeen River" (Siebert, 1967). From this early homeland, the Algonkian peoples expanded through a larger northern Great Lakes area by around 900 B.C.; by 1500 A.D., a diversity of Algonkian languages was spoken over much of the northeastern quadrant of North America (IA in Figure 7.7).

Willard Walker also contributed to the reconstruction of aspects of proto-Algonkian material culture and social life and attempted to relate the linguistic reconstruction of culture history to that of prehistoric archaeology. Tentatively, Walker designated a Middle Woodland culture called Early Point Peninsula, to which archaeologists assign a date of 500 to 1000 B.C., as one that corresponds well—in time span, spatial location, and overall culture content—with that of the proto-Algonkians (Walker, 1975).

TRACKING THE BANTU EXPANSION

A third group of languages that invited comparative study is found in Africa. The more than 300 Bantu languages extend over a large part of the African continent (IIF in Figure 7.5). Most of them show such obvious resemblances that the fact of their common origin has never really been in question. But, at the same time, the distribution of features among the different languages makes it difficult to set up neat subdivisions within Bantu, and the historical picture is obviously complex (Guthrie, 1967).

Bantu was established as a language family through studies done by pioneer Africanists, including German scholars C. Meinhoff (1857–1944) and D. Westermann (1875–1956). Some striking similarities among the languages can be seen in a table of nouns taken from an early survey of Bantu (Werner, 1919). Westermann also observed that there were more remote resemblances that could link the Bantu group to other languages of central and western Africa, but he left the nature of the relationship unresolved. Some years thereafter, as part of a comprehensive classification of African languages, Joseph Greenberg designated Bantu as a subfamily within a large and widely distributed family that he called Niger-Congo. The greatest diversity within the Niger-Congo family is found in west-central Africa, between the Atlantic coast and Lake Chad; the eastern and southern Bantu languages, on the other hand, are relatively undifferentiated. This fact alone would suggest that the earlier base of the family lay in the northwest and that the direction of movement of Bantu was from that region toward the south and east.

The close similarity among the languages of the Bantu peoples suggests that they, like the Algonkians, dispersed at a fairly recent time. This is especially true of a southern extension of the Bantu area, where one language, Swahili, has long served as a *lingua franca* or trade language. This role is facilitated by the low degree of differentiation of the languages, making the learning of one by speakers of the others a relatively easy task.

By 1967, examination and comparison of Bantu vocabularies had enabled such scholars as D. Dalby and M. Guthrie to classify the languages into several subgroups and to suggest routes by which population movements may have taken place. In Guthrie's view, the differentiation and dispersal of Bantu appeared to have occurred within 3,000 years. The starting point lay in the Cameroon region, and a proposed route initially led due east, bypassing the dense equatorial forests to the south. Then, from northeastern Zaire, divergent movements took Bantu speakers both southeast and southwest. These two divisions dispersed and eventually merged, and a final wave of migration carried Bantu languages to far southern Africa. Comparisons of vocabularies indicated that the early Bantus had knowledge of both agriculture and domestic animals; however, the words associated with sheep and cattle suggested that these could ultimately have a non-Bantu source, possibly being acquired in an early stage of the eastward migration.

Bantu terms related to metallurgy—such as *iron, forge,* and *bellows*—aroused special interest. It appeared that a late territorial expansion could have been associated with the introduction of iron-working, a technological innovation that may have enabled the Bantus to advance at the expense of earlier populations. Archaeological evidence put the beginning of the African Iron Age in the first millennium B.C. In the opinion of archaeologist D. W. Phillipson, there was "a marked degree of similarity . . . between the archaeological sequence of the Iron Age in subequatorial Africa and the linguistic evidence for the spread and development of the Bantu languages and their speakers" (1977).

Noun Class	Zulu	Chwana	Herero	Nyanj	Swahili	Ganda	Kongo
1. human being	umu-ntu	mo-tho	omu-ndu	mu-ntu	m-tu	omu-ntu	mu-ntu
2. human beings	aba-ntu	va-tho	ova-ndu	a-ntu	wa-tu	aba-ntu	a-ntu
3. tree	umu-ti	mo-re	omu-ti	m-tengo	m-ti	omu-ti	
4. trees	imi-ti	me-re	omi-ti	mi-tengo	mi-ti	emi-ti	
5. tooth	ili-zinyo	le-ino	e-yo	dz-ino	j-ino	eri-nyo	d-inu
6. teeth	ama-zinyo	ma-ino	oma-yo	ma-no	m-eno	ama-nyo	m-enu
7. thorax	isi-fuba	se-huba		chi-fua	ki-fua	eki-fuba	
8. thoraces	izi-fuba	li-huba		zi-fua	vi-fua	ebi-fuba	
9. elephant	in-dhlovu	tlou	on-dyou	njobvu	ndobu	en-jovu	nzau
10. elephants	izin-dhlovu	li-tlou	ozon-dyou	njobvu	ndovu	en-jovu	nzau
11. wand	ulu-ti	lo-re	oru-ti	u-ti			

Source: After Werner, 1915

Since the 1970s, archaeological and linguistic studies have continued, refining and amplifying the findings of the earlier scholars and revealing a more complex picture of African prehistory. Today, efforts to uncover the origin of the Bantu languages and peoples can be put in the larger context of research on other divisions of Niger-Congo; among these, the relationship of Bantu to a sister subfamily, Ubangi, is of special interest. Further, the Niger-Congo family itself is part of a larger regional picture, and conclusions about the movements of subfamilies such as Bantu must be seen in relation to other groups with which they came in contact. Most notable were the Nilotic tribes that were encountered as they moved eastward and the indigenous Khoikoi

(Khoisan-speaking) peoples, who were the earlier occupants of much of southern Africa (IV in Figure 7.5).

C. Ehret and other contemporary Africanists have overhauled and revised earlier classifications of African languages and developed new perspectives on African history. The overall picture of the Bantu dispersal remains much as was outlined by Guthrie, but the recent work adds many details and, in some cases, makes new interpretations of the data. The most striking revision is that the time depth of Niger-Congo can now be extended as far back as 5000 B.C., with proto-Ubangi and proto-Bantu located as neighboring speech communities in the Cameroon region. Both these groups were slash-and-burn farmers and fishers living in a mixed rain forest and savanna zone; they raised cowpeas, sesame, calabashes, and yams (all West African domesticates). The Ubangi evidently herded goats, while the Bantu also raised some cattle—later to be replaced by the East African humped variety.

Ubangi- and Bantu-speaking populations gradually spread eastward in a roughly parallel fashion. The Ubangi group remained well north of the Congo, hewing to the course of the Ubangi River and its tributaries the Uele and Mbomu; their momentum carried them almost to the upper reaches of the White Nile. The Bantu expansion followed a path between the Congo and the Ubangi. There the population divided, one branch moving south by southwest down the lower Congo to its mouth, and the other following the Luabala southeastward toward Lake Tanganyika. It is in this latter region, bounded by the Luabala, Lake Tanganyika, and Lake Victoria, that Ehret locates the ancestral tongue from which the "modern languages of the eastern half of the Bantu area"—Swazi, Zulu, Sotho, Swahili, and others—developed. Here, significant cultural innovations were adopted—new crops, including grains (sorghum and finger millet); humped cattle, adapted to the grasslands of East Africa; and iron-working.

It should be noted that use of the comparative method makes it possible to distinguish between ancient cultural features, insofar as these are represented by terms present in a proto-language, and more recent innovations. As seen below, a proto-Bantu term for *cattle* can be identified (a); this was lost in some languages and, in some, reapplied to the water buffalo. Later, the ancestral language of the southern Bantus had terms for livestock (b) that are traceable, as loanwords, to (d) Central Sudanic (IIIC in Figure 7.5), suggesting that pastoral Nilotic peoples—ancestors of tribes such as the Nuer and Dinka—were the source of the Bantus' "cattle complex." It may be noted that similar borrowed vocabulary (c) is found in the languages of cattle-herding Khoisan groups:

(a)	(b)	(c)	(d)
			*P-Central Sudanic
*Proto-Bantu	*P-SW Bantu	*P-Khwe (Khoisan)	(Nilo-Saharan)
*nyaka *cattle*	*-twe-gu *bull*	*gu *sheep*	*g'u *animal, livestock*
	* -gu *sheep*		

Source: Ehret, 1982b

MACROFAMILIES AND REMOTE RELATIONSHIPS

Linguists generally agree on using the term *language family* to refer to a group of languages whose historical relationship and common origin are proved beyond doubt by systematic comparisons and the reconstruction of an ancestral language or *protolanguage*. They are far less unanimous about larger groupings—*macrofamilies*, or *phyla*—that assert the existence of more distant relationships between languages and/or language families. For more than a century, there have been suggestions of such relationships, variously based on traditional history, cultural ties, or selected similarities in vocabulary or other linguistic features. Most linguists defer judgment until the suggestions are substantiated by application of the comparative method (and, thus, the establishment of a language-family relationship).

This conservatism is understandable, but is frustrating to those researchers who are seeking a way to bridge the gap between the 6,000 to 8,000 years of time depth yielded by traditional comparative methods, and the 100,000 (or more) years during which *Homo sapiens* has multiplied and languages have diversified. Two recent approaches to this problem have been undertaken by prominent scholars in Russia and the United States.

THE NOSTRATIC HYPOTHESIS

A project begun by V. Illic-Svityc and continued under the leadership of A. Dolgopolsky builds on earlier suggestions that link the Indo-European family with Uralic (Finno-Ugric), Altaic (Turkic), and/or Afro-Asiatic (Hamito-Semitic). These four groups, plus the Dravidian family, Kartvelian (Georgian and related languages of the southern Caucasus), and Korean make up the proposed macrofamily known as *Nostratic*.

The Russian scholars have extended the comparative method, using reconstructed protofamily lexicon and selectively focusing on lexemes identified as "conservative" or stable (i.e., least likely to change); these words, if retained as *archaisms*, may provide clues to ancient history. The most stable vocabulary includes pronouns, especially the first- and second-person singular; interrogatives, such as "who?" and "what?"; verbal negatives and prohibitives; locatives, body parts, and certain kinship categories.[7]

The complex chain of proposed phonological correspondences supporting the reconstructed Nostratic forms are not discussed here; however, three relatively simple (and highly recognizable) examples may be examined:

1. Nostratic **mi "I": IE *me-; Kart *me/*mi; AA *mi,-*mi; Uralic *mi; Altaic *bi/*mi-n.

2. Nostratic ** k'udi "tail": IE *kaud- (Latin cauda/coda); AA *k'dr; Kart *k'wad-/k'ud-; Alt *k'udi-rga; and so on.

---

[7]It may be recalled that M. Swadesh's lexicostatistics employs a similar distinction between noncultural (and presumably stable) and cultural (and variable) lexicon.

3. Nostratic ** bari "take": IE *bʰer "take, bring, carry"; AA *br- "sieze, catch"; Alt *bari- "take"; Drav *per- "pick up, gather. . . .

A "WORLDWIDE WEB" OF LANGUAGES

Joel Greenberg approaches the problem of language taxonomy on a continent-wide and even a worldwide basis, drawing vocabulary from individual languages. Thus, he may skip—or postpone—the reconstruction of protolanguage forms at the family level while at the same time assessing evidence for wider connections linking families. The work of Greenberg and his colleagues has been controversial, exciting great interest (especially among nonlinguists) while drawing fire from conservative linguistic scholars, who generally insist on the traditional comparative method as a check on the validity of proposed relationships.

In *The Languages of Africa* (1967), Greenberg undertook a broad classification of African languages into four macrofamilies (Afro-Asiatic, Congo-Kordofanian, Nilo-Saharan, and Khoisan). Although deemed radical at the time, these groupings are now generally accepted (see Figure 7.5). In *Language in the Americas* (1987), Greenberg put forth even more sweeping proposals, consolidating the roughly 1,500 languages of North and South America into three macrofamilies, only one of which—Amerind—is confined to the New World, and suggesting links between Old and New World groups (building on earlier suggestions by Edward Sapir and others).

Assessing the implications of Greenberg's work, Merrit Ruhlen indicates that "the world's languages can be classified into as few as a dozen [macro]families." These may be listed as:

1. Khoisan
2. Niger-Kordofanian (a. Kordofanian, b. Niger-Congo)
3. Nilo-Saharan
4. Australian
5. Indo-Pacific (= Papuan)
6. Austric (a. Austroasiatic, b. Miao-Yao, c. Daic, d. Austronesian)
7. Dene-Caucasian (a. Basque, b. Caucasian, c. Burushaski, d. Nahali, e. Sino-Tibetan, f. Yeneseian, g. Na-Déné)
8. Afro-Asiatic
9. Kartvelian
10. Dravidian
11. Eurasiatic (a. Indo-European, b. Uralic, c. Altaic, d. Korean-Japanese-Ainu, e. Gilyak, f. Chukchi-Kamchatkan, g. Eskimo-Aleut)
12. Amerind

(Ruhlen, 1994)

The fact that Greenberg and Dolgopolsky arrive at remarkably different assessments of the affiliation of several language families should serve as a caution against accepting either uncritically.[8] Nonetheless, Greenberg's proposals have been heralded by geneticist Luca Cavalli-Sforza and other researchers, who support their own theories of human biological origins by pointing to a rough correspondence between boundaries defined by gene frequencies and macrofamily linguistic groupings.

PROTOWORLD

The trend in taxonomic research by Greenberg and his colleagues is clearly toward reduction of diversity, to ultimately arrive at a demonstration of the monogenesis of the world's languages; in this respect, it is the counterpart of Greenberg's pioneering work in language typology (as discussed in chapter 3). In a recent publication, John D. Bergstrom and Merrit Ruhlen list 25 proposed "global etymologies" that appear to override family and macrofamily divisions. As an example, the listing under KANO "arm" includes vocabulary drawn from roughly 100 languages, including:

!Kung	//kau "branch"
Swahili	m-kono "arm, forearm"
Iraqw	kun-day "foot"
English	hand "hand"
Hungarian	hon "armpit"
Yukaghir	xanba "hand"
Yeneseian	*ken "shoulder"
Vietnamese	canh "arm, branch, wing"
Blackfoot	kin-sts "hand"
Piro	kano "arm"
Botocudo	kinaon "shoulder"

Intriguing as such resemblances may be, it should be remembered that each set of potential cognates represents a tiny fraction (in most cases, less than 1%) of the world's languages. Most linguists would caution that chance may play a role, that the influence of lexical borrowing must be recognized, and that only systematic comparative research can establish connections beyond doubt.

INTERNAL AND EXTERNAL INFLUENCES IN LINGUISTIC CHANGE

As already described, the comparative method is the accepted approach for demonstrating relationships among languages. It is based on the occurrence of *internally motivated* changes—changes that occur within each speech

---

[8]Both Eurasiatic and Nostratic include Indo-European, Uralic, Altaic, and Korean; to these, Nostratic adds Afro-Asiatic, Kartvelian, and Dravidian, while Eurasiatic adds Japanese, Ainu, Gilyak, Chukchi-Kamchatkan, and Eskimo-Aleut.

LINGUISTIC INNOVATIONS IN LOKONO

In my file of Lokono vocabulary, I can identify roughly 6% of the entries as loanwords—a fairly typical number. Almost all of these can easily be traced to three European languages, reflecting the history of European exploration and colonization. Spanish ships explored the northeastern coast of South America around 1500, and Amerigo Vespucci led an expedition through the the Guianas soon thereafter. Dutch intrusions began around 1590, followed by settlements, and the Dutch East India Company made claim to most of the region in 1621. By the mid-18th century, land concessions had been granted to British planters from the West Indies, who established plantations along many of the major rivers. In 1831, following a series of treaties, Britain purchased territory from Holland and established the colony of British Guiana. This became the independent nation of Guyana in 1966; English is the dominant language, while Dutch continues in use in neighboring Surinam.

LOANWORDS

The obvious Spanish influence on the Lokono language appears to be, in large part, a heritage from early times, although some continuing contact (direct or indirect) with Spanish speakers may continue in the ill-defined Guyana-Venezuela border region. Numerous Spanish loanwords can be identified, as the names of common items of material culture, domestic plants and animals, and so on: *kauaiu* horse, donkey; *karina* chicken, hen; *poroko* pig, swine; *kaburitu* goat; *pero* dog; *puratuna* plantain; *kimisa* cloth; *sapata* shoe; *senta* ribbon; *akosa* needle; *molo* mill; *uela* sail; *semana* week; *epaniol* Spaniard. The Spanish component is a stable part of Lokono vocabulary; similar items (such as *sambuleru*, hat and *kampana*, bell) are also present in the Lokono spoken in coastal Surinam.

One loanword is of special interest: *arakabusa*, gun. The matchlock harquebus was the first gun that could be easily carried and fired by a single individual. It was invented in Germany in the mid-15th century and was in wide use by European armies until supplanted by the flintlock musket, roughly a century later. Harquebuses would have been carried by some of the earliest European invaders of the Indies and the mainland of South America. The form of the Lokono word suggests that the Spanish *arcabuza* was its source, rather than the Dutch *haakbus* or English *hackbut*. Thus, linguistic evidence attests to contacts in the late 15th or early 16th century—probably the period of the strongest direct Spanish influences on Lokono language and culture.

Words of Dutch origin are also numerous. Like the Spanish loans, they provide the names of domestic animals, plants, and artifacts of European origin: *lepele* spoon (*lepel*); *hemede* shirt (*hemd*); *hemode* jacket (*hemd*);[9] *sepo* soap (*zeep*); *tafolo* table (*tafel*); *sikapu* sheep; *kopero* brass or copper pot (*koper*); *sikaro* sugar (*suiker*); *sopi* rum (*zoopje*); *paipa* pipe; *kana* jar, can; *planka* board, flooring; *skulu* school; *risi* rice (*rijst*); *kofi* coffee. The last six words could come from either Dutch or English; however, it seems likely that such common cultural items would have been introduced early, under Dutch influence, rather than later—though English may have reinforced the use of these words.

One set of words evidently began as borrowings from Dutch, later to be reshaped by English influence: the days of the week, for example, *mondaka* Monday, *uensdaka* Wednesday. Here, -daka appears to come from the Dutch -tag, while the initial syllables have been modified toward English models. Today, Lokono speakers in Guyana are as little aware of the Dutch

---

[9]Note that the Lokono words have evidently become differentiated, subsequent to the original borrowing of a single Dutch model.

influences in their language as they are of the Spanish. By contrast, the Lokono of Surinam appears to contain more recent Dutch loans, reflecting the continuing use of the Dutch language there.

Unlike the Spanish and Dutch borrowings, which have been thoroughly assimilated to the Lokono phonological system, English words can be heard in the speech of bilingual individuals in fairly unmodified form—dates, product names, names of the months, holidays, and so on. A few probable English borrowings appear to be older, stabilized vocabulary—for example, *iono* onion; *aleti* lamp, light; *diara* jar; *tioti* church; and *blu-* blue. The words *mama* and *papa* (as kinship terms of address, not reference) could be from Spanish, Dutch, or English; as might *aransu* orange and *koko* coconut.

Loan Blends

A rough test of the integration of loanwords into the lexicon is that they occur in inflected forms. In Lokono, borrowed nouns are found in combination with pronominal prefixes and the suffix that indicates possession: thus, *dakartan* my book; *deperon* my dog; *daborokon* my trousers; *demeden* my shirt; *dabaskitan* my basket; *dakosate* my needle; *dasepoia* my soap; *dafrenia* my friend.

The adjective *blu-*, like other color terms, usually occurs with the suffix *-to*: *bluto* (it is) blue. *Danki* thanks, thank you could come from the Dutch "dank u" or from English—perhaps an archaic "thank ye"; this salutation is the base for a derived Lokono verb *dankida* to thank. Similarly, *odida* to greet may be have its source in English "howdy."

With native Lokono bases, the suffix *-da* serves to derive verbs from nouns, as in

arua tiger, *aruada* to creep. It is especially productive in combination with borrowings—be they salutations (as just mentioned), adjectives, verbs, or nouns in the source languages. Additional examples are: *plantiada* to iron; *uelada* to sail, *remoda* to row; *leseda* to read (from Dutch "lesen"); and *sportdua* to debauch (from English "sport"). The method of forming Lokono verbs was evidently well understood by 19th-century English missionaries; biblical texts yield, for example, *praiseda*, *prophiseda*, *circumciseda* and *sacrificeda*.

Numerous compound terms blend native and borrowed nouns: *karinasa* (*karina* + *osa* child) hen's egg; *aletira* (*aleti* + *ura* juice) lamp oil; *sikaroko* (*sikaro* + *oko* pus) sugar-cane sap; *poroko kihi* (*poroko* + *kihi* fat) pork; *baka siroko* (*baka* + *siroko* flesh) beef.

New Formations

A nominalizing suffix *-kuanahu*, *-kuana-* provides a convenient way to form new vocabulary; this might be compared with the English suffix *-er*, which can be added to a verb to derive an instrumental or agentive noun. Some examples are: *arukuanahu* (*aruka* cut) scissors; *akaratokuanahu* (*akarata* bury) coffin; *daridakuanahu* (*darida* run) bicycle; *adukuanahu* (*aduka* see) mirror; *uamaritakuanti* (*ua-* our + *marita* make + *kuana-* + *-ti* masculine) God (literally, "our creator").

Loan Shifts

Several common Lokono nouns have been extended in meaning to apply to new culture items: *simara* arrow, gun; *hikihi* fire, match; *kasakabo* day, Christmas Day; *uatinati* our father; God.

community, as the cumulative result of countless instances of unconscious variation in the speech habits of individuals. These changes eventually give rise to regular phonological correspondences among sister languages; in turn, the correspondences provide tangible proof of the relatedness of the languages.

But internal developments are not the only influences that lead to change in languages. Changes, large and small, also originate in sources external to the language and speech community. The most obvious type of *externally motivated* changes consist of the borrowing of vocabulary from one language to another. These *loanwords* usually accompany and mirror the diffusion of culture traits. When new ideas—technological innovations, religious movements, medical practices, fashions in clothing or cuisine—are adopted, terminology may be borrowed at the same time. In the past, such events might be assumed to result from direct contacts between communities or nations; today, cultural and linguistic innovations can spread very rapidly by way of modern communications media.

Still, borrowed terms that have become a stable part of vocabulary often do provide evidence of past cultural contacts and even give clues to the time and nature of the contacts. Though less obvious than outright borrowing of vocabulary, other linguistic innovations may also occur. This usually happens under circumstances of prolonged cultural contact: *loan blends*, when borrowed and native morphemes are combined; *loan shifts*, when the meaning of native terms is modified in order to accommodate to cultural changes; as well as the outright coinage of new terms.

THE HISTORY OF THE ENGLISH LANGUAGE

Like all languages, English has been shaped over time by many different influences; some of these can be identified, while others cannot. The fact that English has a centuries-old written tradition certainly makes it possible to trace its evolution in more detail than can be done in the case of Bantu, Algonkian, or Arawakan. However, inference still plays a role, and unrecorded events (such as the time or circumstances of contacts with speakers of other languages) must sometimes be reconstructed from the available linguistic evidence. The English lexicon is rich in words that attest to such events and that mirror economic, social, and political currents over many centuries; a staggering 75% of the vocabulary comes from foreign sources.

Archaeologists trace a history of the British Isles that begins with hand-ax cultures of the Lower Paleolithic period, at least 200,000 years ago. The linguistic identity of these early Britons and their Upper Paleolithic successors, who began the construction of the great stone circles at sites like Stonehenge and Avebury, must remain a mystery. Celtic speakers may have brought Neolithic culture to England, on the westernmost margin of the great Indo-European dispersal. By the time Caesar's legions arrived, more than 2,000 years ago, the islands were occupied by a number of different Celtic-speaking peoples.

OLD ENGLISH

English is a western Germanic language. Its history begins at the end of the Roman occupation, around 400 A.D. The Romans had built Hadrian's Wall to defend their northern frontier from intermittent attacks by Celtic tribes and frequently had to beat back the attacks of Germanic raiders along the eastern coast. When the legions withdrew, the invaders from across the channel began to arrive in large numbers and establish permanent settlements. Speakers of several western Germanic dialects were represented, all usually identified simply as Anglo-Saxons. As these newcomers arrived, the remaining Celts retreated or were assimilated; Celtic languages survived in the extreme west of England, in Scotland, Ireland, and Wales, and in Brittany in northern France. Very few Celtic words were borrowed by the Anglo-Saxons of this period—a handful of terms for landscape features, including *tor* (a high peak), *crag* (a rock formation), and several place names. Many Irish and Scots words have, of course, entered the English vocabulary in more recent years (*clan, kilt, shillelagh, brogue*).

Historical linguists divide the history of English into three stages—Old English (450–1150), Middle English (1150–1500), and Modern English (after 1500). In the first of these periods, the separate tribal identities of the original Germanic invaders gradually became submerged. Early dialects still recalled the continental regions from which they derived, and the country became divided into seven kingdoms—Angles in Northumbria, Mercia, and East Anglia; Jutes in Kent; and Saxons in Essex, Sussex, and Wessex.

By the eighth century, the country as a whole was called Englaland, and its people, despite their regional divisions, shared a distinctive culture and language. This language was still close to continental Germanic in its complex systems of verbal conjugations; inflections of adjectives, articles, and pronouns; and declensions of nouns, with three gender categories of masculine, feminine, and neuter. Nouns exhibited a great variety of plural formations—many with unpredictable vowel mutations (retained today in a few words like *feet*, *men*, and *mice*), others with -en (as in *children* and *oxen*), and still others with -s.

Dialectal variation, in vocabulary and in grammatical features, became less important over time. The population increased, and intermarriage and interregional trade served to link what had been disparate groups. New influences came from the continent of Europe; one of the most significant was an intense wave of Christian missionizing that began with the arrival, in 601, of St. Augustine and a group of 40 monks. This marks the beginning of a long history of Latin influences on English; however, Old English was highly productive in forming new vocabulary through compounding and derivation. Words such as *eahrring* (earring), *gladmodnes* (gladness), and *ealohus* (alehouse) date from this period, as do religious terms such as *god-spell* (gospel), *Halig Gast* (Holy Ghost, based on the Latin *spiritus sanctus*), and *pre-osthad* (priesthood). A byproduct of the Latin influence was the gradual acceptance of the Roman alphabet. Roman and Anglo-Saxon writing systems coexisted for many years, with the older Anglo-Saxon lettering especially common on signboards in public establishments; but by the end of the millennium, Roman script was in general use.

Toward the end of the eighth century a new invasion began, which would interrupt the development of Anglo-Saxon civilization and would have a major impact on the English language. Scandinavian raiders—called Vikings, or Danes—sailed across the North Sea in longboats, attacking outlying villages and sacking the monastaries that were the leading seats of learning. The full force of these attacks came in the ninth century, when it became clear that the objective was conquest; fleets of Viking ships sailed up the rivers, and Danish settlements became established throughout the north of England. Finally the advance was halted by King Alfred the Great, who rallied an army and led a counterattack to regain English territory. Following Alfred's victory in 865, the invaders retreated to the north of England, a region that became known as the Danelaw. Danes and English eventually intermarried; the Danish settlers adopted Christianity, and new churches and monastaries were built. However, education and literacy had suffered a tremendous setback, and the influence of Latin declined. Beginning in Alfred's reign, English developed as a language of literary expression, and educated people began to use English rather than Latin.

Many English placenames still reflect the Scandinavian influence—for example, those ending in *-thorp* (village), *-thwait* (piece of land), or *-by*, from *-byr* (farm)—thus, Althorpe, Micklethwait, Rugby, and so on. In England, such names are still concentrated in the former Danelaw, but they have been spread worldwide by English migration. The ninth and tenth centuries, following the coming of the Vikings, saw changes in the English language that went far beyond the borrowing of vocabulary. As Danish and English speakers began living side by side, their dialects (northern and western Germanic, respectively) began to merge—with consequences that no linguist would have predicted and that make English unique among the Germanic languages.

The Danish and Anglo-Saxon dialects of ninth-century England may have been, to a degree, mutually intelligible. Many of the word bases were similar, or even identical; what set them apart and interfered with intelligibility were the endings—the case declensions, verb inflections, plurals, and so forth. The English language that came out of this encounter of dialects could be considered a sort of western Germanic *pidgin* that retained what Danish and Anglo-Saxon had in common and dropped the confusing parts—the endings. As a result, the grammatical structure of English was radically overhauled and simplified; it now stands apart from all of its linguistic kin in its relative lack of inflection, which became reduced to the indication of number in nouns and tense in verbs.

At the same time, as a consequence of this simplification in word morphology, English became increasingly reliant on syntactic rules. This means that word order had to provide the sort of information about word relations that was formerly carried by inflectional morphemes. Therefore, word order is less flexible than it is in Latin or German, and phrases are sometimes necessary, to do the work that an instrumental or ablative case form might do more concisely.

Roughly 1,000 common words in modern English are of Scandinavian origin—for example: *axle, dirt, freckle, awkward, happy,* and *sly*. There are a fair number of doublets—Danish and English forms of the same Germanic root—that give us similar words with only slightly different meanings: *no, nay; whole, hale; shatter, scatter; wagon, wain* (hay-wagon).

MIDDLE ENGLISH

The Middle English period opened with a new tide of influences from the mainland of Europe. Normandy, on the French coast, had been overrun by Viking invaders just as England was. Over the intervening two to three centuries, these Vikings (Norsemen, or Normans) had adopted French customs and the French language while still retaining political ties with their kin in England. The prominence of Norman advisors in the English court began with the reign of Edward the Confessor, who came from Normandy to take the throne. On his death, an English prince, Harold Godwin, was crowned as king. However, William of Normandy, Edward's cousin, raised an army and crossed the channel to press his own claim. He defeated Harold at the Battle of Hastings in September of 1066 and took the English crown on Christmas Day.

For several decades thereafter, relations were strained between the Norman court of William the Conqueror and an older English nobility, who generally spoke no French. However, William gave favors to his supporters and siezed many properties that were then distributed to a new Norman elite. Soon, Normans had become entrenched in the positions of prominence in government and the church. For three centuries, all the kings of England spoke only French, and the sons of the nobility were generally sent to Normandy to be educated. The French language was a status symbol; Englishmen of Norman ancestry "had nothing but scorn for local customs and language." English declined as a written language; works of literature, diplomatic correspondence, royal edicts, and public records were generally composed in French, while Latin kept its place in the church and universities. Only the *Anglo-Saxon Chronicle*, begun by Alfred the Great and continued by the monks of Peterborough Abbey, continued to record events in the English language (Barnett, 1970).

To judge by the written evidence, English might appear to have become almost extinct during these years; but actually, it was never really threatened. Between the 11th and 14th centuries, a type of *diglossia* situation prevailed in English society, in which two languages coexisted, each used in a different set of contexts. French was the language of higher prestige, the language of education and literature, used in teaching and in formal situations. English was the language of the common people, the home, and most informal settings. Relatively few people outside the royal court were native speakers of French, but an ability to use French was necessary for the achievement of status and for employment in respectable occupations. There was, therefore, a great impetus for socially ambitious people to learn French. French-English bilingualism was especially typical of individuals in middle-status positions—local government officials, businessmen, military officers, or parish priests—who had to deal both with ordinary people and with higher authorities.

By the 13th century, the sharp divide between English and Norman had begun to be modified, through intermarriage and social mingling at all levels except the court and high nobility. On the continent, King Philip II of France took possession of Normandy in 1204; this influenced the English ruling classes to gravitate away from their orientation toward France. At about the same time, there was a sense of social revolt in the older English country elite and the middle classes that encouraged the increased use of English in public affairs. By the mid-14th century, official proclamations were routinely issued in both French and English. Some schools had also begun to permit English as a language of instruction; this became commonplace by the end of the century. It was in this milieu that Geoffrey Chaucer became the first prominent author to write in English rather than French; with this as a precedent, most popular literature came to be composed in English. By the end of this century, Parliament had ruled that all public business should be conducted in English; French, which was still needed in international diplomacy and commerce, had to be taught as a foreign language. Henry IV, who came to the throne in 1399, was the first king in almost 400 years whose first language was English. By this time, English had clearly prevailed over French.

Many traces of the period of French influence are still to be seen in the English language. Overall, around 10,000 French words "slid unobtrusively into English speech." Much of this vocabulary is concentrated in the areas of religion (including *prayer, friar, clergy, saint, miracle,* and even the word *religion* itself); government (*reign, parliament, minister, prince, duke,* and *nation*); and law (*justice, judge, marriage, property,* and *real estate*). French vocabulary is also prominent in the arts (*color, design, ornament*); sports (*chase, quarry, sport*); and games (*dice, cards,* and virtually the entire vocabulary of card-playing—*ace, deuce, trey, suit,* and *trump*). Finally, there is a long list of culinary terms, including *sauce, pastry, soup, jelly, cuisine, dinner,* and *supper.* It has been pointed out that the French names of various animals came into the English vocabulary to refer to meats, while English words still name the living animals: *beef, veal, mutton, pork,* and *venison* are of French origin, while *ox, cow, calf, sheep, pig,* and *deer* are from Old English. Thus, the English language was enriched and given greater expressive power by the infusion of French vocabulary. Chaucer chose to write in English, but roughly 50% of the words in his literary works are of either French or Latin origin—about the same as in modern usage.

Earlier trends still continued to shape English in the years after the Norman invasion. The tendency to grammatical simplification that had begun with Old English continued. Grammatical gender categories were lost, and a single article—*the*—now remained to do the work of three (*der, die, das*) in German. In this period, also, the -*s* plural, which had already become standard in northern dialects, prevailed over the -*en* plural that was more common in the south of England (*eyen, shoon,* and *housen* became *eyes, shoes,* and *houses*). This particular leveling may have been influenced by the fact that an -*s* plural is standard in French.

Several French derivational endings became productive in English, often added to English bases. Thus, we have -*age* in *acreage* and *breakage;* -*ess(e)* in *goddess;* -*ance* in *forbearance;* and -*able* in many words, including *kissable, readable,* and *understandable.* The French suffix -*e* became -*ee* in English, as in *trustee* and *mortgagee.* An example of the patchwork nature of the English vocabulary can be seen in the word *trusteeship*—*trust* is a Scandanavian contribution, -*ee* is from French, and -*ship* is an Anglo-Saxon word ending.

MODERN ENGLISH

Besides the obvious external influences, seen in the legion of loanwords that have entered the English language, a slow accumulation of internally motivated phonological changes has never ceased—changes of which the speakers in any given generation are completely unaware. Comparison of earlier and later spellings give a rough index of the time and rate of these changes, even though it may be impossible to recover the phonetic details of actual speech. Such a change took place, for example, when initial *sk-* in Anglo-Saxon words became *sh-* in Middle English; Scandinavian words with *sk-,* coming into English around 900 A.D., do not show this change. Thus, the Anglo-Saxon *scyrte* gives us *shirt,* while the nearly identical Scandinavian *skyrta* became *skirt.* Similarly, *ship, shall,* and *fish* are of Anglo-Saxon origin, while *sky, scrub,* and *whisk* come from the Scandinavian lexicon.

The most striking sound changes, which might well interfere with our ability to understand Old or Middle English, affected the quality of vowels. Between Chaucer's time and and Shakespeare's, there occurred a series of sweeping phonological changes known to linguists as the Great Vowel Shift. The effects of this "shift" are seen most clearly in long vowels, which were generally raised. This seems to be simply the consequence of a gradual change in habits of articulation—words came to be pronounced with a higher elevation of the tongue. Other changes during the same period include simplifications of diphthongs and a tendency to weaken short vowels (to a central) or, in word-final position, to drop them entirely. Thus, "name" in Chaucer's Middle English was pronounced [na:mə]; a few hundred years later, it was [ne:m], as it is today. Middle English "clean" was [klɛ:nə]; by Shakespeare's time, it was [kle:n], and since then it has been further raised to [kli:n]. These and other changes amounted to a complete transformation of the vocalic sounds of English—another striking point of contrast to the continental Germanic tongues.

At the end of the 15th century, an important technological innovation made its appearance: the printing press with movable type, which had been invented around 1450 in Germany by Johannes Gutenberg. In 1474, William Caxton set up a press at Westminster, where he printed Chaucer's *Canterbury Tales* and around 100 other works, including the first English encyclopedia. Caxton and other early printers began to establish uniform conventions of spelling. Because these were based primarily on the dialect of London and its environs, this central dialect soon gained status as the correct or standard form of the English language.

The dominant intellectual movement in the early Modern period was the Renaissance, a new awakening of interest in classical literature and philosophy—works that the printing press made accessible to the educated public. As one result, a new wave of Latin and Greek words and phrases came into English and the continental languages. Unlike earlier external influences, this one spread more through print than by word of mouth. From the 16th century up to the present day, these ancient languages have been a rich source for scientific and literary terminology. From Greek we have scientific and scholarly terms—*arithmetic, logic, rhetoric,* and *astronomy*—and a large body of words related to the theatre, such as *prologue, scene, climax,* and *critic.* The input from Latin is especially large and expands the resources of English both for expressing fine semantic distinctions and for setting the tone in writing or speech. Terms derived from Latin are often considered more scholarly or formal, while the shorter Anglo-Saxon words seem simpler or more informal—thus, magnitude versus size, or ponderous versus weighty. (Most of the "four-letter words" used in swearing are, in fact, Anglo-Saxon.)

The 16th century also launched the Age of Exploration. England competed with Spain, Portugal, France, and the Netherlands in a search for new trade routes, resources, and territories. From this time forward, the English vocabulary has been enriched by many borrowings that come, directly or indirectly, from hundreds of different languages, including the native tongues of Africa, the Americas, and the Pacific. Many of these loanwords provided the names of exotic plants and animals, hitherto unknown in western Europe. The first known English borrowing from a Native American language was "arrathkune," an Algonkian word first recorded in 1610 by Captain John Smith; a variety of spellings appeared, but *raccoon* eventually became the standard form. Words like this have become international vocabulary, some by way of English, others via Spanish, French, and other world languages. A number of words from Nahuatl, the language of the Aztec civilization of Mexico, came to English from Spanish—*tomato, chocolate,* and *avocado,* for example.

By 1700, the English vocabulary already included words (almost all of them nouns) from at least 50 different languages. Other languages share the tendency to borrow vocabulary, but English is especially open to the process. The absence of gender classes and case affixes makes it easy to take in foreign words, and the simplicity of inflection means that those words can be used immediately (whatever their grammatical status or functions in the source language). The Inuit word /iɣlu/ could have been borrowed (as *igloo*), supplied with the proper English plural suffix ([-z]), and used with complete freedom by any speaker of English; the fact that the plural in the source language is /iɣlut/ is completely irrelevant.

VERB-ADVERB COMBINATIONS: A RECENT TREND.   The frequent use of verb-adverb predicates is a striking development in recent English. Combinations of this sort were not unknown in earlier centuries but were usually literal in their meaning—*climb up, get up, fall down*, and so on. In 20th-century English, the great majority are figurative or idiomatic—*catch on, clean up, knock off, crack down*. The verbs are typically short—more often Anglo-Saxon than Latin. Baugh and Cable (1993) list 20 verbs that occur in more than 150 combinations: *back, blow, break, bring, call, come, fall, get, give, go, hold, lay, let, make, put, run, set, take, turn, work*. The most productive adverb appears to be *up*, though *down, in, out*, and *off* are also very common, and two or even three adverbs sometimes occur in sequence (*give up on, go through with, fall out with*, and the like). Many of the same combinations are also used as nouns; these are usually (but not always) hyphenated when written: for example, *break-in, breakdown, crack-up, crackdown, run-around, run-down, hang-up, hangout, handout, put-down, runaway*.

Baugh and Cable see the increasing use of verb-adverb sequences as a new development in the general trend toward simplification of word structure and greater reliance on word order that began with Old English. These tendencies may have been interrupted or retarded by the large-scale introduction of influences from French and Latin, but they still have great vitality in English today. The verb-adverb constructions do not replace the longer Latin-derived verbs, which often seem formal or academic; but they can substitute for them. This means that another set of choices is available to speakers of English: *keep on* versus *continue; give up* versus *surrender; set up* versus *establish; take in* versus *comprehend; put up with* versus *endure* or *tolerate*; and so on. Choices of this sort, reflecting the diverse sources and complex history of English, can be drawn upon to define a social setting, adapt to a situation, or set a mood (Baugh & Cable, 1993).

5

LANGUAGE AND CULTURE

A language enables its speakers to relate to the natural and social environment, to describe and identify things and events, to organize and coordinate their activities. However, no language is, in any sense, an exact and perfect copy of the real world. This is inevitably the case because the range of stimuli and sensory experiences encountered by any individual is vast in number and to some extent unique (differing from the experiences of every other individual). Every apple or snowflake, every butterfly or human being can be distinguished from every other; however, the vocabulary of each language names classes of such things. The English word "'apple'," for example, is ordinarily applied to fruit that may be large or small, ripe or unripe, and that comes in varieties that differ in shape, taste, and color. It might not be obvious to someone unfamiliar with this fruit that all varieties, whether green, yellow, or red, are "'apples'"; it is conceivable that another language might use two or more labels to cover this range of variation or might distinguish the several varieties (Rome, Delicious, Winesap, Jonathan, and so on) without a more inclusive term. In any case, the names that are applied stand for generalizations—they lump together an unlimited number of individual specimens on the basis of selected characteristics.

We can go further than this: Because such categories are generalizations based on only a selection from a range of the observable characteristics, there can be differences among languages in the way the categories are defined. In fact, there *are* many such differences, and they contribute to the difficulty that we experience in translating from one language to another. This difficulty is not very great when we are dealing with such things as apples, axes, birds, or fish, or the sun, moon, and stars—all of these are delimited by definite boundaries. More problems arise when we confront the ways in which continuous or unlimited areas of experience are broken up and categorized in different languages. Wholes (like the human body) are divided into parts, time and space are segmented into units for counting and measuring, and sensory experiences like sounds, tastes, and colors are grouped and classified The verbal "maps" for this kind of reality can be remarkably different, exhibiting the kind of incongruities that have made some philosophers claim that real translation among languages is impossible.

A basic similarity, as well as obvious differences, can be seen if we compare the anatomical vocabulary of English with that other languages, for example Lokono (of South America) and Oʔodham, or Papago (of North America). Each of these (like most, if not all, languages) has a special set of terms that segment the body into areas and parts. But there seems to be no natural or inevitable way to accomplish this segmentation. For example, the division between "'hand'" and "'arm'," which seems natural and obvious to the speaker of English, is contrary to the distinction made in Lokono, where *-kabo* refers to the hand and lower arm, *-duna* to the upper arm and shoulder. It is also contrary to the Oʔodham *nowi*, which includes the whole arm as well as the hand. (see Figure 5.1).

Note that differences of this sort can be easily overlooked. A speaker of Lokono who has learned English is likely to simply equate *-kabo* with *hand* and to translate it regularly in that way. The subtle difference in meaning will not usually emerge in direct questioning, which is apt to produce such an exchange as:

FIGURE 5.1

English, Arawak, and Oʔodham terms for the hand and arm.

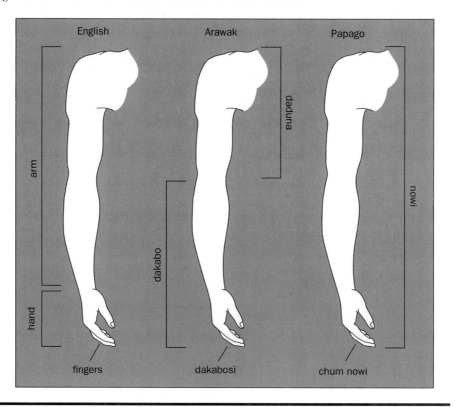

q: "What is the word for 'hand'?"

a: "Dakabo" (Literally, "my hand." In Lokono, body parts, children, and other "inalienable" nouns always require possessive prefixes.)

Or, perhaps:

q: What does "dakabo" mean?

a: It means "your hand." (It is literally "my hand," but the answerer is using the English pronoun in response to the questioner.)

I have elicited Lokono anatomical terms simply by touching or pointing to various areas of the body and recording the words given in response. Other field workers have been known to use anatomical diagrams or models in an effort to get at the meaning of terms while avoiding the kind of influence of one language on the other that could accompany bilingual questioning or the use of a translator as intermediary.

Anthropologists who have done both linguistic and ethnographic research have often remarked on the close connections between particular languages and cultures. Franz Boas, who encouraged anthropologists to study both the languages and the cultures of native peoples, did his first field work in 1883–1884 among the Central Eskimo of Canada. He later published a book on Eskimo culture as well as a study of the language, in which he commented on the large number of words available for naming and referring to such important features of environment as "snow", "ice," and "seal." Years later, in his introduction to *The Handbook of American Indian Languages*, Boas referred to this early study: In the language of the Central Eskimo, "the SEAL in different conditions is expressed by a variety of terms. One word is the general term for SEAL; another one signifies the SEAL BASKING IN THE SUN; a third one, a SEAL FLOATING ON A PIECE OF ICE; not to mention the many names for the seals of different ages and for the male and female" (Boas, 1911). Thus, while English has a single term *seal* and must form compounds (*seal calf, bull seal,* and so on) or use descriptive phrases, the Central Eskimos have a larger, more specialized vocabulary.

Boas's characterization of the Yupik (Eskimo) language has become a classic example, often cited to show a close connection between language and the content of culture. However, it simply illustrates a tendency that can be seen, to some degree, in all languages: Points of cultural emphasis are usually directly reflected in language through the size, specialization, and differentiation of vocabulary. That is, there are more separate terms, more synonyms or near-synonyms, and more fine distinctions in reference to features of environment or culture with which the speakers are the most concerned. There are fewer terms, and they tend to be more generalized when they refer to features that are given less cultural emphasis. "Cultural emphasis" may indicate environmental or economic factors that are critical to subsistence; it can also comprehend aesthetic, religious, and other kinds of values.

LANGUAGE AND WORLD VIEW

The classic anthropological approach to the relationship between language and culture is found in the writings of Benjamin L. Whorf[1] and in later discussion and development of his ideas as the *Whorf hypothesis*. Whorf made the basic assumptions that there is a close connection between language and culture and that the study of a language can give an indication of the categories and relationships—the "world view"—conceived by speakers of the language. This mirrored the opinions of Franz Boas and other founders of linguistic anthropology, perhaps most notably Whorf's teacher, Edward Sapir. However, Whorf went beyond Sapir and most of his contemporaries by assigning a priority to language in this relationship.

Let us return to the observation that the categories in language are, and must be, a sort of generalization based on the selection of a few (out of all possible) features. Whorf recognized this, and drew a corollary about the effects of this classification of experience on the psychology of the speakers of languages. He concluded that the *obligatory* categories in language and the features that speakers must notice condition the way in which they perceive and experience reallty. Each language, then, could be said to enforce its own peculiar logic on its speakers.

Whorf was concerned with English and other Western languages and also with various Native American languages of the southwestern United States. He began his interest in language as an amateur, while holding a professional position with an insurance firm; he had become interested in an apparent connection between the ways that language is used and the occurrence of accidents such as fires and explosions. For example, Whorf noted that "empty" gasoline drums are often treated carelessly, apparently because they are considered *empty* (despite the explosive vapor they still contain). Similarly, a highly flammable material called "spun limestone" was ignored as a fire hazard, apparently because workers assumed that "stone" is incombustible. Whorf proceeded from examples like this to see broader implications about linguistic patterning and its influence on behavior.

The non-European language that Whorf studied most methodically was Hopi, a Native American language of the southwestern United States. He wrote a grammar of Hopi and later published several articles, in both scholarly and popular journals, describing the world view he found expressed in the linguistic materials that he had collected (Whorf, 1956). In his later writings, Whorf often used Hopi as a contrast to what he called SAE (Standard Average European—English, French, German, etc.). Most of these comparisons focused on broad areas of meaning that he felt must be dealt with, in one way or another, by all languages. Whorf asked: "(1) Are our own

---

[1]Benjamin L. Whorf (1897–1941) was an amateur linguist but became highly influential through writings that presented his theories to a popular audience. Whorf studied Hebrew and several Native American languages, including Maya and Hopi.

concepts of 'time,' 'space', and 'matter' given in substantially the same form to all men, or are they in part conditioned by the structure of particular languages? (2) Are there traceable affinities between (a) cultural and behavioral norms, and (b) large-scale linguistic patterns?"

PLURALITY AND NUMERATION

SAE languages can form both "real" and "imaginary" plurals, for example, "ten men" and "ten days." "Ten men" can be seen and counted as a group and is thus a "real" plural; "ten days" is considered an "imaginary" plural because it cannot be objectively experienced as an aggregate. The latter is also an example of what Whorf considered a characteristic tendency of SAE to *objectify* time and treat it as if it were a measurable substance. Thus, we often speak of a "length of time," a "point in time," and "saving time."

Hopi does not form "imaginary" plurals; only objective aggregates can be counted. Units of time are treated as cyclic events, and time is not measured.

TEMPORAL FORMS OF VERBS

"The three-tense system of SAE verbs colors all our thinking about time." With our objectified sense of time, said Whorf, we "stand time units in a row" with boundaries between them, whereas in consciousness there is actually unity. Many non-SAE languages have, basically, two tenses—"earlier" and "later." Hopi verbs are marked by *validity forms*, which indicate whether the speaker reports, expects, or speaks from previous knowledge about the situation at hand; and *aspects*, which indicate duration and other tendencies of the action (see Figure 5.2). There is reference to *time* only when there are two clauses and two different actions, when modes indicate the temporal relationships (simultaneous, earlier, later).

For many readers, a discussion in this vein might have its greatest significance in giving some insight into the limitations of English. By seeing that Hopi may, at times, give a different and possibly more accurate picture of reality than does English or other SAE languages, one becomes aware of the arbitrary and incomplete nature of linguistic patterning, which might otherwise go unquestioned. Whorf argued that the contrasts go beyond the language itself and relate to differences in ways of thinking and perceiving. For individuals, this is the "thought world," the "microcosm that each man carries about within himself, by which he measures and understands what he can of the macrocosm."

The SAE microcosm, according to Whorf, sees the world in terms of "things" and imposes spatial forms on nonspatial aspects of existence. The Hopi microcosm, by contrast, "seems to have analyzed reality largely in terms of events (or better 'eventing')...." Perceptible physical events are seen as outlines, colors, movements; perceptible and nonperceptible events are described in terms of intensity, duration, cyclicity. The characteristics of Hopi culture that Whorf saw as related to these linguistic features is *an*

FIGURE 5.2

Contrast between a "temporal" language (English) and a "timeless" language (Hopi). What are to English differences of time are to Hopi differences in the kind of validity. Reprinted from *Language, Thought, and Reality* by Benjamin Lee Whorf by permission of The MIT Press, Cambridge, Massachusetts. Copyright 1956 by the Massachusetts Institute of Technology.

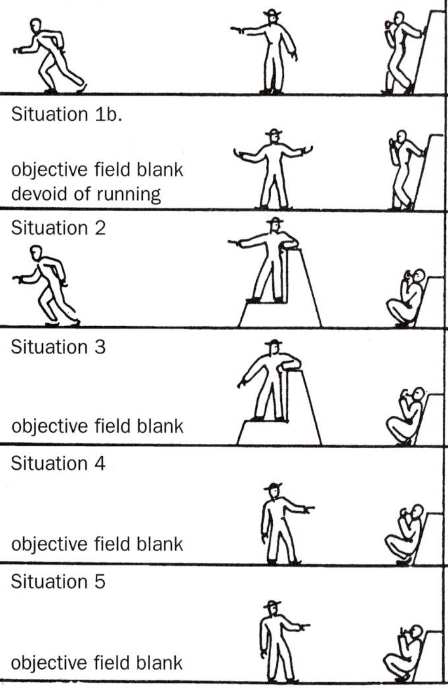

Objective Field	Speaker (sender)	Hearer (receiver)	Handling of topic Running of third person
Situation 1a.			English…"He is running" Hopi…"Wari" Running, statement of fact)
Situation 1b. objective field blank devoid of running			English…"He ran" Hopi…"Wari" (running, statement of fact)
Situation 2			English…"He is running" Hopi…"Wari" (running, statement of fact)
Situation 3 objective field blank			English…"He ran" Hopi…"Era wari" (running, statement of fact from memory)
Situation 4 objective field blank			English…"He will run" Hopi…"Warikni" (running, statement of expectation
Situation 5 objective field blank			English…"He runs" (e.g., on the track team) Hopi…"Warikngwe" (running, statement of law)

emphasis on preparation, especially in relation to religious ceremonials (which include a period of inner preparation in prayer and meditation, public announcement, and an emphasis on correct performance of a number of prescribed steps leading up to the public stage of the ceremonials) (Whorf 1941).

Whorf was not alone in hypothesizing a formative role for language in relation to thinking and cultural behavior. Dorothy D. Lee, Whorf's contemporary, discussed language as the means through which experience is codified, referring to various cultures, including the Greek, the Wintu of California, and the Trobriand Islands of Melanesia. Her views are quite similar to those of Whorf and Sapir (Lee, 1959). Whorf's writings achieved their greatest popularity in the 1950s, several years after his death. More recently, there have been efforts to test and restate the Whorf hypothesis of the influence of language on behavior in a more systematic and controlled way than did its originator (Lucy, 1992; Lucy & Schweder, 1979; see Hill & Mannheim, 1992, for additional references).

LANGUAGE AND CULTURAL EMPHASIS

Benjamin Whorf's goal was to identify parallels between the grammatical categories of language and the "logic" of culture. Assertions of such a relationship can be very persuasive, but they are difficult to prove. There is, however, a much more straightforward relationship between language and culture to be found by studying vocabulary. Here we can find semantic structures that relate closely to areas of cultural emphasis.

LEXICON

A time-honored example was seen in the number of specific terms referring to snow and ice, and to seals, in the Yupik (Eskimo) language as described by Franz Boas, discussed earlier. Eskimo life included a great emphasis on these features of environment, and they have a correspondingly high value in the traditional culture. A report by another famous author related specialized vocabulary to the economic and cultural importance of cattle and other animals in a pastoral society. The British anthropologist E. E. Evans-Pritchard wrote a classic ethnography of the Nuer, an East African society, revealing not only the many ways in which cattle are a focus of interest in the lives of these people, but also some of the linguistic reflexes of this interest.

In the following résumé, economic importance is reflected in the highly technical terminology with which the Nuer identify and endlessly discuss their cattle. Appreciation and concern for the cattle is clearly seen in the individual names and words of praise that are addressed to them; however, the high value attached to cattle herding also comes across—perhaps most strongly—in the transfer of cattle terminology into other areas of reference, such as personal names. Evans-Pritchard studied the Nuer in the 1930s, a time when they lived by a combination of millet farming and cattle herding. In earlier times they kept more cattle and did less farming, and their outlook on life was dominated by their pastoral concerns. They built, one might say, a pastoral ideology. Evans-Pritchard's work gives many examples of ways in which their constant preoccupation with cattle is reflected in the use of language (although he does not discuss language *per se*).

First, the Nuer have a rich and varied vocabulary for the identification and description of cattle and the natural features and cultural traits that have to do with cattle (the equipment and processes of dairy work, for example). A great profusion of words serves to identify individual cattle, especially in regard to their colors and markings. There are 10 "principal colour terms" to describe solid-colored animals (resembling white, black, chestnut, bay, etc.), about 27 terms for various combinations of white and another color, and special terms for rare combinations of more than two colors.

The descriptive vocabulary becomes more complicated, as there are many special words that name patterns of marking and various combinations of colors. For example, the term *rol* indlcates a white shoulder and foreleg, *kwe*, a white face; thus, *kwe rol* is a cow with this combination of markings; *rol kwac* indicates a white foreleg combined with black spots; and *kwe looka* is a mouse-gray cow with a white face. There are several hundred combinations of this sort.

But beyond these terms that have primary reference to the color and markings of the cattle, there are many others that metaphorically associate cattle with other animals, natural features, or objects. Again, the use of the words is based on the color and general appearance of the cattle. For example, spotted cattle can be called "leopard," "python," or "guinea-fowl," depending on the color or pattern of the spots. A black ox can be called "dark cloud" or "charcoal burning." Evans-Pritchard calls metaphoric terms of this sort the "fancy names" for cattle.

Further, there are six different terms for various configurations of horns; these are used in combination with any of the foregoing terms. And a long list of prefixed elements indicates the sex and age of the cattle, such as *tut*, "bull"; *yang*, "cow"; *nac*, "heifer"; *ruath*, "male calf"; or *kel*, "calf which has not begun to graze"; thus, *tut ma kar looka* specifies a "mouse-gray bull with a white back." There are potentially thousands of such terms, probably more than the total number of cattle owned by the Nuer at any given time!

This elaborate system of terminology provides an indication of the economic importance of cattle in the traditional life of the Nuer people. Cultural emphasis is a harder thing to measure, but it is the pervasive cultural importance of cattle to which Evans-Pritchard's discussion returns again and again. It would seem that virtually every activity and every conversation has some reference, direct or indirect, to cattle: "He who lives among the Nuer and wishes to understand their social life must first master a vocabulary referring to cattle and the life of the herds" (Evans-Pritchard, 1940). A few selected examples are noted here:

1. Social relationships are defined in terms of cattle. Like many pastoral peoples, the Nuer formalize marriage by the payment of cattle. Cattle are owned by families, and each son has a right to animals from the family herd. At the time of marriage, a set number of cattle are given to the family of the bride and distributed among her relatives in a prescribed way. Patrilineal kinsmen—fathers, sons, and brothers—live close together and cooperate in caring for the herd. They know the history of each animal (its former owners, when it was obtained, and its parentage), and they are concerned with the future distribution of cattle (when they will be given away and to whom). Ties of marriage, past, present, and future, are directly equated with the payment of cattle from one family to

another. That is why Evans-Pritchard remarks, "I used sometimes to despair that the subject of girls led inevitably to that of cattle."

2. The social use of cattle extends beyond the living. Cattle are sacrificed to the ghosts of the dead, and there are also ceremonies for contacting the dead that might, for example, involve rubbing ashes on the back of a cow. Thus, cattle are the link between the living and the dead. Talk about ancestors, as well as about living kinsmen, nessitates constant reference to cattle.

3. The herds provide the Nuer "calendar" and "clock." The whole course of a year's activities, the moving from villages to cattle camps, and other changes through the year depend partly on the needs of cattle. The round of daily activities is also set by the cattle. Time reckoning is expressed in terms of these annual and daily cycles. Other activities are planned and coordinated by referring to such predictable events as the return from cattle camps, the birth of calves, or, during the day, milking time. There is no expression equivalent to "time" in the Nuer vocabulary; there is, rather, a series of activities focusing around cattle, which constitute both annual and daily cycles.

4. Cattle terminology is extensively used in names and titles of address. This is perhaps the most striking reflection in language of the high cultural value attached to cattle. The Nuer make use of a variety of names and titles of address. A child is given a personal name soon after birth, a name that may be handed down from an ancestor or may refer to circumstances at the time of his birth (like "Heavy Rain" or "Cattle Camp"). Each child also inherits a "praise-name" that identifies the child with his or her father's clan and at times may be called by the praise-name of the mother's clan as well.

Besides these, several names are acquired later in life. One of the most important is the "ox-name": At the time of his initiation into manhood, a boy is given a special ox, which becomes his favorite in the herd. His ox-name is a description of this ox, its markings, or other attributes—for example, *Luthrial*, from *luth* (a bell worn by the ox) and *rial* (a part of an ox's name, indicating a distribution of colors) or *Duhorrial*, from *duhor* (a tassel worn by cattle) and *rial*. Little boys often call their playmates by names of a similar sort, taken from the calves that they care for, in anticipation of the ox-names they will receive at initiation. And older men may take new ox-names when they acquire oxen of which they are especially fond; thus, an individual may have several ox-names, though the one given at initiation remains the one most often used. Ox-names are the ones most used among friends, and they are called out, with embellishments, in dancing and other public events. Men shout their ox-names when attacking an enemy in battle or an animal in hunting.

Girls also may have ox-names, using them among themselves; and married women take cow-names. Both ox-names and cow-names are used in combination with other fancy "dance-names" on festive public occasions.

It can be seen that a Nuer individual is likely to accumulate a number of names in the course of his or her life. There is a definite etiquette in the use of names, as well as in the kinship terms by which a person may also be addressed. Children are apt to be called by patronymics (the father's name), and elderly people by their children's names (teknonymics); generally, relatives try to avoid the use of personal names. Among persons of the same age, ox-names are most commonly used—one of many ways in which terms of address reflect social status (Evans-Pritchard, 1948).

METAPHOR AND THE EXTENSION OF MEANING

Certain linguists whose interests focus on semantics (the study of meaning in language) have called attention to a special way in which language may be related to its cultural context. This lies in the use of figures of speech, including metaphors. Metaphors are words or phrases that have their primary reference to one semantic area but are used, secondarily, in other ways. This is a creative use of language; the secondary or transferred meanings are usually more general or abstract than the primary meanings. A type of metaphor that seems to be virtually universal involves the use of words with primary reference to the human body for talking about inanimate objects or natural features. Thus, in English, we speak of the "eye" of a needle, "mouth" of a cave or a river, "foot" of a hill, "arm" of a chair or of an organization, and "heart" of a problem. Expressions of this sort are found in many languages all over the world—so widely distributed as to suggest a natural inclination in human language.

Some of these usages may be explained by what psychologists have dubbed "physiognomic perception"—a tendency to perceive environmental and other inanimate features as essentially undifferentiated from the viewer. This type of reaction is often seen in the drawings and discourse of children, who may draw a house, train, or mountain with a face or attribute human motives to a tree, stone, or plaything. But adults also tend to describe abstract shapes by comparing them with human forms or movements; the Rorschach test and similar psychodiagnostic techniques make use of this tendency. The suggestion that this is a "primitive" (and, therefore, perhaps universal) type of perception is consistent with the widespread use of metaphors that seem to reflect such a view of the world. Conversely, however, it seems that certain body parts are often named by means metaphors— the pupil of the eye, which may be seen as a small person (a baby, child, or a young student); fingers and toes, which are seen as people, often as members of a family; and muscles, often named for mice (the source of the word "muscle") or other small animals. Using a worldwide sample of 116 languages, C. Brown and S. Witkowski (1981) found sufficient evidence of metaphoric terms of this sort to suggest that "they have been invented over and over again in human languages."

A study by K. Basso demonstrates that a metaphoric extension of meaning can serve, in a changing culture, to provide the lexicon for a technological innovation. Rather than borrowing English words or coining new Apache vocabulary, the speakers of Western Apache extended the range of meaning of familiar terms. It appears that, in the process, cars and trucks were treated linguistically as if they were animate beings rather than inanimate things.

Some Western Apache anatomical terms with extended meanings follow:

		re: man	re: auto, truck
łikǝ		fat	grease
dɔ		chin and jaw	front bumper
wos		shoulder	front fender
gǝn		hand and arm	front wheel
kai		thigh and buttock	rear fender
zɛ'		mouth	gas pipe opening
ke'		foot	rear wheel
yǝn		back	bed of truck
inda'		eye	headlight
ni		face	area from top of windshield to bumper
	či	nose	hood
	ta	forehead	top, front of cab
ɛbiyɨ'		entrails	machinery under hood
	tsǝs	vein	electrical wiring
	zɨk	liver	battery
	pɨt	stomach	gas tank
	či	intestine	radiator hose
	ǰi	heart	distributor
	jisolɛ	lung	radiator

Basso's study documents an instance in which "a body of native words was extended en masse" to cover an introduced type of material culture, namely motorized vehicles. Basso had first elicited the Apache terms in reference to human anatomy, with meanings as in the first column; they apply equally to animals, birds, and other animate beings. He then found that, by extension, they also apply to cars and trucks, as shown in the second column.

It is important to note that the anatomical terms form an organized set and are extended as a set to apply to motor vehicles. This can be seen in the fact that the more inclusive terms (*ni* and *ɛbiyɨ'*) name areas for which there is no single term in English.

Basso offers two explanations, one cultural and the other linguistic, for the extension of anatomical terms to motorized vehicles. The first is the fact that cars, and especially pick-up trucks, have functionally replaced horses. "Since anatomical terms were already used to describe the horse, they were extended to its mechanized successor." The second explanation (which

Basso favors) indicates that motorized vehicles fall into a broader classifica-
tory grouping, *hinda,* which is largely, but not entirely, made up of animate
beings (humans, animals, fish, insects, etc.), and which contrasts with the
category *desta,* covering inanimates such as topographical features and
material objects. The basis for the inclusion appears to be the fact that the
vehicles are "capable of generating and sustaining locomotive movement by
themselves" (Basso, 1967).

There is another type of metaphor that may be universal and is of great
interest because of its evident association with culture-specific themes and
values. German linguist Hans Sperber has observed that "intense interest" in
a subject can lead to its extension into other areas of experience. This is a tan-
talizing idea; however, Sperber and other scholars who discussed his suggestion drew illustrations almost entirely from European history, with relatively little in the way of general information about the use of metaphors in
non-Western cultures (Ullman, 1966). Anthropological linguists should be
able to test the observation as a cross-cultural hypothesis: Do areas of cultural emphasis provide a lexicon of words and phrases that are used more
generally and are applied to other cultural domains? We get a hint of the
possibilities in reading Evans-Pritchard's observations on the Nuer's
extended use of cattle terminology in terms of address; here, words that have
primary reference to cattle are used in the more general context of human
relationships.

Another early observer was Franz Boas, who described the use of
metaphor in Kwakiutl, a native language of the northwest coast of North
America. There are, in Kwakiutl (as in English), many euphemistic expressions for unhappy events; for example, "to grow weak," "to lie down," "to
disappear from the world" are euphemisms in reference to death. There is
also a wealth of formal expressions and actions that are appropriate for ceremonial occasions. Many of these were used in the context of the potlatch
activities—invitations, speeches, feasting, and distribution of wealth. Marriage, with the formal exchange of property that validated alliances between
noble families, was similarly rich in metaphoric formulae. Several cultural
themes are prominent in the metaphoric expressions listed by Boas:

> *Salmon:* The guests of a person as well as wealth that he acquires are called his
> "salmon" . . . a great many guests are "a school of salmon" . . . , and the house
> or village of the host his "salmon weir" . . . into which he hauls . . . his guests.
> The valuable copper plates . . . , the symbols of wealth, particularly are called
> "salmon", and the host expecting a copper plate . . . says in regard to it, "Heavy
> is this salmon caught in my weir here." Potlatch rivals are ridiculed by saying
> that "they are losing their tails (like old salmon)".

> *Warfare:* The invitation to a potlatch in which hosts and guests rival in prodigality
> may be likened to war. The messengers who carry the invitation are called
> warriors . . . and the arriving guests sing war songs. . . . The copper plate is
> also called the "citadelle" of the chief. The orator says: "Behold, now we stand
> on War (name of a copper plate), the citadelle of our chief". . . . When a copper
> is broken, by cutting it with a knife, it is "killed." A marriage formalized by

exchange of property can be called "to make war on the princesses"; another form is "to try to get a slave".

Hunting and animals: Warriors refer to themselves as serpents, thunderbirds, killer whales: "We are the great thunderbirds and we avenge our late ancestors"; "we shall soar and grasp with our talons the Bella Colla." Rivals are demeaned by calling them "little sparrows," "horseflies," "mosquitoes," "old dogs."

Marriage can be ritualized in terms of whaling: A man appears carrying a whaling harpoon which he throws into the house, thus harpooning the bride whom he calls "a whale."

Houses, property: To offer a copper plate "which groans in the house for sale" is called to let it "lie dead by the fire". . . . The purchaser must "take it up from the floor". . . . The term from marrying "means that the property given to the bride's father walks into his house". In the course of marriage transactions, a number of chiefs make the first proposal to the bride's father; then they "go back 'to shake (the bride) from the floor of the house.'" After successive negotiations, she is induced to "move on the floor," to "come right off the floor" to "approach the door," and so on. She is "dressed" by carrying a copper plate; successive gifts of blankets are called "tump line," "belts," "boxes," and "canoes" (values measured in terms of blankets). (Boas, 1929)

Although Boas gave no indication of the relative frequency of the various metaphoric expressions, it would appear such expressions were most often used as components of a characteristic formal or ceremonial style. Salmon fishing, hunting (especially of sea mammals), warfare, and the emphasis on property—the stuff of these metaphors—are prominent in descriptions of Kawkiutl traditional culture. Boas's article, which appears to confirm Sperber's hypothesis, is one of the few anthropological studies of metaphor in a non-Western culture.

A sample of the potential range of variation of metaphoric expressions may be seen in the epithets, or "praise-names," given to chiefs and other individuals of high status in very distinctive, and contrastive, cultural areas:

Kwakiutl: Honorifics given to Kwakiutl chiefs included: Post of our World, Great Mountains Standing on Edge, Overhanging Cliff, Loaded Canoe, and the Cedar that Cannot be Spanned (Boas, 1929).

Iroquois: The Iroquois tribes called themselves, collectively, "House-builders"; individual tribes and villages were named for their geographical location; clans are named for animals. A completely different set of terms is connected with the political League of the Iroquois. This was called "the Tree of Peace"; members of the League, "the great long roots," and "the great black leaves." A chief was "the main root" (Chafe, 1963).

Swazi: The Swazi of South Africa call their king by the title "Lion" and praise and flatter him with epithets such as "The Sun," "The Milky Way," and "Obstacle to the Enemy." The queen (mother of the king) has the title "Lady Elephant" and is also called "The Earth," "The Beautiful," or "Mother of the Country" (Kuper, 1963).

Jukun: This horticultural people of the Nigerian plateau called their king by titles that identified him as the Moon and in ceremonial contexts used the epithets "Our Guinea- corn," "Our Beans," "Our Ground-nuts," "Our Rain," and "Our Wealth." (One of the king's chief duties was control of the weather; through this, he controlled the crops.) (Meek, 1931)

Our Own Metaphors: Metaphors are extremely common in everyday American English and are drawn from a variety of semantic areas. Metaphoric reference to food and alimentation are quite frequent; for example:

1. She's a cupcake.
2. She's a tart.
3. He's just a creampuff.
4. I'm in a pickle.
5. I'm in a stew.
6. That's a fine kettle of fish.
7. That's a tough nut to crack.
8. It's a piece of cake.[2]

Further, Americans are fond of expressions such as "eating up the miles," "eating one's words," "a glutton for punishment," "starved for affection," and "hungry for success" (which has a "sweet taste"). We do not have enough cross-cultural information about metaphors to know whether food and eating are a universal source of metaphoric expressions. They are common in French usage, as in English, and evidently less so—but not unknown—in German; however, similar expressions are widespread.

There does not appear to be any single area of cultural emphasis, and there is no one profession or type of activity that predominates in our metaphoric expressions. This perhaps is to be expected, as there is a great diversity of occupations and interests in American society, and there is no single occupation that carries high prestige (like cattle herding for the Nuer or salmon fishing for the Kwakiutl). One striking fact, however, is the great frequency of metaphoric references to sports and games. It appears that sports constitute a rather neutral area, a common ground in which Americans of all ages, occupations, and social status can meet and share a mutual interest and enthusiasm. This may help to explain why sports can provide figures of speech that are extended in a general way to refer to social and interpersonal relationships. Some familiar phrases are drawn from golf ("par for the course"), card games ("an ace in the hole"), or football ("a Hail-Mary pass").

---

[2]Roughly paraphrased as: 1. She's an attractive girl. 2. She's flirtatious and easily seduced. 3. He has no strength or stamina. 4. I'm in trouble. 5. I don't know what to do. 6. That's a perplexing situation. 7. That's a difficult problem. 8. It's easy and rewarding.

But the most fertile source of all appears to be baseball, the "national pastime," and the game that is longest established and most closely identified with American culture. One can quickly recall using expressions such as:

1. He made *a grandstand play.*
2. She *threw* me a *curve.*
3. She *fielded* my questions well.
4. You're way *off base.*
5. You're *batting 1000 (500, zero)* so far.
6. What are *the ground rules?*
7. I'll be careful to *touch all the bases.*
8. He *went to bat* for me.
9. He has *two strikes* against him.
10. That's way out *in left field.*
11. He drives me *up the wall.*
12. He's *a team player (a clutch player).*
13. She's a *screwball (foul ball, oddball).*
14. This is just a *ball-park* estimate.[3]

Readers can doubtless think of other examples, since expressions of this sort are frequent in idiomatic American English. It would appear that speakers are at times aware, but often unaware, that they are, in effect, comparing life to a baseball game. In this, it seems that American and British usage is quite similar. Compare the following British expressions drawn from the game of cricket:

1. He's *batting on a sticky wicket,* so he'd better be careful.
2. Jones retired last week, so I *move up the batting order.*
3. She was 96 when she died; she *had a good innings.*
4. I *punched him hard,* and *knocked him for six.*
5. I knew she had talked to John, so when she said she hadn't seen him, I *caught her out* immediately.
6. I told him to *work with the team,* but he decided to *work off his own bat.*
7. Since we hired a new worker, we've been *getting along at a great bat.*

---

[3] 1. He did something spectacular in order to get approval. 2. She did or asked something unexpected, hard to respond to. 3. She answered my questions well. 4. You're not behaving properly. 5. All/half/none of your answers have been correct. 6. What are the arbitrary or conventional limitations? 7. I want to do everything that's expected of me. 8. He defended me, argued on my behalf. 9. He is at a great disadvantage. 10. That's very unusual. 11. It is hard for me to cope with him. 12. He cooperates well with others/does well under difficult conditions. 13. She behaves peculiarly/erratically/badly. 14. It's a rough estimate, probably exaggerated.

8. I was going to offer her a slice of cake, but she *took the ball before the bound* and helped herself.[4]

The metaphoric use of language is, potentially, one of the most fascinating links in the interrelationship of language and culture. However, it is a difficult topic to study, and there is still a dearth of cross-cultural information. We do not even know, for example, whether metaphors are rare in some languages and especially plentiful in others (although this seems to be the case), nor do we understand the conditions that give rise to the use of metaphors. Collecting data of this sort demands a very sensitive control of a language, preferably that of a native speaker. Grammars and dictionaries seldom contain systematic discussion of metaphors, and it may be that metaphors, being largely stylistic and requiring "insider" knowledge, are often omitted when communication is difficult (as when an anthropologist is asking questions of a linguistic consultant).

TAXONOMY

It has been a concern of anthropologists in recent years to develop field methods for eliciting and comparing systems of classification, or *taxonomies.* This is the concern of *ethnoscience,* a relatively new subfield of cultural anthropology. It is also of interest to linguists and is an area in which linguistic and cultural study must be coordinated with an eye to discovering parallels between linguistic and cultural categories. For example, researchers have collected exhaustive botanical and zoological vocabularies with an interest both in the rationale and functional basis for each system and in discerning universal features of taxonomic systems. Ethnoscientists want to know how and in what order generic and specific terms develop and to learn why fine terminological distinctions are made in the classification of certain species while gross differences among other species may not even be recognized (as in the English term *weed*).

A taxonomic study by J. A. Frisch examines the internal structuring of the Maricopa category of "food." Maricopa is the language of a Native American people of the southwestern United States. Frisch collected his data at the Salt River reservation in Scottsdale, Arizona. The Maricopa word *čamač* ("food") includes anything edible; it is the most general term in the hierarchy. The domain of *čamač* includes three categories of edible things, which can be easily distinguished since each occurs with a different verb. These categories are: class I, foods that take the verb *maum,* "to eat"; class II, foods that take the verb *cakacum,* "to consume something containing water"; and class III, liquids that take the verb *si:m,* "to drink." (See Figure 5.3.)

[4]1. He's dealing with a difficult situation . . . 2. . . . I move up in the hierarchy. 3. . . . she had a good long life. 4. I presented a strong argument and completely defeated him. 5. . . . I knew she was lying and exposed her deception. 6. . . . he decided to work alone. 7. . . . we've been accomplishing a lot. 8. . . . she was over-hasty. (B. Carey, 1999)

FIGURE 5.3

The domain of *čamač*. Reprinted from J. A. Frisch, "Maricopa Foods," *International Journal of American Linguistics* (1968). Copyright © 1968 by The University of Chicago Press.

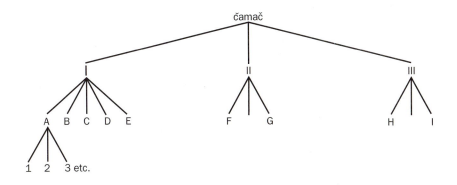

As Frisch notes, a functional consideration in the classification of foods is the amount of water they contain. This is the apparent semantic distinction between classes I and II. "A possible explanation for the importance of the water/non-water distinction ... is that the physical environment of the Maricopa Indians is that of a semi-arid desert with seasonal shortages of water. In aboriginal times such a distinction may have been of prime importance to survival."

The lower levels of the hierarchy include the general and specific terms for various foods. Frisch lists only a limited selection of these. For example, class I includes a. meat (1. beef, 2. pork, 3. deer, etc.); b. vegetables (6. beans, 7. greens, etc.); c. breads; d. canned food; and e. cooked food. Class II includes f. fruits (10. oranges, 11. grapefruit, 12. watermelon, 13. melons, 14. cactus); g. vegetables (15. lettuce, 16. tomatoes). Class III includes h. juice; i. milk; and so on.

In this taxonomy, Maricopa shows both a similarity to and a difference from English. In English, the general class of "food" can be subdivided into solid foods, which select the verb *eat* (bread, canteloupe, a ham sandwich, soup, ice cream), and beverages or drinks, which take the verb *drink* (soft drinks, beer, orange juice, milkshakes). The obvious difference lies in the three-way (rather than two-way) categorization in Maricopa and in the apparent functional basis of the categorization. With this lack of "fit" between the Maricopa and English categories, a completely accurate translation would be impossible since English must translate both *maum* and *cakaum* as "to eat" (Frisch, 1968).

Frisch's study of the Maricopa domain of "food" is primarily a statement about categories in the language but also suggests a practical basis for the categories in the subsistence culture of the Maricopa. His findings are especially valuable because he uses a dual methodology; that is, he bolsters the ethnographic approach of asking for categories ("What kinds of foods are there?" and so on) with strictly linguistic criteria (the fact that the categories select different verbs in the Maricopa language).

COLOR TERM STUDIES

For centuries, the physical nature, perception, categories, terminology, and symbolic uses of color have been of interest to scientists, philosophers, literary scholars, and many others. In the 20th century, anthropologists and linguists seem to have discovered the subject anew and have made color terms the focus of testing and large-scale cross-cultural comparisons. Two facts cannot be denied: (1) Color perception is a human universal; there are no significant differences in ability to discriminate or match hues among human populations; and (2) there are marked differences among languages in the ways that colors are defined and named. Efforts to reconcile and account for these facts have become a significant part of recent anthropological literature and have provided a theoretical model for studies of other semantic fields (concepts of time and space, plant and animal taxonomies, etc.).

We humans are not unique in our ability to perceive and discriminate colors. We have the same visual anatomy and perceive essentially the same range of hues as other higher primates. But color vision occurs very selectively in nature and takes many different forms in the various biological orders. Basically, it is an adaptive complex, most obviously related to diet and the necessity of distinguishing between ripe and unripe or edible and nonedible plants. A type of specialized color vision, very different from that of humans, is found in bees and other insects that gather the pollen of various flowers. Color vision has also evolved in birds that subsist on fruit or flowers and in certain fish. It is absent or little developed in some mammalian orders but is characteristic of the primates, which generally rely on plant foods, especially fruits. In humans, the natural adaptive functions of color vision are subsumed in a legion of cultural elaborations—aesthetic codes, symbolic meanings, and metaphoric associations.

The Western view of the color spectrum was established by Sir Isaac Newton, who conducted experiments with prisms, refracting white light into the range of spectral colors (the colors of the rainbow). Using the seven notes of the musical scale as a model, Newton divided the spectrum into seven segments: red, orange, yellow, green, blue, indigo, and violet. Of these, the term "indigo" has fallen into virtual disuse; the other six are still usually listed as the "primary colors." They are among the most frequently used English color terms, along with brown and the achromatic hues of black, white, and gray. These terms are directly translatable into other Western languages, and their application is virtually identical.

It would be very difficult to persuade most native speakers of English that these divisions of the spectrum are not necessarily given by nature. A child learns to name the colors of the rainbow as red, orange, yellow, green, blue, and violet (or purple) and finds the same colors in a set of building blocks, modeling clay, fingerpaints, and crayons. Other shades are treated as modifications from the focal values of the primary colors (lighter or darker) or mixtures of them (blue-green, purplish red, yellow-orange, and the like).

But the spectrum of visible colors is actually a continuum. Each shade grades into the next, and there are no natural boundaries that delimit color areas. The basic color vocabularies of other languages (the counterparts of our red, blue, green, etc.) often stand for very different ways of dividing up this continuum into more or fewer segments. Even when there is close similarity between languages in color terms, the categories are seldom identical.

EARLY STUDIES OF THE "COLOR SENSE"

A comparative interest in color categories and terminology began with an unlikely researcher, the British prime minister and statesman William Gladstone (1809–1898). In 1858 Gladstone, who was an avid student of the classics, published a three-volume historical study based on the Homeric epics. In an appendix to this work, he discussed the "senses" of beauty, number, and color as revealed in Homer's use of language. He assessed the Greek sense of color as vague and imprecise and judged *melas*, *leukos*, and *eruthros* to be the only terms used with consistency (being, at least, consistently translatable by English *black*, *white*, and *red*).

Gladstone's conclusion that the "organ of colour and its impressions were but partly developed" in ancient Greece evidently reflected the phrenologists' view of the mind as made up of some 30 separate "organs," including the "organ of color." (Gladstone, 1858, p. 448) According to phrenology (considered a highly reputable science in the England of Gladstone's youth), these organs have developed over time, modified by use, thus accounting for differences among individuals and races. Gladstone's time frame was based on biblical chronology, and he considered the Homeric Greeks to stand very close to the "childhood of the race." His assessment of the Greek color terms was consistent with this view.

Whatever Gladstone's merits as a historian, his comments on Homer's color vocabulary evidently attracted considerable interest. Within a few years, several studies had appeared, dealing with the color vocabulary of other early literature—the Bible, ancient Sanskrit hymns, Anglo-Saxon and Celtic epics (for example, Geiger, 1878; Hopkins, 1883; Mead, 1899). At the same time, anthropologists and other students of non-Western languages had become aware of color vocabulary as a point of interest and, at times, a source of difficulty in translation.[5] By the end of the 19th century, the "color sense"—as studied through terminology—was an established research topic and was usually discussed in the broad context of evolution. It became standard practice to use colored paper or yarn samples to elicit terms and to test the ability of subjects to match and discriminate among colors. Around 1880, H. Magnus, a German ophthalmologist, circulated a set of 10 color tiles (white, black, red, green, yellow, blue, purple, brown, pink, and orange) to missionaries, colonial administrators, and other correspondents who helped him gather terms from speakers of 61 languages. Magnus found marked variation in the number of terms and observed that a degree of "confusion" was characteristic of most non-Western languages (as, for example, merging orange with red or blue with green). He and his contemporaries debated whether the problem lay in perception (as Gladstone had suggested) or in a "deficiency" in language itself.

Two decades later, in 1898, W. H. R. Rivers became the first researcher to investigate color vision and terminology in the field. Rivers, who would become a well-known anthropologist (but had been trained as a neurologist and psychologist), was a member of the Cambridge University expedition to the Torres Strait region of Melanesia. In Melanesia, Rivers used the latest ophthalmic methods to test visual acuity, peripheral vision, myopia, and color blindness. In these respects, he found that the native populations fell well within the range of variation typical of European populations—an important finding, since it countered widespread stereotypes of racial inferiority. In addition, he tested color identification and discrimination and recorded color terminology in Miriam, Mabuiag, and several additional Papuan and Australian languages. For this, his materials included a limited selection of colored papers, similar to those used by Magnus, plus a set of yarns for the matching test (Rivers, 1901).

Back in London, Rivers assessed his findings in a public lecture delivered early in 1900. In four of the languages studied (Seven Rivers, Kiwai, Murray Island, and Mabuiag), he declared that "we have progressive stages in the evolution of color language; in the lowest there . . . [is] only . . . a definite term for red apart from white and black; in the next stage there are definite terms for red and yellow, and an indefinite term for green; in the next stage there are definite terms for red, yellow and green, and a term for blue has been borrowed from another language; while in the highest stage there are terms for both green and blue, but these tend to be confused with one another." This order, he candidly remarked, "corresponds with the order in which (the tribes) would be placed on the ground of their general intellectual and cultural development" (Rivers, 1900).

---

[5]Two traditions of color term studies seem to have developed, both ultimately traceable to Gladstone and his immediate successors—the anthropological tradition is focused on the terminology and semantics of color in different ethnographic contexts; the literary tradition is concerned with the aesthetic and descriptive uses of color by various authors.

What did Rivers mean when he spoke of "definite" color terms? It depended, essentially, on the consistency with which a specific term was applied to a particular color sample. The Miriam (Murray Island) word *mammam* (literally "blood") was a definite term because it was almost always applied to the red sample; another term, *mairmair* ("red ochre"), was only rarely used and thus was considered indefinite or erroneous. *Bulubulu* (from English "blue") was applied to the blue sample by younger—and more acculturated—people; this, in Rivers's eyes, was an advance over the more traditional *golegole* ("dark" or "black"). A century later, we can easily see the ethnocentrism in this approach, which routinely used European terms and categories as a standard by which to evaluate non-Western languages.

TWENTIETH-CENTURY STUDIES

Around the turn of the century, basic changes were under way in the human sciences, including anthropology and linguistics. Sweeping generalizations about human nature, typologies of cultures or languages, and broad theories of cultural evolution—all of these became suspect. The spirit of the times favored objectivity and an emphasis on empirical research. The Torres Strait expedition was an early manifestation of the priority that anthropologists would give to the firsthand collection of data. In North America, Franz Boas set the standard for a holistic anthropology, encompassing archaeological, linguistic, ethnological, and biological subfields. Part of Boas's agenda was a program for studying Native American languages, with the aim of using linguistic categories as a guide for understanding and interpreting cultures.

One of the first American scholars to undertake an extensive study of color terms was Verne F. Ray, an anthropologist at the University of Washington. During the 1950s, Ray collected color vocabulary from speakers of a total of 60 different languages. The methods and materials that were used in this project were quite different from those employed by Magnus and Rivers. Ray collected responses from individual consultants, who were shown more than 100 color samples of carefully controlled pigmentation under uniform conditions of lighting. The test materials were selected to give an even sampling of the spectrum in three different ranges of brightness (light, medium, and dark) and were, thus, not biased in favor of any particular color system. (Note that black, white, and shades of gray were not included.)

One of Ray's published studies used nine Native American languages, along with English, as the basis of comparisons and contrasts. All, including the English, were collected in the northwestern part of North America; to Ray, it was a point of interest to find such variety in the color terminology of people living in the same general geographical and cultural areas. In the chart that accompanied this study (Figure 5.4), the divisions of the spectrum are specified in terms of wavelength (shown on the left, along with approximate descriptive labels in English). Ray noted that the number of terms ranges from three to eight (this variation is also characteristic of the larger sample of languages). English, with six, is close to the average. The number

		English	Salish	Sahaptin	Chinook
	Wave-length	Northwest U.S.	Sanpoil	Tenino	Wishram
Violet-Red	comp 5600	╳	╳		╳
Red	6571	red			
Orange-red	6340		quɩ́l		daɫbȧ́l
Red-orange	6230			lut'sa´	
Orange	6085	orange		m∝́kc	
Yellow-orange	5390				dagȧ´c
Orange-yellow	5870				
Yellow	5793	yellow	kuɤa´i	pa'a´x	
Green-yellow	5710				
Yellow-green	5600		qwɩ́n		qa´naptsu
Green	5164	green			
Blue-green	5050				
Green-blue	4985				daptsȧ´x
Blue	4695	blue			
Violet-blue	4455			l∝́mt	
Blue-violet	4350		qwa´i		
Violet	4210	violet		pu'u´x	
Red-violet	comp 4990				iyaquit'sab∝l
Violet-red	comp 5600		xɛ˙n	╳	

FIGURE 5.4 COLOR CATEGORIES IN NORTH AMERICAN LANGUAGES.

does not appear to relate to the technological complexity of the culture, to color in the environment, or to the artistic use of color. Ray was impressed by the fact that four languages spoken by people living very close to one another (Songish, Chetco, Rogue River, and Santiam—all in Oregon) have color terminologies that "vary as widely as any received" (Ray, 1953).

Salish	Athapaskan	Eskimo	Athapaskan	Takelma	Kalapuya
Songish	**Chilcotin**	**Atka**	**Chetco R.**	**Rogue R.**	**Santiam**
					sa´kwala
			ɫsi´k		utsa··´la
n∝s∝´q^u	τɛlτɛ´l	u´lu·´δax		álc̆ɪ´l	t'sɪ·´lɪlω·
l∝l∝´č			xa´dəgi	Baú∝x	Ba´lamɪ
i∝l∝čalɪs	τɛltso´´	c̆u'mnu´γɪx			tskɪ´tkwu
		či´δγɪx		Gwa´camt	
n∝kwa´i			ɫsu´	tɢic∝´mt	pčɪ´x
či´ɪ'alɪs					
sqwa´iux				kiy∝´x	
n∝kwa´i	τi·lča´n		xa´dətsu´		
kwi´ɪm∝l					

One characteristic of many Native American languages—and, indeed, of non-Western languages in general—was almost always noted by early researchers as a defect or inadequacy. This is the so-called "blue-green confusion," when the range of hues divided between *blue* and *green* in English is covered by a single term. From a Western point of view, this amounts to a failure to distinguish two very different colors—in fact, early investigators (like Rivers) saw this as a "primitive" trait or, perhaps, a kind of "blue-green color blindness" (Rivers, 1900).

A look at Ray's chart shows us that the situation is not that simple. In some cases (Tenino and Chilcotin) a part of the "green" range is covered by a term that also includes "yellow," while the rest falls together with "blue." In other cases (Wishram, Takelma), there are as many terms as in English, but the boundaries are simply different. In still other cases, there are more distinctions than in English. Ray makes a telling point when he comments that, from the point of view of Santiam, English confuses *utsa.'la* and *t'si'lilω.* (both of which coincide with "red"). Similarly, for speakers of Songish, English fails to distinguish between *či'l'alis* and *sqwa'iux*, which are lumped together as "blue."

Thus, Ray's discussion of color terminologies presented a *relativistic* view of linguistic differences. He attempted to show that, despite differences, each system is quite adequate to serve the needs of its speakers. Ray reasoned that "color systems serve to bring the world of color sensation into order so that perception may be relatively simple and behavioral response, particularly verbal response and communication, may be meaningful." For color and other areas of sensory perception, all natural languages appear to accomplish these same ends quite adequately (Ray, 1953).

THE "INSIDER'S VIEW" OF CULTURE

It is difficult to compare any semantic area across language boundaries since each culture has its own organization, its own way of categorizing things and of putting the pieces together. For example, in many languages the words that we translate as color terms have their primary reference to vegetation (as do some of our own, like *lilac* or *avocado*); in others, the references are anatomical (*red* may be the same word as *blood, yellow* as *bile,* and so on); and in still other cases, terms relating to light and shades of brightness may be the source of color vocabulary. All of this is lost in the translation when we simply equate these words with our *red, yellow, blue,* and so forth.

Roughly contemporaneous with Ray's cross-cultural research, Harold Conklin explored the internal organization of a single system of color nomenclature and examined its place in the culture of the Hanunoo people of the Philippines. Conklin was inspired to collect and analyze color terms while conducting an ethnobotanical study. He found that the four primary categories into which the Hanunoo group colors are closely tied to their view of the plant world.

The primary categories are labeled by the following terms (which include the prefix ma-, which means "having or exhibiting"):

ma-bi:ru	". . . darkness, blackness"
ma-lagti?	". . . lightness, whiteness"
ma-rara?	". . . redness, presence of red"
ma-latuy	". . . greenness, presence of green"

STUDYING LOKONO COLOR TERMS

I became interested in color vocabulary while studying Lokono, the coastal Arawakan language of the Guianas. I recorded several color terms on my very first day of field-work, as direct translations of English terms:

koreto	"red"
subuleto	"yellow"
imoroto	"yellow"
bluto	"blue"
bunaroto	"brown"
karimeto	"black"
harirato	"white"

All of this seemed simple and straight-forward, an exact matching of terms in two languages, Lokono and English. However, a few days later I heard my Lokono con-sultant translate the word *bunaroto* as "pur-ple"; previously, it had been "brown." Soon there were other puzzling develop-ments that suggested that some of the terms did not stand exclusively for colors; *koreto* could be translated as either "red" or "ripe," and *imoroto* and *bunaroto* also seemed to have secondary meanings—"unripe" and "over-ripe," respectively. My curiosity was aroused—what was going on here? Like several other anthropologists in similar circumstances, I had stumbled on the "color term problem."

What did these words really mean? Obviously, they didn't simply divide and label segments of the spectrum in the way I had taken for granted! My reaction was to devise an *ad hoc* test. Using some watercol-ors that I had with me, supplemented by bits of colored paper torn from magazines and can labels, I put together a set of 30 color samples (more varied than Rivers's, less so than Ray's). These were presented in random order for identification, first by my local consultant and later by several residents of a Lokono village located some distance into the interior. In the process, I discovered something that I would other-wise not have suspected. There is no direct Lokono translation for the English word "color"; thus, my question, as I displayed each color sample, had to be phrased as *"Hama-dianto tora?"* (literally, "What is this like?").

The results of my experiment were both exciting and confusing. In identifying the color samples, Lokono speakers used two types of words or phrases. The primary terms, already recorded as translations of English color terms, were, on the whole, the most frequent responses. All, with the exception of *bluto,* were applied to a wide range of shades, but a range that is quite different from that of the corresponding English terms.

Lokono Term	Applied (by Various Individuals) to
koreto	red, pink, wine, rust, brown, yellow
subuleto	bright shades of yellow, blue, pink, orange, green
imoroto	medium to dark green
bluto	dull, dark blue or indigo (denim blue)
bunaroto	brown, purple, deep yellow-orange, buff, gray
karimeto	black, dark brown, dark blue
harirato	white, pale yellow, buff, light gray

It appears that these seven terms form a cohesive set *only* as they have been equated with and influenced by the categories of European languages (English, Dutch, and Spanish). Objectively, however, it is a com-posite set, built of two groups of semanti-cally related native terms, plus a loanword.

1. Three terms have primary reference to the maturation of vegetation (*imoroto* unripe, immature; *koreto* ripe, mature; *bunaroto* overripe or burnt).

2. Three terms appear to have primary reference to a range of brightness (*hari-rato* light, white; *subuleto* bright; *karimeto* dark, black).

3. The need for a translation equivalent of "blue" (*bluto,* borrowed from English) may have arisen as *subuleto* became

identified with English "yellow." However, *bluto* is used hesitantly and was applied only to a dark denim-blue; most individuals chose descriptive terms to identify the lighter "blue" samples.

As in Hanunoo, descriptive terms can be more specific than the primary terms, identifying or comparing a color sample with an object or material of distinctive hue. Two kinds of constructions are used: (a) words consisting of a noun plus the adjectival suffix -to, for example, *balisiato* gray (from *balisi* "ashes"), *heheto* pale yellow (*hehe* "urine"), and *iauareto* pink (*iauare* "rainbow"); and (b) constructions with the comparative suffix -dian- "like, similar to," plus -to. Examples are: *karakori-dian-to* metallic yellow (*karakori* "gold"); *koriuaka-bara-dian-to* light blue (*koriuaka* "parrot," *bara* "feather"); *kakau-(u)da-dian-to* rust-brown (*kakau* "cocoa," *uda* "skin").

Several years after I had published a description of the Lokono color system in a

brief publication, I came across Conklin's study of Hanunoo color categories. I was struck by the obvious similarities as well as differences between the two.

1. In neither language is there an abstract term for "color."

2. In both languages, primary categories are defined by two kinds of natural phenomena—ripeness of vegetation and variation in brightness. In Hanunoo these dimensions are coded as oppositions (fresh versus dry and light versus dark), while in Lokono each is divided into three terms (green, ripe, over-ripe; and pale, bright, dark).

3. Both languages provide ways to form descriptive terms, based on identification or comparison with natural objects or materials in the environment. In all of these characteristics, both undoubtedly have much in common with many other natural languages (Hickerson, 1953; 1991).

These words might be roughly translated into English as *black, white, red* and *black*; however, they provide the Hanunoo with a four-way division of the spectrum that can accommodate any shade or mixture of colors. The four terms divide the spectrum into unequal parts; the largest is *ma-bi:ru,* which includes not only black but many deep shades (dark blue, violet, green, gray, and various mixtures). The range of *ma-lagti?* includes white and many very lightly pigmented shades. Thus, these two terms—*ma-bi:ru* and *ma-lagti?*—can be understood as an opposition of dark and light.

The other two, *ma-latuy* and *ma-rara?,* express an opposition of freshness or succulence and dryness or dessication in plants. In terms of color, *ma-latuy* corresponds roughly to light green, yellow, and light brown, and *ma-rara?* to red, orange, yellow, and mixtures in which these predominate.

Hanunoo native arts feature indigo-dyed textiles and beadwork, with red being the preferred color of beads; native aesthetics place an emphasis on the categories *ma-bi:ru* and *ma-rara?.* By contrast to these, *ma-lagti?* and *ma-latuy* are seen as weak, faded, and colorless. The shades of green that are the most visible features of the natural environment are considered unattractive, and green is not used decoratively.

The Hanunoo language can also designate colors more specifically, by descriptive terms derived from nouns such as *ashes, turmeric,* or *gold;* both these "descriptors" and the primary terms can be combined or modified. The four inclusive primary terms, however, provide the main framework in which color is categorized and discussed (Conklin, 1955).

THE SEARCH FOR UNIVERSALS

In Western languages, color terms exist at an abstract level—that is, color is dissociated from natural objects or materials and from sources of pigment. Divisions of the spectrum are labeled by words that stand for color and nothing else. The most common English color terms (except, perhaps, *orange*) are words of this sort, which B. Berlin and P. Kay have called "basic color terms." These authors believe that basic color terms are found in all languages and that they are added (or "emerge") in a predictable order.

Research on this subject began in a seminar at the University of California, with a pilot study of 20 languages; the students who participated in the seminar investigated 19 languages in the San Francisco Bay area, while one was studied by B. Berlin in Guatemala. A testing procedure was developed, in which consultants first provided a list of the color terms that they considered "basic" or essential. They were then asked to map the areas of reference of the terms on a chart of the color spectrum. Finally, they were asked to point to the *focus* (the "best example") of each term. In these 20 languages, the number of basic color terms (*BCTs*) was found to range between 3 and 11, with "black," "white," and "red" present in all. Further, it was observed that there was remarkable similarity in foci. For example, the "red" area in language A might be larger or smaller than in language B, but the focal shades of red in A and B could be close or even identical. Observations of this sort led to hypotheses about universals, which then were tested through library research on a second sample of 78 languages, described by earlier scholars (including Gladstone, Rivers, and Conklin). Cross-cultural comparisons yielded a list of categories, labeled by English glosses—*black, white, red, green, yellow, blue, brown, pink, purple, orange,* and *gray.* Berlin and Kay argue that these 11 terms identify universals—"basic perceptual color categories"—that "emerge," in the history of a language, in a predictable order (see Figure 5.5). According to their 1969 formulation:

1. All languages contain terms for "white" and "black" (stage I).
2. If a language contains three terms, then it contains a term for "red" (stage II).
3. If a language contains four terms, then it contains a term for either "green"[6] or "yellow" (but not both) (stage IIIa and IIIb).
4. If a language contains five terms, then it contains terms for both "green"[7] and "yellow" (stage IV).

---

[6]Later called "grue."
[7]Later called "grue."

FIGURE 5.5

Berlin and Kay's "basic perceptual color categories."

5. If a language contains six terms, then it contains a term for "blue" (stage V).

6. If a 1anguage contains seven terms, then it contains a term for "brown" (stage VI).

7. If a language contains eight or more terms, then it contains a term for "purple," "pink," "orange," "gray," or some combination of these (stage VII).

Berlin and Kay converted their ranking of languages according to the number of basic color terms into a corresponding series of stages (numbered I–VII). Thus, they asserted an evolution of color terminology that is, at least superficially, similar to that advocated by 19th-century theorists such as Rivers. They point out that many of the stage I, II, and III color systems (Hanunoo would be classified as stage III) are found in languages spoken by technologically simple societies, while stage VII is largely (but not entirely) restricted to modern industrialized societies (Berlin & Kay, 1969).

A number of inconsistencies and apparent exceptions were pointed out by critics of Berlin and Kay's initial formulation (Newcomer & Farris, 1971; Hickerson, 1971; Conklin, 1973). Subsequent discussion led to revisions, both by the original authors and by others who continue this research (including Kay & McDaniel, 1978; Kay, Berlin, & Merrifield, 1991; McLaury, 1992); as a result, the definition of "stages" has become somewhat less rigid. Much early discussion focused on the categories *yellow, green,* and *blue.* Stage III (four-term systems) had, at first, two variants, IIIa *(black, white, green, yellow)* and IIIb *(black, white, red, green).* This was followed by IV (with both *yellow* and *green*) and V (with the addition of *blue*). The reporting of many exceptions (including Lokono) and the fact that a number of languages have a single category spanning the "green" and "blue" range of the spectrum led to the introduction of the term *grue.* The upshot is, in effect, an acknowledgment that the occurrence of *yellow, green,* and *blue* categories is quite variable across languages and even, at times, among individual speakers of a language. Further, *gray* and *brown* were soon recognized to be "wild cards" that can emerge at any point; and no particular order of occurrence is assigned to *purple, orange,* and *pink.*

Berlin and Kay were also criticized for their lack of attention to the possible influence of bilingualism and the borrowing of vocabulary from one language to another, especially under conditions of close cultural contact (Hickerson, 1971; Caskey-Sirmons & Hickerson, 1977). However, the main outlines of their formulation have been generally accepted, as tendencies if not as inevitable developments: (1) Basic color terms may develop and become more numerous over time; (2) the contrast of *dark* and *light* (or *black* and *white*) is expressed in vocabulary everywhere and may take precedence over the appearance of color terms based on contrasts in hue; (3) words that can be translated as *black, white,* and *red* are the most widespread categories—universal, or nearly so. Red is, in physical terms, the most salient area in the spectrum. (4) Beyond these three, there is a great deal of variety in color terms, and translation problems make it difficult to equate the categories found in different languages; the use of English glosses is sometimes suspect, as, for example, when a broad opposition of "dark" and "light" is glossed as *black* and *white*.

One of the most valuable aspects of the Berlin and Kay study was the distinction that was made, in the initial study of 20 languages, between *focus* and *field of reference* in the mapping of color categories. In this, they were influenced, as earlier researchers had been, by the materials and methods used by their contemporaries in other fields of study, including experimental psychology. Rivers's test materials were those that had been developed by Galton and other psychologists of his day; Ray's methods owed as much to behavioral psychology as to cultural anthropology. Similarly, Berlin and Kay adopted methods and test protocols that were pioneered by cognitive psychologists such as Eric Lenneberg. Lenneberg and his colleagues employed the concept of "prototypes" (the best or most typical examples of cognitive categories) in experiments that tested accuracy and speed of response. They demonstrated, for example, that communication is less ambiguous and response time shorter when the stimulus is closest to the prototype—that is, the "best example." This concept, as "focus," was adopted by Berlin and Kay for comparative study of color-term categories; the possibility that color foci are more universal than color categories deserves further study.

Berlin and Kay argue that the order in which color terms "emerge" in any language is determined by human anatomy—by sensory receptors and neurological processes—as well as by the physical properties of the spectrum. If this were entirely the case, the color categories of all languages would be essentially the same. Studies such as that of V. F. Ray have long indicated that there is much variation; points of difference between these findings and the "natural order" proposed by Berlin and Kay remain to be resolved.

Berlin and Kay and the numerous researchers who have followed and been influenced by their work have called attention to the fact that the perception and categorization of colors, like any other part of human behavior, is at least partly determined by human biology (the kind of animal we are), as well as by culture and the conditions under which we live. The categories into which languages classify colors do not vary in a random way; there are general, universal tendencies. Still, there is also a measure of arbitrariness—each system has its unique, individual characteristics.

In a broader perspective, this influential study of the categorization and naming of colors was part of a wave of interest in human universals and cultural evolution. It inspired emulation and stimulated efforts by other researchers to investigate the principles of taxonomy and naming in other semantic fields—life-forms, time concepts, counting systems, and the like (for example, Brown, 1981; Brown & Witkowski, 1982; Berlin, 1992; Wierzbicka, 1992).

THE LEXICON OF ENVIRONMENT

Color-term studies deal with the relationship of vocabulary to a continuum, the "color space" or "color solid," with three dimensions of hue, brightness, and saturation. This continuum is best considered as an abstraction, since it is not ordinarily a part of direct human experience. After all, elaborate color charts and precisely controlled samples of pure color are artifacts of industrial civilization; such things are foreign to many traditional societies. The use of these charts and samples in testing provides a corpus of data that are uniform and comparable; but it has a negative side, in the fact that the data are divorced from their normal cultural context and are obtained in an unusual situation or setting. It is possible that, at times, informants may have invented vocabulary for the test situation that would not be used in everyday life.

Another kind of continuum can be found in the physical environment, the terrain, landforms, vegetation, and hydraulic features that people do have direct contact with and must deal with in order to survive. Environment is always present and is always something that people talk about (though they may not always talk about the colors in the environment). Every society exists in a complex reciprocal relationship with its natural environment; the environment provides sustenance and resources and is, in turn, manipulated and reshaped by human exploitation. Perception of the environment—the "environmental image"—derives from this relationship. It is influenced by technology, the means of subsistence and the division of labor, the size and complexity of the community and its ideology, and many other factors. It must be assumed that the environmental lexicon of any language is, in some sense, adaptive, since it is shaped by and facilitates the total interaction between people and nature.

It has been pointed out that even among peoples as culturally similar to one another as are the speakers of modern European languages, there are noticeable differences in the categorization of environmental features. These are sometimes sufficient to cause problems in translation. For example, English *river* must be translated by one of two French words, *fleuve* (roughly, a major river that empties into the sea) or *riviere* (a tributary). English classifies topographic relief features as *mountain* or *hill;* the two words can be roughly matched by German *Berg* and *Hugel,* or by French *montagne* and *colline.* However, in each case the match is inexact. Some large hills, for example, would fall into the *Berg* category; and German has an additional term, *Gebirge,* to use for very large or extensive mountains. English complicates matters by borrowing terms from other languages (like *butte, mesa,* and *veldt,* from French, Spanish, and Afrikaans) to apply to particular types of terrain.

Geographer Kevin Lynch observed that "different groups may have widely different images of the same outer reality" (Lynch, 1960). Underlying this observation is the conviction that if different groups utilize the same environment in different ways, they will experience it differently; they may select different features as important or unimportant and give names to some and not to others. Each group will have, to use Lynch's term, an *environmental image* that is consistent with a particular adaptive strategy.

Such differences have been demonstrated in the man-made environment of cities, where different urban population groups live markedly different lives. Commuting office workers, ghetto children, and down-and-out tramps do not perceive or talk about the urban landscape in the same ways; an abandoned building, for example, might be variously perceived as an eyesore, as an exciting play area, or as a "flop" or sleeping place (Spradley, 1970).

A more striking illustration could be drawn from the geographical names given to a natural area that has been utilized by more than one distinctive cultural group. Contrasts in the cultural meaning of the environment and the imagery that the environment evokes will be reflected in the geographical terminology and place names that each group applies to the same geographical continuum. Information of this sort is available from the southwestern region of the United States, where a number of different peoples (Spanish-speaking and English-speaking populations and several Native American groups) occupy adjacent (and sometimes overlapping) areas. Two of these groups are the Hopi and Navajo nations, whose territories have impinged on each other for generations. An examination of place names in these two languages reveals both similarities and differences:

Navajo place names usually have the form of a noun preceded or followed by a qualifying or descriptive term; the most common are those built on the nouns *rock, water, mountain,* and *house* (used in reference to prehistoric ruins).

tó tso	Big Spring/Water
tó dich'ii	Bitter Spring/Water
tó naneesdizi	Tangled Water (Farmington, NM)
hasbidi bito'	Mourning Dove's Spring
tsé ch'izhi	Rough Rock
tsé łichii'	Red Rock

Most of these place names apply to two types of environmental features—either to sources or bodies of water (springs, rivers, and the like) or to prominent landscape features such as mountains, large rock formations or canyons, and prehistoric ruins, which also stand out as important land-marks. These two groups of terms—landmarks and sources of water—have an obvious importance to a seminomadic people like the Navajo. Their traditional habitation sites are less permanent and are named only by reference to the environmental features (although in some cases, as can be seen in the list, the names have been transferred to contemporary communities).

The Navajo have long been known as a peripatetic people. In the recent past, they have migrated and relocated several times and have had a reputation as raiders and guerilla warriors. Their subsistence activities include movement of their flocks from one pasture area to another, seasonal shifts from one habitation site to another, and trading expeditions over a wide area.

Ethnographic and linguistic studies speak of the Navajo "passion" for geography and for movement. Navajo myths are filled with references to landscape features and locales; the mythological heroes are constantly in movement, traveling over the mountain ranges and canyons of the Navajo world (Wyman, 1957; Witherspoon, 1977). The telling of these myths (the basis of all ceremonials) is at the same time an assertion of Navajo claim to territory. It is also, for the young, a lesson in the terrain, routes, and land-marks that are recounted in the telling.

Hopi place names are often marked as such by the final element *-pi* (also written as *-bi* or *-vi*); it is a suffix that can be translated as "place." Other place names can end in *-pa* (or *-ba*) "spring"; *-ki*, "house"; *-mo*, "mound"; and several other suffixes (Voegelin & Voegelin, 1977). These suffixed elements are added to bases that are often the names of animals or insects, body parts, or even manufactured objects:

Awatobi	Bow Place
Boliki	Butterfly House
Chubmobi	Antelope Mound
Hochokoba	Juniper Spring
Sikyatki	Yellow House

Superficially, these place names do not seem, in translation, very different from the Navajo names. They are, however, very different in their cultural meaning, since they have a direct connection to the important units in society; each refers to, or has a traditional association with, a Hopi clan or a clan-related ceremonial group.

The Hopi have a long history as a sedentary farming people. Their residence in the Southwest can be traced, archaeologically, for many centuries. Most of the Hopi place names refer to locales within or clustered in the vicinity of their villages; some also refer to the prehistoric ruins that have for the Hopi (as they do not for the Navajo) a historical association as their ancient homes. Each of these named places is linked with a certain clan, which may have the responsibility for rituals performed at the various springs, peaks, ruins, and other sites associated with clan history. Many Hopi place names are actually applied to two or more locales; one may be a distant spot, such as a hill that figures in mythology, while another may be a shrine within a village, named for the more distant place. Thus, *chubmobi,* "Antelope Mound," is a hill sacred to the Antelope clan; it is the starting place for foot races held during certain ceremonies; it is also the name of a village site used by the ceremonial society associated with the same clan. In effect, virtually all named places are apportioned to one or another of the matrilineal clans that are the basic units in Hopi social organization.

The prominence of the clan in Hopi society is confirmed by an examination of mythological texts. There is, in fact, no unified body of Hopi sacred literature; there are simply the myths of the several clans. Each clan's mythic traditions recount the acts of ancestral beings, the times and routes of their migrations to their present homes, and events that explain or justify their present position. This is especially true for politically powerful groups like the Bear or Corn clans that hold leadership positions (Eggan, 1950). The events are localized in specific ancient or modern villages, and action takes place principally at sites within the villages, in houses or, most often, in *kivas* (ritual centers). There is traveling, but it is usually defined and named by the beginning and ending points; there is not the same concern with landscape features or the events of travel as is seen in Navajo mythology. While Navajo narrative gives the impression of preoccupation with movement, the Hopi seems to concentrate on locale or situation (Hickerson, 1978).

The form and meaning of place names, then, appears to be consistent with the view of environment and spatial orientation of each cultural group (Stewart, 1975). The Navajo names apply, above all, to prominent landmarks and springs that are widely spaced along historical travel routes. The places named by the Hopi are most densely clustered within, and in the vicinity of, their villages. The Navajo terms are characteristically descriptive, while most Hopi place names derive from their association with the clan divisions of society. It might be noted that while both Hopi and Navajo have a matrilineal clan organization, many of the Navajo clan names are derived from geographical locale, while the reverse is the case in Hopi.

PERSONAL NAMES

All languages give their speakers ways to identify and talk about themselves and others. One type of vocabulary that is found in every human society consists of kinship terms—words like *father, mother, cousin, grandmother,* or *uncle,* which classify individuals according to their common descent or connections through marriage. Anthropologists have a long-standing interest in this kind of vocabulary since kinship systems have proved to be a useful guide for the study of the organization of society. There is a rich anthropological literature on kinship, some of it concerned with the analysis of the terminology itself as well as the social relationships in which kinship terms are used. Another universal domain of language, which also provides resources for identifying and categorizing individuals, has less often been discussed by either linguists or anthropologists; this is the lexicon of personal names.

Let us consider how names are acquired and used in our own contemporary society. In English-speaking countries, most individuals have a single surname and one or more given names (a first name plus a second or "middle" name; in some European countries the second name is a patronymic, but in others, includlng the United States, it is chosen as arbitrarily as the first). The *surname* is one of the principal indicators of a patrilateral bias in our society because it is passed on from father to children and because a wife traditionally assumes her husband's surname at marriage (there have always been some exceptions to this rule, and women have increasingly rejected it in the 1990s). English surnames may be analyzable words. Compound or derivative forms, like Johnson or Armstrong, are common; sometimes they are even identical to words in the regular lexicon of English (as Baker or Cook). Some are directly imported from other languages (Müller); or they may be phonologically modified (Muller) or translated (Miller). But whether or not a surname can be analyzed into meaningful elements, we are accustomed to disregarding its apparent meaning; names are a special category of vocabulary. It is true that an unusual name (such as Boozer or Hogg) can be the basis for jokes, but this would be considered rude and childish.

Given names are simultaneously arbitrary and personal; that is, names are chosen without any restrictions, usually on the basis of personal taste, and they become an inseparable part of an individual's sense of identity. Most Americans have names that are drawn from a very restricted set. There are about a dozen most common men's names and around 20 women's names, each of which is borne by a million or more members of the American population. The number of "Johns" is approximately 6 million, and there are almost as many "Williams," while "Marys" (the most common women's name) number about 4 million (Smith, 1970). The selection is a matter of choice, usually a decision made by parents before or immediately after the birth of a child; the basis for the decision varies from one case to another. We are all aware that there are fads in naming: Political figures, movie or television stars, athletes, and other public figures play a part in bringing certain names into vogue. (In the 1940s, the name "Gary" became popular, in emulation of actor Gary Cooper; similarly, in the 1960s, the name "Elvis" was chosen by a number of families; neither of these names was common in previous years.) Once chosen, the name usually remains unchanged for a person's entire life and is considered a very personal possession; there are times when one must prove his identity or defend his right to use a particular name. We like to assume that our own name is unique—or at least not too common. It is unusual, certainly, if one's own combination of first, middle, and last names is duplicated in the same community or circle of acquaintances.

Typically, our given names are unanalyzable and appear to be essentially meaningless; whatever their origin, they are names and nothing else. Most of them are gender specific; in fact, an indication of sexual identity is the one bit of information that we can almost always get from hearing a person's name. Names do have connotations; some are considered especially "strong" or "manly"; some sound very "dainty," "sweet," or "ladylike"; they may be selected because of these or other connotations. Some names have associations with class or region or ethnic group. However, most of these associations or connotations are fairly fluid and change over time. Everyone, certainly, can claim an inalienable right to freedom of choice in naming the baby. Whatever choice is made, the recipient is stuck with it for life; he or she may not like it but probably will not change it.

It is very likely the workings of this English, and generally European, system of naming that have led to some of the general statements Western writers have made about the nature of names. For example, the philosopher John Stuart Mill called *names* (both personal and geographical names) "meaningless marks" that are given to things and people to distinguish them from one another. It appears, in such a definition, that the form or literal meaning of a name is unimportant; the association between persons and their names is arbitrary, and the main function of the name is simply to identify or distinguish individuals (Gardiner, 1957).

But if we examine the forms and uses of personal names in other societies, it would appear that there is a wide range of variation in both. Names are seldom strictly personal, they are not usually meaningless or arbitrary, they are not often given by free choice, and they are rarely individual "possessions" in the way that we may be accustomed to regard them. In many cases, the names given to individuals are drawn from ordinary vocabulary and may be identical with words or phrases that are in everyday use. Further, even though an individual is given such a name, it may be that it is not used freely—a person's "real" name may be kept secret, with kinship terms or supernumerary names (what we would call "nicknames") used as terms of address or reference.

SANUMA NAMING

An account by A. R. Ramos illustrates the kind of cultural and social meaning that names have for the Sanuma (a division of the Yanomamo) in northern Brazil. The Sanuma are a horticultural people who also rely heavily on hunting and gathering; they live in small villages of 30 to 50 people. Their social organization is patrilineal, and each person has a patronym that is passed from father to children (both male and female) and that indicates membership in a patrilineage. Besides this, each person has a "real name" that is individual, which is bestowed soon after birth. There are several possible sources for these, but the one that is preferred is the name of an animal species. It is obtained through a ritual hunt undertaken by the father.

After the birth of a child, both parents are subject to certain restrictions on their activities and to taboos on the eating of certain foods, which protect the child from supernatural harm. Hunting is one of the activities that are forbidden during this time, with the exception of a ritual hunt, which the father undertakes alone in order to find an animal that will provide both a name and a guardian spirit for the child. When killed, the animal (which must be one that is not taboo, as a food, to the father's lineage) is treated with great respect and must not be touched directly. It is tied in a bundle and carried home, where its spirit eventually comes to live in the child's coccyx; this "coccyx spirit" will provide protection against malevolent spirits. The *humabi* name thus acquired, like all personal names, is never used in direct address during the bearer's lifetime. Once the animal has been brought home and the name bestowed, the meat is cooked and sampled by someone in another household who is not a lineage kinsman of the father. This is an oracle of the child's fate: If the meat is good, the child will live—if not, the child will die.

Typical of the names acquired in this way are Obo (Armadillo), Wisa (Woolly Monkey), Paso (Spider Monkey), and Pakola (Grouse). The only restriction is the avoidance of animals that are forbidden as food to the father's lineage. The main determinants, then, are chance and the father's skill as a hunter; a certain percentage of hunts end in failure, and the name is obtained in another way.

It is especially desirable for a first child to obtain a *humabi* name, apparently because mortality is somewhat greater for a firstborn and spirit protection is therefore more desirable. But there are other names; the most common are based on physical or behavioral characteristics, such ae Short, Feverish, or Brown Eyes. These can also take the form of animal names: Kazu (Capybara) for a child with eyes as big as those of that rodent, or Kutadaima (Tree Frog) for one who is very small. Another common source of names is found in events or places: place of birth, such as Waikia (a child born during a visit to the Waika), or events at the time of birth, such as Oka (one born at the time of a raid). Such names are fairly common and provide a sort of chronology of important events, since the occurrences can be correlated with the age of individuals who bear these names.

Names in the last two categories can be given with fewer restrictions than the *humabi* names, and they can also be taken to replace a *humabi* name that is judged to be "bad" (if, for example, the child becomes sickly or if the father dies). Incidentally, whatever Sanuma names are based on, they are not based on sex. With few exceptions, there seems to be no basis for associating certain names exclusively with boys or with girls.

Ramos emphasizes that the *humabi* naming ritual is the Sanuma norm; even though many names are actually obtained in other ways, this is considered to be the *best* way to name a child. Ramos finds particular interest in the parts of this ritual that dramatize the mutual dependence between the patrilineal kin group (to which both father and child belong) and outsiders— between the father, who kills the animal and obtains the name, and those nonrelatives who sample the meat and thus determine the child's fate.

On another level, we might note the prevalence of names drawn from animal species, the same species that are hunted and used for food. It is intriguing that even though the Sanuma derive their main subsistence from their gardens and also make use of wild plants, they do not include plant species in their roster of names (Ramos, 1974).

The French anthropologist Claude Levi-Strauss has called attention to another widespread type of naming system. This involves a fixed relationship between a group of people, such as a clan, whose members have a strong sense of common identity and unity, and a set of names that are used exclusively by members of that group. To cite an example used by Levi-Strauss, the Osage (Native Americans of the North American plains) had clans with animal names, such as Turkey, Fox, Deer, and so on. Clan membership was indicated by the way in which children's hair was cut and was also symbolized by the names they were given. Each clan's roster of names made reference to "habits, attributes, or characteristic qualities" of the clan animal. Thus, for the Black Bear clan, some of the names were Flashing Eyes, Tracks on the Prairies, Ground Cleared of Grass, and Fat on the Skin. Each such name, then, would serve both to identify an individual and to give an indication to others of his clan affiliation; the supply of names was finite, and they were reused in successive generations (Levi-Strauss, 1966).

This sort of naming system was widespread in traditional Native American societies. It is also typical of aboriginal Australians, whose names are usually associated with ancestral spirits that are reincarnated in the members of a clan or similar group who trace their descent from these ancestors. And they can also give the anthropologist some clues to cultural beliefs about the nature of humans and their place in the universe. Typically, the names seem to reflect beliefs about souls or spirits that have been termed *animistic*.

As Levi-Strauss puts it, names have the linked functions of particularizing and universalizing; that is, they relate the individual to the larger world and the social contexts in which the person has a place. Naming systems—the number of names, the way they are selected and bestowed—also appear to be at least partly determined by the size and cohesiveness of social groups. In small-scale societies, there may be an assumption that names should be unique, either invented anew for each individual or reused only after a previous bearer of the name has died. The bestowal of the same name in successive generations serves to emphasize continuity in descent and is often associated with a belief in reincarnation. In larger societies, especially in those of the Western world, the same reservoir of names is used and reused; we have learned to dissociate them from other contexts. After all, the group of people who are named "Bill" or "Mary" probably do not have anything in common besides their names.

NAMES AND HISTORY

An examination of the history of English surnames can give an indication of the kind of changes that can occur in this limited segment of language as social and cultural conditions change. Historian C. M. Matthews describes a series of stages and transformations in the evolution of English names.

In the centuries before 1100 A.D., Anglo-Saxon names were single words, either simple or compounded; they were easily analyzable, usually drawn from ordinary vocabulary, such as: Aelf (elf), Frith (peace), Wine (friend), Snelgar (bold warrior), Aethelgar (noble warrior), Aethelstan (noble stone), Bealdgyth (bold battle), and the like. There were, Matthews observes, an enormous number of such compounds because the names were prevailingly individual. They were not to be repeated, at least not within the same community. They were not passed on from one generation to the next; the same name might be coined again, but not intentionally. The Anglo-Saxons, according to Matthews, "honored their ancestors by leaving their names severely alone" (Matthews, 1966).

After 1066, the date of the Norman Conquest, the naming system changed rapidly. French names and naming practices were introduced, and Anglo-Saxon names fell into disuse. The total inventory of names became smaller, since the Normans used names to show loyalty or respect; a child might be named after his father or a deceased ancestor, or after a lord or patron. Somewhat later, saints' names came to be used in the same way: A peasant's child might be named Dennis in honor of the lord of the manor while, at the same time, both peasant and lord showed their respect for Saint Dennis. The great popularity of saints' names caused many older names to be abandoned.

With the increasing repetition of a relatively small stock of names, the use of *by-names* was quickly established. This resulted in a double name, consisting of a personal name followed with the by-name, which might be a patronymic, a designation of occupation or locality, or a personal description. Thus, "Richard the Son of Gilbert" could be distinguished from "Richard the Barber," "Richard the Stout," "Richard the Fainthearted," and so on.

The transformation of by-names into inherited *surnames* took place in a brief period, between the late 13th and early 14th centuries; it coincided with changes in laws affecting the registration, tenure, and inheritance of property. Like most property, surnames came to be patrilineally inherited.

There have been few changes in English surnames between the 14th century and the present. The second, or middle, name became popular in the 18th century. The double surname was adopted by a number of British families in the 19th century, giving us hyphenated names such as Radcliffe-Brown and Pitt-Rivers. Both of these developments seem to be adaptations to the increasing difficulty of maintaining unambiguous individual identification in an ever-expanding society. (We can see our increasing reliance on numerical codes—social security numbers, licenses, credit card numbers, and so on—as a further adaptation to the same dilemma [Matthews, 1966].)

SOCIOLINGUISTICS
AND THE ETHNOGRAPHY
OF SPEAKING

On the world map, the United States appears as one of several English-speaking nations; brought into closer focus, it falls into a number of regional dialect areas and also includes a large array of minority languages. Most Americans can identify with fair accuracy the dialects characteristic of New England, the Midwest, or the deep South and can easily detect the "foreign" accents of non-native English speakers. If we bring the focus still closer and zoom in on a single community, the picture does not become simpler. Instead, new levels of complexity are revealed. There are patterns of variation in ways of speaking, sometimes too subtle to be detected by outsiders but understood by insiders as meaningful within their own social context.

English is the dominant language in most American communities, but not in all; in some towns near the Mexican border, Spanish is the language most often heard. Native American reserves, settlements of recent immigrants, and even certain religious orders add to the mix of languages. In urban areas there are neighborhoods where minority languages such as Spanish, Italian, Polish, or Chinese become dominant. Linguistic pluralism is not as prevalent in North America as in many parts of the world—India, West Africa, or eastern Europe, for example—but here, as elsewhere, there is always some degree of speech diversity.

In some regions of the United States, English and Spanish are part of the experience of most residents, who are acquainted with local varieties of both languages and with the situations in which one or the other is normally used. In certain towns on the plains of west Texas, where English is recognized as the dominant language, most individuals can be identified as "Anglo" or "Chicano." The relationship between these two languages, here as elsewhere, is linked to the history, the occupations, and the hierarchical relationships of persons of Anglo and Chicano identity. Unlike neighboring New Mexico, the Texas plains do not have a long-established Hispanic population; there are few third-generation Spanish speakers, and many individuals are recent immigrants, either from Mexico or from border regions such as the Rio Grande Valley.

In many Texas communities, Chicanos are residentially segregated. They often hold unskilled and semiskilled positions (as agricultural workers, custodians, short-order cooks, shop clerks, and so on); they usually speak Spanish to one another on the job and to obviously Hispanic clients and customers. English is the language of official functions and of education and has, overall, a higher status than Spanish. Many Chicanos use both English and Spanish; some appear to be coordinated or "balanced" bilinguals, fluent in both languages, while some have only active control of English words and phrases for a few necessary transactions (at work, on the bus, and so forth). Bilingual education programs (mandated only in districts with a high ratio of Hispanic to non-Hispanic students) underline the necessity for Spanish speakers to learn English, but not the reverse. Proportionally, far fewer Anglos know any Spanish at all. Even though educators often pay lip service to the desirability of dual language skills, only a marked increase in the economic and social power of the Mexican-American population could make it seem really important for Anglos to study Spanish.

Chicanos are apt to overestimate their knowledge of English, while Anglos tend to deny or minimize their knowledge of Spanish. However, observation of Chicano family groups would suggest that there is often a three-generation passage from Spanish to English dominance: Grandparents may speak Spanish almost exclusively; their grandchildren use English among themselves and to their parents; while those in the middle generation switch between Spanish and English, as uneasy translators between the older and younger generations. Anglos are accustomed to hearing Spanish spoken, but they appear to disregard it as "background noise." They are, in other words, conditioned to a third-party role when Spanish is spoken; their relationship to it is passive. While most Anglos would be taken aback to be directly addressed in Spanish by a store clerk or receptionist, Chicanos need to make active use of English, though their usage may be specialized for use in a limited set of situations. They are, in the status structure of the total community, rewarded or penalized according to their mastery of an Anglo variety of English, rather than for bilingual ability.

In the United States, the relative prestige of English and Spanish, the numbers of speakers of each, the number of bilinguals, and many other factors vary from one region or community to the next. The sociolinguistic situation in the southwest differs from that found in California or in northeastern urban areas such as New York, where the majority of Spanish speakers may be of Puerto Rican rather than Mexican origin or ancestry. Throughout the world, similar complex and unequal ethnic and cultural relationships often find their most obvious expression in the juxtaposition of distinctive forms of linguistic expression. From about 1960 on, linguistic anthropology has seen a rapid development of methods for studying and describing speech behavior in its social context.

LANGUAGE AND SOCIETY

During much of the 20th century, students of language were guided by the distinction that Ferdinand de Saussure drew between *parole* (or "speech") and *langue* (or "language") and gave priority to the latter as the object of study. In the words of William Labov, language was seen as a "structured set of social norms . . . shared by all members of the speech community" (1972). Even though linguists gathered their data from individual "informants," they usually directed their efforts toward the description of this generalized system—"the language"—and rarely gave systematic attention to individual variation in speaking. Yet this variation, always present, has long invited study. Over several decades, sociolinguistics has emerged as a productive interdisciplinary research field that takes speech variation as its focus.

In earlier years, research that dealt with speech variation had usually focused on regional dialectology, or the geographic distribution of selected lexical and phonological features that could be explained by reference to the history of settlement, extra-areal origins, and other diachronic influences; the *Word Geography of the Eastern United States*, edited by H. Kurath (1949), is an example of this type of research. By contrast, sociolinguistics offered a new paradigm; this was essentially a synchronic approach, combining linguistic field methods with a sociological perspective on structural factors such as role and status, ethnicity and gender. There is an underlying premise that people who interact on a regular basis will acquire and use similar language patterns; thus, networks of interaction, whether based on ethnicity, gender, residential patterns, social categories, or other influences, are reflected in verbal behavior. According to Labov, language, while itself a form of social behavior, "may have a special utility for the sociologist as a sensitive index of many other social processes. Variation in linguistic behavior does not itself exert a powerful influence on social development, nor does it affect drastically the life chances of the individual; on the contrary, the shape of linguistic behavior changes rapidly as the speaker's social position changes. This malleability of language underlies its great utility as an indicator of social change" (Labov, 1972).

The primary objective in sociolinguistic research is to trace connections among linguistic and social variables, and thus to use language as a source of insights for the study of society. The framework in which these variables can best be studied is the speech community. Sociolinguistics takes the community, rather than the broader and more diffusely defined language, as the basic unit for study. A speech community is a real social unit within which speakers share a repertoire of "ways of speaking"; that is, they share rules and conventions for using, evaluating, and interpreting speech that are rooted in their shared experiences and traditions. A speech community may include speakers of one or several languages; it is a localized nexus that crosscuts the wider distribution of regional, national, and world languages.

LANGUAGE VARIABLES
AS SOCIAL MARKERS

William Labov, one of the founders of sociolinguistics, is known for the innovative studies in which he demonstrated the use of selected linguistic features as markers of class divisions in society. In 1969 Labov conducted an initial study of the social stratification of English as spoken in New York City;
this research was the basis for his doctoral dissertation. While previous writers had described the speech of New Yorkers as "haphazard," lacking any
regular patterns of pronunciation, Labov succeeded in identifying two
phonological variables that showed a positive correlation with classes as
defined by socioeconomic criteria: (1) the presence or absence of [r] in word-
final position and before consonants, in words like *guard, bared* and *dark;* and
(2) variation between fricative [θ], stop [t], and affricate [tθ] in words such as
thing, through, and *bath.*

Labov selected a sample of lifelong New Yorkers, classified into 10
socioeconomic groups on the basis of three criteria: occupation, education,
and family income. Four types of speech data were recorded during inter-
views: (A) casual speech; (B) careful conversation (the largest part of the
interview); (C) reading; and (D) pronunciation of isolated words. Labov
demonstrated that for all groups, the patterns of stylistic variation are "consistent with the status of /r/ as a prestige marker, and stops and affricates
for /th/ as stigmatized forms." In the distribution of the "th" variable, two
types of variation emerge—first, a tendency characteristic of all socioeconomic class groups for the stop and affricate variants [t, tθ] to occur more
frequently in casual speech, less often in reading and careful speech, and
least often in the slow pronunciation of individual words. Second, grada-
tions within this overall pattern of distribution are consistent with the definition of socioeconomic classes—that is, the stigmatized forms were, overall, used more frequently by working class individuals and less frequently
by those classified as middle and upper class. Thus, this feature proved to
be a reliable social marker—and was used as such in subsequent studies by
Labov and others.

Later sociolinguistic studies have used, and built on, Labov's methodology, combining the use of questionnaires directed toward socioeconomic
variables and tape-recorded interview sessions that are structured to elicit
specified linguistic features. For a study of French in Montreal, D. and G.
Sankoff selected a random sample of native speakers living in a predominantly French area; the sample was stratified in terms of age, sex, and socioeconomic level (based on residential neighborhood). One of the selected linguistic features was the deletion of underlying /l/ in a number of pronouns
and articles (*il, ils, elle, les, la*)—a very complex matter, which cannot be
accounted for by any rule of variation. Like Labov, the Sankoffs used a combination of interview techniques, including free-ranging conversation in a
family setting, and also more controlled interviewing and the reading of a
text in order to assure comparability in the data. Two tendencies emerge:

first, that /l/ is deleted more consistently in certain morphemes (*il*, *ils*) than in others (*la*, *les*). Second, a degree of stratification was found, involving both class and gender as variables; overall, G. Sankoff states that "/l/ deletion follows the order: women professionals < men professionals < women workers < men workers" (G. Sankoff, 1986).

LANGUAGES IN CONTACT

The hallmark of sociolinguistics is the study of speech variation among individuals, socioeconomic classes, ethnic groups, genders, and other social divisions. The most striking variation is seen when speakers of two or more markedly different speech varieties (different languages or dialects) are in contact, living and working together. There are several possible outcomes: individual and community bilingualism; the regular use of different languages in specific contexts or situations; and the development of a mixed language—a *pidgin*—or some other form of *lingua franca*. Early studies of language contact situations predated, and may have inspired, the development of sociolinguistics with its broad focus on speech variation as a general phenomenon.

DIGLOSSIA

An innovator in the study of complex speech communities was linguist Charles A. Ferguson, who described and compared several instances of a linguistic situation that he called *diglossia*. As Ferguson originally used the term, it referred to speech communities in which "two or more varieties of the same language are used by some speakers under different conditions." In such a community, it is typical that there are significant numbers of bilinguals. Indeed, most of the population may be bilingual (or bidialectal), and these individuals feel that each linguistic variety is appropriate in certain situations. Generally, one variety of language is associated with education and literacy.

In defining and discussing diglossia, Ferguson began by describing his own experiences as a visiting scholar in Arabic-speaking countries, where the classical Arabic of the Koran coexists with diversified local dialects (the Arabic of Baghdad or Cairo or Tunis, and so on). He compared this situation with examples drawn from Switzerland (standard German and Swiss-German), Haiti (French and Haitan Creole), and Greece (standard and colloquial dialects). All of these, Ferguson emphasized, are areas in which there is a long-standing stable relationship between markedly different linguistic varieties, a relationship that reflects, and endures in, a stable social situation.

Ferguson labeled the two language varieties in each case as H ("high") and L ("low"). He listed some of the typical situations in which each is used:

	H	L
Sermon in church or mosque	X	
Instructions to servants, waiters, workmen, clerks		X
Personal letter	X	
Speech in parliament, political speech	X	
University lecture	X	
Conversation with family, friends, colleagues		X
News broadcast	X	
Radio "soap opera"		X
Newspaper editorial, story, caption, or picture	X	
Caption on political cartoon		X
Poetry	X	
Folk literature		X

As an outsider, Ferguson was keenly aware of the distinction between H and L, although insiders did not usually perceive these as different codes. Instead, they generally judged the forms and constructions characteristic of H to be "purer" or more "correct." But in fact, all speakers know and use L; it would not be unusual for a professor to deliver a lecture in H and then to lapse into L while chatting informally with colleagues. According to Ferguson, any speaker "is at home in L to a degree he almost never achieves in H" because L is everyone's first language. Adults use L when speaking to children; children may overhear H being used, but they use L in speaking to one another. The actual learning of H comes through formal education; those who have little or no formal education do not become skilled in using H. Thus, both level of employment and social standing are closely tied to fluency in H.

Diglossia, as described by Ferguson, is characteristic of speech communities that have a body of literature of high (or sacred) reputation; a small, long-established literate elite; and limited social mobility. Predictably, in his opinion, the relationship of H and L varieties will change if social conditions change. Increasing public education, with an increase in the contexts in which H is used, will eventually diminish or erase the distinction between H and L; there may be a movement toward language standardization. On the other hand, if there is a revolutionary or radical populist movement, L can rise in prestige and displace H, coming to be considered appropriate in any situation (though borrowing vocabulary from H in the process) (Ferguson, 1959).

Ferguson's deliberately narrow definition of diglossia as the use of "two or more varieties of the same language" was soon extended by other scholars, and the term has been widely applied to a variety of situations in which distinct or even unrelated languages coexist in a hierarchical relationship. Thus, for example, Joan Rubin (1972) described the linguistic situation in Paraguay, where Spanish (H) was established under colonialism as the official language, superposed on a native language, Guaraní (L). Today, both languages are widely used—Guaraní to a greater degree in rural areas, with Spanish more common in the cities. Another variation on the definition of H and L speech varieties will be seen in Migliazza's study of Yanomama diglossia, discussed later in this chapter.

BILINGUALISM

An alternative way of describing the relationship of languages in contact puts the focus on the linguistic skills of individuals. Linguists usually define *bilingualism* as "native-like" control of two languages; however, this is a rather subjective definition, and one that would be hard to apply uniformly (after all, how can native-like control be evaluated?). Many applied linguists who are involved in second-language teaching prefer to treat bilingualism as a gradient; there are degrees or stages of bilingualism that can be evaluated based on performance—the ability to understand and to produce meaningful utterances in the second language.

In a diglossic society, there are by definition a high percentage of bilingual individuals, fluent in both linguistic varieties (different languages or, in some cases, highly divergent dialects). But bilingualism (we will use the term to cover the ability to use *two or more* languages) prevails in many countries in which the relationship between language varieties does not conform to the diglossic pattern. The situation in a plural society such as India, where there are hundreds of languages in use, is too complex to be described simply in terms of diglossia. The number of languages and the contexts in which they are used varies from one state or region to another, and many individuals must use two, three, or more languages. Hindi and Urdu are very similar, though written with different scripts; these two Indo-European languages are used to some degree throughout the nation; the related ancient language, Sanskrit, is important in connection with the Hindu religion and classical literature. Other Indo-European languages such as Bengali, Gujarati, and Assamese predominate in regions of eastern and northern India. Speakers of languages of the highly diversified Dravidian family are in the majority in much of the south; and there are also regional enclaves of Austroasiatic languages, as well as isolated tribal languages. Depending on the region, it would not be unusual for an individual who is a native speaker of a minority language (such as Toda or Santali) to acquire the dominant language of the region (Bihari, Kannada, Gujarati, for example) in primary school and to continue his or her education in Hindi (important for participation in national affairs) and English (essential for international travel and communication). This would also entail, depending on the language mix, mastering at least two and perhaps four different writing systems.

Multiculturalism and multilingualism has probably prevailed in the subcontinent of India since prehistoric times; as a single administrative unit, the subcontinent was unified under British colonial rule, and English was imposed as an official language. As such, English was essential for civil service and other public functionaries and became the main language of education at the university level. Since the end of colonial rule, English has continued to have a place in Indian society; it is one of 12 languages with official status and serves to some extent as a neutral *lingua france*—an important role in a multiethnic nation in which rivalries often involve language loyalty.

Despite periodic fluctuations in national language policies, India in general presents a picture of *stable bilingualism*—a situation of bilingual equilibrium that is perpetuated generation after generation. This is also characteristic of Switzerland, a nation in which German, French, and Italian predominate in separate regions. Most Swiss citizens are fluent in more than one of these tongues, and many speak English as well. *Unstable bilingualism* could arise, for example, in a situation in which military conquest or political events result in language shifts. The island of Palau, for example, has a complex linguistic history: Palauan is a unique Austronesian language with no close ties to any other; at various times between 1885 and World War II, Palau was a colony of Spain, Germany, and Japan; after World War II, it became a U.S. trust territory. This has entailed radical shifts in education and a linguistic rift between generations. In 1960, H. G. Barnett wrote: "Quite literally, young people are . . . learning to speak a different language from that of their parents, some of whom know Japanese, some only Palauan, very few English. . . . [P]arents who were partly assimilated into Japanese life are becoming intellectual strangers to their Americanized children" (Barnett, 1960).

INCIPIENT BILINGUALISM. In a small village in western Mexico, Richard Diebold investigated an early stage in the development of contacts between the national language, Spanish, and a native language, Huave; he termed this stage incipient bilingualism. The official census counted over 80% of the Indian population in this area as monolingual speakers of Huave. Six percent were found to be coordinate bilinguals, and about twice as many were classified as subordinate bilinguals (that is, they could use Spanish, but imperfectly and with a strong Huave accent). Diebold knew that, as a general rule, native languages in rural Mexico are giving way to Spanish; his study was directed toward understanding the process of change and the place of individuals who vary greatly in their language abilities in this process.

Using a 100-item list list of Huave words, Diebold found that men who had been classified as bilingual were able to give Spanish equivalents for 90% or more of the words. Those in the subordinate bilingual group ranged from 61% to 94%, with a mean of 89%. However, even the monolinguals could translate a large number of the words; their ability to provide Spanish equivalents ranged between 11% and 68%, with a mean score of 37%. Diebold noted that many Spanish loanwords have been borrowed into Huave and are known, as Huave vocabulary, to monolinguals and bilinguals alike. Other Spanish vocabulary has also been learned by many monolingual speakers of Huave, probably indirectly from those who are bilingual.

All of this goes to show that contact between languages (linguistic acculturation) is a complex processs that involves the speech community as a whole. It can also be seen to involve every individual; even those who are functionally monolingual are found to be in an "initial learning stage" of bilingualism and are thus more than passively involved.

The Huave community of San Mateo, which Diebold studied, is located in a remote rural area, but it was coming into increasing contact with and participation in national life. Men from San Mateo must use Spanish on the occasions when they visit the nearby Spanish-speaking community that serves as a regional administrative and marketing center. Active use of Spanish was largely a male skill; Huave was uniformly the language of the home, and women rarely spoke Spanish. Indirectly, however, they were being programmed for change. Diebold has predicted that this change can lead to either of two outcomes: (1) the extinction of the native language, or (2) a stable coexistence, with both Huave and Spanish in use (comparable with the diglossia situation described above). This prediction could be extended far beyond the Huave villages and far beyond the borders of Mexico. Native peoples in all parts of the world are subject to similar pressures and must cope with similar necessities, affecting both the way they will live and the languages they will speak (Diebold, 1961). *Language death* has increasingly become a topic of concern for linguistic anthropologists.

Pidgin and Creole Languages

The words *pidgin* and *creole* have long served as labels for what were traditionally regarded as marginal or illiterate varieties of "standard" Western languages, usually varieties that developed and were used in colonial or frontier regions. Racist and paternalistic attitudes toward non-Western peoples went hand in hand with the assumption that they were simply incapable of speaking "proper" English or French. Most linguistic scholars devoted their research to the mainstream varieties of language and gave little attention to those they considered simply incorrect. But pidgins and creoles have become a focus of interest to modern linguists, especially as a source of insight into processes of language development and change.

A pidgin, as today's linguists use the term, is a *lingua franca* that comes into use in situations where a group of individuals with no language in common find a need to communicate. What develops is a kind of minimal language, with a vocabulary adequate only to the particular situation and little or nothing in the way of grammatical inflection. Pidgins have sometimes been developed to facilitate trade—indeed, it is thought that the word *pidgin* itself dates to the opening of Western trade with China, from the English word *business*. Pidgins also arose during the years of the slave trade, in the early stages of colonialism, and in settings such as mines, plantations, and maritime ports, where workers might be recruited from a number of linguistic and cultural backgrounds. Dozens of pidgin languages have been noted, but only a few of them have been studied in detail, in areas such as West Africa, Melanesia, Australia, and the West Indies.

A pidgin is, by definition, a mixed language. However, the bulk of the vocabulary is usually drawn from the language of the dominant power. The explanation is simple: Workers, whatever their background, must obey orders and respond to questions in the language of their masters. Thus, exposure to a colonial language—English, Portuguese, French, or the like— is the shared experience from which the raw material of the new language develops; the creativity of the speakers provides the rest.

Robert A. Hall, one of the linguists who introduced pidgin languages as a subject for serious study, provides some examples of vocabulary drawn from Melanesian pidgin (today known as Tok Pisin or Neo-Melanesian), along with the (presumed) models from the source language (usually English in this case). A typical pidgin may have a vocabulary of around 800 to 1,500 words, compared with 10,000 or more in a "full-size" language. The tendency seen here, to adopt very specific words and to broaden or generalize their meanings, is a distinctive characteristic of pidgin languages.

Melanesian Pidgin	Source word	Meaning
ars	arse	bottom, base, cause, reason, source
bagarap	bugger up	wreck, ruin
bilong	belong	of, for
disfela	this + fellow	this
faitim	fight 'im	strike, beat, hit
gras	grass	anything bladelike growing out of a surface (grass, whiskers, etc.)
haisimap	hoist 'im up	lift, raise
long	along	to, at, with, by
mi	me	I, me
mifela	me + fellow	we, us (not including the hearer)
pinis	finish	already
yu	you	you (sing.)
yufela	you + fellow	you (pl.)
yumi	you + me	we, us (including the hearer)

(Hall, 1959)

A few sentences:

Mi gat trifela buk.	"I have three books."
Em i lukim mi.	"He looks at me."
Mi lukim em.	"I look at him."
Em i digim boret hariap olsem mi.	"He dug the trench as fast as me."
Em i digim boret hariap long mi.	"He dug the trench faster than me."
Dispela man i kam asde em i papa bilong mi.	"This man who came yesterday is my father."
Mi ritim Wantok niuspepa pinis.	"I have finished reading Wantok (newspaper)." (Lyovin, 1997)

Many pidgins are shortlived; they quickly fall out of use when the need has passed. The word *creole* is often paired with *pidgin;* many linguists, like Hall, treat the two as stages in a kind of evolutionary process of language development. If a pidgin remains in use, it may be expanded to serve the whole range of functions necessary to a speech community; thus, it gives rise to a creole language. Over the course of two or more generations, the various native tongues of the first generation are forgotten or lapse in importance, and the creole is the first, or "native," language of the descendants. In the process, the vocabulary is greatly increased by continued borrowing from the original source language or from others; by compounding and other processes of word derivation; and often by incorporating vocabulary from one or another of the native languages of the original speakers. Thus, for example, Hall's list of Melanesian pidgin vocabulary includes *pato* "duck" and *pikinini* "child," from Portuguese; *tambu* "prohibited, forbidden" from Polynesian; *karabau* "water buffalo," from Malay; and *balus* "pigeon, airplane" and *kiau* "egg" from a local language of Melanesia.

More fundamental, perhaps, is the increasing complexity and regularity of grammatical processes. In many cases, there are influences of earlier languages to be seen in the grammatical patterns; for example, the Melanesian pidgin *mifela* (or *mipela*) and *yumi* preserve a distinction between exclusive and inclusive first person plurals that is typical of Melanesian languages but absent in English. Typically, creole languages are fairly uninflected, while placing great reliance on word order and syntactic rules. However, it remains difficult to draw a clear line between pidgin and creole—where does the one end and the other begin? The Melanesian variety that Hall studied in the 1950s could be properly identified as a pidgin; it was no one's native language. Today, its descendant, Tok Pisin, is a creole language; it still serves as a *lingua franca* for speakers of mutually unintelligible languages, but it is also the primary language of several thousand speakers.

Both Bickerton, who studied pidgins and creoles in Hawaii, and Duval, who conducted dialect studies in Jamaica, found a continuum of variation from the most rudimentary "pidgin" to more elaborated "creole" varieties. It may be preferable to speak of *pidginization* and *creolization* as processes—the first, the formation of a minimal language, reflecting the common core shared by the first speakers; the second, the expansion of a pidgin as a fully complex language. In many world areas, creoles and "standard" varieties of language are present in the same speech community—for example, English and English-based creole in Jamaica and French and French-based creole in Haiti. This is a common type of diglossia. In this type of situation, public education and various socioeconomic pressures may eventually lead to *decreolization*—modification of the creole in the direction of the standard and to the point that some or all of its distinctive characteristics are lost.

The brief history of pidgin and creole studies, over little more than a century, presents an opportunity to examine the range of interpretive frameworks that have been applied to a single problem. The acknowledged "father" of pidgin-creole studies was Hugo Schuchard (1842-1927). Schuchard was a critic of the comparative-historical approach, which dominated linguistics in the late 19th century. In his *Kreolische Studien,* he argued that creoles were *mixed languages* and thus should be seen as exceptions to the accepted "family tree" model of language origins. However, Schuchard to the contrary, few linguists of the time gave serious consideration to creoles. Some would have seen them as imperfect imitations of correct models, while others—Leonard Bloomfield, for one—suggested that they might be essentially correct imitations of poor models.

Bloomfield favored the so-called "baby-talk" theory, suggesting that European masters improvised a simplified form of language to communicate with their servants and slaves, and that this was, in turn, imitated to create the pidgin and creole languages of the West Indies and other colonial areas. This idea, as well as the suggestion that departures from European models were inspired by African influences, soon fell by the wayside. This was largely the result of analytic studies that revealed (1) that there is no widespread or systematic "African" substratum in Caribbean and West Indian creoles (not to deny the presence of specific vocabulary and other features in individual languages); and (2) that there are remarkable parallels among pidgin and creole languages worldwide, regardless of their individual backgrounds.

Several investigators have suggested, partly on the basis of a few widespread vocabulary items like *savvy* (or *sabe*) "know" and *pikni* (or *pikinini*) "child," that Portuguese—an important language in early Western exploration and colonization—played a major role in the formation of pidgins throughout the world. K. Whinnom carried this idea further by proposing a monogenetic origin for all European-based pidgins, beginning with Sabir, the original *lingua franca* of the Mediterranean (which may be as old as the Roman Empire).

By contrast, Robert A. Hall has been a proponent of the view that pidgins arise more or less spontaneously, when the need is present. He emphasizes the sociopolitical environments in which pidgins develop and the simplification that sets them apart from the language or languages from which they are derived. More recently, Derek Bickerton has interpreted the general similarities among pidgins and creoles as evidence for the workings of a universal human "bioprogram" for language.

Beginning in 1959, this generalizing perspective has been furthered by a series of conferences, held in Jamaica, that provide a venue for comparisons and dissemination of information among the scholars involved in this field. Contributing to the recognition of pidginization and creolization as general phenomena is the realization that there are, and undoubtedly have been in the past, many such languages that are neither the products of Western colonialism nor based on European languages. The Chinook Jargon of northwestern North America, Lingoa Geral of central South America, and Bazaar Malay of Malaysia and Indonesia are three well-documented examples.

THE ETHNOGRAPHY OF SPEAKING

The presence of two or more languages in the same community is the most obvious type of linguistic diversity. As shown in Ferguson's study, bilingual individuals can be observed to switch, in different situations, from one language to the other. A person may speak one language at home, switch to a second at school or work, switch again while lunching with friends, and so on. But monolinguals also switch codes (or styles of speaking) in different situations, though the changes may be less noticeable. The study of diglossia and bilingualism has helped call linguists' attention to the more general phenomenon of situational variation, or code switching, as a normal part of social behavior.

For practical reasons, it seems impossible to record and explain all the variation found in speech, even in the speech of a single individual. Every individual has a unique speech repertoire that reflects his or her own experiences—the languages used in the home, school, and community, the changes acquired in moving from one community to another; the influence of personal acquaintances, reading, media, and the like. Out of this repertoire, which makes up the individual's competence or general knowledge, speech behavior is selected as appropriate to any given situation. In other words, an individual's performance shows a range of variation, since he or she is able to switch from one style of speaking to another.

The reasons for switching are obvious. We use speech to transmit, simultaneously, two types of message. One of these might be called the purely "linguistic" message, the sum of the information contained in the morphemes, the raw material, from which an utterance is built up. The other, more personal, type of message is conveyed by the ways this raw material is selected, combined, and delivered. It includes information on the identity of the speakers, their feelings about other individuals, and their interests and attitudes. And because each individual plays different roles and acts in different situations, the verbal clues that are given can vary from one moment to the next.

Dell Hymes is an anthropologist who has worked to encourage and facilitate research of the sort that he calls the "ethnography of speaking"—the descriptive study of the use of language, deeply embedded in its cultural context. Hymes's approach is built on (but goes far beyond) those of earlier researchers like Labov and Ferguson. Labov focused attention on the speech variation that he saw primarily as a reflection of societal variables; Ferguson highlighted code switching by individuals, describing this switching as a response to certain situational variables. Hymes took a more comprehensive perspective, realizing that a great number and variety of factors influence the use of language; he made this point by the use of an acronym based on the term SPEAKING:

S—Setting and scene: the time, place and psychological setting

P—Participants: the speaker, listener, audience, and any other participants

E—Ends: the desired or expected outcome

A—Act sequence: how form and content are delivered

K—Key: the mood or spirit (serious, ironic, joking, etc.)

I—Instrumentalities: the dialect or language variety used by the speech community

N—Norms: conventions or expectations about volume, interruption, hesitation, etc.

G—Genres: different types of performance (speech, joke, sermon, etc.)

Hymes not only calls attention to the complexity of speech behavior and to its multifaceted interrelatedness with its social setting; as an anthropologist, he also brings cultural variables into the mix. He sees it as important to acknowledge that individuals make active use of their linguistic skills to influence others and to achieve culturally defined ends. The effect has been to heighten awareness of the central role of language in its cultural setting, in ethnographic fieldwork, and in the anthropological curriculum as well (Hymes, 1972).

Under Hymes's aegis, the focus on the speech community has been sharpened and supplemented by the addition of a number of tool concepts, including speech situation, speech act, and speech event. The smallest of these units is the *speech act,* a single uninterrupted utterance by, in most cases, a single individual. A *speech event* consists of one or several speech acts; it is defined and governed by the rules and conventions of the speech community—for example, exchanging greetings, making an apology, telling a joke, ordering a meal or a drink, delivering a sermon or a lecture. A *speech situation* is not an event or series of events but the setting and circumstances in which people speak—or, in some cases, refrain from speaking: a birthday party, a scholarly convention, a family reunion, and so on. Speech events and speech situations cannot be defined in absolute terms, primarily because they are culturally variable. However, application of these concepts provides a basis for dividing the stream of human behavior into manageable segments for close study and, eventually, for comparison. And comparison can reveal underlying similarities as well as differences.

SPEECH EVENTS

Even among people who use the same language or dialect, speech behavior varies in ways that reflect the social context. One way of examining this variation is to observe how individuals behave in a specific, culturally defined situation. In Western societies, an exchange of greetings is a most ordinary, everyday sort of occurrence; it does not require conscious planning and seems almost automatic. Most Americans greet acquaintances spontaneously, and some even greet complete strangers.

1. "Hi there, Mr. Jones!"

   "Hello, Tommy. How are you?"

   "Fine, thanks."

2. "Good morning, Mrs. Goldman."

"The same to you, Dr. Stevens. Nice weather."

3. "How's it going, Sam?"

"Not bad. How's it with you, Mike?"

"Could be worse."

4. "Good morning, Jenkins."

"Good morning, sir."

5. "Hello, Louise."

"Oh. Hi."

6. "Mary! How are you? You look wonderful."

"Nancy! It 's so good to see you!"

7. "Bill."

"Dick."

8. "Morning, Dr. Brown. Pretty day, isn't it?"

"Oh, hello, Susan. Yes, it's nice—going to be a scorcher, though."

9. "Mommy! Mommy!"

"Hello, Johnny! Have you been a good boy?"

10. "Good evening, Senator."

"Hello there. Nice to see you."

Any of these speech events could be taken as an example of what the British anthropologist Bronislaw Malinowski termed *phatic communion*. That is, they are exchanges of words and phrases that are important less for their literal or referential meaning than for their social functions. Malinowski emphasized the importance of social context in his discussion of meaning in language; this becomes especially critical when translating from one language to another. Malinowski's experience in fieldwork in the Trobriand Islands of Melanesia had convinced him that words cannot be translated in any absolute sense but are meaningful and can be understood only in the context of a particular society (Malinowski, 1923).

In Western societies, we use verbal exchanges, such as an exchange of greetings, to establish or reaffirm social ties, to show that we are aware of and value one another. We know, in our familiar social context, that "How are you?" or "How's it going?" is not a serious request for information about the condition of one's health or the state of world affairs; rather, the inquiry is an acknowledgment of one's existence and importance. It could be very upsetting to find oneself ignored. Exchanges of greetings are often accompanied by a wave or nod, a smile or other gesture of recognition; such nonverbal salutes alone can sometimes suffice to serve the same functions.

Phatic communion is a social function of language that can easily be separated or abstracted from the literal meaning of the words used in any individual verbal exchange. But there is more information contained in these brief verbal exchanges than might seem obvious at first glance. From the previous list of speech events one can guess, among other things, that in (1) and (9) the speakers are an adult and a child; that in (4) and (8) there is a difference in status and that in (8) the speakers may be employer and employee; that in (3) and (7) they are well acquainted with each other and probably friends; while in (5) and (10) the second speaker does not know or does not remember the first. In short, from such brief and fairly "rneaningless" snatches of conversation, something can usually be inferred about the social identity, relative age, and status relationships of the parties involved.

We can do this because we, as well as they, are privy to a code that is expressed through the use of names and other terms of address. The intricacies of this code have been explored in a number of sociolinguistic studies. One of the earliest and most perceptive of these, by psychologists Roger Brown and Marguerite Ford, examined the use of terms of address in business firms and other institutions in the eastern United States. The system that they described still seems generally applicable, though variations could undoubtedly be discovered in different regional and social settings.

Brown and Ford dealt especially with status ranking in American society. This is a feature of American life that everyone is aware of, though the awareness may be heightened in certain settings, such as military organizations or business offices. Relative status, or "pecking order," affects the way individuals behave toward one another—who does a favor for whom, who pays the luncheon check, who asks for advice and who offers it, and so forth. Perhaps the most explicit recognition of relative status and the best source of information about status for an observer can be found in the terms of address that individuals use in speaking to one another. The number of these used in American English is small; as Brown and Ford point out, the main choices are the use of a first name (FN) or a title combined with a last name (TLN). There are three possible ways these terms can be used in the interaction of two individuals: reciprocal use of FN, as in example (3) above; nonreciprocal use of FN and TLN, as in example (1); and reciprocal use of TLN, as in (2).

What determines our choice among these three options? There are two reciprocal patterns, TLN/TLN and FN/FN. Of these, the first is certainly more formal; two people who are introduced with TLN are apt to move away from this and to assume the FN/FN pattern as they become better acquainted. For example, they will go from "Mr. Smith" and "Ms. Campbell" to "Mike" and "Sue" rather than the reverse. Both of the reciprocal patterns might be said to assume relative equality of status; or at least, they do not express inequality.

The nonreciprocal pattern, TLN/FN, is used: (a) when there is a marked difference in age, between children and adults or between younger and older adults; (b) when there are differences of rank or status within an organization, as between a supervisor and a clerk or an officer and an enlisted person; or. (c) when someone in a service occupation wishes to express helpfulness or subordination to the wishes of a customer. In American society, any of these relationships may move toward the reciprocal FN/FN pattern;

however, it is considered appropriate that the older person or the one with higher status take the initiative in making such a change—to do otherwise might be considered overly familiar or "pushy."

There are many deviations away from these general patterns, and there are also other terms of address. For example, a title alone (T)—such as Sir or Ma'am, or Professor, Judge, Colonel, and so on—is usually felt to be even less intimate and somewhat more formal than TLN. Last name only (LN) is sometimes used as a substitute for FN but may be a bit more formal; in this sense, it is common in military usage (Brown & Ford, 1961).

STATUS MANIPULATION IN WOLOF GREETINGS

The study of greetings and the use of titles and other terms of address has proved to be a useful means of gaining insight into power and authority relations and other aspects of social structure. This was seen in Brown and Ford's pioneering study and is a focus of attention in Judith T. Irvine's more recent examination of the greeting routines of the Wolof, an Islamic people of Senegal.

Wolof greetings occur frequently—they are part of every social interaction. In principle, according to Irvine, "a greeting must occur between any two persons who are visible to one another." The only exception to this rule is that when there are persons of high status to be greeted, one of relatively lower status may be neglected. Initiating a greeting sets up a dyadic interaction; even in a gathering, an individual will greet individuals in turn, rather than the group as a whole. Ideally, the greeting is initiated by the person of lower rank—one "greets up." Age, sex, social caste, achievement, and moral character all play a role in the assessment of rank. Usually, the allotment of roles is clear but is, at times, subject to manipulation.

Irvine describes the routine of greeting as falling into three stages:

1. Salutation: Person A approaches B and extends his hand. Conversation opens with an exchange of Arabic formulae and continues in Wolof with an exchange of names, each party stating first his own name and then that of the other.

   A: *Salaam alikum.* (Peace be with you.)

   B: *Malikum salaam.* (With you be peace)

   A: (A's name).

   B: (B's name).

   A: (B's name).

   B: (A's name). Yes, (A's name).

2. Questions: Questions may be few or many, but the first two exchanges are obligatory; this is the point at which A may attempt to manipulate the situation to his advantage with a long series of inquiries or B may try to turn the tables by becoming the questioner.

A: How do you do?

B: I am here only.

A: Don't you have peace?

B: Peace only, yes.

. . . (open ended)

The initial questions and responses are stereotyped; if B is ill or has news to impart, it would not be reported at this point, but only after more prolonged inquiries. Further questions by A could concern the whereabouts and state of health of B's household and family. Prolonged questioning by A emphasizes his respect and concern for B and is, thus, a way of minimizing his own importance and accentuating that of B. Omitting these questions entirely cuts the greeting short— perhaps A is pressed for time, but he may simply wish to reserve his time for greeting someone of higher rank.

3. Praising God: Like the salutation, this is formulaic, consisting of the repetition of Arabic phrases.

A: *H'mdillay.* (Thanks be to God.)

B: *Tubarkalla.* (Blessed be God.)

A: *Tubarkalla.*

B: *H'mdillay.*

At this point, questioning may begin again, returning to stage 2 and prolonging the conversation. This would be followed by a repetition of stage 3.

Both speech and activity are seen as duties that lower-status persons perform for those of higher status—thus, it is normally a lower-ranking A who approaches B, initiates the greeting, and takes the initiative in every phase. Voice modulations also express the status relationships: The speech of nobles is stereotyped as low in pitch, low in volume, slow, and terse; that of low-caste persons is high in pitch and volume, rapid, and wordy. Use of these styles accompanies the exchange of greetings, even when the two parties are of the same caste—the initiator is marked by his verbal behavior, as is the responder.

Variations on the greeting routine are possible; between certain persons who stand in a joking relationship to one another, it can incorporate an exchange of insults. It can also provide a setting for a type of one-upmanship, as individuals jockey for advantage with strategies that Irvine describes as self-lowering and self-elevating. Since noble rank entails an obligation of charity, A may wish to emphasize (perhaps falsely) his low status, implying that B should give support or financial aid. The more repetitions and extensions of questioning, the more emphasis on the presumed difference in status. On the other hand, B can subvert A's strategy by moving quickly to seize the initiator role in the salutation phase or can attempt at some point to switch roles. B might simply ignore one of A's questions and ask one of his own. This would be considered rude unless done very adroitly; more likely, B would wait until the third stage to interject a question after the first exchange of praises, returning to stage 2 and continuing to the end in the role of interrogator. Despite these and other possibilities for manipulating the routine, Irvine observes that it maintains the established caste relationships between nobles and griots (commoners). If a griot adopts the voice modulations appropriate to the B role, he will automatically disqualify himself for any aid or assistance; if a noble assumes the vocal style associated with a griot, he will be seen as lacking dignity or self-control and thus jeopardize his own reputation (Irvine, 1974).

WESTERN APACHE SPEECH—AND SILENCE

Are personal names and titles invariably used as terms of address? This is by no means the case; in many traditional societies, personal names are little used and kinship terms are the norm, even between people who are not closely related. For the Apachean peoples, Navajos and Apaches, personal relationships are traced in terms of clan membership; the relationship between one's own matrilineal clan and that of one's father, for example, can affect the nature of the relationship between individuals. Age differences are also important, and older people are universally respected. Personal names are seldom used, and then only as terms of reference, not of address.

Keith Basso describes Western Apache encounters, not so much in terms of speech as of silence. In many encounters, according to Basso, the "decision to speak or keep silent" lies in the nature of the relationship and the situation. In some circumstances, say the Apache, ". . . it is right to give up on words." Basso enumerates several such circumstances:

1. When meeting "strangers"—non-Apaches or Apaches from a distant community, who cannot be identified in terms of kinship. There is no formal introduction; instead, silence is maintained, perhaps for several days, until the two individuals have become sufficiently accustomed to each other to begin speaking.

2. In the initial stages of courtship, when the couple is "shy"; they may spend their time together in silence, eventually begin speaking, and later—perhaps after several months—begin to have long conversations.

3. When an individual returns home after a long absence, most often a child returning home from boarding school. There is a period of silence, perhaps 10 or 15 minutes, before the child takes the initiative in speaking; parents may listen attentively but say very little until several hours have passed. In the meantime, they watch for signs that the child has been adversely affected by contact with strangers and the outside world.

4. When "getting cussed out." Persons who are enraged or "crazy" (often when intoxicated) are apt to engage in tirades, accusations, or threats. In this case, it is considered unwise to try to reason with them and best to remain silent.

5. When a relative of a deceased person emerges from a period of mourning, it is considered courteous and considerate to refrain from conversation. In this case, too, there may be a feeling that such a person could be unstable or unpredictable so that it is best to avoid speaking.

6. When a person is the patient in a curing ceremony; conversation breaks off when the healer begins to chant. Throughout the ceremony, which may continue intermittently over several days, it is inappropriate for anyone except the medicine man to speak to the patient. The explanation given is that supernatural power, from the healer and the forces that he invokes, could make contact with the patient dangerous.

Basso sees the common thread in these situations as ambiguity and/or unpredictability. Speech is curtailed, not so much by the situation or activity involved as by the status of the focal participant, who is either unfamiliar or perceived as being in a liminal or dangerous state. In summary, "keeping silent among the Western Apache is a response to uncertainty and unpredictability in social relations" (Basso, 1979).

Apache attitudes toward and behavior during encounters are quite different from those of the Anglo-American outsiders that Apaches often must deal with. In *Portraits of the Whiteman*, Basso provides a sample of Apache humor that enables the reader to reflect on this contrast. Joking imitations of the "Whiteman" are replete with parodies of behavior that is, from the Apache point of view, "flagrantly wrong." Anglo-Americans are portrayed as "gross incompetents in the conduct of social relations":

> The setting is the living room of an Apache home in Cibecue. There is a knock at the door; J opens the door and greets L, who is standing outside. J speaks, using a rapid, high-pitched voice, in a monologue that is interrupted by gestures and body-language.
>
> J: Hello, my friend! How you doing? How you feeling, L? You feeling good? Look who here, everybody! Look who just come in. Sure, it's my Indian friend L. Pretty good, all right! (J slaps L on the shoulder, looks him in the eyes, and shakes his hand .)
>
> J: . . . Come right in, my friend. Don't stay outside in the rain. . . . Sit down! Sit right down! Take your loads off you ass. You hungry? You want some beer? Maybe you want some wine? You want crackers? Bread? You want some sandwich? How 'bout it? You hungry? . . . (J has seated himself, with a look of bemused resignation on his face; K, J's wife, has come into the room and is looking on with amusement). . . .
>
> J: You sure looking good to me, L. You looking pretty fat! Pretty good, all right! You got new boots? Where you buy them? Sure pretty good boots! I glad. . . . (J and K dissolve in laughter; L shakes his head and smiles. The joke is over.)

In commentary, Basso points out that J's rapid, loud delivery is a parody of "Whiteman" talk; to Apaches, Anglo-Americans seem to be "angry even when they're friendly." J's repeated use of "my friend" reflects Apache opinion that Anglo-Americans use this phrase too often and, at times, hyporitically when they want something from someone else. Inquiries about feelings and other personal matters are considered invasions of personal privacy; L might choose to reveal his feelings, but J certainly should not inquire about them. In addressing L by name, J is violating an Apache taboo on using personal names in direct address; and the slap on the back, handshake, and other physical contact are seen as violations of personal space. In Apache culture, prolonged eye contact is an act of aggression or defiance; Anglo-Americans are considered to be "entirely too probing with their eyes and hands."

The repeated use of imperatives—"Come in!" "Sit down!"—is resented: "some Whiteman talk like they bossing you around." The string of rapid-fire questions is also seen as rude and coercive; Apaches feel that Anglo-Americans ask too many questions, leaving no time for carefully considered replies. And unsolicited observations and queries about a person's health, physical state, or possessions violate a traditional Apache reluctance to stand out or call attention to oneself. Further, praising a person's possessions (in this case, the boots) is taken to be the equivalent of a request, obliging the person to either hand them over or to appear stingy (a technique that traders have used in the past to obtain valuable items that could be sold for profit) (Basso, 1979).

The "Whiteman portraits" are, of course, insiders' jokes that ridicule the cultural outsider—comparable to Polish jokes and the like. They are also political humor, expressing the frustrations of a conquered people who feel themselves to be an oppressed minority. They reflect a perception of Anglo-Americans as insensitive to Apache culture, condescending, and blind to the effect that their actions have on others. On a more positive note, by singling out points of contrast between Apaches and their Anglo-American neighbors, they demonstrate how little in human behavior can be taken for granted. What seems perfectly natural and ordinary to the Anglo-American is loaded with cultural significance to the Western Apache observer.

LANGUAGE AND GENDER

A type of variation that seems to be universal characterizes the verbal behavior of men and women. Some differentiation of gender roles is found in all societies, whether stratified or egalitarian; this differentiation is reflected in different norms for male and female speech. In some cases it is simply a matter of the frequency of usage of words and phrases within a range of variation, while in other languages there are clear-cut differences in sounds, grammatical forms, and/or vocabulary. As a general phenomenon, it is likely that the existence of different speech codes for men and women is related to two kinds of social forces—those that keep men and women apart (a division of labor between men and women, separate social spheres based on gender) and those that encourage social solidarity among males and females, respectively (single-sex work groups, social networks, residential rules, and so forth). Overall, it appears that male and female speech is more differentiated where these factors are strongest and less so where men and women mingle during work and socialize together. However, despite a growing wave of interest in speech variation, there is little solid cross-cultural documentation on the topic as it relates to gender. In part, this reflects the inadequacy of information about women's culture in the older anthropological literature; in part, it reflects the *modus operandi* of traditional linguistic research. In the past, linguistic studies were often based on data collected from a small sample of speakers—sometimes only a single speaker. In such cases, little or nothing can be learned about speech variation of any kind—a great deficiency, since many non-Western languages are rapidly becoming extinct.

GENDER DIALECTS

An early description of formal differences in men's and women's speech is found in Edward Sapir's study of Yana, a native language of California. In Yana, the lexicon of word bases was evidently the same, but different word endings were used by men and women. One of Sapir's students, Mary Haas, described an elaborate system of this sort in Koasati, a Native American language of the lower Mississippi Valley. As in Yana, the differences are mainly found in verb forms, which differ systematically according to the sex of the speaker (Haas, 1944). For example:

	Women Say	Men Say
he is saying	ka:	ká:s
don't sing	tačilawan	tačilawâ:s
lift it	lakawhôl	lakawhós
he is building a fire	ó:t	ó:č

In a number of other languages, both phonological and lexical differences have been noted. While doing an ethnographic study of the Chuckchi of Siberia, the Russian anthropologist Waldemar Bogoras observed that several consonants [r, č, k, g] that were distinguished in men's speech fell together as [š] in the speech of women; for example, "people" was ramkičɪn in the men's version, šamkɪsšɪn in the women's. To Bogoras (who may primarily have worked with and become accustomed to the speech of Chukchi men), "the speech of women, with its ever-recurring š, sounds quite peculiar" (Bogoras, 1911). Similar situations have been described in a number of Native American languages. Typically, the most highly differentiated speech appears to be that of older men and women.

When James Goss studied the language of the southern Utes, around 1962, he realized that there were marked phonetic differences in the speech of various individuals. Earlier investigators had despaired of finding order

in Ute phonology and simply described these differences as "free variation"—that is, as random or unsystematic. However, order appeared in
Goss's data when he took into consideration both the age and gender of the
speakers. In summary, he found the speech of young people to be relatively
undifferentiated. Differences begin to be noticeable by around the age of 30,
and these become progressively more numerous and fixed with increased
age. His adult male acquaintances claimed that they alone "spoke the language as it should be spoken." Goss was tempted to agree: It is in the speech
of men in their 40s that the phonological rules are most regular. There are
fewer omitted or reduced vowels than in the speech of younger people, and
articulation is clear and deliberate. In elderly men, beyond the age of 50,
some of this clarity declines, and there is a tendency to merge stops with
affricates (/t/ becomes [ts]).

By contrast, in the speech of older women, voiceless stops and affricates
become voiced (/t/ becomes [d], /ts/ becomes [dz]); some phonemic vowel
contrasts are lost; and vowels become increasingly nasalized, to the point
that the speech of women over 50 can be characterized as a "voiced nasal
drone."

Examples of southern Ute phonological variations for /tuk utsi/ "mountain lion" would be:

[tʊk uts] in the speech of males and females under 30;

[tsʊk ʊʔtsI/ in the speech of males over 50; and

[dug undz] in the speech of women over 50.

It should be noted that individual speakers of Ute are well aware of this
variation and sometimes use it creatively—thus, a young man may adopt the
"old man" style when speaking respectfully to tribal elders; and in telling a
myth, the narrator (male or female) will use a mixture of styles appropriate
to the characters—male or female, old or young—as well as mimicking the
special speech characteristics attributed to animals and supernatural beings.

Some gender differences in the selection of vocabulary are to be anticipated in any speech community, since the cultural knowledge and activities
of men and women always differ to some degree. In certain languages, however, the lexical differences are not just a matter of selection and relative frequency of usage but appear to be exclusive. A classic example is seen in the
long-extinct language of the so-called Island Carib, a native people of the
West Indies. Here, there were a large number of doublets, pairs of words with
the same meaning; thus, for many meanings, the missionary Father Raymond
Breton recorded a pair of entries—men's words and women's words:

	Women Say	Men Say
rain	kuyu	kunobu
sun	kači	hueyu
canoe	kuriala	ukuni
manioc	kawai	kiere

In 16th-century Island Carib, such doublets were so numerous that explorers reported that men and women "speak different languages"—a report that is sometimes repeated to this day. But this was not actually the case. In fact, much of the vocabulary and almost all of the grammatical system were shared by all speakers. The main differences lay in the first- and second-person pronouns and in many of the most common nouns. Comparative research eventually revealed that the women's vocabulary and the basic grammatical structure identify the language with the Arawakan, rather than the Carib, language family; it is closely related to the Lokono language of the Guianas (see Figure 7.9). The prominence of Carib loanwords in the men's vocabulary suggests that frequent, possibly warlike, contacts took place between the Arawak Igneri and their Carib-speaking neighbors. In the opinion of Douglas Taylor, an authority on languages of the West Indies, the special vocabulary of the "men's language" may reflect the influence of a Carib-based *lingua franca,* or trade language, that was used in an extensive network that linked these islanders with others and, perhaps, with the mainland of South America. It is this borrowed vocabulary that led to a misidentification of the language, as is still reflected in its name (Taylor & Hoff, 1980).

GENDER DIGLOSSIA

The story of the Island Caribs is known primarily from descriptions and lists of individual words compiled by early explorers and missionaries. Little is known of the social setting in which their language was spoken prior to the Spanish conquest of the Indies. However, there still are, on the mainland of South and Central America, aboriginal societies that resemble the bygone tribes of the Indies in at least three respects: an emphasis on trade and other types of exchange; a reputation for aggression, with a frequent involvement in warfare; and a differentiation of language along gender lines. Differences between men's and women's language have been noted in groups as widely separated as the Jivaro of Ecuador and Peru, the Karaja of central Brazil, and the Yanomama of Venezuela and northern Brazil. Ernest Migliazza, who studied the Yanomama language between 1958 and 1971, provides a close examination of the *wayamo,* a special "men's language."

Migliazza has adopted Ferguson's diglossia concept but modifies it in one important respect in order to apply it to the Yanomama. As defined by Ferguson, diglossia was limited to literate societies, and the H code was sustained by the existence of an established literary tradition. For the Yanomama, Migliazza sees the respect directed toward the *wayamo* as playing a comparable role in maintaining and supporting the H variety of language. In his opinion, the emphasis on correctness and skill associated with the *wayamo* has kept its forms relatively unchanged over many generations, while an original L code has diversified into the several Yanomama dialects. Thus, for Migliazza the relationship between the *wayamo* and the regional dialects is analogous to the relationship between, for example, classical

THE YANOMAMA WAYAMO

The Yanomama people are horticulturalists and hunters, numbering some 12,000, who live in about 200 villages scattered over approximately 100,000 square miles of forested territory. Two varieties of Yanomama language are in use; each has definite functions, and there are restrictions on the use of each. The dry season (October to March) is a time during which many social gatherings are held and there is visiting between villages, with formal feasting, trading, exchange of news, and forming of alliances. Alliances are important because feuds, raiding, and small-scale warfare between families and villages are also common. Such visiting and alliance-making necessitates the use of the *wayamo*, a *lingua franca* used exclusively by men. (Students who have viewed Napoleon Chagnon's *The Feast* or other films of Yanomama village life may recall the chantlike cadences of the *wayamo*, heard when the arrival of visitors was announced, when headmen conducted negotiations, and in other scenes.)

Migliazza characterizes the *wayamo* as an archaic form of Yanomama that is mainly used as a "trade and news language" in intervillage communication. It is also a "manhood language" that gives prestige to young men as they learn to use it; it is never used by women or young children—women are not even supposed to understand it. Thus, adult males know and use two linguistic codes, while women and children use one.

The *wayamo* is uniform throughout the Yanomama area, superposed on a number of local dialects, some of which are not mutually intelligible. Because of this superposed relationship, Migliazza refers to the *wayamo* as H ("high") and to the local dialects as L ("low"). H is distinguished from all varieties of L by lexical, phonological, and syntactic features. (1) A special set of idiomatic words and phrases is used in H; for example, "sharp thing" is a euphemism for "axe." The vocabulary is small, limited to "cultural situations common to all Yanomama." (2) Although H is phonologically closer to the dialect of certain central villages, it differs from all in having a more regular syllable structure and somewhat simpler sound rules. (3) The most characteristic feature is a chanted intonation and regular sentence rhythm, facilitated by lengthening and repetition of syllables. (4) Sentences are short and syntactically simple; there is more repetition than in the ordinary use of L.

Although the *wayamo* has an obvious utility in dealings among speakers of different dialects, it is also used in encounters between neighboring villages that use the same dialect and on certain occasions by people within the same village. It is considered appropriate to particular situations—roughly, to formal situations—even within the local community. Migliazza summarizes the use of H and L in the following situations:

	H (men only)	L (everyone)
Formal invitations	X	
News, trading, intervillage complaints	X	
Shamanistic practices	X	
Song improvisation	X	X
Everyday life		X
Evening talks and stories	X	X

Ethnologists have characterized the Yanomama as a society with strong male dominance. Villages are involved in chronic feuding, sometimes with high casualties; abduction of women is the usual expressed motive, though competition for horticultural land and hunting territories may be a more fundamental cause. Males are highly valued as warriors, and female infanticide is frequent. Mastering the *wayamo* is seen as a mark of manhood, of superior status, and serves to set men's concerns clearly apart from those of women: ". . . a man will boast before the visitors of his strength and fierceness in wars and beating contests, of his ability as a hunter; he can ask the other how many women lovers he has and the visitor must answer the truth; he can ask how many people he has killed or outwitted in his life, which people he likes or dislikes; he can

offer his sister or daughter for one or more times to the other in exchange for goods or other women. Women listen to the men's H and although many understand it, they do not complain about what is transacted during it And whether women understand or not, they claim that they do not" (Migliazza, 1972).

Arabic and the vernacular Arabic spoken in countries such as Morocco, Egypt, and Iraq.

The type of *gender diglossia* described by Migliazza may find parallels in other traditional societies in which an exclusive "men's language" is associated with male social dominance and political leadership. In such cases, children typically acquire and retain L, the speech pattern of their mothers; this constitutes the main language or dialect of the speech community. As boys reach manhood, they acquire the prestigious H dialect that is primarily used in public and extracommunity affairs in which women have little or no participation. It may be noted that in unacculturated Yanomama villages, Migliazza found that boys were highly motivated to learn to use the *wayamo*—their "greatest ideal in life" was to emulate the prominent men who were skilled in its use (literally, "tongue-clever"). The situation is changing, especially in border areas, where Yanomamas have low status in relation to the more numerous and more acculturated Caribs. In these areas, Yanomama rituals are ridiculed, Yanomama boys are reluctant to practice chanting, and the use of the *wayamo* has rapidly declined.

In their use of formally differentiated speech codes, the Yanomama exhibit similarities to a large number of societies, including the Kuna of Panama, as described by Joel Sherzer. Sherzer's study, undertaken as a comprehensive ethnography of speaking, uses native categories to define a variety of styles and genres characteristic of both men and women.

KUNA WAYS OF SPEAKING

Joel Sherzer undertook a thoroughgoing application of Hymes's ethnographic perspective in a long-term field study of the San Blas Kuna people of Panama. Sherzer describes the Kuna as an egalitarian society, with distinctive economic and social roles allotted to men and women. Their subsistence is largely based on small-scale agriculture and fishing; women contribute substantially to the economy through the production of *molas*, unique textiles that are widely exported. There are several speech genres associated with each sex, though with some degree of overlap in actual usage. Speaking ability is highly valued and can be a source of prestige for anyone, male or female. Political leaders and specialists in healing are usually male, and formal political oratory and healing chants are typically male genres. Women's special genres are infant lullabies and mourning chants for the dead and dying.

"Language," in Kuna, is *kaya*. Many different varieties can be distinguished: *tule kaya*, literally "people's language," is the everyday language of the Kuna themselves. There are also the languages of other peoples, including *waka kaya*, "Spanish language," and *merki kaya*, "English language." Different styles of speaking are also named: *kuento kaya*, the speech of storytellers; *ome kaya*, the speech of women; *arkar kaya*, the formal speech of the chief's spokesman; and so on.

Three kinds of men's ritual language are designated: *sakla kaya, suar nuchu kaya*, and *kantule kaya*. Taken together, these three varieties might be compared with the Yanomama *wayamo* in that they are men's codes that are markedly different (in phonology, morphology, syntax, and/or vocabulary) from everyday language. But the three also differ from one another, and each is associated with a particular ritual or set of rituals. By contrast, two genres performed by women use colloquial Kuna, though with special grammatical and stylistic features that set them apart from everyday speech.

(1) "Chief language" (*sakla kaya*) is formal oratory, delivered in a chanting style. It is most often used in the "gathering house," which is the vital center of Kuna social and political life. Here village business is transacted, including decisions about public works, accusations of wrongdoing, and resolutions of quarrels. The greater part of the time, several nights a week, is devoted to formal chanting.

In a typical session, two chiefs sit suspended in their hammocks; one of them takes the lead in chanting, while the other interjects periodic responses; this dialogue may go on for hours, followed by an interpretation by a chief's spokesman (*arkar*). The chanting chief may hold forth on Cuna historical traditions, politics, or current local events, and may predict future events; there will also be exhortations on proper behavior, hard work, and obedience to Kuna tradition. The chanting chief and the responder are flanked by other chiefs, either in their hammocks or on the adjacent benches, and by *arkars*, who rise to speak in commentary on the chiefs' words once the chanting has ended. Surrounding these participating chiefs and *arkars* are several rows of benches, with women on the inner rows and men on the outer, surrounding the women.

CHANTING CHIEF: God sent us to this world in order to care for banana roots for him.

RESPONDING CHIEF: It is so.

CC: . . . in order to care for taro roots for him.

RC: It is so.

CC: . . . in order to care for living yams for him.

RC: It is so.

CC: . . . in order to care for living squash for him.

RC: It is so.

CC: . . . in order to care for pineapple roots for him God gave us this world.

RC: It is so.

Some of the characteristics of *sakla kaya,* the language of formal chanting, are the inclusion of vowels that are elided in ordinary speech; the use of special "framing" morphemes that set off each clause; syntactic rules that result in a great deal of redundancy, repeating phrases that are omitted in ordinary speech; and the use of special terminology not found in ordinary speech (for example, "currasow" is *sikli* in *tule kaya* but is *olo-kupyakkile* in *sakla kaya; olo-* is a morpheme that distinguishes the chief's chanting, prefixed to a number of different nouns. The cumulative effect is a way of speaking that requires considerable learning on the part of both interlocutors and audience. In some stylistic features, this exclusively male genre, with its chanted delivery, specialized vocabulary, and dialogue format, recalls the Yanomama *wayamo.* However, Kuna women, far from being excluded, are very much a part of these events. Sherzer observes that "the congresses in which chanting occurs are thought of as being especially for the women . . . they literally surround the chanting and in turn are surrounded and seemingly protected by the men."

(2) "Stick doll language" (*suar nuchu kaya*) is a form of chanting used in curing rites. The "stick dolls" are small wooden figures that represent benign spirits, placed beneath the hammock of the patient. The healer (*ikar wisit,* literally "ikar-knower") addresses his chants to the stick dolls, using a special variety of language that the patient and others within earshot understand poorly if at all. In phonological, morphological, and syntactic rules there are many differences from ordinary language, and there are special words and metaphors that are used only in curing chants. This is said to be language that only the "stick babies" understand. Men learn their curing ikars by rote; they are passed from teacher to student. Unlike the chanting in the gathering house, in which innovation and creativity play a part, each curing text is fixed, and verbatim performance is essential to the cure. Certain women have visionary experiences, and some of them diagnose and treat illness; but they do not chant, and they do not use special linguistic forms in their verbal formulae.

(3) *Kantule kaya* is the language of the *kantule,* the director of the girls' puberty celebration, the most elaborate and most distinctive of Kuna ritual events. When a girl reaches puberty, she is the focus of a private rite conducted by a female specialist and her assistants. Her hair is cut short, in the style of an adult woman, and a gold ring, also symbolic of adult status, is inserted through her nasal septum. This is the essential rite of passage; it is normally followed by public festivities, as long and elaborate as can be afforded, sponsored by the girl's father. The central event during these festivities is a long *ikar* (text) performed by the *kantule* and his assistants; this may continue for two to three days. The texts are performed in a special shouted style and addressed to the spirit of the *kammu,* a long flute used in this and certain other ritual events. This variety of language is the most

different from everyday speech and the most difficult to understand of all of the ritual varieties. It is also "the most immutable. . . . It is repeated identically, including every single phoneme and morpheme, each time it is performed." As in the other ritual varieties, there are special phonological and grammatical forms and a large body of special vocabulary unique to the *kantule* genre. Essentially, the texts are detailed descriptions of the paraphernalia and events of the puberty rites:

> The girl goes quietly.
> Along the path of the river.
> Walking along the path of the river.
> She arrives at the river.
> She stands up in the river.
> She bathes in the river.
>
> The young girl undresses and bathes. . . .

Again, it may be noted that while males monopolize the roles of sponsors and ritual specialists in this central cultural event, the ceremony itself focuses on an event in the female life cycle, in a matrilineal society. There are no corresponding rites for males.

(4) *Koe pippi* (literally, "little baby") are lullabies. Women, from young girls to grandmothers, improvise these songs that are addressed to babies: The baby is told "not to cry, that it will soon grow up and perform adult tasks and that its father is off working in the jungle or fishing." The singer also describes her own activities and those of other family members and devises lyrics to fit the actual situation of the baby and its family:

> Little baby.
> Your mother is sitting with you in your hammock.
> Little baby she is sorry to see you cry.
> Mmmm. . . .
>
> Father is not here I see.
> He went to the jungle.
> 'I am going to clear out the coconut farms.'
> Father said as he left.
> Mmmm. . . .
>
> Little girl.
> You will stay in the house.
> You will make a little mola [a child's mola].
> You will also sit beside your mother.
>
> You will wash clothes.
> You will go to the river.
> With your relatives. . . .

These songs, clearly aimed at educating and socializing children as well as at quieting and putting them to sleep, are performed in colloquial Kuna, but in a special style. As in the men's genres, vowels that are elided in ordinary speech are not deleted; and a special suffix (-ye) is added to mark the ends of lines. The inserted "Mmmm," which marks the end of stanzalike units, is unique to the lullabies.

(5) "Tuneful weeping" is a second women's genre. Mournful songs are performed by groups of women, directed toward a dying individual. The songs continue after death, while the body remains in the hammock and during the canoe trip that conveys it to a cemetery on the mainland for burial. Like lullabies, these songs are sung in colloquial Kuna; the stylistic devices are similar, with a high frequency of certain suffixes that mark the structure of the lines. They also resemble the lullabies in being fairly stereotyped in content but tailored to fit the details of the lives of the individual dead. Thus, a young girl mourns her grandfather:

> It pains me to see grandfather.
> My grandfather died.
> He will be underground.
> I say.
>
> He would always go with us [to the mainland].
> In order to get medicine.
> 'I am going to get medicine.'
> He said to us.
>
> I am sorry to see you, grandfather.
> Lying in the hammock, dead.
> Under the ground you will rot, grandfather.

GENDER STYLES IN AMERICAN ENGLISH

Although much has been written about gender and language in American society, linguistic research has generally failed to reveal any clear-cut patterns of phonology, syntax, or vocabulary that are distinctively "male" or "female." In a comprehensive review published in 1978, Kramer, Thorne, and Henley observed that "unlike some languages where there are 'sex-exclusive' linguistic distinctions, sex differentiation among English speakers is, at most, a matter of frequency of occurrence." Yet there is an abundance of popular stereotypes on this matter, many of them directed at women's speech and usually derogatory.

Psychologist Cheris Kramer set out to investigate these stereotypes and to test their validity. She noted that women are often characterized as talkative (the crux of many jokes) and that female speech is sometimes described as "weaker" or less effective than male. Women are sometimes said to speak less forcefully than men, to use fewer exclamations and less profanity, and to weaken the impact of what they say by using qualifiers before expressing an opinion ("I may be wrong, but . . .) or by following it with "tag questions" (such as ". . . isn't it?" or "don't you think so?"). A rising, or questioning, intonation may convey the same impression.

Kramer confirmed the existence of such stereotypes of women's speech by showing the captions taken from a number of magazine cartoons to a group of college students (25 men, 25 women) and asking them to identiy the sex of the speaker in the cartoon. The students were able to do this easily, with almost total accuracy. Kramer then went on, in a second test, to ask a group of male and female students to write paragraphs describing two photographs; she then asked a panel of judges to identify the writers as male or female. The judges were not able to accomplish this task with any success, though they sometimes called on their own stereotypes to justify their decisions, finding "sensitivity" in a paragraph judged (incorrectly) to have been written by a woman or "objectivity" and detailed description in one attributed to a man (Kramer, 1974).

Kramer's experiment demonstrated the strength of stereotypes about the way women use language, while also casting doubt on their validity. Printed captions and written descriptions, of course, are not the same thing as speech. Writing is often a more formal medium than speech and does not provide the intonation and emphasis used in speaking. But the study suggests, at least, that no regular and obvious differences were found in the way college men and women used English in their writing.

It may be that Kramer's college-student participants were at the age and in a situation in which they might be expected to show few differences in the use of language. As students in a coeducational institution, their interests and activities were probably much the same. On the other hand, when and where women's interests and occupations are separate and different from men's, their use of language would be expected to show more divergence. The language of rural or suburban housewives, then, might have come closer to the steretype than that of college coeds or women in business or industry. Further, the "weakness" that Kramer found to be a stereotyped feature of women's speech would be more characteristic of those in a subordinate social position than of women in general. It is likely, even in the quarter-century since Kramer's study, that this stereotype is on the decline; predictably, it should disappear when women, as a group, achieve social equality with men.

Besides selection of vocabulary and grammatical structures, styles of speaking involve the use of pitch, hesitation, and "tone of voice"—the vocal behaviors that linguists sometimes lump together as "voice qualifiers." According to S. McConnell-Ginet, intonation—"the tunes to which we set the text of our talk"—may be "the chief linguistic expression in American English of (relative) femininity and masculinity." Part of the picture is simply the pitch and quality of the voice. We can usually identify a voice as male or female, partly by its basic pitch and partly by the effect of the overtones that influence the quality of speech sounds, especially vowels. Are these differences biologically determined—simply a matter of anatomy?

It is true that, because of the larger size of the larynx and vocal resonators, there is, on average, a difference in the vocal range of adult men and women. Larger vocal cords vibrate more slowly, producing a lower basic pitch in adult males. The average male voice is, thus, naturally deeper than the average female voice; but there is considerable overlap, especially since neither men nor women will necessarily speak at the upper or lower limits of their vocal range. But it seems that there is also a cultural component and that the natural differences can be minimized or maximized; according to McConnell-Ginet, "different cultures settle on different parts of the possible pitch range for actual use in speaking by each sex." Men and women can use virtually the same vocal range, minimizing any natural differences, or differences in pitch can be exaggerated. And this is also something that can be, consciously or unconsciously, manipulated by individuals—in American society and, no doubt, in others (McConnell-Ginet, 1983).

Linguists describe the intonation of American English by indicating three basic pitch levels (1 = low, 2 = mid, 3 = high), plus an optional fourth (4 = extra-high) that is more rarely used. As described by H. L. Gleason, the commonest English intonation contour is /(2)31 ↘ /—that is, any syllables before a stressed syllable are at a neutral or medium level 2, the pitch goes up to the higher level 3 on the stressed syllable, and it falls at the end of the sentence, for example:

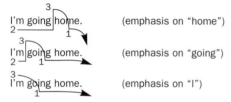

I'm going home.   (emphasis on "home")

I'm going home.   (emphasis on "going")

I'm going home.   (emphasis on "I")

Use of the "extra-high" level 4 is said to convey a degree of surprise or impatience—thus:

I was going home, but it rained.   (extra emphasis on "rain")

Pitch level 4, according to Gleason, is "much rarer than the others." He gives no consideration to the issue of the speaker's gender (Gleason, 1961). McConnell-Ginet cites a number of studies that indicate that women use a wider pitch range than men and that the extra-high register is much more common in women's speech than in men's. In general, men use a narrower range with less frequent shifts in both pitch and loudness; women's speech is characterized by more frequent shifts and can be described as more "dynamic." Again, this is a matter of tendencies and not a clear-cut difference; men and women use the same devices, but the overall impression is different.

Many speakers, male or female, seem never to use the extra-high register, but women do so far more often than men—and those who use it more are perceived as being more "feminine." Further, when used by men it is apt to be perceived as a marker of effeminacy (and for this reason may be used deliberately by some gay men). McConnell-Ginet suggests that men "lose by sounding woman-like, whereas women do not lose (perhaps they even gain in some contexts) by sounding man-like." Whether this is a valid generalization or not, it does appear that intonation is a feature that can be manipulated to adapt to an individual's occupational setting or life-style (McConnell-Ginet, 1983).

Rather than structural features of language itself, it is the pragmatics of verbal interaction that have been of interest to an increasing number of sociolinguists. Deborah Tannen writes about problems of communication in which differences in assumptions, motivations, or expectations appear to affect the outcome. In writing for an American readership, Tannen is careful to explain that these differences are largely cultural—that assumptions about gender roles, for example, are variable and reflect cultural tradition rather than (as is often assumed) human nature. Examining children's socialization, she finds that girls are generally encouraged to downplay their accomplishments or abilities, to be compliant, and to achieve ends through verbal manipulation. By contrast, boys' individual achievements are more often applauded, and both physical and verbal assertiveness are accepted as the norm.

In *Talking from Nine to Five*, Tannen examines women's and men's conversational styles in the workplace. She observes that "one conversational ritual that can cause trouble at work is apologizing." Men and women tend to use and to understand apologies in different ways. Women tend to use the phrase "I'm sorry" as a "conversational smoother"; when her words are misunderstood over the telephone, for example, a woman will say something like, "Oh, I'm sorry! I must have just been unclear." In a similar conversation, a man is less likely to apologize and may express irritation. The purpose of the woman's apology in this case is not so much to admit guilt as to show consideration and put the other person at ease. However, to a male employer or co-worker, the apology is apt to come across as self-deprecating and to suggest lack of confidence or insecurity. Therefore, frequent use of apologies can mask a person's true competence and can work to an employee's disadvantage.

For women, Tannen observes, an apology may be simply "the first step in a two-step routine: I say 'I'm sorry' and take half the blame; then you take the other half." When a typist has made a mistake, she could say, "Oh, I'm sorry. I'll fix it." Her boss might counter with, "Well, I wrote it so small it was easy to miss." Thus, the ritual works as a mutual face-saving device, to share the blame. With this sort of expectation, the woman who makes an apology can become resentful it the unanticipated response is "I accept your apology" or—worse yet—"Okay, just make sure it doesn't happen again" (Tannen 1994).

Although Tannen writes for a popular audience, her observations reflect the interests of many other researchers. The insights that can be gained through detailed, contextualized study of speech events—apologies, compliments, verbal genres such as jokes, verbal dueling, and the like—have given ethnography a new vigor and brought it to a new prominence as a research metholodology of wide applicability. Studies of this sort can involve field-work in settings such as business firms, school or university classrooms, military bases, or hospital operating rooms. Verbal interaction, in any setting, is worthy of study; and analysis of verbal interaction can often reveal the source of problems and suggest ways of dealing with them. (For an example of ethnographic research on language acquisition, see chapter 2.)

LANGUAGE, NATIONALISM, AND ETHNICITY

It is generally recognized that language has an important value as a symbol of national and ethnic identity. In the United States, we may be especially aware of this function of language since ours is a nation made up of a great variety of peoples, with English as our common language. For much of its history, this nation has maintained its image as a "melting pot." The image reflects not only the diversity of the peoples who have come into it, but also a process of change—a process that tends to reduce differences and produce uniformity.

In the past, it seemed almost inevitable that immigrants would rapidly lose their old ways and accept new ones. They would be "Americanized"—if not right away, then at least in the course of a couple of generations. An important part of this process was the learning of English and, along with that, the loss of the immigrants' original language. It was the policy of the American government to insist that English be the only language or instruction in the schools, and adult immigrants were expected to learn English (often by attending night schools) as quickly as possible. President Theodore Roosevelt expressd a widely held opinion when he said, "It would be not only a misfortune but a crime to perpetuate differences of language in this country" (Gonzales, 1955).

Roosevelt proposed that immigrants be given a period of 5 years to learn English, with deportation as the penalty for failure. No such policy was ever put into effect; however, many immigrants were eager to learn English. Since they were gaining a new nationality and leaving behind their old, they often insisted that their children speak only English. Thus, many of us who have German or Italian or Russian names and who know when and from what foreign place our grandparents or great-grandparents came to America do not know one word of the language that they spoke. We are the product of the melting pot. For those immigrants and for their descendants, the English language—American English—has stood as a symbol of our identity as Americans.

However, there is another side to this picture. The United States of America still contains more diversity than the image of the "melting pot" would suggest, and this ethnic diversity has its expression in linguistic diversity. There are some groups in our society who never have wanted to become completely "Americanized" and others who have lately found a need to rediscover or reassert their ancestral traditions and cultural heritage. Similar movements are going on in many areas of the world outside the United States. In Africa and Asia, colonial peoples have worked for and achieved independence, and minority groups in many nations also speak of the right to self-determination.

Such movements are a powerful political force in our time, and one that still has momentum. Recent political separatist movements—by the Irish Republican Army, the Quebecois in Canada, Basque separatists in Spain, Chechens in Russia (to name only a few)—all express the desire of minority peoples to maintain a separate identity and not to be completely absorbed or assimilated into a homogeneous larger nationality. In each of those cases, language plays a prominent role. In fact, these separatists are struggling, to a considerable extent, for the right to retain and use their own languages and to teach them to their children.

The American society is a pluralistic one, and many of our familiar social problems involve some type of conflict or disagreement over cultural tradition and language. When large numbers of people of the same nationality immigrated to the United States, they often settled in the same general area and retained their language, at least for several generations. There are pockets of this sort—ethnic and linguistic enclaves—throughout the United States: Germans in eastern Pennsylvania and central Texas, Scandinavians in Minnesota, "Cajun" French speakers in Louisiana, Japanese and Chinese in California, and many others. One of the largest of the ethnic blocs is made up of the Mexican-American population that is concentrated most heavily in southwestern border states and is increasingly represented in urban areas elsewhere. In such concentrated ethnic areas, German or Japanese or Spanish may be used in the home, in shops, and in other local settings; but English is the language that must be used with outsiders, the official language, and the language of most media (though there may be local radio stations and newspapers that use the minority language). It is also, for the most part, the language of the schools, although bilingual education programs have been developed in most states.

Typically, in ethnic enclaves, children learn to speak English more fluently and with less "foreign" accent than their parents. Children may also tend to lose fluency in their parents' languages, especially if jobs or higher education attract them away from their home communities. However, there is also a resistance to complete assimilation by many members of distinctive ethnic communities, a conservative movement to maintain their traditions, cultural identity, and language.

Native American peoples have a special position in relation to the larger national society. In most cases, their communities are small, economically depressed, and culturally marginal to dominant groups in American society; and their cultural traditions are generally ignored or misunderstood by other Americans. During the past three centuries, some Indian tribes were destroyed, displaced, or dispersed, while others suffered military defeat at the hands of the advancing Euro-American population of North America.

Nations like the Cherokee and Creek were forcibly removed from their homes; others, like the Hopi and Pima in Arizona, found themselves confined to only a small portion of their ancestral lands. Along with this, populations were much reduced in numbers, often decimated by disease. Defeated tribes were subjected to restrictive and discriminatory legislation that limited their freedom—including the freedom to use and maintain their own languages.

The United States government, through the Bureau of Indian Affairs, has consistently favored the assimilation of native peoples. Official policies have promoted the breakdown of tribal lands, integration of native communities into the larger society, and the learning of "American" ways. Native American schools are usually conducted in English, with the objective of reinforcing its use and hastening the extinction of native languages; in the past, children were often forbidden to use their native tongue. Many Native American languages have been lost; of perhaps 500 spoken in 1600, fewer than 200 are in use today. But most of these persist stubbornly, and in some cases programs have been undertaken to increase fluency. Beginning in the 1930s, something of a renaissance movement developed as Native Americans gained the right to revive and practice traditional ceremonies and religious rites. Native American communities have organized to resist cultural assimilation; efforts to preserve their languages are, in this case as in others, just one part of a larger struggle for human rights and self-determination.

Many anthropologists, whatever their own national or ethnic origins might be, feel that they have a vested interest in the survival and well-being of minority cultural groups and languages, in this country and elsewhere in the world. One reason for this feeling is found in the training and professional involvement of anthropologists: Most of us have lived and worked (sometimes almost as adopted members) in minority communities and have come to understand, respect, and value their traditions. If we value them, it becomes our duty to assist in maintaining them, and a number of anthropologists have undertaken to do so. One way in which linguistic anthropologists have contributed is seen in their efforts toward developing practical writing systems and teaching materials and in the promotion of literacy in Native American languages.

Kenneth Hale, a respected linguistic anthropologist who has worked with Navajo and other tribal educators in projects of this sort, emphasizes the important role of native knowledge in this partnership. Another linguist, I. Goosen, is the author of a series of introductory lessons in the Navajo language and has developed a practical Navajo orthography for use in textbooks and other materials for Navajo schools. The objectives of this work include, on the one hand, the preservation of the Navajo language by increasing the situations in contemporary life in which it can be used. On the other hand, both Navajo and non-Navajo teachers are encouraged to make education more rewarding and useful for Navajo children by drawing on the knowledge of their own language and culture that they bring into the classroom (Hale, 1974; Goosen, 1967).

Similarly, linguists Dean and Lucille Saxton have worked together with several Papago collaborators, publishing a dictionary, collections of myths and tales, and other cultural materials . Their work is printed in a practical O?odham orthography and is designed to be of use to the Papago people as well as to researchers in fields such as anthropology and linguistics. Some scholars in these fields have, in the past, been drawn from native communities, and more will be in the future; recently, an annual series of summer workshops, held at the University of Arizona, has encouraged cooperation between Native American educators and professional linguists. It might be noted that the Saxtons dedicated their publications to, and see them as the continuation of the work of, an earlier scholar, Juan Dolores, who was a native O?odham speaker (Saxton & Saxton, 1969, 1973).

LANGUAGE PLANNING

Language planning is a relatively new field of applied linguistics, oriented toward assisting political, educational, and other public agencies in dealing with problems that involve language. Decisions about language matters have often been made by heads of state and other official agencies, in early times as well as in modern, as means to a variety of ends: to achieve national unity, to heighten patriotism or nationalism, to suppress or accentuate ethnic distinctions, to improve internal or external communication, to facilitate literacy, to purge unwanted influences from the media, and so forth.

In the present century, the need or desire for language planning appears to have increased by leaps and bounds. This can be at least partly explained by such developments as the rise of new nations, large-scale immigration, and crises that result in refugees and displaced populations—the general phenomena of multiethnic and multilingual societies. And while some of the earlier efforts to solve language problems may have been undertaken by individuals, with or without linguistic training, language planning on a national or international scale requires not only cooperation between official agencies with political power, but also academically trained language experts.

Many variables must be considered in developing a language plan on a national scale. In discussing the problems that arise and the kind of measures that may be adopted, Carol Eastman distinguishes three types of nations:

> Type A, or *amodal nations*. These are linguistically complex nations with primarily oral traditions. Language planners may have to make choices among local vernacular language varieties for standardization and the development of educational materials. One or more languages will be selected for official use, as regional or national languages. In addition, in developing nations, a non-indigenous language may be

designated as the language of wider communication, for use in diplomacy, trade, and other external relations. In many cases, the language of a former colonial power that is already established in the area is retained for this function, for example, English in Nigeria and French in Senegal.

Type B, *unimodal nations.* In developing nations in which there is an indigenous language with a literary tradition, this is the likely choice for modernization and use as the national language. Again, history plays a role in designating the language of wider communication. Tanzania (discussed later in this chapter) is an example.

Type C, *multimodal nations.* These are nations with more than one language with a literary tradition; one must be selected for modernization, to serve as a national language. Others remain important at the regional level, and bilingualism is encouraged. India is the leading example of this type.

Among the earlier agencies of language planning are official language academies that were first established in several European countries in the 17th century. These were, in part, a response to an emerging need for standardization of language, following the invention of the printing press and the burgeoning of printed media. The most famous and perhaps most influential of these bureaus, the French Academy, was established in 1635 by Cardinal Richelieu. It has traditionally been a watchdog over the "purity" of the French language, making decisions on the admissibility of word coinage and other innovations and forbidding the importation of "unnecessary" loanwords from English and other languages. Similar language academies were established in Spain, Scandinavia, Italy, and elsewhere; those later founded in several Latin American countries were patterned after and are still linked to the Spanish Academy, serving to maintain a degree of standardization in the Spanish language internationally. The national academies in Egypt, Iraq, and other Islamic countries have long cooperated in maintaining the status of classical Arabic by suppressing loanwords and colloquialisms; their efforts are reflected in the diglossia situation that typically exists in these countries.

In modern language planning, this kind of *purification* may still be an objective; others, as listed by Eastman (1983), are *revival, reform, standardization,* and *modernization.* In most planning projects, two or more of these objectives are usually addressed, though one may be highlighted as the primary objective. Eastman discusses several typical cases in detail; some of her observations are summarized here.

HEBREW

Language revival encompasses efforts aimed at bringing a language, no longer the normal means of communication, back into use. The most successful example is Hebrew; this ancient language, which had survived essentially in the context of religious worship, was successfully revived in the 20th century as the national language of Israel. The movement to make Hebrew a modern all-purpose language was launched around 1880 by European Jews who had begun to settle in Palestine. One of these, Eliezer Ben Yahuda, is credited with the program of action that prepared the way for Hebrew to be made the national language when the state of Israel was founded, in the aftermath of World War II. Ben Yahuda provided an example by using Hebrew in daily life in his own home and founded societies to encourage others to do likewise; he also compiled a dictionary of updated Hebrew, published a Hebrew newspaper, and organized the Language Council, which would eventually become the national language academy.

At first, the Hebrew spoken in scattered Jewish settlements in Palestine was not uniform; the Language Council attempted to coordinate and standardize the various word coinages that emerged as the resources of the ancient language were extended to meet modern needs. The main impetus came in the agricultural collectives, where new immigrants were given intensive instruction by "Berlitz-like" methods. The revival continues as immigrants still arrive from all parts of the world, and many of them must learn Hebrew as a second language. Hebrew is still, in this multilingual society, a unifying force; faulty use of the language is tolerated, and "old-timers" are glad to help out, suggesting words and correcting mistakes. Today, however, the most effective agencies are the schools, government-funded, with up-to-date textbooks and teaching methods.

Of the circumstances responsible for the successful revival of Hebrew, two stand out—first, the symbolic importance of the language in terms of both ethnicity and religion; and, second, its importance as a means of communication for the first-generation settlers who had no other common language. Less successful efforts at language revival have been made repeatedly by ethnic minorities, whose historic language may have much symbolic importance but cannot serve important communication needs on a regular basis— for example, Irish, Cornish, Hawaiian, and a number of Native American languages. In such cases, one might speak of *partial revival*—efforts to instill knowledge of a traditional language as a source of cultural awareness and pride without the objective of use in all phases of daily life. Contributions of linguists in such projects include the preparation of teaching materials that incorporate folktales, songs, and other elements of traditional culture.

TURKISH

Language reform, in the case of Turkish, was stimulated by the nationalist movement led by Kemal Ataturk, who in 1922 became the first president of the Turkish Republic. Turkey had been part of the Ottoman Empire; Ataturk's plan was to build a modern nation and to strengthen ties with Europe. In line with these general objectives, he advocated sweeping changes in the language. This began with the development of a new writing system, using a Roman-style alphabet, symbolically cutting Turkey's ties with the Middle East by replacing the Arabic script previously in use. In modernizing and simplifying the language, Ataturk's policies continued in directions that were already advocated by avante-garde Turkish writers and journalists. An extensive literacy campaign was undertaken; opposition to the new writing system was minimal, as the literacy rate at the time was only around 10%.

In 1932, an official academy, the Turkish Linguistic Society, was formed to continue the work of language reform. At the same time, folklore studies were emphasized to serve as the basis of a national culture that would separate Turkey from the "Perso-Arabic heritage of Ottoman civilization." These studies also contributed to vocabulary reform, replacing both Persian and Arabic loanwords with new coinages derived from Turkish roots. In effect, language reform was aimed at eliminating the diglossia that was seen as a remnant of prerevolutionary society.

Eventually, the campaign that emphasized the weeding out of foreign words slowed down, and the Turkish Linguistic Society was forced to deal with the necessity of incorporating scientific terminology and other kinds of international vocabulary. Language reform is still a concern, both to conservatives who want to avoid foreignisms and to academicians who are concerned with international relations and exchange of information. Applied linguists in Turkey today continue to pursue the objectives of modernization, standardization, and the elimination of illiteracy.

Swahili

Over a vast area of East Africa, the Swahili language has been used for centuries as a trade language. This was the case when European colonies were first established in the area, and there is a long history of bilingualism and multilingualism, with Swahili as part of the mix. At the same time, there was a degree of regional variation in Swahili, reflecting the influence of local vernaculars (such as Kikuyu, Swazi, and Shona) and, especially in the north, the influence of Arabic; further, Swahili had a long written tradition, employing the Arabic script.

Following the end of World War I, several former German colonies in East Africa passed to England, and the entire area was consolidated under British colonial rule. In the 1920s, efforts were begun to standardize Swahili throughout the region to serve as a *lingua franca* linking the colonies, for use in a unified school system, and for church and governmental functions. Christian missionaries were prominent in the East Africa Swahili Committee that was set up at this time; religious bias may explain their decision to adopt the (southern) Zanzibar dialect for official use. Although the (northern) Kenya dialect had the most developed literary tradition, it also reflected strong Islamic influences. Thus, Eastman points out, "a non-literary dialect was transformed into a literary language by non-native speakers." The orthography, two-volume dictionary, reference grammar, and textbooks developed by this committee established the variety of Swahili that is still considered the standard; however, by the 1940s, English had begun to replace Swahili in many functions.

Swahili is still used in the four African nations (Kenya, Tanzania, Uganda, and Zanzibar) of the former British colonial area; it is the national language of two, Kenya and Tanzania. In Tanzania, the National Swahili Council is the language-planning body, charged with modernizing and elaborating the language. Policies include extending the use of Swahili into all areas of education, development of scientific and technical vocabulary from native, rather than borrowed, resources, and expunging the "stilted quality" of language that reflects the earlier non-native influences.

In Kenya, as in Tanzania, governmental objectives include the extensive use of Swahili as a nation-building strategy, while discouraging the use of local indigenous languages in an effort to "detribalize" the country. In this case, perhaps reflecting the fact that "standard" Swahili was not based on the Kenya dialect, there seems to be a kind of diglossia situation, with a "pidgin Swahili" in use in Nairobi among representatives of a number of language backgrounds. Evidently this dialect reflects Kenya's local Swahili tradition and could be the source of changes that will lead to more regional diversification. Nevertheless, Eastman concludes that the "externally standardized Swahili of colonial days is giving way to a consciously planned national Swahili based on policy decisions of the separate countries" (Eastman, 1983).

7

LANGUAGE MAPS
AND CLASSIFICATIONS

No one knows how many languages there are in the world. There are thousands, certainly, but unless all are recorded and mapped and experts have decided on the boundaries that define their limits, an exact count cannot be made. Estimates of the number of the world's languages are usually given in round numbers and range from a low of 2,000 to a high of 5,000 or more. It seems likely that 3,000 is a realistic compromise if we exclude those that have ceased to be spoken within the present century; the higher figure would be more accurate if these dead or dying languages are included in the count. Another reason for uncertainty is the fact that linguists are still ignorant of the speech of many communities. In some areas—central New Guinea, for example—there may not be sufficient information to know whether neighboring communities differ in speech to the extent that they ought to be mapped as separate languages, or whether they are so similar as to be considered local dialects of the same language. Moreover—and this is a more basic consideration—linguists may disagree on how to establish and apply criteria for making this decision: Where should language boundaries be drawn?

LANGUAGES AND LANGUAGE FAMILIES

Some languages in the world have never been the subject of dictionaries or grammars, and some have never even been recorded or written down. However, a great deal of general knowledge has been accumulated, and it is very unlikely that the scholarly world will ever, in the future, be amazed by the discovery of "lost tribes" that speak languages completely different from those already recorded. Still, there are gaps in the detailed study, description, and comparison of the languages already discovered. Much of the excitement of linguistic study lies not in the discovery of new languages, but in tracing the relationships and contacts among languages. These relationships and contacts, all of which contribute to an unraveling of the course of human history, are detected by (1) the recording and analysis of data from individual languages, and (2) comparisons of these data—of vocabulary and grammatical structures—in order to determine the points of resemblance and the differences. By this means, the several thousand languages of the world have been grouped into a much smaller number of language families. The groupings are proposed, in the first place, on the basis of recognizable similarities among the languages. They become established as families of proven relationship after comparative study has revealed regular patterns in the resemblances (as discussed in chapter 4).[1]

CLASSIFYING
NATIVE AMERICAN LANGUAGES

A survey of an area may be undertaken in order to make an initial classification of languages. A major survey of this kind was undertaken during the 1880s when the Bureau of American Ethnology, the federal agency dealing with native peoples and cultures, was established. As one of its first projects, John Wesley Powell, the director of the Bureau, undertook a definitive survey of the native languages of the United States. For some parts of the country, Powell could draw on established knowledge of the Native American tribes, but for other areas, especially in the West and Southwest, the primary data had to be collected. The basic tool used by researchers in identifying and classifying the languages was a word list. With this as a guide, the same types of vocabulary could be collected in one community after another. The parallel vocabularies were then compared to determine the linguistic affiliations and groupings of the Indian communities. Figure 7.1 shows a selection of vocabularies that were collected in California in the late 19th century. Based on resemblances in vocabulary, the local groups listed here were all assigned to a single language, Yurok, which was given the status of a separate language family because no close resemblances to any other language could be detected.

The Powell classification, published in 1891, grouped several hundred tribes into 58 linguistic "stocks" or families (Powell, 1891). Though some of these family groupings rested only on comparison of vocabularies, they have proved to be quite reliable as the basis for further research and comparison. However, further study of the languages and language families in Powell's classification has enabled later scholars to combine some of them into phyla (or "superfamilies"); the families established earlier usually remain as a lower level of classification. For example, Yurok has recently been shown to have a distant connection with the Algonkian family, a group of languages of the eastern part of North America, and both are now included in a larger grouping of related languages, Macro-Algonkian (see Figure 7.1).

---

[1]Further comparisons, of families and of reconstructed ancestral languages, may make it possible to establish more remote relationships and, thus, to extend knowledge of linguistic history even farther into the past. (See chapter 4 for discussion of the work of Greenberg, Dolgopolsky, and others.)

| FIGURE 7.1 | COMPARATIVE VOCABULARIES: YUROK FAMILY |

English	1. Al-i-kwa	2. Al-i-kwa	3. Klamath	4. Yu'-rok	5. Al-i-kwa
1. man	pe-gur'h	pa'-gek	pay-gurk	pe-gurk	pu-gur-uk
2. woman	win-chuk	wint'-suk	went-surf	wen'-tens	win'-chuk
3. boy	mà-werkh	hōkah	meg'-wah	muh'-wah	mà-werkh-sur
4. girl	hak-tchur	wai'-in-uksh	weh-ye-nuf	wurh-yen'-neks	ner-u-luks
5. infant	—	tahai'-nūks	tsaa-noaf	mi-was'-suh	ōk-se
6. father	takht	meg-wa'-she	daat	nek-nep'-sets	takht, ōp-shrekh
7. mother	kak-hus	tsi-ma'-mus	gawk	kok-oss	kak-si
•	•	•	•	•	•
18. head	mōtl-kwa	te-kwe'	oō-mohl	malkh-kob	o-mudtl-kwa
19. hair	lep-taltl	lep-taltl	lep-teilkh	lep-tal'	lep-toikhl
20. face	—	ta'-le	wit-taw-el-aw	me'-lin	we-luu-ni
21. forehead	te'-we	te'-wek	teh-way	wuh'-to-wai	we-te-we
22. ear	wits-pe-gur	spe-gukh	wats-peg-eh	wuts-peg'-ga	speg-gar
•	•	•	•	•	•

GEOGRAPHY AND LANGUAGE BOUNDARIES

Languages differ a great deal in their social and political importance; some are spoken widely, extending across the boundaries of many different countries, while others have only a handful of speakers. English, French, and Russian, for example, are *world languages;* native speakers of these languages are numbered in the hundreds of millions. They are also used as second languages by many persons who have a need to travel or communicate beyond their own national boundaries. Turkish, Estonian, Guaraní, and Nepali could be called "middle range" or *national languages;* they are more restricted in their distribution, though each has several million speakers. Hopi (in North America), Lokono (in South America), Breton (in Europe), and Nuer (in Africa) are *local languages,* spoken by isolated or enclave populations, each with a community of speakers that may number in the thousands or even a few million. Native speakers of such languages could not travel very far and would be quite limited in their knowledge of the world without the use of a second language.

It is clear that the word *language* has a geographical dimension; languages can be defined and delimited in terms of geographical distribution and numbers of speakers. But how is this done? How do we decide where to draw the boundaries between languages? Can we be sure, in a given geographical area, whether people speak the same or different languages? Indeed, how many different languages are present? The phrase "to speak the same language" implies a definite and recognizable similarity in the speech habits of speakers and an ease of communication. However, the degree of similarity may be considerably less in the case of a world language, which encompasses a number of national or regional variants, than in the case of the more restricted local languages. In the first case, the people who claim to speak the same language constitute many separate speech communities, each with internal variety as well as distinctive shared characteristics. The communicative links that bind them all together into a sort of linguistic supercommunity (for example, the English speakers of the United States, Great Britain, Canada, Australia, and many other countries) may today be maintained largely through mass media and a common literary tradition.

At the opposite extreme are certain local languages that are so restricted geographically that the entire population of speakers form a single speech community. For example, Zuni, a Native American language, has, for as long as its history is known, been spoken by a small population in a restricted geographical area; at present, there are approximately 5,000 speakers. In such a geographically and socially compact population, there is little or no local variation in speech (although some variation related to age and status has undoubtedly always been present, as it is today). Linguists refer to Zuni as a "language isolate": It is a single language that shows no close similarities to indicate relationship to any of its historic neighbors (Apache, Navajo, Hopi, and other southwestern tribes); remote connections with more distant languages are possible, but none has been definitely proven.

A clearly delimited and undifferentiated language like Zuni is, however, an unusual case. More typically, we do find a degree of variation within the geographical boundaries of a language and also are able to establish external relationships (its place within a family of languages). Residents of an individual community—a town in Germany, a village in the highlands of New Guinea, a nomadic band in the desert of Australia—are often found to speak almost, but not exactly, like their neighbors. They are aware of distinctive differences and peculiarities in the speech of visitors from neighboring regions, and they can understand some of the speech of certain other communities that are more distantly located. In such cases, it is difficult to decide just where one language ends and another begins. Speakers are able to make judgments about the linguistic similarities among communities, but their judgments are apt to be colored by political or various other biases. Long-time allies may be judged to speak "just the same" (overlooking differences), while chronic enemies may claim complete ignorance of one another's speech (perhaps ignoring similarities).

The language boundaries found on maps sometimes reflect traditional political alliances and divisions rather than purely linguistic judgments. A classic example of this is found in India and Pakistan, where Hindi is written in a script derived from Sanskrit and has religious and cultural vocabulary stemming from that ancient language, while Urdu is written in Arabic characters and has borrowed vocabulary related to the Moslem religion. Hindi and Urdu are mutually intelligible—some linguists class them as a single language, Hindustani. However, speakers of the two express a feeling of linguistic separateness which, in this case as in many others, is as much a reflection of political and religious loyalties as of actual similarity or differences in speech.

On principle, linguists feel that the basis for language boundaries should be *intelligibility*, the ability of members of different communities to speak to and understand one another. If they can do so, they have a common language; if they cannot, they speak different languages. However, this criterion is difficult to apply, especially if one relies on the judgments of the speakers. Attempts have been made to develop objective ways of measuring intelligibility and to use this as a practical basis for drawing language and dialect boundaries. This approach is illustrated by a study, done in 1951, of Iroquoian languages and dialects; the method was developed by C. F. Voegelin, one of the more innovative of modern linguists (Voegelin & Harris, 1951).

A STUDY OF DIALECT DISTANCE

Iroquoian is one of more than 50 language families native to North America. It is a grouping of languages that have been shown (by comparison of vocabulary and grammatical structure) to be historically related and ultimately descended from a common "ancestral" language (see chapter 4). At the time of first European contact, the Iroquoian-speaking peoples were widely distributed in eastern North America, from the St. Lawrence and Hudson River valleys in the north to the southern Appalachians and the coastal areas of the Carolinas in the south and east (see Figure 7.2).

Several divisions of the Iroquois were decimated and scattered as a result of intertribal wars, political events of the colonial era, and the American Revolution; however, seven still maintain their identity. These are the "Five Nations" of the Iroquois confederacy—Seneca, Cayuga, Onandaga, Oneida, and Mohawk—whose historical homelands lie between the Great Lakes and the Hudson River; the Cherokee, native to the southern Appalachians; and the Tuscarora, whose historical location is in eastern North Carolina. Many of the Cherokees were removed from the Southeast to an Oklahoma reserve early in the 19th century, and Cherokees have also migrated, as individuals or small groups, into many other areas. The main body of the Tuscarora voluntarily moved north in 1710, allying themselves with the Iroquois confederacy, and today are mainly to be found in New York State.

The fact that languages are historically related does not necessarily have a direct bearing, pro or con, on the ability of people to communicate with one another. The five tribes of the Iroquois confederacy had, besides a historical relationship, a long tradition of trade and military alliance, social interaction and intermarriage, and common political identity. These facts have sometimes led outside observers, as well as many of the Iroquois themselves, to underestimate their linguistic differences. One contributing circumstance may be the frequent occurrence of bilingualism (that is, of learned rather than native intelligibility). In the past, political and military alliance meant the presence of interpreters who could understand speeches given in the council house by members of other tribes, carry messages between villages, and assist in other intertribal negotiations. There are still numerous individuals who are fluent in more than one variety of Iroquoian. Intermarriage was

FIGURE 7.2

Geographical distribution of Iroquoian peoples. Reprinted by permission from James Mooney, *Historical Sketch of the Cherokee*. Copyright 1975 by Aldine Publishing Co.

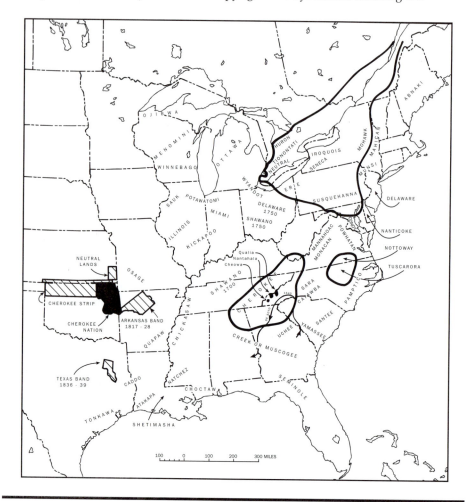

common in the past, as it is also in the present, when communities are probably less homogeneous than they formerly were. Furthermore, during the past century, an ever-increasing fluency in English has reduced the practical problems of communication. (English now serves as a *lingua franca* for speakers of many different Native American languages.)

Our study of Iroquoian languages and dialects involved two stages of fieldwork followed by an analysis of the data. In the first stage, a research team visited the eight reservation communities in New York State and

Canada and recorded the speech of native speakers of Seneca, Cayuga, Onandaga, Oneida, Mohawk, Tuscarora, and Cherokee. This material included a variety of traditional narratives, anecdotes, personal histories, and conversations. All were recorded on tape, and English translations were recorded separately. Two test tapes were prepared, each one including samples from all seven speech communities. The first tape was made up of 2-minute segments and was used in testing general comprehension; the second included 30-second segments that were played a few words at a time, for closer, word-for-word translation.

In the second stage of fieldwork, the reservations were visited again, and the tests were administered to several representatives of each speech community. The 28 individuals who were tested were screened, eliminating those who claimed to be familiar with varieties of Iroquoian other than their own. Then each participant was asked to translate all the tapes; the translations were recorded and were later evaluated for comprehension and general accuracy in translation. In this evaluation, the responses were given a rough percentile score. For the first test, the score was based on a résumé of content in the 2-minute text; for the second, it was based on the accuracy of translation phrase by phrase. The chart below includes the combined percentile scores for all informants in the second test. (This test, since it is easier to evaluate, reflects intelligibility more objectively than the first.)

	S	C	Ona	One	M	T	Ch
Seneca	97	85	30	12	12	½	0
Cayuga	70	100	13	15	16	0	0
Onandaga	30	40	100	23	23	0	0
Oneida	24	23	10	95	75	0	0
Mohawk	5	25	0	86	96	0	0
Tuscarora	2	2	0	0	0	95	0

Figure 7.3 was constructed on the basis of these scores, modified slightly by those scores from the first test. It might be noted that informants were inclined to give a high estimate of their own ability to understand and would sometimes answer the question, "Did you understand that?" in the affirmative, even in cases in which they were able to translate only 25%–30% of the content. However, 75% was chosen as a figure that correlates well with accurate summaries of content (in test 1) as well as specific understanding of vocabulary (test 2). This figure, 75%, was designated as *a percentile definition of intelligibility*. By this standard, speech communities with less than 75% mutual intelligibility constitute separate languages, while those that score above this figure constitute local varieties, or dialects, of the same language. On this basis, the Iroquoian languages were determined to be Cherokee, Tuscarora, Mohawk-Oneida, Onandaga, and Seneca-Cayuga. Mohawk and Oneida, then, are two dialects of a single language, as are Seneca and Cayuga (Hickerson, Turner, & Hickerson, 1952).

FIGURE 7.3

Chart of Iroquois languages and dialects. Reprinted from H. Hickersonn, G. D. Turner, and N. P. Hickerson, "Testing Procedures for Estimating Transfer of Information among Iroquois Dialects and Languages," *International Journal of American Linguistics* (1952). Copyright 1952 by the University of Chicago Press.

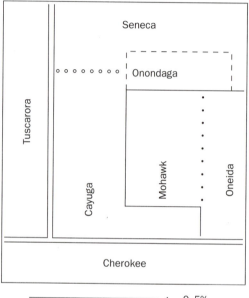

What are the connections among intelligibility, history, and geographical or social contact? We can make some interpretations on the basis of our Iroquoian study. The historical separation of the Cherokee, the Tuscarora, and the northern Iroquois peoples is ancient; an Iroquoian specialist, F. Lounsbury, estimates that these three branches of the Iroquoian family separated well over 2,000 years ago. There are marked differences in vocabulary, though many points of similarity can be detected through close comparison; grammatical and phonetic differences are also reflected in the complete lack of intelligibility between Cherokee and Tuscarora, and between these two and any of the northern Iroquoian group.

The languages of these five northern tribes—Seneca, Cayuga, Onandaga, Oneida, and Mohawk—have a bit more in common. Lounsbury estimates that ancestors of this group established separate identities between 1,200 and 1,500 years ago (Lounsbury, 1959). However, geographical contiguity, political alliance, and continuing social contact have fostered the maintenance of linguistic connections as well. There is a sizable body of shared linguistic material in the presence of cultural vocabulary, such as place names and traditions associated with the natural environment, the names of regional animal species, clan names, and the vocabulary relating to the political institutions that these peoples share. This type of cultural vocabulary is very similar throughout the northern division of Iroquoian and has obviously been borrowed or diffused from community to community along lines of social interaction. Finally, it might be noted that the highest levels of intelligibility, which were interpreted as the division of dialects within a single language, were found between the communities with the closest geographical contiguity: the Seneca and Cayuga, and the Mohawk and Oneida. In these cases, continuing social contacts have clearly served to minimize the divergence of speech, despite the historical existence of separate communities.

The study of Iroquoian languages and dialects shows that it is possible, in theory, to establish language boundaries with precision. In practice, this has seldom been done. Political boundaries are often taken as language boundaries, giving an artificial unity to a variety of dialects. In areas of linguistic diversity or complexity, one or another language or dialect often emerges as a *lingua franca*, the language used in international, intertribal, or intervillage trade and communication. In the case of complex national states, a particular regional or class dialect sometimes acquires the status of a national standard. Used in mass communications, education, and official functions, it may replace other varieties of speech or become specialized to particular situations. *Diglossia*, the use of two or more language varieties, shows us that communication does not stop at the borders between languages.

LANGUAGE AREAS OF THE WORLD: 1500 A.D.

The world today is dominated, linguistically, by languages that have spread as part of the expansion and colonization of large areas by a few European and Asiatic powers. Spanish, English, French, Russian, Portuguese, Arabic, and Mandarin Chinese are among those that have expanded on a global scale in the past few centuries. This linguistic expansion is paralleled by cultural diffusion and movements and mixtures of populations that have taken place during the same historical period.

If we make a mental adjustment and think of the world as it was around 1500 A.D., before the full onset of the colonial era, we will find a clearer and simpler linguistic picture. Up to that time, continental areas were fairly self-contained; distinctive racial, cultural, and linguistic groups developed in relative isolation. It is worth noting that each major world area contained a distinctive set of language families within its natural boundaries and that few and distant linguistic connections can be traced across these boundaries. Within each world area (Eurasia, Africa, North America, South America, and Oceania), we find one or more large groups of closely related languages with wide distribution, which can be assumed to represent a relatively recent expansion and separation of a formerly united speech community. In each world area, there are also marginal or isolated languages that often appear to be survivors or remnants of language families that must have been more widely distributed at an earlier time but have been displaced or pushed aside by the more expansive speech communities.

A primary reason for anthropological interest in the distribution and genetic connections of languages is the insight that they give us into population movements. This is felt especially when linguistic classifications can be related to other types of evidence such as culture complexes or identifiable archaeological horizons. Language family classifications and suggestions about possible, more distant, relations among language families are always of interest to historically oriented anthropologists because they are evidence of the historical connections of peoples. It is very difficult to assess cultural similarities as evidence for historical connections because inventions may spread over great distances simply by borrowing, rather than by direct contact; and similar customs or institutions often develop independently of one another in two or more different locations. Furthermore, cultures that do have a common origin can change so drastically under different environmental or economic conditions that their historical links would be very difficult to discover. The evidence of linguistic affiliations, then, at times may offer the most convincing proof or disproof of the historical origins and movements of peoples. Language family classification is a type of "hard" evidence that can be most valuable to a cultural historian or archaeologist.

It must be emphasized, however, that linguistic affiliations are only one type of historical evidence. Populations can adopt new languages while retaining a particular cultural identity; and, conversely, culture can change without a change of language. It would be a mistake to assume, for example, that contemporary people who speak an isolated or marginal language are direct descendants of an ancient population stratum unless there is other evidence of their special status, such as distinctive cultural retentions or even unique biological traits, that point to the same conclusion.

On the other hand, dominant languages are often adopted by or imposed on groups of people who subsequently abandon use of their earlier language. In this way, for example, Latin replaced a variety of languages in southern Europe. Certain local populations may tentatively be identified as descended from historic tribes of pre-Roman times, but their earlier linguistic affiliations can seldom be inferred.

Linguists use the term *language family* to refer to a group of languages whose historical relationship and common origin are considered to be proved beyond any doubt by close comparisons and reconstruction of an ancestral language or *protolanguage* (see chapter 4). Suggestions of broader or more remote relationships may lead to the grouping of language isolates and/or families into a *language phylum* or superfamily. These larger groupings may have a common origin, but this cannot yet be demonstrated in point-by-point detail because the evidence may be more fragmentary than in the case of an established family. The maps given here (Figures 7.4 through 7.8) display, in some cases, language families; phyla are shown when claims of remote relationship appear to be justified. A third category, *language group,* is used for languages that have been traditionally treated together, even though no strong claim of relationship has been given; these are usually geographically restricted groupings that appear to have great antiquity. In some cases (for example, Paleo-Siberian), a language group may include two or more language isolates. Finally, *language isolates* are single languages (or small families) that have not been shown to have other affiliations (Voegelin & Voegelin, 1964–1966).

In every case, the largest accepted groupings have been mapped: phyla, families, language groups, and language isolates.[2] It can usually be assumed that a family of languages has differentiated from a common origin over the last 2 to 4 millennia. Languages and language families that are grouped together within a phylum may have historical connections at a depth of 3 millennia or more. Language isolates are sole survivors of earlier families or have affiliations so remote that they remain undiscovered. Therefore, in most cases, it can be assumed that language isolates represent populations that preceded the invasion or spread or larger groupings, that is, families and phyla.

EURASIA

I. The *Ural-Altaic* phylum is made up of two divisions. (A) *Uralic,* or Finno-Ugric, is a well-established family that includes Hungarian, Finnish, and Lapp, several small language communities located along the Volga River in Russia (such as Cheremis and Mordwin), and Samoyed and other languages of central Siberia.

The *Altaic* division, which some experts give separate status as a phylum, includes three families: (B) *Turkic,* consisting of Turkish and closely related languages that are scattered over a wide area, including Tatar and Kirghiz of southern Siberia and central Asia, and Yakut in northern Siberia; (C) *Mongol,* a family of closely related languages in Mongolia; and (D) *Manchu-Tungus,* which covers a very large area in Manchuria and Siberia.

---

[2]The phyla are not, in every case, established groupings of great antiquity; some of them express a *proposed* relationship—which may be very likely—which has not yet been *proved.* In such cases the languages included in phyla may actually be historically closer than those included in established families. For this reason, it does not seem important to emphasize the distinction among family, phylum, and (in Figure 7.8) macrophylum, though the distinction will be important if (as Swadesh has suggested) it can eventually be linked to differences in time depth.

FIGURE 7.4 EURASIA.

Both *Uralic* and *Altaic* languages have been dispersed over an extremely large area with few natural barriers to the movements and migrations of peoples. The distribution of these languages is complex, with the different divisions intersecting and overlapping. It is likely that this distribution reflects the famous mobility of these peoples, most of whom are or have been pastoral nomads (the Mongols, Tatars, and Lapps, for example).

II. The *Sino-Tibetan* phylum includes three families, one of which may be questionable. (A) *Chinese* is a family made up of several regional "dialects," which might well be considered separate languages (not mutually intelligible). The most prominent are Mandarin, or Pekingese, of northern China, and Cantonese in southern China; others include Wu, Hakka, and Min.

(B) *Tibeto-Burman* includes Tibetan and several languages of Burma and the Malayan peninsula (Lolo, Kachin, Garo). (C) The *Tai* languages are of disputed status. Some specialists have classified them as an isolated family, while others have suggested a relationship to the Austroasiatic phylum, theorizing that similarities to Chinese are the result of borrowings rather than common origin. Tai includes Thai or Siamese, Lao (of Laos), and other languages spoken in southern China and Indochina (Miao, Yao, Shan, Kadai, and others).

III. *Indo-European* is the largest single family in its geographical expanse and numbers of speakers; it stretches from India to western Europe. There are several extinct languages known only through inscriptions and early written sources; the eight modern branches are essentially regional in distribution. (A) *Indo-Iranian* contains the *Indic* and *Iranian* divisions. The Iranian division includes several dialects of modern Persian. Indic includes the classical language, Sanskrit, and modern languages spoken in Pakistan, India, and Sri Lanka—such as Hindustani, Bengali, and Punjabi—as well as Romany, used by Gypsies throughout the world.

(B) *Balto-Slavic* includes both the Baltic and Slavic groups. The *Baltic* languages are Lithuanian, Latvian, and Prussian (which became extinct in the 17th century). *Slavic* is a large group, including Russian, Czech, Polish, Bulgarian, and other languages of central and eastern Europe. (C) *Greek,* (D) *Albanian,* and (E) *Armenian* each consist of a single modern language. (F) *Germanic* occupies much of northern and western Europe, including the British Isles (where it coexists with Celtic), the Scandinavian peninsula, and Iceland; some of the languages are High and Low German, Dutch, English, Swedish, Norwegian, and Icelandic.

(G) The *Romanic* languages are descendants of Latin and closely related dialects spoken in Italy at the time of the Roman Empire. The modern languages include Italian, French, Catalan, Spanish, Portuguese, and Romanian. (H) *Celtic* languages were once spoken over much of western Europe and the British Isles and have been partly replaced by other languages, Romanic and Germanic. Modern representatives include Irish, Scots Gaelic, Welsh, and Breton (in northern France). Romanic and Celtic are sometimes grouped together, as an Italo-Celtic subfamily.

IV. The *Dravidian* family is made up of several languages of southern India (Telugu, Tamil, Kannada, Malayalam), Pakistan (Brahui), and Sri

Lanka (Tamil). The territory occupied by Dravidian was larger in prehistoric times, before the Dravidian peoples were conquered and pushed back by invading speakers of Indo-European.

V. The *Caucasian* group includes the several dozen languages of a mountainous area in the Soviet Union between the Black and Caspian seas. The relationships among these languages have not yet been completely clarified. They are not necessarily all of one language family, though they have a number of characteristics in common. Some of these languages are Georgian, Azerbaijani, Abkhazian, Kabardian, and Ubykh.

VI. The *Japanese-Korean* phylum is made up of two languages that in the past have often been treated as isolates. If authentic, the genetic relationship is an ancient one; some linguists have also suggested a remote connection of both languages with the Ural-Altaic phylum.

VII. The *Austroasiatic* phylum includes three widely dispersed families: (A) *Munda,* made up of languages scattered in several regions of eastern India; (B) the *Mon-Khmer* family, spread through Burma, Cambodia, and Vietnam; and (C) *Nicobarese,* located on islands in the Indian Ocean. It seems likely that these scattered languages are remnants of a very early Southeast Asian population, now marginal to both Dravidian and Indo-European (in India) and to the several divisions of Sino-Tibetan (in Indochina).

VIII. The *Paleo-Siberian* group includes two small families, Yeneseian and Luorawetlan, and two isolates, Yukaghir and Gilyak. All are located in northeastern Siberia and are spoken by scattered populations of hunting, fishing, or reindeer-herding peoples.

IX. *Basque* is an isolate located in western France and northeastern Spain. Some grammatical similarities indicate that Basque may be very remotely related to languages of the Caucasian group; however, these suggestions still seem highly speculative.

X. *Ainu,* a language isolate of northern Japan, is spoken by people who can be identified with an earlier culture than that of the Japanese. No real connections have been established between Ainu and any other language, though some similarities in vocabulary to several Native American languages have been pointed out.

XI. *Andamanese* is an isolate found on islands in the Bay of Bengal, spoken by a small native population whose simple technology and social organization can be seen as evidence of long cultural isolation. Recently, it has been suggested that Andamanese has language-phylum connections with the Papuan languages of New Guinea (discussed later).

AFRICA

I. The *Afroasiatic* phylum extends beyond the continental limits of Africa, to the Arabian peninsula and neighboring parts of western Asia. Four of the five families that make up the phylum are restricted to Africa, and it seems likely that the earliest dispersal of the group took place within that continent. The divisions are (A) *Semitic,* the most widespread family, which

FIGURE 7.5   AFRICA.

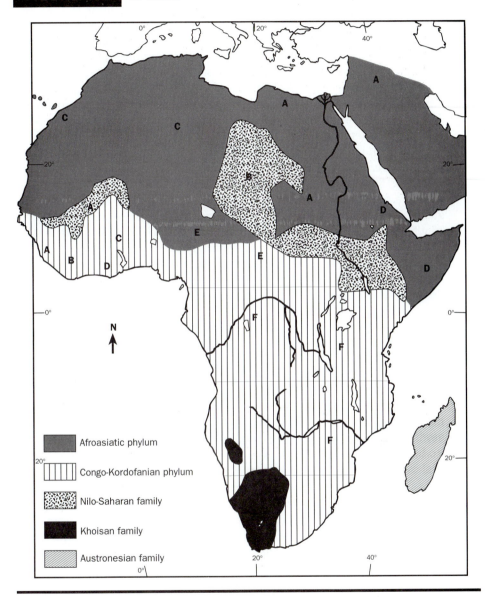

includes in its northern division Hebrew, Aramaic, and extinct languages such as Phoenician and Akkadian; the southern division consists of Arabic (which has spread far in its association with the Moslem religion) and Amharic, the main language of Ethiopia.

(B) *Egyptian* is extinct, surviving only as a liturgical language used by Coptic Christians. (C) *Berber* is spoken by scattered peoples in northern

Africa (Tuareg, Kabyle, and others). (D) *Cushitic* is a fairly large family in eastern Africa; some of the languages are Somali, Galla, and Beja. (E) *Chadic* is a family that centers on Lake Chad in west-central Africa; Hausa is the largest of several languages in this group.

II. The *Congo-Kordofanian* phylum has two divisions; the first is *Kordofanian*, a small group of languages in the Sudan (an enclave in the Nilo-Saharan area). The other, *Niger-Congo*, is an extremely large family dominating most of the African continent south of the Sahara. Niger-Congo includes approximately 300 languages grouped into six subfamilies: (A) *West Atlantic*, including Wolof, Fulani, and other languages of Senegal, Guinea, and Gambia; (B) *Mande*, which includes Mande, Kpelle, Malinke, and other languages of the Ivory Coast; (C) *Gur*, of Nigeria and neighboring countries, with approximately 50 languages including Tallensi and Nupe; (D) *Kwa*, centering in Liberia and Nigeria, containing a number of large language groups such as Akan, Kru, Ewe, Yoruba, and Ibo; (E) *Adamawe-Eastern*, a scattered group of languages east of Lake Chad of which Fulani is the largest and most well-known representative; and (F) *Benue-Congo*, which takes in several languages of Nigeria (including Efik and Tiv) as well as the very widespread *Bantu* languages. As we have seen, Bantu languages are spread throughout the Congo and eastern and southeastern portions of Africa. They are, in general, so undifferentiated that they appear to have spread at a fairly recent time. Ganda, Kongo, Kikuyu, Rauanda, Swazi, and Zulu are among the dozens of Bantu languages, as is Swahili, which has long served as a trade language throughout East Africa.

III. The *Nilo-Saharan* family has a marginal distribution between the Niger-Congo family and the southernmost extension of divisions of Afro-Asiatic. The branches are (A) *Songhai*, located along the Niger River in Mali; (B) *Saharan*, a large group of languages east of Lake Chad; and (C) *Sudanic*, located north of Lake Victoria and in scattered enclaves elsewhere. The best-known representatives are the Nubian and Nilotic languages (including Nuer and Masai).

IV. Languages of the *Khoisan* family are remnants of a group that was probably quite widespread in Africa before the dispersal of the Bantu. The main concentration at present is in arid regions of South Africa where the two main cultural divisions are Bushman and Hottentot; both of these include a number of languages and dialects. There are other scattered enclaves farther to the north, such as Sandawe and Hadza in Tanzania. With few exceptions, speakers of the Khoisan languages are hunting people who appear to be culturally marginal to dominant pastoral and agricultural groups.

V. The languages of Madagascar fall within the Austronesian family; a discussion follows.

OCEANIA

I. The *Austronesian* family is one of the most widespread in the world, reaching from Hawaii and Easter Island in the mid-Pacific, to Southeast Asia, and to Madagascar near the east coast of Africa. It contains roughly 500 languages. (A) The greatest diversity is in the *western* division, which includes

FIGURE 7.6 · OCEANIA ·

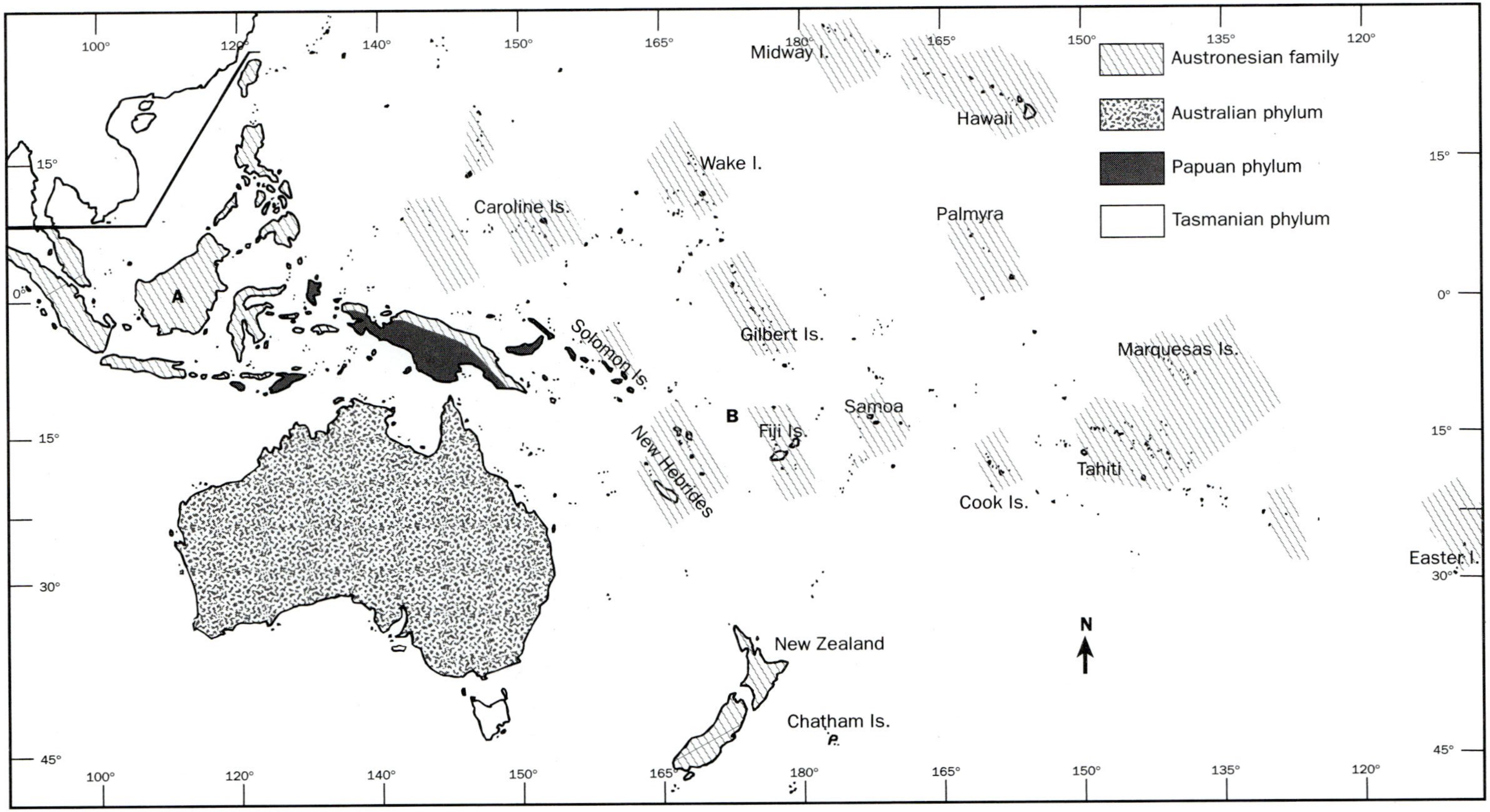

Austronesian family
Australian phylum
Papuan phylum
Tasmanian phylum

N

Easter I.

Marquesas Is.
Tahiti
Cook Is.

Hawaii
Palmyra

Samoa
Gilbert Is.
Fiji Is.
New Zealand
Chatham Is.

Midway I.
Wake I.
Caroline Is.
Solomon Is.
New Hebrides

A
B

15°
0°
15°
30°
45°

100° 120° 140° 150° 165° 180° 165° 150° 135° 120°

Malay, Indonesian, Javanese, and languages of various islands of Indonesia, Tagalog, Ilocano, and a number of other languages in the Philippines; the non-Chinese aboriginal languages of Taiwan; languages of Madagascar; and the languages of several of the island groups of western Micronesia and New Guinea. It seems likely that the Indonesian area is the earlier center of development and diffusion of the language family, from which the languages spread outward to more distant regions and island groups.

(B) The *eastern* division takes in a Melanesian branch that extends to Fiji and includes such islands as New Caledonia, the New Hebrides, parts of the Solomon archipelago, and coastal areas of northern and eastern New Guinea. The Micronesian branch includes Gilbertese, Ponapean, and most of the languages of Micronesia. The far-flung Polynesian branch includes Maori in New Zealand, Hawaiian, Marquesan, Tongan, and Samoan.

II. The *Australian* phylum is a comprehensive grouping of all the aboriginal languages of Australia, numbering more than 200. There are several divisions and a great deal of variety in these languages, apparently reflecting a very long period of isolation and diversification. The greatest number and variety of languages is found in the north; northern languages include Tiwi, Murngin, and Yir Yoront. In the south, central, and western desert areas, population density is low, and language differentiation is not as great; Kariera and Arunta are representative of these areas. All of the languages of Australia that have been recorded appear to be genetically related and may come to be classed in a single family when sufficient comparative research has been accomplished. No definite external relations have been established.

III. The *Papuan* macrophylum also encompasses a large number of languages that are now classified in families, phyla, and isolates—all of which may ultimately be genetically related. However, most of the languages now grouped as Papuan have not been adequately described, and the limits, subdivisions, and internal relationships are not yet established. Papuan takes in several hundred languages of interior, southern, and western New Guinea, as well as scattered non-Austronesian languages in eastern Indonesia (the islands of Timor and Alor) and on New Britain, New Ireland, and some of the Solomon Islands in Melanesia. Papuan appears, in these marginal areas, to belong to an older population stratum than does Austronesian. As mentioned before, a remote relationship of Papuan to Andamanese has been suggested.

IV. *Tasmanian* apparently constitutes a language isolate; no external relationships have been demonstrated. (The one, two, or more languages of Tasmania are extinct.)

NORTH AMERICA

I. The *Macro-Algonkian* phylum unites two large groups of related languages, each of which includes both families and isolates. (A) The largest family included is *Algonkian*, which was spread over much of the northern and eastern portions of the continent. Some of the the Algonkian languages are Ojibwa, Naskapi, and Cree (in eastern Canada); Micmac, Penobscot,

FIGURE 7.7   NORTH AMERICA.

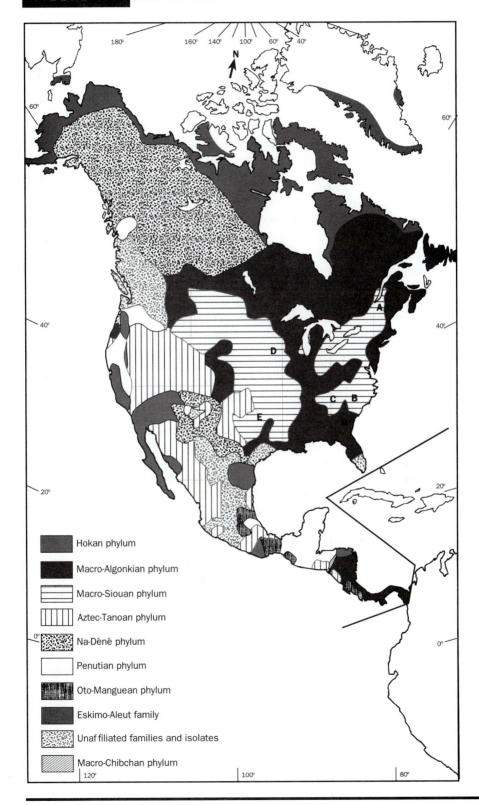

Hokan phylum

Macro-Algonkian phylum

Macro-Siouan phylum

Aztec-Tanoan phylum

Na-Déné phylum

Penutian phylum

Oto-Manguean phylum

Eskimo-Aleut family

Unaffiliated families and isolates

Macro-Chibchan phylum

Delaware, and Powhatan (along the eastern seaboard); Shawnee, Menomini, Fox, and Kickapoo (in the Ohio River valley and Great Lakes area); and Arapaho, Blackfoot, and Cheyenne (in the northern Great Plains). The Algonkian languages were early recognized as related because of close similarities in vocabulary; later, more remote resemblances were found between Algonkian and two isolated languages in California, Wiyot and Yurok, which are sometimes classed together as *Ritwan*. Together, Algonkian and Ritwan make up one of two divisions of the Macro-Algonkian phylum.

(B) The other division also includes a single large family, *Muskogean,* and a number of smaller members. Muskogean covers much of the southeastern quadrant of the continent; some of the included languages are Creek, Koasati, and Choctaw-Chickasaw. Several extinct or nearly extinct languages of the Gulf Coast (Natchez, Tunica, Atakapa, and Chitimacha) have been shown to be related to Muskogean; together they make up a grouping that has been called *Gulf.* Mary Haas, who demonstrated the validity of this grouping of southeastern languages, also established the existence of more distant connections between Algonkian and Muskogean. Thus, we know that a large part of the North American continent was inhabited by speakers of a single group of related languages, the descendants of a single speech community that has fragmented over the course of several millennia. The dimensions of this large grouping of languages may be extended still further; an earlier classification of Native American languages suggested a relationship of Algonkian to Wakashan and several other Western languages (see the discussion later in this section). If these relationships are demonstrated, Macro-Algonkian will extend the length and breadth of the continent and emerge as the most important of the several large phyla in North America.

II. The *Aztec-Tanoan* phylum is made up of two families, *Uto-Aztecan* and *Kiowa-Tanoan.* Uto-Aztecan is a large family, distributed from the Great Basin to central Mexico; it has a prominence in this southwestern quadrant of North America comparable to that of Algonkian in the northeast. Some of the Uto-Aztecan languages are Ute and Paiute (in the Great Basin); Shoshone and Comanche (in the Great Plains); Hopi, Pima, and Papago (in the southwestern United States); Luiseño and Gabrileño (two of several small tribes in California); Cora, Yaqui, and Tarahumara (in northern Mexico); and Nahuatl (the language of the Aztecs, in central Mexico).

Kiowa and Tanoan make up a much smaller family. Kiowa is a Plains language once considered an isolate, and Tanoan is a small grouping of eastern Pueblo languages, including such contemporary communities as Jemez, Taos, Isleta, and San Juan.

III. *Macro-Siouan* is a phylum that, like Macro-Algonkian, unites large language families which, until recently, have been considered independent. The distribution of divisions of Macro-Siouan seems generally to be either intrusive into or marginal to areas occupied by Macro-Algonkian. The interrelationships of the several divisions of these two phyla must play a crucial role in an eventual reconstruction of the prehistory of North America.

The divisions of Macro-Siouan are (A) The *Iroquoian* family, including Huron, Iroquois, and minor languages in eastern Canada and New York, and Cherokee and Tuscarora in the Carolinas (as mentioned earlier). (B) *Catawba* and (C) *Yuchi* are two isolates located in the Carolinas. (D) The *Siouan* family has its broadest distribution in the Plains (with such languages as Dakota, Omaha, Osage, Crow, and Mandan); it is also represented in the southeast (by Biloxi, Tutelo, and Ofo). (E) The *Caddoan* family is mainly located in the southern Plains, where Caddo, Wichita, and Pawnee are the largest representatives.

IV. The *Hokan* phylum is extremely diversified; it includes the *Yuman* family and a number of isolates with a distribution from California to Central America. It has been suggested that these are the scattered remnants of a very early population that was displaced by later immigrants (Penutian and/or Aztec-Tanoan). The Yuman family is located in southern California and along the course of the Colorado River; it includes Yuma, Mohave, and Havasupai. Other members of Hokan are Pomo, Karok, Yana, Shasta, and Achumawi-Atsugewi (all small tribes in California); Seri (in Sonora); Coahuiltecan (extinct, of northeast Mexico); Tlapanecan and Tequistlatecan (in southern Mexico); and Jicaque (in Honduras).

V. *Penutian*, like Hokan, is a phylum that establishes a relationship among several diverse families and isolates of western North and Central America; connections with South American languages have also been suggested. Penutian includes Tsimshian, which is located on the coast of British Columbia; Chinookan, Sahaptian, and Nez Percé in the Plateau area (Oregon and northern California); and several languages of central California, such as Wintun, Miwok, and Yokuts. In Mexico, the large *Mayan* family has recently been shown to be affiliated with Penutian, as have Mixe, Zoque, and Totonacan. Uru-Chipaya, in Bolivia, may also be a related group.

VI. The *Na-Déné* phylum includes, as its largest component, the *Athabascan* family. Athabascan covers most of western Canada (with such languages as Chipewayan, Dogrib, Hare, Kutchin, Sarsi, and Chilcotin) and is also found in northern California and Oregon (Hupa and other small groups), as well as in Arizona, New Mexico, and neighboring areas of the Southwest (Navajo and the Lipan, Mescalero, Chiricahua, and other bands of Apache).

Other divisions of Na-Déné are located along the coast of Alaska and British Columbia. From north to south, they are Eyak, Tlingit, and Haida.

VII. The *Oto-Manguean* phylum is restricted to the mountainous area in middle America. It includes several families, which are quite differentiated: *Zapotecan, Mixtecan, Popolocan, Manguean,* and *Chinantecan.* These appear to be remnants of larger groups that were absorbed or displaced, perhaps by the expansion of the Aztec and Maya empires.

VIII. The *Eskimo-Aleut* family has two branches; Aleut, in southern Alaska and the Aleutian Islands, was the larger in number of speakers but is now almost extinct. In the Eskimo branch, the greatest diversity is in western Alaska; the vast area between Point Barrow in northern Alaska and eastern Greenland shows very little differentiation and may be considered a single language.

There is convincing evidence of remote relationships linking Eskimo-Aleut and some languages of the Paleo-Siberian group; this has been tentatively designated the *American Arctic-Paleo-Siberian* phylum.

IX. The *Wakashan* family is made up of several languages in northwest North America, including Nootka, Kwakiutl, Bella Bella, and Heiltsuk. *Salish* is another family of the western United States and Canada; it includes Coeur d'Alene and Flathead in the plateau area and Squamish, Dwamish, Tillamook, and numerous small language communities around Puget Sound and on the Pacific coast of Washington, Oregon, and British Columbia. *Chimakuan* is a small family in this same area, consisting of Quileute and Chemakum. *Kutenai* is a language isolate of the eastern plateau area.

A classification of North American languages by Edward Sapir (1929) linked these three small families and Kutenai to Algonkian, making up a phylum called *Algonkian-Wakasha;* this relationship still remains as an unconfirmed hypothesis.

X. *Tarascan*, of Michoacán in Mexico, is a large language isolate; there are still several thousand speakers. The Tarascans were almost unique in late prehistoric times in their successful resistance to the Aztec empire.

XI. Other unaffiliated families and isolates include *Yuki,* a small family in northern California, consisting of two languages, Yuki and Wappo. *Keresan* is a language isolate distributed in several Pueblo communities, including Acoma and Laguna; some linguists suggest a remote relationship to Aztec-Tanoan. *Karankawa* is a large isolate (or a family) of the Texas coast. It is extinct, as is *Timucua,* an isolate of southern Florida.

It may be recalled that in Joseph Greenberg's most recent worldwide grouping of languages, all of the languages of South America, plus most of North America, fall into a proposed *Amerind* macrofamily. The exceptions, in North America, are Na-Déné (which is allied with Caucasian and Basque) and Eskimo-Aleut (which is linked to Indo-European and Japanese, among others; see chapter 4).

SOUTH AMERICA

The names of more than 1,000 small language groups have been listed in classifications of South American languages; large numbers of these are extinct, and the status of many of the living languages is unclear. When all of the families, isolates, and unclassified languages are mapped, the picture is quite confusing. In the tropical forest areas, especially, small population groups have tended to migrate and settle by following rivers and their tributaries; this results in very broken distributions. On the other hand, peoples with highly differentiated languages may be situated in a very small map area. The impact of European conquest and settlement has been quite drastic; many native peoples became extinct or lost their tribal identity, while others took refuge by moving farther into the interior, retreating far away from their traditional homelands. There are hundreds of languages known only by name or on the basis of a few recorded words and phrases. Identifying, counting, and classifying them accurately appears impossible, so there are many problems in mapping them.

The map of South America (Figure 7.8) is based on Greenberg's grouping of several previously established phyla and dozens of language families and language isolates into three larger phyla (or *macrophyla*); this is comparable

---

FIGURE 7.8 SOUTH AMERICA.

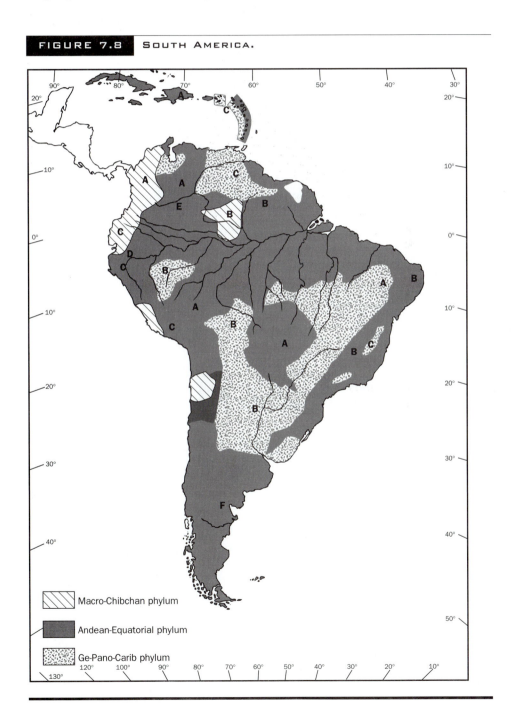

Macro-Chibchan phylum

Andean-Equatorial phylum

Ge-Pano-Carib phylum

to his classification of African languages, though more recent and less widely accepted. One of these large phyla, Macro-Chibchan, includes languages in both Central and South America. The other two, Andean-Equatorial and Ge-Pano-Carib, are widely distributed through South America; the larger families and languages are listed here, but many of the smaller groupings are omitted.

Macro-Chibchan includes as its main divisions (A) the *Chibchan* family, which has its center of distribution in Colombia and extends into adjacent areas of Central and South America. Some of the Chibchan languages are Chibcha, Andaqui, Tunebo, Coconuco, and Cueva in Colombia, Cuna in Panama, and Rama in Nicaragua. (B) The *Waican* languages are spoken by the Yanomama and other peoples in an isolated area along the Venezuelan-Brazilian border. (C) Several more distantly related languages and small families in South America that have been included in Macro-Chibchan are Warao and Yaruro in Venezuela, Esmerelda in Ecuador, and Yunca (or Chimu) in Peru. The distribution of this grouping, thus, is limited to northern and western portions of the continent.

The *Ge-Pano-Carib* macrophylum brings together numerous families and three phyla. One main division is (A) *Macro-Ge*, a phylum that includes *Ge*, a compact family of languages in central Brazil, together with a number of isolates (most of which are no longer spoken). (B) Segments of the *Macro-Panoan* phylum, in which the largest division is the Panoan family, are scattered in separate locations along the border of Brazil and its western neighbors, Paraguay, Bolivia, and Peru. (C) The *Macro-Carib* phylum includes the large *Carib* family and smaller families, the best known of which is *Witoto*. Carib languages are concentrated in northeastern Brazil, Venezuela, and the Guyanas, and they have a more scattered distribution elsewhere, including some of the islands of the Lesser Antilles and isolated areas in southeastern Brazil. Other families included in this macrophylum include *Huarpe* in Argentina, *Nambicuara* in south-central Brazil, and *Bororo* in the Matto Grosso of Brazil and eastern Bolivia.

The *Andean-Equatorial* macrophylum includes large language groups that have extensive distribution in both tropical forests and highland areas of South America. It is more widespread, includes more people, and transcends a greater variety of environments than do the other macrophyla. The large divisions are (A) the *Arawakan* family, which is the biggest in the Americas, including over 100 different languages; the greatest concentration of these is in Venezuela, the Guyanas, Brazil, and the West Indies. (B) The *Tupi-Guaraní* family has its main distribution along the Amazon basin in central Brazil and in a wide area of southeastern Brazil and Paraguay, where Guaraní is an official language. Arawakan, Tupi-Guaraní, and several smaller families (Timote, Salivan, Guahibo) and isolates (including Cayuvava and Trumai) make up the Equatorial division of the macrophylum. (C) *Quechumaran* is a phylum that brings together Quechuan, the language of the Inca empire, with an estimated 6 to 7 million speakers in Peru, Bolivia, and Argentina; and Aymara, spoken by several hundred thousands of persons, mainly in

Bolivia. (D) The *Jivaro* division includes Jivaro, Yaruro, and several language isolates located in northern Peru and Ecuador. (E) The *Tucanoan* division consists of Tucanoan and other small families such as Catuquina and Puinave in northwestern Brazil and Colombia. (F) *Chon* is a highly diversified grouping that includes some of the southernmost languages, most of which were previously classed as isolates: Ona, Yahgan, Alakaluf, Araucanian, and Puelche.

THE LANGUAGE MAP OF THE MODERN WORLD

Before 1500 A.D., there were vast areas of the world about which Europeans knew nothing. There had been little travel or established communications among the separate continents, and Oceania and the New World were essentially unexplored. Since that time, there have been tremendous changes in knowledge and technology, in travel and communication, in economic and social and political life—and more. Changes in language have accompanied all of these other developments. The most obvious linguistic effect of the worldwide expansion of Western culture has been the spread of European languages. Other languages have grown and spread on a global scale as well; Arabic, Sanskrit, and Chinese have had wide areas of influence in the past as well as in the present. However, European languages—Spanish, Portuguese, English, French, German, Dutch, and Russian, in particular—have had the greatest impact on the modern world. These are the languages of the European explorers and conquistadors; of the traders who provided the Western market with furs, precious metals and gems, rubber and hardwoods, and spices from exotic foreign lands; of the imperial powers that, by 1800, had laid claim to vast areas of Asia, Africa, Oceania, and the Americas.

The linguistic consequences of the recent expansion of European powers have been, roughly, of three types. (1) Many languages have ceased to exist; the populations may have died or been absorbed, or their languages may simply have been replaced by the dominant languages. In any case, they are no longer spoken. This has happened most often in areas where large populations of European immigrants have taken over lands formerly occupied by small communities of native peoples (in most of Australia and North America, for example).

(2) Trade or *pidgin* languages usually flourish in areas where speakers of two or more languages are in contact but where neither group adopts the language of the other. This is especially the case when the contact is either short term or limited to certain specific activities—the early spice traders in the Orient, explorers in the Pacific, and traders for ivory, gold, and slaves in Africa have all employed pidgin languages in their dealings with native peoples. A pidgin is a *lingua franca* used only in circumscribed situations for intergroup communication. A pidgin may acquire a life of its own when it replaces the native language or languages of a community of speakers; in

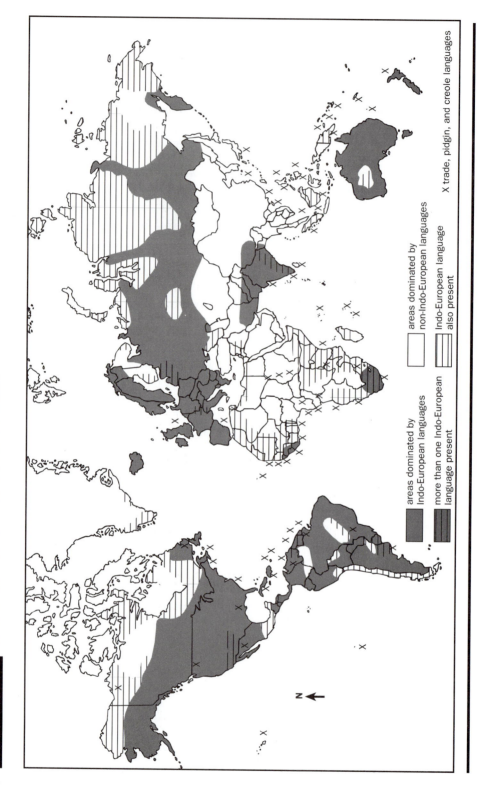

FIGURE 7.9 LANGUAGE MAP OF THE MODERN WORLD.

areas dominated by
Indo-European languages

more than one Indo-European
language present

areas dominated by
non-Indo-European languages

Indo-European language
also present

X trade, pidgin, and creole languages

N

this stage it is called a *creole* language or dialect. A creole may, over time, evolve as a new natural language or may emerge as a dialect of the dominant language (see chapter 6). A variety of examples of creole languages and dialects can be found in the Caribbean area (Haiti, Jamaica, Aruba, Trinidad, and the Guyanas, for example), the variety reflecting the differing relationships among West African slaves, other subject peoples, and several European colonial powers.

(3) Large-scale bilingualism and diglossia are also widespread phenomena in the modern world. In colonial and former colonial areas, it is a common experience that a European language has been imposed on speakers of native languages as the language used in government and education. This was the case throughout colonial areas of Africa, Asia, and the Pacific; it might be compared, as well, to the situation of Native Americans in the United States, most of whom have acquired English as a second language. Even after independence, in former colonial areas such as Africa or India, languages such as English, French, or Spanish have sometimes been retained to serve as a *lingua franca* among several native languages. The retention of a European language is also often favored, at least in higher education, because it is useful as a medium of international communication. For reasons of this sort, English remains in use in India and in several new nations of Africa, and French and Portuguese are widely used in their former colonial territories in Africa, even though very few persons of European ancestry remain in some of these nations.

These three developments are shown, in very general terms, in Figure 7.9. The scope of the modern expansion of languages of the Indo-European family can be appreciated by comparing this map and Figures 7.4 through 7.8.

Instances of the development of pidgin and creole languages are indicated by an X; some of these are known historically from a very early time (those in the Mediterranean area, for instance), while others are in use today (Hancock, 1977).

Areas of large-scale bilingualism are indicated by cross-hatching. In most of these areas, Indo-European languages (principally English, French, and Spanish) are in use, officially or by consensus, for purposes of education and interethnic communication. It is worth noting, when these areas are added to those that are solidly Indo-European, that this language family is truly global in its distribution.

BIBLIOGRAPHY

Andersen, Elaine S., 1996. "A cross-cultural study of children's register knowledge." In Slobin, Gerhardt, Kyratzis, and Guo, eds.

Auel, Jean M., 1981. *The Clan of the Cave Bear.* New York: Crown.

Barnett, H. G.,1960. *Being a Palauan.* New York: Holt, Rinehart and Winston.

Barnett, Lincoln, 1970. *History of the English Language.* London: Sphere Books.

Basso, K. H., 1967. "Semantic aspects of linguistic acculturation." *American Anthropologist*, 69: 454–464 (reprinted in Blount, 1974).

———, 1972. "To give up on words: silence in Apache culture." In Giglioli, 1972.

———, 1979. *Portraits of the Whiteman.* Cambridge: Cambridge University Press.

Baugh, A. C. and Thomas Cable, 1993. *A History of the English Language.* London: Routledge.

Bauman, Richard and Joel Sherzer, 1974. *Explorations in the Ethnography of Speaking.* Cambridge: Cambridge University Press.

Bavin, E. L., 1995. "Language acquisition in cross-cultural perspective." *Annual Review of Anthropology*, 24: 373–396.

Berlin, Brent, 1992. *Ethnobiological Classification: Principles of Categorization of Plants and Animals in Traditional Societies.* Princeton, NJ: Princeton University Press.

Berlin, Brent and Paul Kay, 1969. *Basic Color Terms: Their Universality and Evolution.* Berkeley: University of California Press.

Bickerton, Derek, 1981. *The Roots of Language.* Ann Arbor, MI: Karoma Publishers.

Bloom, Lois, 1973. "Why not pivot grammar?" In Ferguson and Slobin, 1973.

Bloomfield, Leonard, 1933. *Language.* New York: Holt.

———, 1946. "Algonkian." In Osgood, 1946.

Blount, Ben G., 1974. *Language, Culture and Society.* Cambridge, MA: Winthrop.

Boas, Franz, 1911. "Introduction" to *The Handbook of American Indian Languages.* In Boas, ed., 1911.

———, 1929. "Metaphorical expressions in the language of the Kwakiutl Indians." In Boas, ed., 1940.

———, ed., 1911. *The Handbook of American Indian Languages.* Washington, DC: Bureau of American Ethnology, Bulletin 40.

———, ed., 1940. *Race, Language and Culture.* New York: Free Press.

Bogoras, Waldemar, 1911. "Chukchee." In Boas, ed., 1911.

Brown, Cecil, 1981. "Growth and development of folk zoological life-forms in Polynesian languages." *The Journal of the Polynesian Society*, 90: 83–110.

Brown, Cecil and S. Witkowski, 1981. "Figurative language in a universalist perspective." *American Ethnologist*, 8: 596–615.

———, 1982. "Growth and development of folk zoological life forms in the Mayan language family." *American Ethnologist*, 9: 97–112.

Brown, Roger, 1958. *Words and Things.* New York: Free Press.

Brown, Roger and Marguerite Ford, 1961. "Address in American English." *Journal of Abnormal and Social Psychology*, 1949: 454–262 (reprinted in Hymes, 1964).

Carey, Brycchan, 1999. "English cricket metaphors." Personal communication.

Caskey-Sirmons, Leigh and Nancy P. Hickerson, 1977. "Semantic shift and bilingualism: Variation in the color terms of five languages." *Anthropological Linguistics*, 19: 358–367.

Chafe, Wallace, 1963. *Handbook of the Seneca Language.* Albany, NY: New York State Museum and Science Service, Bulletin 388.

Chomsky, Noam, 1957. *Syntactic Structures.* The Hague: Mouton.

———, 1968. *Language and Mind.* New York: Harcourt.

Claiborn, R., 1977. "Who Were the Indo-Europeans?" In Thorndike, 1977.

Comrie, Bernard, 1981. *Language Universals and Linguistic Typology*. Chicago: University of Chicago Press.

———, 1988. "Linguistics typology." *Annual Review of Anthropology*, 17: 144–159.

Conklin, Harold, 1955. "Hanunoo color categories." *Southwestern Journal of Anthropology*, 11: 339–344 (reprinted in Hymes, 1964).

———, 1973. "Review of *Basic Color Terms: Their Universality and Evaluation* by B. Berlin and P. Kay." *American Anthropologist*, 75: 931–942.

Corballis, Michael C., 1989. "Laterality and human evolution." *Psychological Review*, 96: 492–505.

Davis, Flora and Julia Orange, 1978. "The strange case of the children who invented their own language." *Redbook Magazine*, October.

De Waal, F. and F. Lansing, 1997. *Bonobo: The Forgotten Ape*. Berkeley: University of California Press.

Diebold, Richard, 1961. "Incipient Bilingualism." *Language*, 37: 97–112 (reprinted in Hymes, 1964).

Dyen, Isidore and David F. Aberle, 1977. *Lexical Reconstruction: The Case of the Proto-Athabascan Kinship System*. New York: Cambridge University Press.

Eastman, Carol, 1983. *Language Planning: an Introduction*. San Francisco: Chandler & Sharp.

Eggan, Fred, 1950. *Social Organization of the Western Pueblos*. Chicago: The University of Chicago Press.

Ehret, Christopher, 1982. "Linguistic inferences about early Bantu history." In Ehret and Posnansky, eds., 1982.

———, 1982. "The first spread of food production to southern Africa." In Ehret and Posnansky, eds., 1982.

Ehret, Christopher and M. Posnansky, eds., 1982. *The Archaeological and Linguistic Reconstruction of African History*. Berkeley: University of California Press.

Evans-Pritchard. E. E., 1940. *The Nuer*. Oxford: Oxford University Press.

———, 1948. "Nuer modes of address." *The Uganda Journal*, 12: 166–171 (reprinted in Hymes, 1964).

Fenton, W. N. and J. Gulick, eds., 1959. *Symposium on Cherokee and Iroquois Culture*.

Washington, DC: Bureau of American Ethnology, Bulletin 180.

Ferguson, Charles A., 1959. "Diglossia." *Word*, 15: 325–340 (reprinted in Hymes, 1964; also in Giglioli, 1972).

Ferguson, Charles A. and Dan I. Slobin, eds., 1973. *Studies of Child Language Development*. New York: Holt, Rinehart and Winston.

Fishman, Joshua A., ed. 1972. *Readings in the Sociology of Language*. The Hague: Mouton.

Frisch, J. A., 1968. "Maricopa foods: A native taxonomic system." *International Journal of American Linguistics*, 34: 16–20.

Fromkin and Rodman, 1978. *An Introduction to Language*. New York: Holt, Rinehart and Winston.

Gaeng, Paul, 1971. *Introduction to the Principles of Language*. New York: Harper & Row.

Gardiner, Sir Alan, 1957. *The Theory of Proper Names*. Oxford: Oxford University Press.

Gardner, R. A. and B. T. Gardner, 1969. "Teaching sign language to a chimpanzee." *Science*, 165: 664–672.

Gatschett, Albert S., 1979 (August). "Adjectives of color in Indian languages." *The AMerican Naturalist*.

Geiger, Lazarus, 1878. *Der Ursprung der Sprache*. Stuttgart: Vorträge.

Gelb, I. J., 1963. *A Study of Writing*. Chicago: The University of Chicago Press.

Giglioli, P. P., 1972. *Language and Social Context: Selected Readings*. New York: Penguin.

Gladstone, William, 1858. *Studies in Homer and the Homeric Age*. Oxford: Oxford University Press.

Gleason, H. L., 1955. *Workbook in Descriptive Linguistics*. New York: Holt, Rinehart and Winston.

———, 1961. *An Introduction to Descriptive Linguistics*. New York: Holt, Rinehart and Winston.

Gonzales, Josue, 1955. "Coming of age in bilingual/bicultural education: A historical perspective." *Inequality in Education*, 19: 5–17.

Goosen, I., 1967. *Navajo Made Easier*. Flagstaff, AZ: Northland Press.

Goss, James A., 1974. "Gumming to glory: A Ute sociolinguistic note." Paper presented at 27th Northwest Anthropological Conference.

Greenberg, Joseph, 1966. *The Languages of Africa.* The Hague: Mouton.

———, 1978. "Historical background of universals research." In Greenberg, ed., 1978.

———, ed., 1961. *Universals of Language.* Cambridge, MA: The M.I.T. Press.

———, ed., 1978. *Universals of Human Language,* Vol. I. Stanford: Stanford University Press.

Grooms, Steve, 1993. *The Return of the Wolf.* Minnetonka, MN: NorthWord Press.

Gudschinsky, Sarah C., 1956. "The ABC's of lexicostatistics (glottochronology)." *Word,* 12: 175–210 (reprinted in Hymes, 1964).

Gumperz, John J. and Dell Hymes, 1972. *Directions in Sociolinguistics: The Ethnography of Commication.* New York: Holt, Rinehart and Winston.

Guthrie, Malcolm, 1967. *The Classification of the Bantu Languages.* London: International African Institute.

Haas, Mary, 1944. "Men's and women's speech in Koasati." *Language,* 20: 142–149 (reprinted in Hymes, 1964).

Hale, Kenneth, 1974. "Some questions about anthropological linguistics: The role of native knowledge." In Hymes, 1964.

Hall, Rich, 1984. *Sniglets.* New York: Collier Books.

———, 1985. *More Sniglets.* New York: Collier Books.

Hall, Robert A.,1959. "Pidgin languages." *Scientific American,* February.

Hancock, I. F., 1977. "Repertory of pidgin and creole languages." In Valdman, 1977.

Harnad, S. R., H. D. Steklis, and J. Lancaster, eds., 1976. "Origins and evolution of language and speech." *Annals of the New York Academy of Sciences,* 180.

Hays, C., 1952. *The Ape in Our House.* New York: Harper & Row.

Hewes, Gordon, 1973. "Primate communication and the gestural origin of language." *Current Anthropology,* 14: 5–24.

———, 1976. "The invention of phonemically-based language." In Harnad, Steklis, and Lancaster, 1976.

———, 1977. "Language origin theories." (Reprinted from *Language Learning by a Chimpanzee: The Lana Project,* Academic Press, Inc., 1977.)

Hickerson, H., G. D. Turner, and N. P. Hickerson, 1952. "Testing procedures for estimating the transfer of information among Iroquois dialects and languages." *International Journal of American Linguistics,* 18: 1–8.

Hickerson, Nancy P., 1953. "Ethnolinguistic notes from lexicons of Lokono (Arawak)." *International Journal of American Linguistics,* 19: 181–190.

———, 1954. "Two versions of a Lokono (Arawak) tale." *International Journal of American Linguistics,* 20: 295–301.

———, 1971. "Review of Berlin and Kay, 1969." *International Journal of American Linguistics,* 37: 257–270.

———, 1978. "The natural environment as object and sign." *Journal of the Linguistic Society of the Southwest,* 3: 33–44.

———, 1991. "Una reconsideración sobre los términos de color en Lokono." *Revista Latinoamericana de Estudios Etnolingüísticos,* 6: 79–93.

———, 1992. "'Island Carib', Lokono and Goajiro: Relationships among the Caribbean Arawakan languages." *Revista Latinoamericana de Estudios Etnolingüísticos,* 7: 91–106.

Hill, Archibald H., 1952. "A note on primitive languages." In Hymes, 1964.

Hill, Jane H. and Bruce Mannheim, 1992. "Language and world view." *Annual Review of Anthropology,* 21: 381–406.

Hockett, Charles F., 1960. "The origin of speech." *Scientific American,* 203 (3): 89–96.

———, 1961. "The problem of universals in language." In Greenberg, ed., 1963.

Hockett, Charles F. and R. Ascher, "The human revolution." *Current Anthropology,* 5: 135–168.

Hopkins, E. W., 1883. "Words for color in the Rig Veda." *American Journal of Philology,* 4: 166–191.

Hymes, Dell H., 1972. "Models of the interaction of language and social life." In Gumperz and Hymes, 1972.

———, ed., 1964. *Language in Culture and Society.* New York: Harper & Row.

———, ed., 1971. *Pidginization and Creolization of Languages.* Cambridge: Cambridge University Press.

Irvine, Judith, 1974. "Strategies of status manipulation in Wolof greetings." In Barman and Sherzer, eds., 1974.

Jackendoff, Ray, 1994. *Patterns in the Mind: Language and Human Nature*. New York: Basic Books.

Jakobson, Roman and Morris Halle, 1956. *Fundamentals of Language*. The Hague: Mouton.

Jolly, Alison, 1972. *The Evolution of Primate Behavior*. New York: Methune.

Kay, Paul and Chad McDaniel, 1978. "The linguistic significance of the meanings of basic color terms." *Language*, 54: 610–646.

Kay, Paul, Brent Berlin, and William R. Merrifield, 1991. "Biocultural implications of systems of color naming." *Journal of Linguistic Anthropology*, 1: 12–25.

Kellogg, W. N., 1968. "Communication and the home-raised chimp." *Science*, 162: 423–427.

Kramer, Cheris, 1974. "Folk-linguistics: Wishy-washy mommy talk." *Psychology Today*, 8: 82–85.

Krantz, Grover S., 1980. "Sapienization and speech." *Current Anthropology*, 21: 773–792.

Kuper, Hilda ,1963. *The Swazi: a South African Kingdom*. New York: Holt, Rinehart and Winston.

Kurath, H., 1949. *Word Geography of the Eastern United States*. Ann Arbor: University of Michigan Press.

Labov, William, 1972. "The reflection of social processes in linguistic structures." In Fishman, 1972.

Laitman, Jeffrey T., 1976. "The evolution of the hominid upper respiratory system and implications for the origins of speech." In Hamad, Steklis, and Lancaster, 1976.

Lancaster, Jane B., 1975. *Primate Behavior and the Emergence of Human Culture*. New York: Holt, Rinehart and Winston.

Lawick-Goodall, Jane van, 1971. *In the Shadow of Man*. New York: Dell.

Leakey, Richard, 1994. *The Origin of Humankind*. New York: Basic Books.

Lee, Dorothy D., 1959. *Freedom and Culture*. Englewood Cliffs, NJ: Prentice-Hall.

Lenneberg, E. H., 1967. *Biological Foundations of Language*. New York: Wiley.

Lenneberg, Eric H. and John M. Roberts, 1956. "The language of experience: A study in methodology." *International Journal of American Linguistics*, 22 (no. 2).

Levi-Strauss, Claude, 1966. *The Savage Mind*. Chicago: The University of Chicago Press.

Lewis, M. M., 1955. *How Children Learn to Speak*. New York: Basic Books.

Lieberman, Philip, 1975. *On the Origins of Language*. New York: Macmillan.

Lieberman, Philip and E. S. Crelin, 1971. "On the speech of Neanderthal man." *Linguistic Inquiry*, 2: 203–222.

Linden, Eugene, 1974. *Apes, Men and Language*. New York: Dutton.

Lopez, Barry, 1978. *Of Wolves and Men*. Tappan, NJ: Simon and Schuster.

Lounsbury, Floyd, 1959. "Iroquois-Cherokee Linguistic Relations." In Fenton and Gulick, 1959.

Lubbock, Sir John, 1874. *The Origin of Civilization and the Early Condition of Man*. New York: Appleton.

Lucy, John A., 1992. *Language Diversity and Thought: A Reformulation of the Linguistic Relativity Hypothesis*. New York: Cambridge University Press.

Lucy, John A. and R. A.Schweder, 1979. "Whorf and his critics: Linguistic and non-linguistic influences on color memory." *American Anthropologist*, 81: 581–615.

Lynch, Kevin, 1960. *The Image of the City*. Cambridge, MA: The M.I.T. Press.

Lyovin, Anatole V., 1997. *An Introduction to the Languages of the World*. New York: Oxford University Press.

Malinowski, Bronislaw, 1923. "The problem of meaning in primitive languages." In Ogden and Richards, 1923.

Mandelbaum, David G., ed., 1949. *Selected Writings of Edward Sapir in Language, Culture and Personality*. Berkeley: University of California Press.

Marshack, Alexander, 1972. *The Roots of Civilization*. New York: McGraw-Hill.

Matthews, C. M., 1966. *English Surnames*. New York: Scribner.

McConnell-Ginet, S., 1983. "Intonation in a man's world." In Thorne, Kramer, and Henley, eds., 1983.

McLaury, Robert E., 1992. "From linguistics to hue: An explanatory model of color-category evolution." *Current Anthropology*, 33: 137–186.

McNeill, David, 1966. "Developmental psycholinguistics." In Smith and Miller, 1966.

Mead, W. E., 1899. "Colour in Old English poetry." *Publications of the Modern Language Association*, 14: 169–206.

Meek, C. K., 1931. *A Sudanese Kingdom*. Westport, CN: Negro Universities Press.

Migliazza, Ernest, 1972. *Yanomama Grammar and Intelligibility*. Ann Arbor: University Microfilms.

Moskowitz, A., 1973. "The two-year-old stage in the acquisition of English phonology." In Ferguson and Slobin, 1973.

Newcomer, Peter and James Farris, 1971. "Review of *Basic Color Terms* by B. Berlin and P. Kay." *International Journal of American Linguistics*, 37: 270–275.

Ogden, C. K. and I. A. Richards, 1923. *The Meaning of Meaning*. New York: Harcourt.

Osgood, C., ed., 1946. *Linguistic Structures of North America*. *Viking Fund Publications in Anthropology*, 6.

Parisi, Domenico, 1976. "A three-stage model of language evolution: From pantomime to syntax." In Harnad, Steklis, and Lancaster, 1976.

Patterson, Francine and E. Linden. *The Education of Koko*. New York: Holt, Rinehart and Winston.

Phillipson, D. W., 1977. "The spread of the Bantu language." *Scientific American*, 236: 106–115.

Postal, P., 1964. "Boas and the development of phonology: Comments based on Iroquois." *International Journal of American Linguistics*, 30: 269–280.

Powell, John Wesley, 1891. *Indian Families North of Mexico*. Washington, DC: Bureau of American Ethnology, Annual Report VII.

Premack, Ann J. and David Premack, 1972. "Teaching Language to an Ape." *Scientific American*.

Ramos, A. R., 1974. "How the Sanuma acquire their names." *Ethnology*, 13: 171–185.

Ray, Vern F., 1953. "Human color perception and behavioral response." *Transactions of the New York Academy of Sciences*, 16 (2).

Renfrew, Colin, 1988. *Archaeology and Language*. New York: Cambridge University Press.

Rivers, W. H. R., 1900. "Primitive color vision." *Popular Science Monthly*, 59: 44–58.

———, 1901. "Vision." *Reports of the Cambridge Anthropological Expedition to the Torres Straits*, volume II. Cambridge: Cambridge University Press.

Rubin, Joan, 1972. "Bilingual usage in Paraguay." In Fishman, ed., 1972.

Ruhlen, Merritt, 1994. *On the Origin of Languages: Studies in Linguistic Taxonomy*. Stanford: Stanford University Press.

Sankoff, Gillian, 1989. "A quantitative paradigm for the study of communicative competence." In Bauman and Sherzer, 1989.

Sapir, Edward, 1921. *Language*. New York: Harcourt.

———, 1949. "The psychological reality of the phoneme." In Mandelbaum, ed., 1949.

Sapir, Edward and Morris Swadesh, 1946. "American Indian grammatical categories." *Word*, 2: 103–112 (reprinted in Hymes, 1964).

Saussure, Ferdinand de, 1958 (orig. 1916). *Course in General Linguistics*. New York: Philosophical Library.

Savage-Rumbaugh, Sue and Roger Lewin, 1976. *Kanzi: The Ape at the Brink of the Human Mind*. Somerset, NJ: John Wiley.

Savic, Svenka, 1980. *How Twins Learn to Talk*. New York: Academic Press.

Saxton, D. and L. Saxton, 1969. *Papago and Pima-English Dictionary*. Tucson: University of Arizona Press.

Schieffelin, Bambi and E. Ochs, 1986. "Language socialization." *Annual Review of Anthropology*, 15: 163–191.

———, eds. 1986. *Language Socialization Across Cultures*. Cambridge: Cambridge University Press.

Schmandt-Besserat, Denise, 1978. "The earliest precursor of writing." *Scientific American*, June.

Schneirla, T. C. and Gerard Piel, 1948. "The army ant." *Scientific American*, June.

Sherzer, Joel, 1974. "To speak with a heated heart: Chamula canons of style and good performance." In Bauman and Sherzer, 1974.

———, 1983. *Kuna Ways of Speaking: An Ethnographic Perspective*. Austin: University of Texas Press.

Siebert, Frank S., 1967. *The Original Home of the Proto-Algonkian People*. Ottawa: National Museum of Canada, Anthropological Series, Bulletin No. 214.

Slobin, Dan I., 1973. "Cognitive prerequisites for the development of grammar." In Ferguson and Slobin, 1973.

———, 1982. "Universal and particular in the acquisition of language." In Wanner and Gleitman, 1982.

Slobin, D. I., J. Gerhardt, A. Kyratzis, and J. Guo, eds., 1996. *Social Interaction, Social Context and Language: Essays in Honor of Susan Ervin-Tripp*. Mahwah, NJ: Lawrence Erlbaum.

Smith, E. C., 1970. *The Story of Our Names*. Detroit: Gale Research Co.

Smith, Frank and G. A. Miller, eds., 1966. *The Genesis of Language*. Cambridge, MA: The M.I.T. Press.

Spradley, James A., 1970. "Adaptive strategies of urban nomads." In Weaver and White, 1970.

———, 1979. *The Ethnographic Interview*. New York: Holt, Rinehart and Winston.

Stewart, George R., 1975. *Names on the Globe*. Oxford: Oxford University Press.

Stringer, Christopher, 1990. "The emergence of modern humans." *Scientific American*, December.

Stringer, Christopher and R. McKie, 1996. *African Exodus: The Origin of Modern Humanity*. New York: Henry Holt.

Swadesh, Morris, 1959. "Linguistics as an instrument of prehistory." *Southwestern Journal of Anthropology*, 15: 20–35 (reprinted in Hymes, 1964).

———, 1971. *The Origin and Diversification of Languages*. Chicago: Aldine.

Tannen, Deborah, 1994. *Talking from Nine to Five*. New York: Avon Books.

Taylor, Douglas M., 1977. *Languages of the West Indies*. Baltimore: Johns Hopkins Press.

Taylor, Douglas and Berend Hoff, 1980. "The linguistic repertoir of the Island Carib in the seventeenth century—A Carib pidgin?" *International Journal of American Linguistics*, 46: 301–312.

Taylor, Douglas and I. Rouse, 1955. "Linguistic and archaeological time depth in the West Indies." *International Journal of American Linguistics*, 21: 105–115.

Thieme, Paul, 1964. "The comparative method for reconstruction in linguistics." In Hymes, 1964.

Thompson, Stith, 1980. *Tales of the North American Indian*. Bloomington: Indiana University Press.

Thorndike, J. L., ed., *Mysteries of the Past*. New York: Simon and Schuster.

Thorne, A. and M. Wolpoff, 1992 (April). "The multiregional evolution of language" *Scientific American*.

Trager, George L., 1972. *Language and Languages*. San Francisco: Chandler.

Tremayne, Peter, 1997. *The Spider's Web*. London: Headline Book Publishing.

Ullman, S., 1966. "Semantic universals." In Greenberg, 1966.

Valdman, A., ed., 1977. *Pidgin and Creole Linguistics*. Bloomington: Indiana University Press.

Voegelin, Carl F. and Z. Harris, 1951, "Methods for determining intelligibility among dialects of natural languages." *International Journal of American Linguistics*, 11: 322–329.

Voegelin, C. F. and F. M. Voegelin, 1957. *Hopi Domains*. Bloomington: Indiana University Publications in Anthropology and Linguistics, Memoir 14.

Voegelin, C. F. and F. M. Voegelin, eds., 1964–1966. "Languages of the world." *Anthropological Linguistics*, 6–8.

Von Frisch, Karl, 1953. *The Dancing Bees*. New York: Harcourt, Brace and World.

Walker, Willard, 1975. "The Proto-Algonkians." In Kinkaid et al., 1975.

Wallace, Ron, 1989. "Cognitive mapping and the origin of language and mind." *Current Anthropology*, 30: 518–526.

Wanner, Eric and L. R. Gleitman, 1983. *Language Acquisition*. Cambridge: Cambridge University Press.

Washburn, S. L. and I. DeVore, 1961. "The social life of baboons." *Scientific American*, June.

Weaver, T. and D. White, eds., 1970. *Urban Anthropology. Human Organization*, Monograph 11.

Werner, Alice, 1919. *Introductory Sketch of the Bantu Languages*. New York: Dutton.

Whorf, Benjamin L., 1941. "The relation of habitual thought and behavior to language." In Spier, ed., 1949 (reprinted in Blount, 1974).

———, 1956. *Language, Thought and Reality: The Selected Writings of Benjamin Lee Whorf*. Cambridge, MA: The M.I.T. Press.

Wierzbicka, Anna, 1992. "Semantic universals and primitive thought: The question of the psychic unity of humankind." *Journal of Linguistic Anthropology*, 4: 23–49.

Witherspoon, Gary, 1977. *Language and Art in the Navajo Universe*. Ann Arbor: University of Michigan Press.

Wundt, Wilhelm, 1901. *Die Sprache (Volkerpsychologie*, Vol. I). Leipzig: Alfred Kröner Verlag.

Wyman, Leland, 1957. *Beautyway: A Navajo Ceremonial*. New York: Pantheon.